THE ENIGMATIC EDWARDIAN

The Life of Reginald, 2nd Viscount Esher

James Lees-Milne

SIDGWICK & JACKSON
LONDON

First published in Great Britain in October 1986 by
Sidgwick & Jackson Limited

First Paperback Edition October 1988

Copyright © 1986 James Lees-Milne

ISBN 0 283 99738 9

Phototypeset by Falcon Graphic Art Ltd
Wallington, Surrey
Printed in Hong Kong
for Sidgwick & Jackson Limited
1 Tavistock Chambers, Bloomsbury Way
London WC1A 2SG

To Lionel and Christian Esher

'The language of the heart is a thousand times more varied than that of the mind, and it is impossible to give the rules of its dialectic.'
Diderot

CONTENTS

ACKNOWLEDGEMENTS

Firstly, I am indebted to Her Majesty the Queen for her gracious permission to consult Lord Esher's letters to members of the royal family which are among the Windsor Castle archives. And I wish to thank the late Royal Librarian, Sir Robin Mackworth-Young, his successor Mr Oliver Everett and the Registrar, Miss Jane Langton, for their kindness and help.

To Lord and Lady Esher no acknowledgements can be adequate. For not only did Lord Esher put all his grandfather's papers at my disposal, but he has consistently helped me throughout the composition of this biography. To Miss Marion M. Stewart, archivist of Churchill College, Cambridge, I am especially grateful. For nearly two years she allowed me to have on loan all the Esher papers which are now in her custody.

The following, who have either lent me papers or allowed me to look through them in their houses, I thank unreservedly: the Hon. Christopher Brett, Sybil Marchioness of Cholmondeley, the Duke of Devonshire, Kenneth Rose, Earl Lloyd George, Sir Philip Magnus-Allcroft, Dr David Newsome, the Countess of Sutherland and Mrs Ken Thornton (Angela Brett).

I wish to thank a number of friends for almost infinite help and advice, namely: the late (Enid) Lady Adair, the late (Michael) Lord Adeane, Michael Bloch, Mrs Cheyne (Marie Brett), Professor van den Dungen, Lord Egremont, the Hon. Mrs Crispin Gascoigne, John Harris, Sir Rupert Hart-Davis, Derek Hill, Regius Professor Sir Michael Howard, H. Montgomery Hyde, Robert Rhodes James, MP, Viscount Lambton, the late Anita Leslie, the Hon. Lady Lindsay of Dowhill, the late General Sir James Marshall-Cornwall, Professor

J.D.B. Miller, Lady (Frances) Phipps, Stuart Preston, Colin Simpson, Timothy d'Arch Smith, Dr P.L. Strong (Eton College Collections), A.J. Sylvester and Humphrey Whitbread. I only wish I were allowed more space in which to record precisely how much I owe to each.

The staffs of the following libraries have given me every facility, for which I am indeed beholden: the Bodleian Library, the British Library, the London Library, the Liverpool University Library and the National Library of Scotland (Manuscripts Department).

Finally, for their patience, perseverance and skill I gratefully thank my editors at Sidgwick & Jackson, Robert Smith and Mrs (Esther) Jagger and their staff. And how truly fortunate I am that Douglas Matthews has consented to compile the index for me.

J.L.-M.
Bath, 1986

1

CHILDHOOD AND CHEAM

1852–1865

Unlike Hilaire Belloc's Godolphin Horne, Reginald Baliol Brett, 2nd Viscount Esher, was not, strictly speaking, nobly born. Nevertheless he grew to be a man upon whose shoulders the purple fell, to fit him like a perfectly tailored mantle. He came of a long line of small squires of no fixed family seat. The Brett lineage can be traced far back, but its first member of any interest is Joseph George, born in 1760. Although not Irish, he came from Dublin to England and was a banker connected with Calcutta houses. Joseph George married Isabella, daughter and heiress of George Forbes of Edinglassie and Auchnerrach in Aberdeenshire. Her great-grandson, the 2nd Viscount Esher, was to be very proud of this ancestry, which he believed accounted for his great love of Scotland where he was in later life to make his favourite home. And on every possible occasion he sported the Forbes tartan, whether or not he had the right to do so at three generations' remove.

The eldest son of this union, born in 1790, was also called Joseph George. He married Dora, the auburn-haired, pretty, high-spirited daughter of George Best of Chilston Park, Kent, and his wife Caroline, *née* Scott, of Scotts Hall, also in Kent. Joseph George junior was a decent but rather feckless fellow who, for want of an income, entered the Church when his father-in-law offered him the curacy of Lenham, a village on the Chilston estate. In due course the Bretts moved with their eight children from Lenham vicarage to Ranelagh, where Joseph George had inherited property from an aunt. From 1831 to 1852 he was the incumbent of the Hanover Chapel in Regent Street.

The second but eldest surviving son of this marriage was born at Lenham in 1815 and christened William Baliol after Alexander de

Baliol, hereditary Chamberlain to the Scottish monarchs in the thirteenth century. The Chamberlain was the elder brother of one William le Scott, from whom Caroline Best was directly descended, and this ancestry was greatly venerated by the Scott family.

Having been educated at Westminster School and Caius College, Cambridge, in 1839 Baliol Brett was admitted a student at Lincoln's Inn. His career was distinguished by his absolute probity and extraordinary memory, and he excelled at the Bar through sheer pertinacity and hard work. Elected a Bencher of his Inn in 1860, he was appointed a Queen's Counsel in 1861. From 1866 to 1868 he was Conservative Member of Parliament for Helston, Cornwall, serving for a few months as Solicitor-General in Disraeli's short-lived administration of 1868. From Serjeant-at-Law he rose to be one of the Justices of the Common Pleas, and in 1876 one of the Lords Justices of Appeal and a Privy Councillor. His final achievement was the Mastership of the Rolls, which he held from 1883 to 1897; he was created Baron Esher in 1885, and on resigning office in 1897 1st Viscount Esher.

Baliol Brett was said to have been a bit of a dandy in extreme youth and a hedonist in his bachelor days. It is true that he liked boats, and for three years rowed at Cambridge in the University Eight. He also played the flute, and he learned to speak French. But in his twenties he fell in love, once and for all, and after his marriage became a serious man with few recreations. The object of his adoration was a Frenchwoman of great beauty, who, when she finally accepted him, made him keep their engagement secret for eighteen months and wait another eight years until he had earned enough money to support her. From the tone of the letters she wrote before her marriage, one deduces that she was not the least in love with her suitor; but gradually respect for his character developed into tolerant affection. Baliol invested her with every virtue: he called her his enchantress, cosseted her indifferent health – she lived to be ninety – and generally spoiled her.

Eugénie's antecedents were shrouded in obscurity. Of her father nothing is known beyond his name, Louis Mayer. Her mother, Fanny, claimed to have been the widow of this man whom she followed to Waterloo with her daughter Eugénie, born the year before the battle – 1814. Fanny herself was one of four extremely attractive daughters of a Monsieur Kreilssamner, or Kreissamer, a small landowner near Mulhouse in Alsace. (Oliver, 3rd Viscount Esher, liked to make out that the father was a peasant and Fanny a *vivandière*, and that Eugénie had been born on the battlefield of Waterloo.) At all events, when Monsieur Kreilssamner died the four sisters settled in Paris. Isabelle, the most beautiful, formed an association with Alexandre Dumas *fils* and was always referred to by her family as '*la malheureuse Belle*'; Mariette, a poor little cripple, was found strangled in her Paris apartment during the Commune of 1871; and Esther married a rich member of the lesser nobility, Monsier Béjot de Nointel. During the First World War Reginald Esher visited the Château de Nointel, which he described as a miniature Versailles. He added that his mother had lived there as a child a hundred years earlier.[1]

It was not long before Fanny, with her raven hair, blue eyes and laughing, mischievous manner, found an English husband. As a young man Colonel John Gurwood served throughout the Peninsular campaign, distinguishing himself in 1812, at the age of twenty-two, by capturing the Governor of Ciudad Rodrigo, for which he received the congratulations of the Duke of Wellington and the Spanish Governor's sword. On being promoted brevet-colonel he immediately married Madame Mayer in Paris. His greatest subsequent achievement was a commission from the hero of Waterloo to edit the Wellington despatches. When this task was completed, in 1837, he received a much needed pension from the Crown and was made Deputy-Lieutenant of the Tower of London at £400 a year.

All his life Gurwood suffered from lack of money – he was a proud, cold, embittered man with a permanent chip on his shoulder. He was also a fearful snob. Although devoted to Fanny, by whom he had several children, he never allowed her to enter society. He would not, for instance, let her meet his confidante Mrs FitzHerbert, the Duke of Wellington or any of his important English friends. On visits to London he left her in their hotel when invited to luncheons and dinners. Furthermore he made her leave Eugénie behind in Paris, thus casting a slur upon the child's legitimacy. (Reginald Brett, who was not a snob, nevertheless pretended in middle age that Gurwood was his grandfather.) Eugénie never forgot or forgave the insult to her mother and herself. One disagreeable consequence of her stepfather's behaviour was that eligible young suitors whom she met before Baliol Brett came on the scene did not ask for her hand, but expected her to consent to be their mistress. Society did not deem her suitable for the marriage market.

In 1838 Colonel Gurwood left France to live in London, where he became more and more unbalanced. Finally in 1845 he cut his throat, in the belief that people were questioning the veracity of his heroism at Ciudad Rodrigo. Fanny lived on at the house in Lowndes Square until 1873, a kind and indulgent mother. Released by her husband's death, she blossomed. Gurwood's friends, from whom she had been kept at arm's length, rallied to her. She even held a *salon*, which he would certainly not have approved, and frequented Gore House, where Lady Blessington – herself not received by London society – presided over a cosmopolitan circle of artists, writers and musicians. Here Fanny mingled with the Count d'Orsay, Prince Louis Napoleon (of whom she was a fervent admirer), Bulwer Lytton, Samuel Rogers and Benjamin Disraeli. To this distinguished and intellectual group she introduced Eugénie, whose portrait by Winterhalter was included in Lady Blessington's *Book of Beauty*, published in 1848. Years later Eugénie described her hostess as an old lady with black ribbons tying up a row of double chins, just as her granddaughter was to describe her, Eugénie, as a frightening old lady in a brown wig with no traces of her former stunning beauty.[2]

After their marriage Baliol and Eugénie Brett took a house, 19 Prince's Terrace, Kensington; here, on 30 June 1852, their eldest child, Reginald Baliol, known to them and his family as Regy, was born.[3] He was followed by a daughter, Violet, and a son, Eugene. Baliol became a devoted family man and had few interests that did not include his wife and children. The theatre, the opera and occasional yachting were delights to be shared with Eugénie. Yet his work frequently took him away from home. It brought him into contact with eminent landowners such as the Earls of Derby and Lonsdale, in whose country houses he often stayed when on circuit and to whom he endeared himself by his affability and his skill as a raconteur. In the evenings he would write to his wife, protesting that his only happiness was his home and that his professional path was pursued solely for her and the children's sake. To judge from the homesick Baliol's letters, his adoration of Eugénie was cloying; whereas hers suggest that she was slightly bored by it. Yet as the years went by the tone of her letters became increasingly affectionate, while remaining strictly practical. She never relaxed her exhortations that he must forge ahead in his career. Gently she chided his diffidence. 'If my husband is too modest it is his only fault; he has too good an opinion of men, and he thinks that it requires too much perfection to lead them,' she wrote to him.[4]

Regy's first baby letters to his father are written in a clear, steady hand. At the age of seven he takes up Eugénie's refrain in urging his absent father to get many briefs and make much money. Regy was devoted to him, more so than to his mother who, he confessed to his elder son when a boy at Eton, had always been *'difficile'*, and a bit of a trial.[5] His childhood was a happy one, spent between London and Heath Farm, the Bretts' modest country house near Watford, interspersed with visits to his mother's relations in Paris and to Lowther Castle in Westmorland, the home of his father's friend, the 2nd Earl of Lonsdale.

It seems that Eugénie remained on good terms with her sister, '*la malheureuse Belle*', for Regy records how he met in her Paris apartment Alexandre Dumas *fils* and the Comte de Flahaut, whose black, stocky cravat and hat taller than any encountered in those days of 'chimney-pots' remained vividly in his memory. He even recalled sitting on the lap of a little wizened old man who had played the violin to Marie Antoinette.

Summer holidays spent at Lowther Castle left an indelible impression upon him, and first aroused his appreciation of natural beauty and literature. Lord Lonsdale was the original of Lord Eskdale in Disraeli's *Coningsby*, a Whig nobleman survivor from the eighteenth century. The castle itself, with its oil lamps and hearty English fare, belonged to a past age; its tranquillity was so marked that no resident cared to break the silence by raising his voice above a whisper. Regy would climb the tall library steps to reach the late Greek authors and what he called the 'sulphurous pages of Caroline poets'. Books became an early passion. Before he was seven he had read Goldsmith's 'The Deserted Village'. On his tenth birthday he was given Shakespeare's collected works and acted *Henry IV* in the nursery. By the age of twelve he had consumed all Scott's Waverley novels except *Redgauntlet*, which he never could stomach, and Hume's *History of England*. His favourite reading of all was Southey's *Life of Nelson*. To Stanhope's *Life of Pitt* he attributed his lasting respect for that statesman and his enduring interest in history.

For some reason – probably his father's reluctance to part with him – Regy was not sent to a preparatory school until 1863, when he was eleven. Although on arrival at Cheam he found himself somewhat behind the other boys of his own age, he soon caught them up. He was pursued by letters from his parents – over-solicitous ones from his father and slightly nagging ones from his mother. 'My own darling Regy', some of Baliol's letters began, ending, 'a thousand kisses to you, my darling boy'; and sometimes 'Darling of my soul', ending 'Your affectionate father'. Since they were seldom dated, one cannot be certain which of these letters was addressed to Regy at Cheam and which to him at Eton; but they all abounded in fatherly advice: not to get hurt at football, not to quarrel, not to tell lies, and above all to say his prayers. 'I hope you will recollect and observe all the cautions we gave you,' his doting father wrote. 'Beware *wet* and *pastry*.' Mrs Brett likewise concentrated upon health, urging him not to bathe in cold weather and to avoid draughts. She also stressed moral issues, warning him in 1865 that God might forgive dishonourable behaviour, but men never. She counselled him not to hate people who disagreed with him, and reproved him for admiring Gladstone.

Regy had barely settled down at Cheam when it was time to prepare for Eton. Arthur Campbell Ainger was to be Regy's tutor and Baliol was unhappy about this because he was one of the youngest masters and therefore unproven. The boy was to board in the house of Sam

Evans, the drawing master, which was reputed to be most comfortable. Ainger, an Old Etonian whose entire life was dedicated to the school, was to be Reginald Brett's scholastic guide and guardian of his welfare. Lean and active, with a gaunt face and fine features, he had a grim mouth until it broke into a smile and his blue eyes twinkled over lined cheeks. He had a dry and ready irony, but was never harsh. Ainger could seldom be induced to set punishments, and his relationship with the boys was paternal – he was either not very observant or else dismissive at times of what went on under his nose. Reginald became very fond of him and in due course sent his two sons to Ainger's house, his old tutor having become a house master in the interval.

By sending Regy to Eton in 1865 Baliol Brett was consciously intending to improve his son's social standing. 'You will make your friends', he wrote to Regy in one of his undated letters, 'of nice, good, gentlemanly fellows, and will not let anyone persuade you to do anything that is wrong. . . . You will at every period of your life be thrown with the boys who are now at Eton with you, so that if at Eton a boy does anything wrong or dishonourable it is always recollected against him all his life.' This stern warning was an echo of Eugénie's. Yet the judge had an eye to his son's material advantage, hoping that he would one day move in exalted circles, so long as those circles were worthy ones. At the same time he cautioned him: 'Remember what I told you that, as you and I were not born Dukes with large estates, we must work.' In a few years' time he would fear that Eton had taught his son to disregard this sage counsel.

2

ETON AND CAMBRIDGE
1865–1874

When Regy Brett went to Eton in January 1865 the school was just coming through a crisis. The Public Schools Commission Inquiry of 1864 had introduced sweeping reforms to which Dr Balston, the headmaster, had taken exception and resigned. The reason for the current state of affairs was that the 1850s had witnessed a decline in the standard of teaching and a corresponding emphasis upon games. Before 1850 the education at Eton may not have been first rate, but it was the primary reason why a parent sent his son there. In those days the boys for the most part invented their own forms of recreation, and when not working would go for long rambles into the surrounding countryside. With the 1850s, however, things changed. Games became an honoured part of the school curriculum, and prowess at them transcended learning. Rowing was taken seriously and cricket matches against rival public schools assumed gigantic importance. To be good at games made a boy a 'swell', and the swells ruled the roost, often intolerably so. In Chapel packets of raisins and almonds were distributed among the noblemen seated in the stalls; the swells came into Chapel at the very last moment, jostling each other and creating considerable disturbance.

But there were exceptions among both masters and boys. The boys in the highest social stratum, which happened also to be the highest intellectual one, included some who combined a keen interest in rowing, cricket and football with a yet keener enthusiasm for learning. Belonging to an older group than Regy Brett's were the Wood brothers, most notable the elder, Charles, who was to succeed as 2nd Viscount Halifax, and the fourth, Frederick; also Archibald Primrose, Lord Dalmeny, who became the 5th Earl of Rosebery and later Prime

Minister. These and many others of England's *jeunesse dorée* owed much of their culture – and were proud to admit it in after life – to one of the most remarkable schoolmasters of all time. Regy, too, was to be strongly influenced by this man.

William Johnson, born in 1823 of a Devon family, was educated at Eton and King's College, Cambridge. In 1845 he returned to Eton, remaining there for twenty-six years. Johnson never kept a boarding house, and his freedom from such binding duties suited his independent and morbidly eccentric character. This scholar, poet and aesthete was a misfit among the majority of his Eton colleagues. Extremely absent-minded and near-sighted, he wore three pairs of spectacles one on top of the other. One apochryphal story relates that he was once seen pursuing a hen down Windsor Hill, making futile grabs at it under the belief that it was his hat.[1] He had a tongue like a razor and was both shy and rude, given to taunts and sarcasm, 'versed', as one of his ex-pupils put it, 'in the vocabulary of contempt'.[2] Yet the same writer admitted that he was 'the most remarkable man I ever knew or am likely to know'. The eminent historian G.W. Prothero called him 'the most brilliant Eton tutor of his day'; and Arthur Coleridge, who taught classics at the school, assured Regy's father in 1866 that he was 'the wisest master who has ever been at Eton'.

The secret of his influence was that he was the first master to treat boys like human beings. In his manuscript *Hints for Eton Masters*,[3] written in 1863, Johnson advocated the revolutionary idea of the master deferring to the pupil in almost all cases: 'If a boy stammers, do not scold him, but civilly ask him to take a full breath.' And then, 'Treat everyone in the class with more or less respect; let them feel that your looking over their exercise is done in the way of a personal attention, as well as a matter of routine.' He went on to suggest that after repeated misdemeanours a boy should not be given the same punishment. Logical remonstration should be applied so as to make the wilful wrong-doer understand that he was mistaken – 'Don't use the word *sin* whatever you do.' Johnson's precepts come close to the policy of the most advanced thinking in academic circles today.

Finally Johnson touched upon the relationship between master and boy, the matter most outstanding in his reforms and the one which ultimately brought him to disaster.

Suppose there is in one's division a lad of good behaviour and good manners, whom one cannot help liking – *a fortiori*, if one sees that one is naturally liked by him – is the acquaintance to cease, or to be limited to occasional recognition, after the lad has passed into another division? This is a sad, serious question for a Fifth Form master. I cannot answer it for other people. . . . I will only say then that I should be very sorry if

I had given no affection to any other Eton boys besides my own pupils, and that I should never have known the goodness of the place, if I had been shut up, as some men shut themselves up, in a miscellaneous set of forty boys, instead of enjoying some little freedom of selection from the hundreds outside one's pupil-room.

Unfortunately for him he let his special likings lead to notable favouritisms and infatuations.

Johnson took it for granted that those who became his pupils were friends of a mental calibre potentially equal to his own. If he discovered that they were not, he dropped them at once. He was also among the first to recognize the intellectual equality of men and women. In politics he was a Whig, believing passionately in the Pax Britannica and the Englishman's God-given right. His heroes were the younger Pitt and Nelson. He believed that western Europe's supreme age was the present, just as he claimed that Tennyson was greater than Milton and the French dramatist Sardou superior to Shakespeare. History was in his opinion still being taught as a 'tissue of homicide and perfidy' instead of a chronicle of the noble deeds, thoughts and arts of the greatest recorded minds. It was nonsense to claim that the age of chivalry had been that of the Crusaders, or the Black Prince – common brigands. On the contrary, it took place during the Italian Quattrocento when the Greek torch of honour was carried into the Renaissance. If the Renaissance had been the age of chivalry, then the present was the age of romance.[4] Greek philosophy was the backbone of his particular form of paganism, and his faith is neatly summed up in his poem 'Mimnermus in Church', addressed to the orthodox Christian teachers:

> You promise heavens free from strife,
>   Pure truth, and perfect change of will;
> But sweet, sweet is this human life,
>   So sweet, I fain would breathe it still;
> Your chilly stars I can forego,
> This warm kind world is all I know.
>
> You say there is no substance here,
>   One great reality above;
> Back from that void I shrink in fear,
>   And child-like hide myself in love:
> Show me what angels feel. Till then,
> I cling, a mere weak man, to men.

Johnson made the Greek and Latin classics and his approved modern literature spellbinding to his pupils. And to crown his appeal he deprecated the tyranny of organized games and sports. He urged his pupils to read voraciously along scientific lines. In short, it was impossible to come under his tuition without being inspired to seek knowledge and enjoy the fruits of it.

In 1867, the year when Reginald Brett first came to his attention, Johnson claimed that he was more thoroughly Etonian and more interested in his chosen pupils than ever before. Regy struck the very climax of the assistant master's Eton career. The subjects in which he ostensibly went to Johnson for guidance were political economy, Greek and French history.

In June that year Regy had his fifteenth birthday. When the summer 'half' was over his tutor, Ainger, wrote to the boy's father, now Conservative MP for Helston, that, despite his abilities, Regy had done badly in trials, the annual school examination. Regy had in fact reached that disturbed and disturbing phase of puberty when boys' sensibilities are easily swayed, and often permanently affected, by the deeply held principles of an older and respected person. With Regy that person was William Johnson, and the gospel he preached was summarized in a book of poems he had published in 1858 under the title *Ionica*. As Regy was to write to his younger son in years to come: 'The atmosphere of Eton changed during his [Johnson's] sway, and *Ionica* marked an epoch and created a spirit which stole into every nook and corner of Eton, unrecognized but not the less powerful.'[5]

Johnson's philosophy and teaching, which had such a radical influence on Eton in the mid-nineteenth century, derived from deep reading of the Greek classics, which had been expurgated by post-Renaissance schoolmasters and were to remain expurgated in schools for the ensuing hundred years.[6] Pindar, Theognis, Plato, Heracleides Ponticus, Theocritus, Anacreon, Meleager, Callimachus, Strato and even Homer are among the philosophers and poets on whom Johnson drew to vindicate his thesis. Pindar taught that the first objective to be striven for was happiness, and the second an honourable reputation among men. Theognis put health as the first happiness, and the attainment of what one loved as the second. The great Greek thinkers stressed sensuality as a major element in the happiness of cultivated man: voluptuousness was reserved for the governing classes, whereas work and toil were the lot of slaves and the poor.

Plato's *Symposium* was a hymn of Eros unique in the literary history of the world. 'A perfect virtue', he wrote, 'is absolutely unthinkable in women.' Greek sex was always dignified by the desire of beauty, and this over-riding ideal was to be found in the young male – one who had reached puberty, an ephebe. Heracleides Ponticus, Plato's pupil, affirmed that marriage was for the Greeks a means to an end – the procreation of children to succeed the husband, and the trustworthy management of the household affairs by the wife. The Greeks were decidedly bi-sexual. Having consummated the marriage, the husband could with a good conscience return to his male lover and the aesthetic and intellectual higher life. The ethic of the Greek love of boys, far from being an occasional and reprehensible aberration, as even the most unblinkered Victorian schoolmasters were obliged to proclaim, was held to be ennobling. It cultivated the manly virtues: for lover and beloved to die together in battle was the ultimate heroism in ancient Greece. If an ephebe failed to find an older friend, a boy was considered to have some concealed moral taint.

From this basic philosophy of life William Johnson stripped the blanket of bowdlerism imposed by distant school preceptors and maintained until recently. The conditions of the Greek paedophiliac ethic, however, should be borne in mind. They were that the accepted form of male love was not hostile to marriage and the enduring affection between husband and wife; and that prostitution and even promiscuity among males were generally frowned upon. Socrates, who had an eye for boyish beauty and intimate companionship with the ephebi, abstained as far as possible from physical activities. He certainly advocated abstinence as an ideal for others, although he did not require it from all. Johnson accepted these conditions in principle, but how far he deviated from them is a matter for speculation.

Regy Brett's tutor, Ainger, saw no harm in his pupil being taken up by the master whom he regarded as a man of genius and a first-rate scholar. Besides Ainger was not unsympathetic to boy-friendships provided they were kept within the bounds of discretion. William Johnson was his friend, whom he positively encouraged to invite suitable – by which is meant brilliant – boys to the Cabin and the Trap, as Johnson's pupil-room and lodgings respectively were known to the few boys who belonged to his esoteric circle. It was in the cosier Trap that the group would gather in the long winter evenings, to rummage among the master's portfolios and borrow without request whatever books took their fancy.

The first reference to Regy Brett in Johnson's journal of 1868 ('I have a new friend who plays tunes on my piano.') is undated. But since for health reasons Regy was sent home for several weeks of the summer half it was probably written during the Easter half, in February or March. From an early age Regy had been musical. In London he attended concerts, and he played the piano well and with enthusiasm, which provoked his father to sound a note of warning.

I believe the piano to be the only instrument for a gentleman in our days. The professional musicians are so adroit and so numerous that it is not worth while for a gentleman to endeavour to equal them in the mechanism of playing. All that he should do is to be able to recall the idea of music and put it into his own finer taste and feeling.

During the summer half Johnson wrote letters to the absent boy. They began with unexceptionable advice and encouragement: 'Be unworldly; don't worship celebrities; like simple people, honest people – *loyal je serai.*' Regy should improve his French, which colloquially was perfect but grammatically not so. Johnson told him what books to read. Regy's life, he declared, was more like that of a Provençal troubadour than any he had seen. 'Sweet and pretty it is. I doubt whether there is enough backbone to it.' But very soon the letters dealt with more intimate matters. With Regy Johnson was affectionate and bantering, but never sentimental – although he certainly was about others, including some of Regy's special favourites. In July he wrote: 'Your Charlie came the first morning to get some breakfast and was odd, stuffed up somehow; not communicative, but he liked sitting to be looked at and stood up on a chair to look at his reflection in the glass when I hinted that his trousers were baggy; he would not have a flower.' This he attributed to his having taken rather a dislike to B.F. [Bevill Fortescue] 'probably for pulling him about too coarsely'. He went on to say, 'At 9 I shall once more feed my sweet Elliot and your darling who does not like me as much as Elliot does.'

The topic and the phraseology in a letter from master to boy may seem unorthodox. A year older than Regy, 'my sweet Elliot', later Sir Francis Elliot, GCVO, and Minister to Athens, was Johnson's ideal – 'the quintessence of virtue', he called him – as he was of all the Eton masters. He was spartan, hard-working and intensely reserved. Since his father was at the time abroad Elliot spent part of his holidays with Johnson. Regy found him a dry stick, although he was not averse to receiving his favours during their early acquaintance. Johnson worshipped Elliot. 'I envy you being kissed by him,' he wrote to Regy. 'If I were dying like Nelson I would ask him to kiss me. I kissed his dear foot last Tuesday on the grass of Ankerwyke.'

The Charlie ('your darling') referred to was Charles Williamson, a year younger than Regy and known by his friends as Chat, short for Chatterbox. From their first meeting at Eton, Regy was to love and cherish him throughout Chat's erratic career. In youth beautiful, endowed with disarming charm and intelligence which he never succeeded in harnessing to a constant purpose, Chat ended up being dependent on Regy's bounty for a livelihood. In these early days Johnson foresaw him developing into a butterfly, for he did not read or reflect. Regy's enduring devotion to Chat is possibly the pre-eminent example of his intense loyalty to those whom he took to his heart. To begin with, the errant Chat did not reciprocate the love which Regy lavished upon him, although any news of his admirer through an intermediary was welcome to his vanity.

Towards the end of the August holiday and the finish of a walking tour with two Eton ushers Johnson stayed with the Williamsons at Lawers, near Loch Earn. The laird, a foolish father, fostered Chat's premature egotism by reading to Johnson, in front of his son, the boy's childish letters and his school reports. Chat and his adorable mother sang together,

> . . . the boy with his Scotch cap far back on his head, his strong rich hair in luminous swathes making a free crescent, his eyes like mountain pools, condensing under sunlight into jewels, his mouth smiling in the very making of the sounds, his voice springing but not hurrying, crisp and elastic, and his duly reserved but joyful mother sitting next him and supporting every rise of his voice as a lady eagle bearing up her eaglet.[7]

The Williamsons took him for a picnic on Loch Earn, which he detested: 'I hate the dirty plates and the perpetual dread of sitting down on a bottle of salad mixture.'[8] The Eton tutor must have made a curious spectacle on the Scottish moors.

Regy was at Eton in September for the winter half, and Johnson was present at his and Chat's reunion after eight weeks. 'It was good to see them together again,' he noted.'Yet there was a little cloud of shyness between them, just perceptible.' On 8 October he wrote: 'Beloved Brett and Chatter came to see me for a visit, such as I never got in old times. One played, the other entangled himself in my great chair. Is it possible he should like me for my own sake?' In fact Chat never cared for Tute, as the boys called him, as much as others of the clique did.

On 28 October Regy recorded in his journal an expedition to Skindles at Maidenhead, where they dined. At last some inroads upon the volatile Chat's affections could be registered.

> Returning Chat got on to the box seat with me and drove, making me put my arm round him to keep him warm and hold him on. After supper at the Trap Elliot and I lay together on the long morocco sofa. He put his dear strong arms round me & his face against mine. Chat, not very well, sat near the fire. . . . W.J. [Johnson] in the big red chair close to our sofa. We kept on calling for Chat, & finally he was lifted on to us, nestling in between Elliot and me. My arms were round him, & Elliot's were round him and me. Chat liked our both breathing in his ears. We kept on repeating this. All things must end.[9]

The occasion was celebrated by a poem in free verse by Regy, addressed to 'Charlie W', containing the lines: 'My prayer is heard. . . . For hours we stood together, his dear voice thrilling through every vein, passing his hand caressingly upon my head, showing me, O longed for joy, my love returned at last.' A note attached explains: 'Written when strongly under the influence of love for C.D.R.W.'

On the last day of the year Johnson wrote that he wished Chat was as fond of Regy as he ought to be, but he was certainly attached to him. He commended Regy for the poetical and rapturous affection, without passion, that he displayed. If he could keep it up he would be happy – for passion, disturbing the reason, turned sweet to sour. But in the next paragraph the master, as though forgetful of his Greek precepts of restraint, referred to 'the dear events of the last day at Eton . . . your last kissing of Elliot, his statuesque attitude in the chair with his arm round you, sitting still to be kissed and cherished'. One cannot help wondering how passionless these cub-like embraces were.

With the turn of the year 1869 Regy was caught up in a mesh of romantic friendships which for the remainder of his Eton career were to engulf him, somewhat to the detriment of his academic achievement. William Johnson was not slow to recognize this: 'It seems as if being in love at Eton was fatal to school work.' Yet he finished his letter to Regy with the observation, 'How little do the wiseacres know that this sentiment is actually part of the staple of life at a school.'[10]

Ainger may have been suspicious of what was going on and he was not – at this time of his life, anyway – a complaisant spectator of these schoolboy romances. He would certainly not have confided in his journal what Johnson wrote in 1868: 'I have seen young lovers interlacing like honeysuckle, rose and jessamine, romantic chivalrous friendships forming under my eye, to which I am almost admitted as a partner.' On the contrary, during the holidays of January 1869 Ainger saw fit gently to rebuke Regy by letter for spending too much of his time on extra-scholastic pursuits. He begged him to write and let him know if he wanted elucidation of his Latin and Greek reading. He clearly had a high opinion of his pupil's ability if only he would apply it, and in March was predicting that he ought to take a good classical degree at Cambridge.

The summer half of 1869 was arduous for Regy on the river. The previous year he had already 'got his boats' in *Britannia*, and there is a photograph of him wearing a straw boater crowned with a wreath of flowers over a broad Eton blue ribbon, marked *Britannia*, dangling over his left ear. It is probably this photograph which reminded his mother of the well-known portrait of Byron wearing Albanian dress, which she and her husband had just seen. Both thought that their son resembled the poet in his looks, and certainly the photograph shows a handsome boy with fine eyes, a firm nose and full, sensuous lips. This year he was promoted from *Britannia* to *Victory*, and for a short time endured rigorous training for the Eight. He also began to express that interest in politics which never deserted him. He wished, he wrote, that the Conservatives would stick to the old term, 'Tories'; then they would win more votes. He also displayed a loving concern for the welfare of his brother Eugene, who had followed him to Eton. The bucolic jaunts with Tute were resumed. 'Yesterday being a holiday Mr Johnson and my tutor took me to Marlow with some others, and we rowed to Medmenham Abbey and down to Maidenhead.' It all sounded quite innocent and innocuous. The Brett parents could surely congratulate themselves that Regy was making a number of suitable young friends among the scions of the nobility. For this they had very largely to thank that nice Mr Johnson.

Tute, unencumbered with a wife who might not have been welcome in the houses of the great, was a constant visitor to the parents of his favourite pupils. The Halifaxes entertained him at Hickleton, while the Northbrooks welcomed him at Stratton Park, Hampshire, and the Portsmouths at Eggesford Park in Devon. At Haverholme Priory in Lincolnshire he was doted on by the widowed Lady Winchilsea,[11] who shared all his romantic notions without understanding the depths of his philosophy. She soon became acquainted with Regy Brett, admired his good looks and intelligence and was impressed by his sophisticated tastes. She invited him to stay in Lincolnshire with her sons, Murray, Henry and Harold Finch-Hatton.[12] 'I delight in Reginald Brett,' she wrote to Johnson.

> He is like a beautiful summer day too sweet and bright to last . . . I do not think there is any youth out of your own family that would have interested and pleased you so well . . . so much mutual love and admiration, so much beauty and youth and music with so little that was otherwise than beauty and sweet is rarely seen . . . you would have seen them sitting with all the dogs on their knees and their arms linked and wound round each other. We were invited to dine out one day and I took Reginald and Murray and Henry. The three boys sat holding hands and worshipping each other.

She only trusted that Reginald would not become spoilt, for if he did she would have been largely responsible. Regy looked upon Lady Winchilsea as the kindest and most true-hearted of women.

In other words Regy had a way with him. Older women, such as his friends' mothers, were captivated by his attentions, his charm and enthusiasms. His school contemporaries were often amused and not a little jealous of the success which this paragon achieved in their homes. Julian Sturgis, his contemporary at Eton, was not deceived by his friend's susceptibility to admiration and flattery. He had a notion, he told him, that Regy only cared for people who made themselves pleasant and agreeable to him, in which case he tolerated them.[13] And again: 'You know that you are one of fortune's favourites who gains a great deal of affection at the expense of going about with a pleasant smile & an engaging manner, receiving a great deal as your right, and giving very little.' He added that Regy was a great liar and that he, Julian, never believed a word he said. Regy, knowing that his friend's straight talk was largely true, took these criticisms in good part. He professed himself not altogether satisfied with the way he was conducting his last two years at school, although it was all such fun and so romantic. To Ainger he admitted self-pityingly that he had wasted his life, but his tutor would not tolerate such nonsense, replying that Regy lacked sufficient self-discipline and was allowing the counter-attractions of Eton to prevent him from working hard enough. He reminded him that he would never find a better teacher anywhere than William Johnson; and he had only himself to blame if he did not take advantage of the great privileges he enjoyed.

In January 1870 Regy Brett returned to Eton for his last half, in the course of which he went to Cambridge for the entrance examination to Trinity College. On 1 February he was able to tell his mother that he had passed, but the prospect of leaving Eton was devastating. Regy clung to his beloved Tute who understood, and was himself still mourning Elliot, who had departed the previous summer. 'I have loved other Eton boys,' Johnson had written to the Troubadour, as he called young Brett,

> but none was so *great* as he, so devoted to the public good, so exalted above me. Some day, not long hence, *you* will be steeped in love for a woman as not to comprehend the old affection for boys. Meanwhile come to me and be friendly, for though old I am just like a boy in feeling. . . . Mentally I kiss your dear face and throat. Write to Elliot at once floods of love – he wants it all, being so lonely and starved.[14]

Regy was only too ready to come to the Trap, which he did daily, for comfort as well as intellectual sustenance. But Johnson was misreading him if he supposed that Regy would ever become so enslaved by women as to cease cultivating the old affection for boys. Regy never grew out of Eton; never grew away from it. It had done something to influence the whole course of his life. Distinguished and powerful though he was to become in later life, in this one respect he did not change: he never perfectly grew up.

When Reginald Brett's elder son left Eton in 1898, apparently without sorrow or emotion, his father was deeply shocked. He assured him that when he had left in 1870 he went straight to his parents' house, Heath Farm, where he spent miserable hours in his bedroom for days, even weeks on end. 'For not only did I leave a passionate friendship behind me at Eton, but I was devoured by the green-eyed monster, from whom (according to you) you are free.' Regy's passionate friendship was not for Reggie Paget, Arthur Wickham, Arthur Hervey, John Oswald, Edward Russell, Cyril Oliphant, Richard Greaves Townley or Ernest Bickersteth, to all of whom he wrote and received in return tearful missives of farewell and promises of unbroken friendships ahead. Nor was it for Alfred Lyttelton, that paragon of adolescents, a king among boys and of unbounded popularity with masters. Though these friendships were fervent, they were not all-absorbing, and did not arouse in Regy Brett the green-eyed monster. The cause of his disturbance was Chat Williamson.

Regy's memory was mistaken in recalling that he had gone straight from Eton to Heath Farm, there to eat his heart out in haunting nostalgia and jealousy. In fact he went by train from Paddington to Devon, in the company of William Johnson and Chat, to stay at Halsdon House which Tute had just rented from his elder brother. The low, irregular, comfortable Victorian house still stands on its small plateau above a long, steep slope to the River Torridge, murmuring in the woods below. Between groups of larch trees almost surrounding the house one open side allows a distant view of bleak, cold Dartmoor, pencilled faintly blue. The place is a remote oasis in barren moorland, approached by long, winding lanes within primrose- and fern-garnished banks, some eight to ten miles from Eggesford station and a mile and a half from the nearest village.

This was the first of several visits to Halsdon which in the years to come remained for him vivid dreams of tranquillity – albeit often of turbulent romance, and always intellectual stimulus. He was delighted with the cosy, old-fashioned air of the house with its panelled dining room, the bedrooms each bearing an esoteric name on its door – Bellew, Whey, Mr Pitt, Torrington, Wellington, Stourton and Zoar – the billiard room, with its ancient furniture, family portraits and relics, and the devoted old servants.

Days of unadulterated bliss ensued. One evening 'Chat and I slipped out of the window. A gorgeous moon overhead.' It was very still, an owl occasionally hooting.

We had one long kiss under the moor-shadows. We have stood lip to lip, under the woodland and by the murmuring Torridge. I have kissed him in every room in Halsdon. Five days of free and unconfined love. Our rooms are opposite and he wanders in and out quite easily and simply. Today we strolled down along to the river, through the oak copse. His arms were round my waist. He was dressed most sweetly, a flannel shirt, wading trousers, a bright tie and my Victory cap. I carried a plaid and the basket. I put up his rod and arranged his flies, then he fished and I read on the bank. Every fish he hooked I jumped down to land for him; so for three hours . . . . it is a delicious life, so easy and quiet, canvas shoes, and flannel shirts, astrachan caps and flannel coats. Chat has thrown himself altogether into our rapturous love and Halsdon is Elysium for me.[15]

The following day Francis Elliot arrived to stay, no doubt to Tute's joy. Regy did not record his sentiments beyond writing: 'Our positions are curious with regard to Chat', who had at Eton been attracted to Francis before turning to Regy. After dinner that evening Regy and Chat lay together on the sofa: 'My head has just left his shoulder,' Regy wrote, 'my lips his hair, my hand from clasping his; so we have been lying, and so the last evening is passing, the last for ever in these relations, in the free love of so many days.' There is a hint of finality in these words. Was he trying to face up to the fact that, with Eton now in the past, such boyish love ought regretfully to cease, or were the pangs of jealousy assailing him again?

On the day of Regy's departure Tute was unwell, and stayed in bed. However, he presented Regy with a locket, 'With Lalos and Kissos woven within it . . . . Chat and I said good-bye faintly enough in his room . . . . Our lips met for the last time at the foot of his bed, and so I saw the last of him I love best.' As the waggonette rolled slowly and noisily down the gravelled drive Chat rushed upstairs to his window, remaining there until it was out of sight.

Regy's condition did not pass unobserved by his friends or indeed his parents, who presumably did not understand it. His friends at first wrote him affectionate and sympathetic letters in reply to his lamentations at having left Eton. One rebuked him for being over-sentimental,[16] a charge that cannot be gainsaid. Allowing for the fashion of the time, the nicknames some boys chose for themselves were slightly ridiculous. Ernest Bickersteth, for example, was known to his intimates as either Beak or Ivy. Regy asked his special friends to call him June, a girlish name which luckily did not stick. His parents were perplexed by the depth of his unhappiness and his discontent at home. Sir Baliol, as his father had now become, had written to him at Halsdon: 'It is a grief for you to leave Eton I know but you must bear it cheerfully. Come to us soon.'[17] He admitted to being a little jealous of Johnson. 'I think you are right to go, but having pleased him, please us.' He told him not to be morose. To succeed in life one had to be popular, which meant mixing with all sorts, not merely with old school friends; Sir Baliol was fond of giving good advice. In June he was harping on the same subject. In his letters to his son he begged Regy to pay attention to his parents' advice and return the love they felt for him: 'You are now a man!' This was the one thing that Regy did not then like being.

As it turned out, life was not all lamentation and boredom. By the end of April Regy was in Paris staying with French relations, probably the Béjots. It was an exciting time to be there, on the eve of the Franco-Prussian War, swiftly to be followed by the Commune. Paris was a city of unrest and discontent, in which fear stalked. The citizens carried revolvers and sword-sticks. Diseases, including smallpox, were rife. Regy spent one day with Monsieur Husson, a very learned antiquarian who took him to the Panthéon and several churches, and conducted him round the whole Quartier St Germain. Patti was singing in *La Traviata* and he watched her take her curtain call smothered in bouquets. At the last ball ever given by the Emperor Napoleon III at the Tuileries he was introduced to Madame de Pourtalès, then one of the reigning beauties and a friend of the Empress Eugénie. He saw too the Empress, on the last public occasion before the waves closed over her splendour. 'She was radiant, without a jewel of any kind. Everyone else was emblazoned. The Emperor, half stupefied with morphia, inscrutable-eyed, and mightily unimpressive. The Tuileries [soon to be destroyed] gorgeous and crammed with the smartest and some beautiful women.'[18] On 11 May he watched troops being picketed in the streets of Paris, barricades smashed down, omnibuses and cabs overturned, and a *sergeant de ville* disembowelled. By 11 July France and Prussia were at war. Regy bitterly lamented the fate of Paris, identifying the destruction of the capital of his mother's country with 'leaving the spot on earth that was dearest to me' at a time of bodily anguish and suffering 'in which my beloved boyhood fled away'.[19]

The rest of the summer was spent watching his old school win the Eton and Harrow match, visiting Lord and Lady Ripon on the Isle of Harris where he shot stags and killed salmon, and staying with the widowed Lady Winchilsea at Haverholme where that susceptible lady stroked his hair amidst the old helmets and suits of armour. On 4 September came the seemingly irrelevant entry, 'Nothing to prevent me and Harold [his hostess's fourteen-year-old son] lying together on the sofa which we did in the evenings.' It was a mere interlude in the long hours of brooding over Chat. 'How true', he wrote in his journal, 'the idea that has floated through centuries of song: that the hours of youth are worth all the laurels of a lifetime.'

Regy took up residence at Cambridge in the Michaelmas term of 1870. In October he informed his mother that he was settling down happily. Suddenly he found himself plunged into adult society where nothing was taken for granted, where there was less heartiness, but also less openness, and yet more freedom of action than at school. In this tranquil and isolated haven of beauty, minds were pitted against minds. Every subject under the sun was submitted to the most logical scrutiny. The absorbing topic of games could be dispensed with. Sport took their place, but not to the exclusion of more important cerebral concerns. Regy did not excel at physical recreation, although he was a good swimmer; nor did he excel at work. In 1874 he acquired a second class degree, and two years later became an MA. Like innumerable undergraduates who have not yet decided upon a profession or career, he frittered away his time in an agreeably leisured manner. The mornings were mostly spent in reading and playing the piano;[20] the afternoons in wandering round the Backs or further afield; the evenings at dinner parties, rehearsals for plays and in moonlight walks with a favoured friend, such as Charlie King who had 'a divine voice and bright grey eyes'.[21]

But Halsdon and Chat, still at Eton, held him in thrall. In April 1871 the visit of the previous year was repeated. Their Etonian colleague Ernest Bickersteth, known as Beak or Ivy, accompanied them. On the train to Eggesford Regy chartered a private carriage in which he sat opposite Chat who 'slept wrapt up in my plaid; he wore my seal-skin cap. Then Beak wore his plaid.' Beak, a delicate boy greatly beloved by the group, was a special favourite of Johnson's. He was much in love with Chat, who did not then reciprocate. Next day Regy and Chat, arm in arm, looked for wild daffodils, anemones, violets and primroses. They played billiards and read Latin prose. Then they fished. Chat waded in his stockings, so Regy walked to the house to fetch him dry stockings and a towel. 'I found Chat at the same spot; he paddled in the stream; and I pulled off the wet socks; wiped his pretty white feet dry and reclothed them.' The two boys cut their names on a window sill. 'Chat is young for ever; bright as ever and brilliant. Gay, original, perfectly rapturously lovely. . . . His eyes are pools of life to me. Beak is the Ivy of yore; more manly; but bright, fresh and young still.'[22]

On the 18th Regy was back at his father's house in London. 'Chat again. Chat everywhere. I think of him ever; dream of him sleeping and waking. Would I could tell the story of our friendship.'[23] The remembrance of his pools of wit and cleverness and the brilliance of his mind, combined with the beauty of his person, eclipsed the most extravagant ideal.

Sir Baliol rescued the nineteen-year-old Regy from the hectic London season by making him accompany him on circuit to Salisbury in July. Regy was pleased, because the season was becoming a slight disappointment to him. 'Somehow it is not the sight of old friends so much as young friends that excites me. The old friends are so different to what they were.'[24] In other words they were growing up and leaving him behind emotionally. His journals this summer are interspersed with quotations from poems about youth.

From the Bishop's Palace at Salisbury Sir Baliol wrote a long letter to his wife, beginning, 'Of course the fact that you are not contented with Regy makes me unhappy.' Lady Brett was under the impression that her elder son was a wastrel, consorting with the idle rich and, in short, above himself. It is true that he found communication with his mother awkward. He found himself writing somewhat pompous clichés in his letters to her, such as 'Gold is but little use to man in his own native home. Transfer it to the surface and, see it may be dross.' She found this affected. And when he told her, 'I am older than you think,' she detected presumption. Sir Baliol did his best to make excuses for Regy.[25] He explained how his father, the Revd Joseph George, had risen to a better place in the world than *his* father. He, Baliol, had in turn reached a better place than his father – for her benefit. He and she were equally ambitious for Regy. So they had sent him to Eton and encouraged him to make acquaintance with boys of birth and rank, which he had duly done. Sir Baliol admitted that Regy was over-conscious of the equality between them at present. But he would soon grow to recognise the difference. It would continue until by his own exertions he raised himself to their nobility and status.

This well-intentioned letter did not entirely reassure Eugénie Brett. Within a year she was rebuking Regy for his depression. It was absurd to fancy he was old at twenty. She too had wished to die when she was twenty-three; it had been wicked and foolish. 'So long as you have these wild ideas you are very young, and I hope you won't remain so very long.'

The year 1872 opened with scandals at Eton which culminated in disaster for Johnson. In March Regy visited the school, where he learned that a boy called Probyn had been expelled in company with four admirers. A friend of Regy's, Reggie Herbert, was in a similar scrape after a master had discovered a foolish letter from him written to another boy. Some Chapel choristers, too, were implicated in clandestine affairs and had been given severe warnings by the governing body. At the end of the month Regy went to Halsdon and found Tute very gloomy, taking a morose view of life in general and Eton boys in particular. On 9 April 'Tute talked to me all the morning. He has resigned his Eton appointment and offered to take me on here until June.' Regy gave no reasons for William Johnson's decision which came as a great surprise and mystery to all his friends.

It has been suggested that in the aftermath of these various affairs the headmaster, Hornby, who had long regarded Johnson with suspicion, dismissed him. It was rumoured that a compromising letter from him to a certain boy had been found by the boy's parents, who sent it to the headmaster for an explanation. At all events Johnson was extremely upset and made out that he had resigned his mastership voluntarily. Regy's journal entry for 14 April goes on: 'I am to stay with Tute and give up my Cambridge term. Tomorrow I go to town and Eton to arrange Tute's affairs.' Indeed he went and packed up all Tute's 'valuables', bidding a final goodbye to the Trap and the Cabin. Writing from Cambridge, Regy's friend Albert Grey[26] reproached him, telling him that it would defer his degree. 'I cannot understand for the life of me why you have taken this droll fancy into your head, & stay away this term.'[27] The reason was that Tute was too unhappy to be left alone, and Regy had agreed to be his companion until he could travel abroad. For a young man of twenty this was noble behaviour, and one of very many sacrifices and hardships that he was willing to incur in the future for his friends.

In June Regy returned to London where he manoeuvred for a commission in the Duke of Rutland's Regiment of Militia; he was to receive it in the following year, being gazetted a lieutenant. At the beginning of July Tute left for the continent, taking Chat and Bickersteth, who had just left Eton. The idea was to make a break with England for several months until the gossip about his dismissal from Eton had died down. But the expedition was to be cut short by tragedy.

Meanwhile Regy again accompanied his father on circuit. After Carlisle Assizes father and son took the train to Patterdale, which seemed to Regy more like home than any other place – barring Eton – because in his childhood he had spent most of his summer holidays at Lowther Castle. Once again they were the guests of Lord Lonsdale. One Sunday evening he walked down to the lake, boarded a boat, paddled in solitude until the moon rose gloriously over the hills, and composed some verses. By the end of the month Sir Baliol was in Manchester, and it was here on 4 August that Regy received news which caused him great distress. 'Before I was out of bed I received a letter from Chat at Baden, telling me of Beak's illness, a slight fever. On going down to breakfast I got another . . . telling me of our dear boy's death.' The death of this young man – intelligent, sensitive and aspiring to the loftiest ideals – was a severe blow to his little group of worshippers. It was the first tragedy in Regy's life, and he took it badly. As for Chat, who had been in attendance upon Beak during his sudden illness and demise, he was shattered – though his grief was to some extent enhanced by misplaced guilt because he felt that he had not sufficiently returned the boy's ardent love.

Regy straightaway caught a train to Cambridge; his purpose was to retrieve from Beak's room certain letters 'which would have pained his relatives'.[28] In his journal he poured out a lament over the loss of his young friend. He had few regrets over his past relations with him, but the thought of one so young and beautiful now lying inanimate was too dreadful to contemplate. Alfred Lyttelton was similarly devastated, and wrote to Regy:

> As yet I cannot realise the full force of the blow . . . . All clouds are gone and I can only remember him, as you and I knew him, bright, fond and lovely. I hardly know what I am saying . . . . I cannot dare think whether I was to him a good or an evil influence, whether, if he turned his thoughts on me he could think of our love with pleasure or with a wish that it had never been. O Regy I am very miserable.[29]

Tute was, of course, heartbroken. He assured Regy that throughout his illness he had treated Ivy as though he were his own child. Chat, he informed him, had become very devout as a consequence of their friend's death. He thought Chat might end up a clergyman or one of those laymen who live with the clergy until they marry. The odd thing was that this response to the death of his companion was not temporary. It changed Chat's carefree, sybaritic outlook on life into a permanent inward-looking search for convictions which he never captured. Tute recognized the depth of the blow and told Regy that he feared Chat might wish to break with him after the catastrophe at Baden, as though he had been responsible for it.[30] On the contrary, by the end of the year Chat was back at Halsdon, showing more affection to Tute than formerly.

In October Johnson told Regy that he had changed his name by deed poll to Cory, his grandmother's name. His stated reason was that it would save time in writing. Furthermore, he announced that he was resigning his King's College fellowship. He could not see that he had the right to take £200 or £300 more from the founder's alms, although the Kingsmen were pressing him to return to them. 'Please to say this for me in case anyone deigns to notice the little event,' he wrote. Clearly he had taken the Eton business very much to heart. At any rate he believed he might still afford to go on living at Halsdon; but whether parents would continue sending their sons to him for tuition, he thought, was another matter.

At Heath Farm Regy was suffering terrible nightmares. Hiding in a cupboard, he found Beak beside him. 'I seized him in my arms and kissed his cheek, which was icy cold. It was his dead body.'[31] At the same time, as though to counter Chat's thrilling letters about his desire to be a clergyman ('He has a Catholic mind. Would make a perfect Jesuit.') and moved by the revelations of Charlotte Brontë's *Villette*, which he had recently read, Regy reflected upon the nature of women. 'There is one thing to be discovered yet,' he wrote, as Isaac Newton might have done about the law of gravity after discovering the composition of light. 'Perfect sympathy between men and women. How to keep morality without the aid of religion.'[32]

As a boy and a young man Regy had appealed strongly to older women; he was attentive and sympathetic and quickly gained their confidence. Lady Winchilsea had taken a strong fancy to him while he was still at Eton. Lady Ripon was to do so while he was at Cambridge, and he stayed again this autumn with her and her husband at Fincastle on the Isle of Harris. Known to her intimates as HAT, an acronym formed from the initials of her Christian names, Henrietta Ann Theodosia, Lady Ripon became a regular correspondent and treated him as a son. She was a kind, sweet semi-invalid, who appeared little in the public eye owing to a disfiguring ailment, and spent much of her time reclining on a sofa. An extremely rich woman, she was perceptive without being clever and always at the service of those in distress. Although she belonged to no religious group she was strongly in sympathy with the Christian Socialists and shared her husband's advanced radical views. It was largely through the Ripons' influence that Regy came to reject his father's Toryism and adopt the Whig principles that would lead him to join the Liberals. Lady Ripon became the intimate adviser of the future Liberal politician Sir William Harcourt in the years between his first and second marriages. Being wise and tender-hearted, she gently curbed the precipitate impulses of that incautious, quick-tempered but good-hearted man. It was during this visit to Fincastle that Regy met Harcourt, a friend of his father's, and his son Lewis, or Loulou, then a boy of nine.

William Harcourt, who had been called to the Bar in 1854, was now a brilliant advocate. Since 1869 he had been Whewell Professor of International Law at Cambridge, his duties entailing the delivery of a few lectures a year. On the strength of the appointment he had been granted rooms in Trinity; he now agreed to relinquish them to Regy, in whom he took a paternal interest, on condition that he might occupy them during his occasional periods of residence in the college. Regy was delighted with the spacious rooms in Nevile's Court, which were close to those of his friends, Bertie Grey and Arthur Lyttelton. Nevile's Court made a deep impression upon him. The peace and architectural symmetry, the narrow lime avenue, the lawns sloping to the River Cam, and the quiet cloisters were what his soul craved. All his life he was haunted by the sound of the Trinity clock striking the hours, the Chapel bell and the tinkling of the Great Court fountain.

In January 1873 Tute went on a cruise to Alexandria, taking with him Harold Finch-Hatton. Fanny Winchilsea was a loyal friend prepared to entrust her beloved youngest son to the tender mercies of the ex-Eton master, whom she still revered. At the end of the month Regy went on a visit to Studley Royal in Yorkshire, another of the Ripons' homes. He saw and approved the new church in the park, which William Burges was in the course of building 'with his usual good taste'. He attended the Ripons' only son Olly de Grey's coming-of-age celebrations, and enjoyed balls, feasts, concerts and skating parties. At a tenants' dinner for 250 farmers Lord de Grey spoke well. On the last day of March Regy went to Halsdon in Tute's absence to keep an eye on the place. He took with him Albert Grey, accounted one of his best Cambridge friends, who was much liked by Tute when he met him at Trinity. In after years Regy remembered with affection his 'transparent utterances, his varying moods, his constant principles, his choking idealism'. The son of Queen Victoria's first secretary, Bertie Grey was an ardent Liberal; he would argue with his contemporaries deep into the night as he rushed with exultant glee or rage from one set of rooms to another in Nevile's Court. Sparkling and fervent, he enjoyed life immensely. His Cambridge letters to Regy were gossipy and rather facetious.

An event in May which impressed itself strongly upon Regy was a visit to Cambridge by George Eliot. Regy had been taught by his father to consider her books not as fiction but as careful philosophical thoughts expressed in the form of novels. He was captivated by her presence and wrote:

> Her low sweet voice thanked me for giving her tickets for the Choir Festival at King's, to which she, taking interest in every or any religious service, took her husband who had not entered a church for years. . . . Her face reminds me of Savonarola's bust and pictures at San Marco, Florence. She exuded Agnosticism.[33]

Regy did not seem to mind this, but Sir Baliol, had he known, would most certainly have minded. Once again in the summer the son accompanied his father on circuit in the Midlands. They stayed in a series of country houses, including Knowsley with Lord Derby, whose eccentricities made him a difficult conversationalist. He would pause for long intervals before answering, so fearful was he of not expressing exactly what he meant. Moreover he had a positive horror of touching – he thought hands were dirty things. Lord Odo Russell, the Minister in Berlin, was also a guest and alarmed Regy by telling him that Germany could muster one million men, if need be, in less than a fortnight. These days Regy's head was full of metaphysical gleanings. He was worried, too, by Chat's behaviour. Chat was for ever mourning for 'our Adonais', Beak Bickersteth, the experience of whose sudden death (from galloping consumption), he explained, had terrified him and scarred his life. In September he established himself in a mission church where he read the lessons in a cassock and surplice. After a visit to Paris Regy was back at Heath Farm, bored and pining nostalgically for Halsdon and Chat, now more than ever alienated from him by his newly acquired piety.

Regy soon became a member of a distinguished intellectual circle of Cambridge undergraduates which formed a sort of Platonic symposium. It consisted of Frank and Gerald Balfour, younger brothers of Arthur, the future Prime Minister, and in those days both considered more brilliant than him; S.H. and J.G. Butcher, scholars and men of letters; Albert Grey; Edmund Gurney (of musical renown and founder of the Society for Psychical Research) and Alfred Lyttelton's brother, Arthur, a man marked for the highest offices of the Church but who died prematurely. In addition there was F.W. Maitland, of whom Leslie Stephen once said to Regy, 'Whatever Maitland tells you, you may be sure is as near to truth as we can hope to get.' He became Downing Professor of Law at Cambridge. Hallam and Lionel Tennyson, the Poet Laureate's two sons, completed the group. Regy thought at the time that of the lot Gerald Balfour and Maitland would achieve most fame in the long run.

Without deserting their undergraduate companions, Regy and Bertie Grey began to see much of three dons: Henry Jackson, Regius Professor of Greek, R. Claverhouse Jebb, a Greek scholar, and James Stuart. Professor Stuart, who helped found the university movement for extending education to destitute districts of London, lured Regy into joining a small band of graduates who under his supervision delivered lectures on history and economics in Bermondsey. In this way Stuart introduced him to a stratum of society of which he had hitherto been unaware. Compassion for these people confirmed his developing Liberal instincts. Yet another influence upon him was Henry Bradshaw, the university librarian and a Fellow of King's. Bradshaw became a father figure, an affectionate and sympathetic friend rather than a teacher. His Sunday afternoons before Chapel were a tradition. Bradshaw's learning seemed universal and Regy regarded him with profound reverence. But if his erudition attracted many, his standards excluded all but a few: before acceptance the aspiring disciple's voice, manners and appearance were closely scrutinized and assessed. Of ruddy complexion and stocky build, Bradshaw reminded Regy of a tawny, plump cat, who purred when something pleased him and showed his claws when he was displeased. After Regy went down from Cambridge he turned more and more towards Bradshaw as his mentor, while becoming increasingly remote from

Meanwhile Tute continued to correspond regularly. His letters dealt with every subject under the sun – the unacceptable power of upper-class parents over their offspring; the necessity for Balzac's novels 'as substitutes for conversation with intellectual people'; Wordsworth's 'Excursion', the music that passed into the face of nature; and the way to avoid old age being to love the young. His letters were becoming more and more diffuse, his political views more and more erratic.

The summer term of 1874 was Regy's last as an undergraduate at Cambridge. The chief event was the entertainment of his father at the Master's Lodge at Trinity, with Alfred Lyttelton acting as the Judge's Marshal. Regy basked in reflected glory. In May he went to camp as lieutenant with his Militia and on 20 June took his degree. This was celebrated by an expedition. On the 25th he rowed with friends down the Thames from Henley to Windsor, sweetly reminiscing about Eton. They passed Hurley, where Chat had thrown flowers into the branches of sycamore trees.

Now he had come to the end of his allotted phase as an undergraduate at Cambridge, where life had been more adult and only a little less agreeable than at Eton, which was always to retain his first allegiance. To Regy the charm of childhood, with the rapid germination of noble ideals, was more appealing than early manhood, in which these ideals can be watched slowly fading until they are lost in convictions, fixed opinions and the sundry shibboleths of maturity. As an undergraduate, it is true, he had cemented some old friendships and made new ones, but without the accompaniment of romance. For the romantic friendships essential to him, Regy would have to look elsewhere, away from the monastic courts and cloisters.

3

YOUTH IN DISARRAY

1874–1877

Sir Baliol Brett's cherished scheme was, not unnaturally, that his elder son should follow in the paternal footsteps and read for the Bar. Regy complied with his father's wishes to the extent of not positively dissenting. But from the first he did not foresee a legal career as the fulfilment of his talents and tastes. What were his ambitions? Truth to tell, at this stage of his life – he was twenty-two – he had none. He did not know what he wanted to do beyond lead a social life in the country and London houses of the great people with whom he had made friends, at his father's request, and felt at ease. Nor could Sir Baliol complain that any of the sprigs of nobility with whom he had become intimate at Eton and Cambridge were undesirable. Vaguely Regy wanted to write prose, and less vaguely poetry, for which he had an easy facility but little genius, to play the piano, and to improve his mind by reading. His condition was that of many young men of his class with the education of Eton and Cambridge behind them, plenty of prospects in the future and very little ready cash in the present.

Meanwhile, in July 1874 he went on yet another four weeks' circuit with his father, this time to the West Country. On 4 August they were at Axminster. Regy recorded it as 'the saddest day of the year to me. The anniversary of our great loss. It was two years ago that we first kept that melancholy day.' The mid-Victorians were tremendously addicted to melancholy anniversaries. Arthur Lyttelton sent him some verses about Bickersteth, and Regy composed a sonnet, 'Quo Desiderio', in which he pictured Beak Bickersteth on either the football or the cricket field:

And through my tears I watch once more the game,
   And see him dash across that southern field,
Stop sharp, and toss back with a haughty fling
   His rebel hair into delicious curves
And then impetuous as hawk on wing
   Dart back again with sudden bird-like swerves
Which send my blood leaping as it leapt then.

Two days later father and son were at Wells, staying at the Bishop's Palace. Here Regy had another momentous encounter with a youth who for the next six or seven years was to make a heavy tax upon his affections, though never to the extent of Chat or Beak. Ernlé Johnson, then fifteen, was the elder son of the Dean of Wells, a mathematical scholar and great friend of Archbishop Tait of Canterbury. A photograph taken while at school at Malvern shows an oval face, not strictly handsome; but he had fair, wavy hair and raised eyebrows which gave him a questioning aspect. He was small and rather delicate. Tormented, like so many sons of Victorian ecclesiastics, by problems of original sin and lack of response to prayer, he looked to Regy, as an older, experienced man of the world, for help and guidance. Yet he had a mind of his own. Strongly Tory and monarchist, he would not be converted to Whiggery by his friend. He was a good correspondent and Regy thought fit to have his letters from 1875 to 1882 typed and bound in two volumes, to which he gave the title *A Schoolboy's Letters*. He had them scrupulously expurgated in the process.

Ernlé was brought by his younger brother Basil, a promising pianist, from the Deanery to the Palace. The two boys listened ravished by Regy's rendering on the episcopal piano of Bach preludes and the Louis XIII gavotte. Then Regy persuaded Basil to accompany Ernlé singing some sentimental ditties. Ernlé's sweet voice reminded him of Chat's and reduced him to tears; the susceptible postgraduate's heart was smitten. Before being whisked off by Sir Baliol the following day he promised to send Ernlé songs by Gounod.

Father and son spent the night of the 9th at Longleat as guests of Lord Bath. Regy was deeply impressed by the luxuries of this great house, notably the rosewater provided in the bedrooms for washing. Lord Malmesbury[1], and Disraeli, who had been Prime Minister since February, were among the guests. Lord Malmesbury who was rising seventy, had been Foreign Secretary in Lord Derby's first Government. Full of gossip about George IV's marriage with Caroline of Brunswick, he possessed the King's affidavit taken on the third day of his married life. It affirmed that the monarch had been to bed with the Queen only three times in all, on the first night after he had drunk much wine, on the afternoon of the second day, and again that night. Each experience was more beastly than the previous one. She was definitely not a virgin when she came to him, and her manners were extremely coarse. When she put her hand on his person exclaiming, '*Mon Dieu, qu'il est gros!*' even King George was taken aback and vowed never to sleep with her again. He kept to his oath. Regy found Dizzy enchanting. He put the company into fits of laughter talking about his scheme for a Channel tunnel; even his silences were droll. He took young Regy into the garden for a stroll. Remarking on personal attacks and political hatreds, he said, 'I never trouble to be avenged, but, when a man injures me, I put his name on a slip of paper and lock it up in a drawer. It is marvellous how men I have thus labelled have a knack of disappearing.'[2]

In the middle of August Regy went to Scotland, taking the train to Aberdeen. From there he walked up the Dee to Ballater, a knapsack over his shoulder, and passed Balmoral. He stopped at tiny shops for lemonade and bannocks, and slept in lonely inns, sometimes on sofas. The children he passed walked barefoot. Eventually he reached his goal, Crieff in Perthshire. After depositing his luggage at the station he walked to Lawers on the road to Loch Earn, to stay with the Williamsons and Chat. He ambled up to the front of the sturdy Palladian house, with its long matching wings at either end and projecting colonnades, all of purple stone; while he stood observing the large ancestral house he heard the rattle of a drag and four horses drawing up at the front door. So he hid in the bushes to give Chat, in a red tartan kilt and grey plaid over his shoulder, a head start. After an interval he advanced, pulled the bell – which came away in his hand – and waited. Chat answered the door. 'He was not shy,' wrote Regy. 'I forgot whether we shook hands or not. His mother was upstairs, and we got our greetings over before going to dress. On coming down I met his father. Dinner was lively, owing mostly to the chaff of Mrs Williamson.'[3] Regy could not but admire the father's appearance. 'Extraordinarily handsome. His hair is black as jet and his teeth and eyes very beautiful. In a kilt his whole person is shown to great advantage.'

Mrs Williamson was still young and pretty, he thought; she might have been eighteen. As for Chat he was unchanged, except for being taller and broader. 'Intellectually he is brilliant beyond comparison. His social qualities are more eminent than I could have believed possible. Still his speech is like music, and he still retains that touch of tongue, that art of leaving things unsaid, which made his boyhood so lovely.' The old magic persisted. It was only after bedtime, when Chat sat with him for an hour and talked about 'the subject which is nearest his heart', namely his religion, that Regy realized their relations could never again be on the same footing. He spent a week at Lawers, walking and talking. 'Many sweet talks with Chat and songs from his mother. . . . Her last song was "Farewell to Lochaber"; his last word was a promise, unfulfilled.'[4]

On his return to London Regy had to make a show of taking life seriously. He began his first term reading for the Bar; it was not inspiring, and he could not pretend it was. He sought relief in concerts and plays. He listened to Rossini's *Stabat Mater*, heard Joachim playing in a Mendelssohn quartet and saw Henry Irving as Hamlet.

In December he again went on circuit with his father to Stafford and Worcester. In the latter city he watched the schoolboys in the cathedral playground at the old game of Base. 'It was delicious to watch the beautiful curves of the boys' figures, swerving and turning sharply to avoid capture. It was as good as Miss Farren[5]. . . . Shall I live to see the education of children forced upon parents? Why cannot it be done now? That great good which must come.' Even when caught by aesthetic reverie Regy could turn his attention to the lot of the underprivileged. Political perfectionism was stirring within him. This month he wrote a letter to *The Times* about the Brussels Conference for the rearrangement of the rules of warfare; it may be taken as the first intimation of his public career. In spite of the disappointing announcement of his second-class degree Regy decided, under the influence of S.H. Butcher, to stay up at Cambridge for at least another two years. He became a regular lecturer for Professor Stuart's University Extension movement in the East End of London.

By the spring of 1875 he had abandoned all pretence to study law. Instead John Stuart Mill's *Logic* and *Political Economy* were his preferred reading and subjects for discussion. Another was military strategy. He found himself questioning opinions which previously he had taken for granted, and this left him in a state of perplexity. Although he still stayed at Halsdon and corresponded with Tute, his new sympathies no longer always accorded with those of his old mentor. Tute's didactic pronouncements were becoming increasingly perverse. It irritated Regy to be told that Sir John Millais's paintings were more poetical than all those of the Renaissance put together, and that Shakespeare's *King Lear* was the most ridiculous play ever written. He read through Tute's early letters to him, 'so full of tenderness they made me weep, and then the thoughts which crowded after into my mind, thoughts of those golden years which form the great trilogy of my life, 1868, 1869, 1870. Then came the war, and soon after the death of our darling [Bickersteth] and sorrow and misery and coldness and age.'[6]

Matters were not improved by the receipt of a letter on 4 February from Chat, announcing that he had been received into the Catholic

Church. Regy went hurriedly to Lady Ripon, who was subconsciously aware of his feelings for Chat. She was in a good position to proffer comfort, since her husband had caused great consternation in political circles by becoming a Catholic the previous autumn. From this tender-hearted woman Regy departed with the conviction that his friend's step was not necessarily deplorable. 'My soul is with Chat. . . . There are so many strong links to bind me to him,' he decided.[7]

Regy had not reckoned with Tute's reaction. The latter had never been able to remain intimate with a friend who turned Roman Catholic, and was furious with Chat: 'A man who loves the priests more than his country, a man who wishes no good to Italy . . . a man habitually reckoning on Purgatory and Penance as a sort of hedging or insurance, such a one I can hardly respect enough for friendship.'[8] These were reactionary words coming from a man who all his life preached liberal principles; the truth was that he regarded Chat's conversion as a rejection of his teaching. But the old kindliness soon reasserted itself. When he learned that Mr Williamson had cut his son's allowance and refused to allow his wife to borrow money from her Tredegar relations to keep the boy alive, he sent him £50 in spite of Chat having written him a curt note saying that henceforth he wished to keep Tute at arm's length, and having returned the necklace Tute had given him. It was spontaneous acts of generosity such as this which never failed to arouse Regy's admiration for Tute. Tute so far forgave Chat that he took him for an afternoon to Greenwich where they admired a Turneresque sky. He even canvassed friends to get him elected to the St James's Club, where at least he could eat a square meal; then he offered to pay his subscription. He went to Oxford and walked to Shotover and back with Chat, talking about his hopes in the Church he had just joined.

Distress over the step Chat had taken did not prevent Regy cementing his friendship with Ernlé Johnson – perhaps it even encouraged him. If Chat no longer wanted his love and intimacy, here was a schoolboy who did. Regy's journals for the next six months are almost exclusively devoted to Ernlé. He arranged assignations to meet him in the holidays under the monument to Pitt in Westminster Abbey. In termtime he made excursions to Malvern where he took the boy from school for long walks on the hills, endeavouring to instil in him some of the high thoughts which Tute had taught him – liberal notions and principles of freedom. Ernlé disclosed his problems, which amounted to little more than a belief that his school-fellows did not care for him because his political convictions were too Tory, and that his ill health was due to hereditary causes. Regy was much touched by these adolescent banalities and wrote in his journal:

As no human eye will ever, I trust, see this I may record his sweet expression of gratitude when I sent him away with a gift of two bright sovereigns, a bottle of rose water for his eyes, and one of my Venetian photographs. His fair face lifted up with a look which you dream of upon the face of Raphael's violin player. . . . Ernlé's fair hair haunts me, and his voice modulated as it is almost into a theme. . . . He is as pure and simple as Ivy was when he used to stand under the moonlight in the open window of my dame's passage in 1868. I could write a symphony upon the melody of Ernlé's expression, poor dear little fellow.[9]

And so the reflections continued. Whereas there was something natural and robust about Regy's boy loves at Eton, among his contemporaries or near contemporaries, another side of his repressed sexual nature is manifested in the simpering affection of this twenty-three-year-old man for a weakling schoolboy of sixteen.

Regy was gently feeling his way. When Ernlé begged his more worldly-wise friend to tell him his faults and throw light upon the cause of his unhappiness, Regy rejoined that were he to tell the inmost truth about his own, Ernlé would be scandalized. To this he received the reply, 'This is impossible, so please let me know at once.' Regy did so, while at the same time urging Ernlé to concentrate less upon theories such as predestination and original sin and instead to throw his cap over the windmill. Ernlé expressed gratitude to Regy for releasing him from bigotry, narrowness and pedantry.

Meanwhile Lady Ripon was wondering how she could help Chat. By April she had persuaded her husband – who, although he had recently resigned all offices, was to resume an active public life, becoming Viceroy of India in 1880 – to engage Chat as his private secretary. Regy urgently summoned Chat to London, told him of his good fortune and took him to be interviewed by Lord Ripon, who, favourably impressed by the applicant, pitied his predicament and straightway engaged him. At the beginning of May Regy accompanied Chat to Studley Royal where his friend took up his duties. During the visit Chat agreed with Regy that 'there are intimacies between friends who have known Tute which cannot exist between others. An outsider would think a great many things very peculiar "in one of us".'[10]

During the summer of 1875 Regy was launched on London's social life. A personable young man, son of a successful and highly respected father, he was welcomed in the houses of the great and grand. He stayed with the flamboyant Lady Waldegrave at Strawberry Hill, where the atmosphere, more political than literary, was slightly tinged with Revivalism. Exclusively social was a ball at Grosvenor House. He and Albert Grey escaped from Cambridge without leave, returning at dawn by the milk train – for Constance, Duchess of Westminster, had urged the flagging band to yet one more waltz in the early hours. The carrying of heavy luggage was an encumbrance. At this date men changed their evening coats between dinner and a ball if they had been in contact with tobacco smoke. Girls carried bouquets of lilies to a dance, while young men wore gardenias or a tuberose in place of 'orders', which were then restricted to the blue sash of the Garter or the red ribbon of the Bath. The fragrance of exotic flowers, mingled with the stench of sweat – for deodorants were unknown – was often overpowering in a ballroom. The month of July marked the peak of Regy's social ascent. On the 21st he attended a ball at Stafford House, the first of many visits to the Duke and Duchess of Sutherland's great town house, to meet the Prince and Princess of Wales. On the 26th he was invited to Marlborough House itself; he could hardly go higher. He wore knee breeches and enjoyed it enormously, for he actually danced with the ravishing Princess of Wales at three o'clock in the morning.

In August, the London season being over, Regy Brett considered what progress, if any, he had made in life. Yes, there had been a little, and that little must in all fairness be largely attributed to Tute. On the other hand he wondered if the influence of one powerful mind was not weakening for a man because the impression it left was perhaps too marked. In his humility he asked himself what results should be expected from a life spent calmly, with no compelling desire for riches or power, with 'only a hope to be of service to a few friends'.[11] This was a theme which persisted through the whole of Regy Brett's life. He decided with a modicum of satisfaction that he had added a little to his store of knowledge. But morally he felt obliged to confess that his vicious inclinations had intensified and virtue passed out of him. From 1868 – that is to say when he was sixteen – 'My whole soul has decayed. Bad habits have increased their hold, good wishes have given place to worldly ones. Perhaps I have escaped the commission of one irremediable sin. Perhaps there never was any great danger of it being committed.' The ambiguity in these words can be clarified by the sentence which immediately follows. It probably does not relate to sexual intercourse, which it is hard to suppose he had not yet experienced. 'However *she* will live to find a better life-mate than I should have made, and a true one, I hope. It is a bitter reflection.' The 'she', a guarded and coy substitute for 'he', must be Chat, and the explanation that Regy had refrained from dissuading Chat from turning to God and clinging to him. And, he continued, 'in looking over these two years of my life I cannot recall to mind a single pure and disinterested action. . . . I am thinking of all those who have been the stars in the firmament of my life.'[12] The self-deprecation is excessive. Yet it is proof, if proof be needed, that the writer was not a hardened egoist or a complacent voluptuary. He was fortified by reflecting upon the fact that Ernlé, with whom he kept up almost daily correspondence, was as yet unsullied by worldliness and could claim to be motivated by the loftiest ideals – so haunted was Regy by the lost innocence of his own youth.

In September, with his family in Switzerland, he composed love-sick verses. He found that in idle moments there was no sweeter way of employing the mind than in dwelling upon the memory of some friend and throwing the picture into the form of verse: 'giving it a tangible shape as a sculptor does his conception. It prevents the mind flapping vainly to and fro like a loose sail in the wind.'[13] A letter from Chat wondering why more people did not read St Augustine and enclosing a poem addressed to the Virgin Mary, and several letters from Ernlé assuring him that so far he had managed to avoid immorality 'and the odious vice called *fastness*', left him curiously unmoved. What put him into 'a stage of stormy emotion' was the sculpture gallery of the Louvre, visited on the family's return journey to London.

When he got back to Cambridge for the Michaelmas term he compounded his impatience with Chat's new-found religious fervour by visiting him in cheerful rooms next to a monastery in Oxford and reading poetry with him in anticipation of his examination for a degree – it was to be a third. 'Near to one of those dearest to me on earth', he wrote piously, 'I feel that immortality, such as I can imagine it; free from temptation, free from anxiety.'[14] Yet he could not refrain, on picking up the first book he had given Chat, in 1868, from recalling nostalgically how at the time he had not dared sign his name as the giver, so smitten had he been with desire for him. He compounded his irritation with Ernlé's perpetual protestations (Was it wrong to work on Sundays? It was in order, was it not, to look for hope in the vast consolatory power of nature in Wordsworth's poetry at a time when his own religious faith was waning?) by heartening that tormented boy, who reposed all his capacity for love and his hopes of salvation in Regy, now addressed by his Christian name, Reginald, instead of Brett. Regy much enjoyed explaining to Ernlé the meaning of Tennyson's 'The Palace of Art' (an uphill task) and sympathizing with his distaste for Cicero and indifference to Terence and Plautus. Nothing gave him more pleasure than instructing those whom he loved.

Just as 1868 had been Francis Elliot's year, 1869 Chat's and 1870 Beak Bickersteth's, so 1875 had been Ernlé Johnson's. The rest of his life would be guided by Ernlé's pure influence exerted unconsciously like the mask of moving water over mountains, or the wind through trees. Regy was aware of telling him more than he really intended. 'Perhaps everyone has always felt the presence of two distinctly different natures, one sometimes standing in a neutral and critical attitude towards the other.'[15] He asked Ernlé to keep their friendship dark from the world which contaminated and destroyed, and to avoid discussing him with others. His affair was not altogether free from guilt, which was confirmed by Howard Sturgis a few years later. 'You and I, Rex[16] dear', Howard wrote, 'were the youthful vices of that young man who has shaken himself free and into the Heaven of the Blessed, under the auspices of a very chubby angel with a most *un*-cherubic continuation.'[17] In other words Ernlé had fallen in love with a schoolfellow of his own age who was, however, to prove a disappointment. No doubt Ernlé's discovery of a contemporary who could for a time requite his copious affection weaned him from the attentions of older suitors: by 1890 he was a civil servant in the Home Office and in love with a girl. After a long interval he wrote to his old admirer for a loan of £100, which was promptly given him. Regy never dropped Ernlé, always keeping in touch with him. Meanwhile Ernlé's sufferings on Regy's account were not yet quite at an end.

In January 1876 Robert, 2nd Lord Lytton, son and heir of Bulwer Lytton, the novelist, poet and statesman, was appointed Viceroy of India. Regy's Aunt Adèle Gurwood, one of Lady Brett's half-sisters, who all her life was devoted to her nephew, revealed that through her friendship with the new Viceroy's father she might get him the job of private secretary, were she to ask for it. Regy was within an ace of allowing his aunt to do so, but knew his father would not approve on account of the climate and fear that his son's health was not up to it. Indeed long afterwards Regy recorded that Robert Lytton had been prepared to take him. Thus he missed an early opportunity to launch himself into politics, and the next did not present itself until two and a half years later.

Regy was going through one of his recurrent bouts of Halsdon sickness. Chat was there staying with Tute, and his letters to Regy gave his friend cause for grave concern. They intimated that, in direct opposition to his father and even his adoring mother, he was about to join St Philip Neri's Order of Oratorians which J.H. Newman had lately introduced to England. They reproached Regy for his persistent paganism. Regy was saddened that he could not think as Chat thought. With his mania for anniversaries he recalled on 8 April that six years ago to the day he had been walking with Chat at Halsdon in perfect happiness, untrammelled by any tiresome religious prohibitions.

In June he stayed with the Ripons at Nocton Hall. Chat also came, wonderfully cheerful, from a retreat. He announced that he had settled to go to Newman's Oratory in Birmingham as a priest. Since their two bedrooms adjoined they were in and out, arguing and discussing, far into the night. What worried Regy about the chances of Chat's future contentment and, indeed, purity of mind was that, as Chat confessed to his lover, his old desires were unweakened. The following month, while at Malvern with Ernlé, Regy wrote his confession to Chat. He told him that he was without faith; that he had no religious convictions, no beliefs at all.

> I do not feel that there is any hope of a life beyond this. I do not feel that there is any power guiding the destinies of mankind. . . . I live on from day to day, without any great aim, but having a few small aims; accepting the experiences of mankind as guides in the choice of this or that: resisting what I am taught are temptations when I can, and when I fail, giving in with a feeling that, it is so arranged, and the consequences must be borne.[18]

Regy made the same confession to Ernlé, who was all noble solicitude. Ernlé's advice to Regy was 'to cling to the last chance for Chat, marry him if you possibly can; scheme; intrigue, practise on his emotions. All this is fair to save a man from himself.' But if this tactic were not successful, then 'it is best to look sorrow in the face, to take her, if need be, for a bride. . . . Dear friend, it is impossible that your life should be spoilt by this.'[19] All the comfort that he, Ernlé, could derive from the situation was to occupy second place in Regy's affections.

In September Regy was at Studley Royal. Cardinal Manning, next to whom he sat at dinner, was a guest. Regy hated him for indirectly ruining the life of his dearest friend. He would never forgive the Catholic Church for her opposition to patriotism (in other words putting God before country), domestic ties, friendship between man and man, and, strangely, the acquisition of knowledge. Regy was in despair. To his journal he committed the lament:

> I know of a love that combines the passionate devotion and persistent fervour of one (a mother's), with the forgiving tenderness and self-sacrifice of the other. The sort of love rhymed about by the ancients, and idealised by the noblest Greeks. Something like it, during ten years, I have felt. I courted for a year. For a second year I worshipped. Then came those years of passion, intensified by marvellous aids from books and art and music. Then a breakage of hopes until I floated into smooth waters. After next Tuesday we shall be nothing to each other, except in my dreams. Still for this week he is with me. His room opens into mine. We can talk each other to sleep, and I can hear him breathing through the night. And this is '*meorum finis amorum*'.[20]

The following week Chat departed for the Oratory. Ernlé, Francis Elliot, the lamented Beak and the other loves of yore now meant nothing to Regy. They were eclipsed by the one over-riding love about to be lost to him forever. 'I am not sanguine about [Chat] returning to the world,' Regy recorded in his journal. 'He let me kiss his hand before the train took him away. . . . I have seen as much as possible of him during the week. Perhaps our friendship ends more poetically so.'[21] On the 26th he received a stiff, cold letter from Chat; it signified that they had better not write any more, and should think of each other as little as possible. Regy did his best to forget, and he more or less succeeded, but there could not fail to be traces everywhere of Chat's previous existence. It was agony to be reminded of his present whereabouts. Howard Sturgis, for example, wrote three months later, 'The other day going down Piccadilly in a hansom, I saw a beautiful face that seemed familiar surmounting a queer muslin collar and long black garment; it was Chat looking more lovely than I ever remember to have seen him since he was quite small. I did not recognize him till I got past. I am so sorry.'[22] Regy was deeply upset.

Regy's loneliness and sense of desertion were not improved by the marriage that month of his sister Violet to William Humble Dudley Ward, a tall, good-looking young man with a fair moustache. Spoilt and brought up to expect the inheritance of the barony of Dudley, Ward never got over the marriage of his uncle (who became 1st Earl of Dudley) in middle age and his procreation of six sons. Violet was adored by her father and mother and her two brothers. Eugénie disliked her son-in-law from the start, and showed it. In due course Regy pronounced him drunken and fiendish, with no redeeming qualities at all.[23] He was certainly neurotic and uncontrolled. When his pet parrot, which he had teased, bit him, Ward proceeded to wring its neck, stamp on it and behave like a lunatic. This nasty scene was followed by a fit of remorse, when he kissed it and buried it by torchlight in the garden.

Politics were concerning Regy more and more. Mill's hatred of oppression was weighing heavily upon him. He particularly deplored at this time the contempt shown by the white man for the natives in India, foreseeing that the Indians would seize the first opportunity to escape from the British yoke. He asked his friend Albert Grey to put him up for Brooks's Club, which was tantamount to declaring himself publicly a Liberal.

This Michaelmas term a new friend came into his life in the person of George, Lord Binning, the son and heir of the 11th Earl of Haddington. Of all the friends of Regy's postgraduate Cambridge years, Binning, four years younger and just up from Eton, became the closest and dearest. He did not belong to the Halsdon set and was unknown to Tute. Although he was to get a first, Binning was not an intellectual; his interests were mainly sporting. He was an intelligent, affectionate, extrovert, madcap charmer. Regy was intoxicated by his splendid physique, which Binning had taxed by games and – so he liked to pretend – uncontrolled abandon to his desires at Eton. In fact Regy believed that he was already a physically broken man. He admired his new friend's half-conscious irony, combined with a most lovable manner, and his mind stored with music and romance. These qualities aroused Regy's protective instincts. Evening after evening he spent quietly with Binning, delighting in ordering him to bed promptly at ten o'clock for his health's sake. Binning reciprocated the affection, although slightly bewildered and gently amused by his friend's adoration. When he came to leave Cambridge to go into the Army he asked him, 'What strange whim induced you to take up the shy, gruff, hunted-looking animal (your description) you found, and by what strange process you have transformed it into a fairly decent member of society (your description again) I will not enquire.'[24]

Regy Brett was not the first or the last person of either sex whom George Binning's deep brown eyes and piquant smile were to enslave. But none remained so constant and loyal a friend, or so tireless in helping him out of scrapes. It was not long before George's promiscuity led to contraction of venereal disease. Throughout the 1880s he was a martyr to painful cures in a series of Austrian nursing homes. The disease deferred his marrying, which his parents kept requesting him to do. Regy, who had ingratiated himself with his friend's mother, acted as a mollifying go-between when Lady Haddington finally discovered the cause of her son's indisposition.

Regy continued to write almost daily letters to Ernlé, and to receive his replies. He noted that the eighteen-year-old boy was showing advance in imagination and wisdom. But he told him he should not make use of terms such as 'coarse passion' without defining what he meant. Possibly what he called 'coarse passion' might one day be considered the least sordid of all human desires. Ernlé was referring in a coy way to his hopeless love for the schoolfellow at Malvern. By the end of the summer term the unrequited passion was over and done with, and the object of it had left the school. In the autumn Ernlé was established in rooms in Peckwater Quad at Christ Church. He still loved Regy more than anyone else, he wrote, thought of him every day, dreamed of him when he dreamed at all and slept with his letter under his pillow, kissing it often in the night. He was his dearest teacher and cleverest friend. He begged Regy to meet him either at Oxford or in London: 'Let us sleep in the same room.' He was delighted that Regy's friend Howard Sturgis, to whom he had been introduced and found a little alarming, seemed to like him too.

Howard Sturgis, whom Regy first met at Cambridge in the autumn of 1875, was Julian's younger brother, and three years Regy's junior. They were the sons of a Bostonian father, a partner in Baring Brothers, the bankers, who had settled in England, taking a house in Carlton House Terrace. Howard, familiarly known to his friends as Howdie, 'Owdie and even Doody, had been educated at Eton. He was now a rich bachelor, intelligent, delicate, witty and intensely kind. While an undergraduate and for some years afterwards Howard lived at home with his parents and, when his father died, with his mother from whom he was inseparable. Plain, verging on ugly, he suffered acutely in his emotional relationships. Not being of the marrying sort, he nevertheless remained circumspect, although after his mother's death in 1888 he took to live with him at his house, Queen's Acre, overlooking the Long Walk at Windsor, a young man called Willie Haynes-Smith. Commonly referred to as 'The Babe', he was a housekeeper-cum-confidential friend. Sturgis wrote three novels, two of which caused something of a stir. The first, *Tim* (1891), a maudlin and embarrassing tale about the love of a small, frail boy for a handsome, stalwart one, good at games and a school hero, was considered by pre-Oscar Wilde society to be extremely tragic. Gladstone, an innocent man, was moved to tears by the reference to a pet dormouse, whereas Lord Rosebery, more knowing, pronounced the book distasteful. Regy, to whom the author sent it in manuscript fourteen years before it was published, liked it more than he would admit. The second novel *Belchamber*, far more mature, subtle and cynical, yet without homosexual undertones, is today considered a minor classic. However, when it came out in 1904 it was considered scandalous. Regy for some reason found it 'a very painful, disagreeable book . . . cruel, sordid and generally odious'.[25]

Howdie was utterly without pretension or cant, and freely teased Regy Brett, to whom he wrote amusing letters which were blatantly candid in praise or criticism. He would never allow the Hon. Reginald Brett or the Viscount Esher to disguise his homosexual propensities in his presence. At Quaggers, or Qu'Acre, as his house was affectionately known, he loved to entertain his friends, including Henry James, Edith Wharton and Percy Lubbock, with the last of whom he had had a romantic friendship when a boy at Eton. For hours on end he would sit indoors, contentedly gossiping while he knitted, sewed or did embroidery, pricking his patterned canvas with long white fingers. Whenever anyone in his circle was ill or unhappy Howard Sturgis would rush to give comfort or help which, if it were financial, he would go to great lengths to conceal from the beneficiary. Through Regy Sturgis met Ernlé Johnson, whom as a lame puppy he befriended, visiting him at Malvern in termtime and taking him sightseeing when the boy passed through London.

Julian Sturgis was of rather different metal. He too had been at Eton where he excelled at games and was very popular with masters and boys. He was outward-looking and good-natured. In March 1877 he suggested that he and Regy should rent and share a small house on the Thames at Brayfield, a few miles upstream of Eton, which belonged to his American cousin, Madame Van de Weyer, and was next door to The Hut, where her daughter Louise lived. Madame Van de Weyer was the widow of Sylvain, Belgian Minister at the Court of St James and the principal founding father of the Belgian kingdom, of whose dynasty Queen Victoria's Uncle Leopold was the first monarch. She lived then at New Lodge in Windsor Forest and was much favoured by Queen Victoria who received her at the Castle. Of the four Van de Weyer daughters Louise, or Lou, became a maid of honour to the Queen. Regy readily accepted Julian's proposition. He would go to Brayfield in the long vacation. He would take plenty of books for study while his companion wrote[26] and painted.

The summer term at Cambridge passed uneventfully. The highlight was Regy's second meeting with George Eliot, in whose company he spent four hours one afternoon. Her talk was arresting,

> like the best parts of her books, the parts where she analyses without dissecting; the parts out of which compilers get her 'wise, witty and tender' sayings. Her presence would be one of the glories of life were it not for her amusing vain mountebank of a husband. She is truly and wonderfully thoughtful even in trifles. I was late for luncheon, an embarrassing thing in a small party, and I noticed that she avoided looking my way for a minute or two even *à la dérobée* for fear of increasing my confusion. It was considerate controlling of a strong animal instinct. She shut up George Lewes when he tried to talk about her. She does not seem vain, nor fond of adulation. She adores Charles Darwin, because of his humility. I suppose it is an event to have spent the day in her company.[27]

Brayfield was a great success. Regy brought with him from Cambridge an Old Etonian friend, John Oswald,[28] to help him arrange his books and the pictures of those he loved and admired. It was during the Brayfield sojourn that Regy made the acquaintance of George Curzon, still at Eton. He was instantly struck by his singularly acute brain and mystified by his aloof manner. In his impulsive way Regy undertook to befriend Curzon. In an early letter[29] Regy warned him against flattery from people desiring to please him, advice which Kenneth Rose thinks would have come better from somebody else.[30] Certainly Curzon was not the sort to respond to any sentimental advances, as his total indifference to Oscar Browning's makes clear.[31]

On several occasions Regy accompanied Julian to play tennis and dine with Madame Van de Weyer at New Lodge. And it was there that he first saw and was attracted by the youngest of her daughters, Eleanor, who was to become his wife. Tute, ever vigilant, even from Devonshire, must have been told about the fascinations of New Lodge, for he wrote strongly, reproving Regy for taking what he called a cottage at Monkey Island: 'How mean, and absurd, and indiscreet and muggy: all weeds, midges, gudgeons, shandygaff and spoonery of the stalest kind.'[32] On this curmudgeonly letter Regy noted in pencil at a later date, 'Yet it was this that led to my knowing Nellie and to all the subsequent turn of my life.' Tute's resentment was irrational, considering that his recent letters had been almost exclusively about the local ladies to whom he was giving lessons in the classics, for no remuneration. By the end of the year he was writing: 'For the second time in my life I have undergone the sweet astonishment of finding a person fond of me; really fond. I had a true love letter today from a girl of 20.' The letter implied that the first love to be returned was Bickersteth's. 'I have heard startling news from Halsdon,' Regy noted in his journal,[33] 'but I dare not write what it is: for fear of the matter falling through.' By January 1878 Tute was engaged to Rosa Carolina Guille from Torrington, thirty-four years his junior. In April he took her to Madeira, married her and remained abroad for the next four years; she bore him a son, Andrew.[34]

Although Tute and Regy continued to correspond for many years and Brett remained a faithful and generous friend during his old tutor's declining years, finding a house for him in Hampstead and regularly supplying him with books, their relations were no longer to be on the same confidential terms. Yet Regy never overlooked the fact that he owed his fundamental philosophy of life to his old tutor, as the last stanza of a poem, 'Tan-yr-Alt', addressed to Chat in September 1891, testifies:

> Suffice that we do not forget
> a teacher's voice, so well obeyed,
> whose old tradition lingers yet
> beneath that dear Athenian shade.
> Enough that when the sun declines
> Your soul, with his and ours, entwines.

The sad truth was that Tute went to pieces after leaving Eton in 1872. As Regy wrote to Chat, the *dégringolade* was caused by humiliation. 'The whole tone of his mind underwent a change henceforth. Flashes of the old W.J. cropped up now and again; but the prison-house shade was about him always.'[35]

In September Regy had received a letter of a serious kind from his father.[36] Sir Baliol warned him that he could not – because he ought not to for his son's good – increase his allowance of £400 a year. In any event he was going through anguish, thinking how little he could leave his wife were he to die suddenly. He reminded his son that he was now twenty-six and it was high time he adopted a profession. On the 25th Regy was making a first reference in his journal to Lord Hartington, then out of office during Disraeli's second Tory ministry. 'He was too calm, too moderate, to have succeeded as an ordinary man . . . his passions, which blind the perspective of his mind, do not stand in his way as a politician, but they prevent him from being a great statesman.' On the other hand, although now an avowed Liberal, Regy could not withhold his admiration from the Prime Minister's mastery of his Cabinet, his wit, mystery and imagination, attributes which Hartington conspicuously lacked. Ever since the visit to Longleat he had been captivated by Dizzy's charm. On 15 October, while still at Trinity, he asked himself, 'Could I be of any use to Lord Hartington? That is the question.' In desperation Sir Baliol appealed to his old friend William Harcourt to use his influence with Regy to break with Cambridge. Harcourt approached his parliamentary colleague Hartington. Was he prepared to take his young nominee as an extra private secretary? Lord Hartington was, and Sir Baliol wrote in ecstasy to Harcourt, 'As for Lady Brett and myself we cannot really adequately express how grateful we are.' It would be, he added, the saving of Regy from some false steps. 'He has some great qualities and a good manner.'[37] He at once telegraphed his son at Halsdon, where he was staying for the last time with Tute, telling him to come to London. Regy did not leave immediately. His journal entry of 30 December records: 'I am not elated.' And that of the 31st: 'So ends 1877. It is 12 o'clock. Tute and I are sitting quietly in the music room at Halsdon. He is preparing me for my new career: my tutor still, the wisest, and the kindest of tutors.'

4

POLITICS AND MARRIAGE

1878–1885

Reginald Brett considered that during his seven years at Cambridge he had acquired sufficient political training to render him as well fitted as anyone to be the private secretary of a man of Lord Hartington's eminence. He was glad to be serving an honest, straightforward man, said to be wanting those human kindnesses which he, Regy, would be able to supply.

In writing to congratulate him on the new job his friend Alfred Lyttelton did not hesitate to refer to his youthful pretensions: 'What is most likely to be a drawback to you in public life when speaking and readiness are wanted is a certain superfluity of self-consciousness, which clogs every young man's footsteps, which you seem to have an extra share of.' Then he dwelt more kindly on his merits: 'You will now have a real opportunity of displaying what is your peculiar genius (for no other word expresses it), the great faculty you have in influencing people, upon a man who will be worth influencing . . . in matters about which you have special knowledge.[1]

On 14 January 1878 Regy Brett reported for duty at Devonshire House, Piccadilly, where Lord Hartington, as the eldest son and heir of the 7th Duke of Devonshire, had a suite of apartments. It was difficult for contemporaries to decide which was the more unkempt, Devonshire House or the Marquess. Of the former, the silk walls and upholstery were faded and in tatters, the gilding tarnished, the family portraits blackened and hung in no apparent order. As for the Marquess, his clothes were of shabby tweed, unpressed and baggy, and he wore an old hat which was said to have belonged to Goethe. He was no respector of persons.

He had a broad-browed dog called Roy which enjoyed the privilege accorded to his master of breaking every social rule; whether to Buckingham Palace or to the House of Commons, wherever Hartington went, Roy went too; and his habits, which were as leisurely as his master's, accentuated more than ever that utter disregard of time which was Hartington's most notorious characteristic.[2]

He was vague and imprecise. His letters to his private secretary, invariably courteous if distant, might begin by asking him to look up a few papers, or read a book for him on some topical matter which bored him, but would always end in a dissertation on his racing ventures. He occasionally wrote asking Regy to remind him if he had answered an important letter to the Prime Minister, and he would forget to post letters to the Queen. Except during a crisis, which was rare, Regy's duties were not onerous. His chief, although leader of the Opposition, would make long visits to country houses even when the Commons was in session, shooting and fishing on his father's numerous estates, or racing.

Lord Hartington's chief political concern was the events leading to the outbreak in November of the Second Afghan War, aimed at checking increasing Russian incursions in the Middle East. Lord Hartington personally was opposed to the war but would not move an amendment to condemn it in case he embarrassed the Government, which was fearful of a Russian occupation of Afghanistan and smarting from the Emir's refusal to accept a British agent although he had admitted a Russian envoy. Hartington's inactivity led to the dissatisfaction of some Members, and trouble from Joseph Chamberlain in particular. Brett supported his chief, although inwardly he believed that to keep the Russians out justified the British invasion of Afghanistan. 'A less calm, less self-controlled, less patriotic, vainer man than he would have given up long ago,' he said. 'He sticks to his guns.'

Regy threw himself heart and soul into his new job, forming contacts with influential persons, whether Liberal or Conservative, and taking much upon himself. This was remarked upon by the leading Radical, Sir Charles Dilke, with whom Regy dined on 3 March:

> He was the ablest secretary, except Edward Hamilton [Mr Gladstone's], that I ever came across; but he was far from being a model secretary, because . . . he always behaved as if he held delegated authority from Hartington to represent Hartington's conscience when it would not otherwise have moved, and 'Hartington's opinion' when the Chief had none.[3]

Nevertheless Dilke conceded that in all he did Brett kept the public good in view.

Regy had plenty of time to enjoy the delights of the London season, which included a masked ball at Strawberry Hill. His journal discloses a new interest in women: 'Mary Dawson Damer has grown into a lovely girl.' His name was being coupled with that of Lady Hilda Charteris.[4] He went twice to see Ellen Terry as Olivia in *Twelfth Night*. He even wrote poems addressed to women, of which one began:

> What promise lay half uttered in her eyes,
> Who came unsought and led me in my dreams,
> Through life's turmoil and battle.
> O dear hand, soft hand. . .

which may well have been Nellie Van de Weyer's.

But Regy was not neglecting his male friends. He composed a long and careful letter, almost an essay, to a new Cambridge friend, Samuel Whitbread, pointing out that Byron was a far from virtuous man. What virtue he had stemmed from his Harrow friendships and love for the choirboy John Edleston. Regy kept up a regular correspondence with Ernlé, who told him that Oxford was haunted by the prospects of war. He hoped Regy would not consider that he was growing impractical and sentimental if he heard that sometimes he went to see Oscar Wilde, a true poet, although a non-Christian and a republican. And Tute from Madeira kept up a bombardment of political advice to be tendered to Lord Hartington.

> I think occupying Kabul would be like squatting on an ants' nest when aiming at a target. I believe the Afghans living in clans are less . . . likely to swing into position on the change of centre of gravity (that is when the symbol of supremacy is seized by a new power) than any set of people in Asia. They are not like the apathetic Asiatics.[5]

In August Regy was invited by the Ripons to Studley Royal to be with Charlie (not referred to by them as Chat). They walked in the garden and Regy told him 'of my trouble. . . . He says we are absurdly shy with each other, considering our friendship is of ten years' growth.'[6] The reason was that hitherto their conversations had always concerned Chat's soul and perplexities, never Regy's. Now, on the verge of his third Oratorian year, Chat's vows prevented him from laying bare his soul to an old friend. 'He seems to regret it. So do I.'[7] On the 16th Chat left, in tears.

Regy took infinite pains over drafting speeches for his chief, who made several on important themes in January and February 1879. On 31 January, for instance, Hartington gave an address to the University of Edinburgh on his inauguration as Lord Rector. It had taken months of preparation, and Regy even consulted Tute. While staying at Panshanger Regy totally rewrote his master's latest draft. Hartington never bore the slightest resentment and always welcomed a better turn of phrase than his own. When finally delivered in Hartington's casual manner, the speech received a tremendous ovation.

On 7 March Regy went to the Haymarket Theatre to join a party including Miss Lindsay and Marion, Ellen Terry's sister. Miss Lindsay was the beautiful Violet, to become Lady Granby and Duchess of Rutland. Regy, very taken by her beauty as well as her wit, was until August playing with the idea of proposing marriage. And yet for months past he had been confiding in friends that he had an understanding with Nellie Van de Weyer to marry her. Whatever his true feelings, Regy had reached that point in his life when he considered it was right to take a wife. Everyone did it once they were established in a career or vocation. He hinted to George Binning in May what his intentions were, without mentioning Nellie's name. On the 13th George wrote to him:

I need hardly say your letter has roused my curiosity. Is this feeling you complain of, this icy shroud of matrimony which is creeping nearer and nearer, merely a general sort of discovery that society is rot, races a delusion & – false? or is it a specific complaint? Who's the victim? how? when? & why? do let me know.[8]

Binning's 'icy shroud' implies that Regy's affections were not deeply rooted.

When precisely Regy Brett and Nellie Van de Weyer became engaged is uncertain. Regy must have told Tute fairly early in July, since Tute wrote from Madeira on the 31st acknowledging the news. He thought it was a good Liberal connection, but was no more enthusiastic than that. Ernlé Johnson knew on the 18th. He wrote congratulating his friend, full of speculations about the bride and whether she could possibly be good enough for Regy. The news had taken Ernlé by surprise, and he could not help feeling jealous of her. A few days later he wrote again. He had had a sort of breakdown: the news had been a greater shock to him than he had at first supposed.

Regy wrote Ernlé many reassuring letters during his engagement and encouraged him to continue writing poetry. His verses, he said, had become more adult. He sent Reginald, as he called him, a poem:

O love, it haunts me the old pain!
    And since I may no more caress
    Those graceful curls of your dear head
To live in grief, to die were gain,
    And, if I may not love you less,
    But still must sorrow for love fled,
    I pray harsh love to strike me dead. . .[9]

Few letters between Regy and Nellie survive. Her first mention of her future husband is some diary notes written in Pisa in 1875 when she was thirteen. They show spirit, and they also throw a light upon their subject.

Mr Brett sends word that I shake hands in a most unbecoming fashion; that is neither pretty or taking. This is very likely. I have never studied the becoming, which he apparently does to a very great extent, both in himself and others. . . . He wishes to improve himself and everybody: he is quite right. . . . Some men have such capacities for loving too. But I think I should wish the same privileges allowed to me – and this is just what men are not strong enough to give. All women should take this view of married life and not be so exacting. The greatest praise a husband of mine could give me would be to say that he did not feel in the least tied down; or any more encumbered than when he was a bachelor. This is not speaking with the ignorance of a girl for I shall act up to it when married, if I do marry.

How perceptive the girl was in noticing that 'Mr Brett' wished to improve himself and everybody else he came in contact with. Although she was only seventeen when she married Regy, her son, Oliver, was wrong when he came to state that his father had to break in his young wife like a recalcitrant horse. In some intuitive way Nellie Van de Weyer had a shrewd idea of what she was taking on, and she never regretted it. From the very first she worshipped Regy, to the extent of alienating most of her children in years to come. She made allowances for him. She deferred to him without being subservient. She chose to be his background. And she thought him the cleverest man in the world. She is reported once to have said that a wife's office in life was to make the tea kettle exciting.

One letter from Regy to his future wife survives – at least transcribed in Nellie's hand, because the original fell to pieces in 1935, five years after his death, having been carried everywhere in her reticule. It is a touching tribute to her loyalty and an oblique confession of his weaknesses.[10]

Why you have thrown yourself away upon one who is the converse of you in all things still remains a mystery. Very sincerely I feel quite unworthy of you, and I think you must be a kind of St Theresa, a reforming soul. Some day, like [George Eliot's] Romola, you will find me out and you will hate me. Are you prepared for this?

It astonishes me that I can write to you so easily and in this strain. You are the only girl with whom on writing I have felt on equal terms. I mean that I am sure of your not misunderstanding me and there is no necessity for elaborate detail. Does this please you or not? It is, I am sure, very unusual between a man and a woman who have anything to hide. True confidence is a heavy burden and very few men and women can bear that of those they love. But you have led me to think you stronger than most women and I have very little fear for the future. Do nothing and say nothing lightly to weaken my faith in you. . . .

Do not, I ask you, start thinking too well of me, for I dread the disenchantment.

Nellie must have found him out, sooner or later. If Regy's protestations are slightly intransigent, at least he never pretended to be other than he was in all the long years during which they lived happily together and brought up four children. On 2 August he wrote to her again, giving her the option to change her mind and retract the vows she had made to him the day before. He ended by making the odd and not very opportune statement that the happiest period of his life had ended in 1868 – the year in which his love for Chat was at its climax. She was a brave and trusting child, for on the eve of her wedding she wrote of her love for him, adding, 'And do not think to frighten me with your two-sided character – show me which side you please. I should like you as much when your whole life was laid bare as I do now, when, as you say, you have humbugged me.' Regy could not have made a wiser choice. His bride was well educated, cosmopolitan in outlook, tolerant and moderately pretty. She was extremely music-al, frequently went to concerts and played the piano well. She thought her bridegroom perfection, and yet she had a mind of her own. Lawrence Burgis was right in pronouncing her a very clever woman.

Lord Hartington sent his secretary one line: 'When does your melancholy event come off?' It came off on 24 September in Winkfield church. The reception was held in Nellie's old home, the gabled house which her father had built in the Jacobean style. Her mother had died in 1878, and New Lodge had become the property of her brother Victor. The honeymoon was spent in Paris. Exactly a decade to the day after their wedding Regy wrote to his wife, 'I expected ten years ago, happiness in subsequent times; but not such *uninterrupted* happiness.' And again on 24 September 1918: 'You have been everything to me, the love and joy of my life. Mistress and wife.'

In spite of George Curzon's prognostications that Regy would find his honeymoon boring and irksome, the young couple's time passed happily enough. It was an uneventful two months in which they endeavoured to get to know one another. They had a piano in their hotel suite on which Nellie played. They read together George Eliot's *Silas Marner*, *Daniel Deronda* and *Romola* 'and her sorrows'. They went shopping; Regy ordered a dress from Worth[11] and a fur cloak for her, but she was too shy to buy herself a bonnet. He supposed that this shyness would wear off in time – after all she was still a mere child. They met Gladstone in an antique shop on the Quai Voltaire, searching for ivories. He was wearing the worst hat ever seen, presumably to impress the shopkeepers with his poverty.

To his chief Regy wrote after the wedding, 'I am pretty well considering; not feeling much the worse for the gloomy proceedings two days ago. . . . I am beginning to feel that the worst is over. . . . Marriage is a curious game to play at.'[12] To his journal he confided, 'It is difficult to describe the past ten days, sown as they have been with conflicting emotions';[13] and a few days later, 'I have written *sub sigillo* to my two best friends, an account of this first month of our married life. It is very smooth. The torrent's smoothness perhaps!'[14] Who the friends were he does not specify.

The correspondence with Ernlé by no means slackened. Regy had proposed leaving all his letters and papers in his will to Ernlé, who declined on the grounds that he was not a fitting person to deal with them. Ernlé had been very ill, and his parents had come to Oxford to look after him. He thought that one of the sadnesses of becoming a man, and leaving off being a child, was that half the wonder and mystery of one's older friends' characters was taken away.[15] He supposed that he too would have to marry.

Back in England the first thing Regy Brett did was to make an offer for the freehold of No.1 Tilney Street, Mayfair, which he came upon by accident. This long, nondescript Georgian house was once lived in by Mrs FitzHerbert. The Bretts did not move in until April 1880. Thereafter it was to be their London house, off and on – for it was frequently let – until in 1914 they acquired the adjoining and smaller No.2, which was to remain theirs until the end of their lives.

In November Regy returned to Paris alone, this time on a self-imposed mission to Gambetta,[16] President of the French Chamber and an admirer of Lord Hartington's, which had been arranged for him by Sir Charles Dilke. Gambetta advised Regy that the Liberal party would do well not to be returned to power in the forthcoming general election. The moment was not propitious, for Gambetta did not see what the Liberals could do with '*ces gens-là,*' meaning the Irish nationalists.

Notwithstanding Gambetta's views, the election had to be fought because the term of Disraeli's second ministry was expiring. Lord Hartington wrote rather pusillanimously to his secretary that Gladstone was exhibiting such extraordinary energy in putting forward a programme on every conceivable issue – notably unequivocal opposition to Hartington's supporters and their policy of peace with Afghanistan at any price – that it seemed best to let him resume his proper position as leader of the party.[17] Regy did not at all agree, and was not slow to convey to his chief his opinion. If a Liberal Government was to hold office, he said, it could not possibly be presided over by Gladstone, whose Midlothian campaign had completely reopened the question of the leadership of the party. Gladstone had renounced his intention to take office, and must be held to this decision. Lord Hartington under-rated his own influence and power. If he were to form a Government with a resentful and disloyal Gladstone in the wings, it certainly would not endure long. But on going to the country, Regy went on, the country would put Lord Hartington back with an enhanced majority. He hoped his chief would discuss the matter with Sir William Harcourt and others. But in no eventuality should he hold office under Gladstone; he should only do so under Lord Granville.

On 16 December a meeting was held at Devonshire House, which Lord Granville attended. Supported by Harcourt, Granville persuaded Hartington to take no action, but try and extract from Gladstone what his intentions were. They were quite clear. The following year the Liberals were returned, and the Grand Old Man assumed the Prime Ministership for the next five years.

Just before Christmas Lord Northbrook[18] suggested that Regy should stand for his old seat of Penryn and Falmouth, about to become vacant. After Lord Hartington had persuaded him that it would be of assistance to him having his private secretary in the House of Commons, Regy sent an affirmative answer to the local Liberal committee. At the general election early in February 1880 he was successful. It had never been Regy Brett's ambition to become an MP and ultimately a minister, nor did his short experience of the House of Commons make him change his mind. He was not a fluent speaker and he did not enjoy the hurly-burly of debate. He was essentially a committee man, preferring to deliberate and weigh his arguments carefully before committing himself to a considered opinion. Yet by becoming an MP he widened his acquaintance and contact with men of influence, which stood him in good stead for the rest of his political career. Moreover, he flourished in a society where intrigue, plot and counterplot were the machinery of daily life.

The victorious Liberals took almost a month to form a Government. The Irish dilemma was the cause of the delay. Lord Hartington was convinced that Gladstone must be supported because, although the Grand Old Man sympathised with Irish grievances generally, he was committed to maintaining the supremacy of the imperial Government; also it was his policy to suppress disorder while removing agrarian discontent in Ireland. In these circumstances Hartington was prepared to serve under Gladstone, who was in his opinion the obvious man to become Premier. So when the Queen sent for him to form a Government he declined, giving as his reason Gladstone's renewed popularity and overwhelming prestige. He did so despite the agreement with his colleagues to fill the vacancy on Gladstone's resignation in 1875, and against the advice of his private secretary. Accordingly Gladstone took office and Hartington went to the India Office. Even Regy changed his tune. He soon realized that Gladstone was most unlikely to take office under someone else, and that if he did he would prove an impossible colleague. On the other hand he hoped that his chief would have been offered the Foreign Office. Harcourt reluctantly consented to take the Home Department, while advising Hartington that the new Government should wait until it was defeated before resigning.

Regy held strong views about Ireland, which was the over-riding issue of the moment. He hoped the Government would not introduce coercive measures. He did not believe that 'the land question' was at the root of Irish disaffection, although he wanted to see the whole system of land tenure in Ireland changed by breaking down the laws of entail.[19] It was the Catholic issue, he felt, that was paramount. England would do no good until she recognized the Catholic supremacy of the Irish people. He did not hesitate to express his views to his friend, Willie Compton,[20] private secretary to the Lord-Lieutenant of Ireland, and to Lord Cowper, the Lord-Lieutenant himself, to whom he deprecated the screening of sedition and railed against the stupidity of the English middle-class prejudice against Irish claims. As the year went by Parnell's National Land League, on the specious plea that the land belonged to the Irish Republican Brotherhood, led to repeated outrages against landlords and those who resisted it. Parnell's methods were totally revolutionary and, as leader of the Home Rule party in the Commons, he was responsible for innumerable boycotts and murders. The rejection by the Lords in August 1880 of the Compensation for Disturbance Bill aggravated his discontent. Parnell told any tenant who took a farm from another tenant who had been evicted that he ought to be treated 'as if he were a leper of old'. In October W.E. Forster, the Chief Secretary for Ireland, recognizing the virtual impossibility of checking outrages and repressing disorders, resigned.

He was not the last minister to wash his hands in despair over the intractable business.

With the appointment of his chief to the India Office Regy benefited from first-hand experience of Eastern affairs which was greatly to influence his future services to imperial defence as well as to widen his interest in the Empire's outposts.[21] Furthermore, the appointment enabled him to exercise for the first time his own influence in politics, and to set in motion that extraordinary ability to manipulate from behind the scenes which was to be the most important achievement of his later years. It was largely through him that Lord Ripon was made Viceroy of India, an extraordinary appointment – successful though it turned out – considering the Marquess's conversion to Catholicism combined with his extreme Radicalism. It was certainly owing to Regy that Lord Ripon took his younger brother, Eugene Brett, as his ADC.

Lord Ripon had a high regard for Regy Brett and was himself largely responsible for his present job. Indeed, he had told Lord Hartington that he feared he might think his recommendations of Brett exaggerated, whereas they were from the heart. For the four busy years of his viceroyalty Ripon found time to keep up a regular correspondence with Regy on political matters.

Lord Hartington's relations with Queen Victoria were always ambivalent. While she did not detest him as she detested Gladstone for what she considered his rudeness, and disregard of her feminine feelings, she believed the Marquess's vagueness and neglect of authority reprehensible. Indeed, although Lord Hartington always intended to be absolutely respectful – and his loyalty to the Crown was irreproachable – he was known to complain to his intimates at times that 'these royalties are a damned nuisance', a phrase which in modified terms reached the Queen's ears.

This was particularly true in the Marquess's dealings with the old Duke of Cambridge, the Commander-in-Chief of the British forces. The Duke's conservatism and opposition to any proposed change were a thorn in the flesh of the Secretary of State for India. Lord Hartington was now fighting a battle with the Duke about the command in India. The Duke strongly objected to the Secretary of State's nominee, Sir Garnet Wolseley, and enlisted the Queen's support. She too looked upon Wolseley as an upstart. Brett agreed with his chief that Wolseley was the only clever soldier he knew of. A glorious opportunity now arose for Regy to act as mediator. Harting-ton told him that he deplored the Queen's habit of ignoring discussions with her ministers on matters which were disagreeable to her. Regy, on the other hand, thought she was right. He realized she knew full well that in an argument either she or her ministers must give way,

and that she never could and never would in any circumstances go
against her united Cabinet. Therefore she was wise to avoid argument
altogether on any matter she felt strongly about, since her advice was
bound to be fruitless.

Already through his marriage to Nellie Van de Weyer Regy had
been brought to the notice of the Queen. He made the most of the
connection, and as soon as he was appointed private secretary to
Hartington opened a correspondence with the Queen's secretary, Sir
Henry Ponsonby. Gradually, off his own bat, he began forwarding
confidential memoranda he had drafted about India Office matters.
The Queen acknowledged them. After his first of three memoranda he
told Hartington what he had done. 'I suppose you have no objection to
my sending occasionally explanations to Sir Henry Ponsonby. I think
it is useful.'[22] His easy-going chief expressed no disapproval; it merely
saved him the bother of doing the job himself. Thus the private
secretary established a relationship with his sovereign which was to
grow ever closer. The better she got to know him, the more she was
charmed by his engaging manner.

Lord Hartington's two-year session at the India Office was marked
by renewed Russian activity in the Trans-Caspian area. In 1879
British control over Afghanistan's foreign relations, strengthened by a
British resident in Kabul, had been established. The arrangement
broke down when he was murdered. General Roberts, at the head of
an avenging force, entered Kabul. Summary executions and burning
of villages by the British caused intense resentment. In December the
Afghans recovered Kabul and Lord Roberts, beset by 30,000 hostile
Afghans, was obliged to withdraw. On assuming office, Lord Hartington was in favour of British troops evacuating the country immediately. His view was that Britain had merely succeeded in bringing
about the disintegration of a buffer state between India and Russia,
which she needed to see strong and friendly. But Hartington did not
achieve his objective at once. General Roberts again avenged the
setback to British pride by marching into Kandahar. Only in November, under Lord Ripon's pressure, were British troops ordered to
withdraw from Kandahar. What the Second Afghan War had
achieved was a very temporary halt to Russian interference in the area.
Towards the end of the year correspondence between Regy and Sir
Henry Ponsonby intensified. The withdrawal from Kandahar was
glossed over by the preparation of campaign medals to be awarded by
the Queen, who took a keen personal interest in the design, the
mottoes and motifs they should bear.

The year 1881 opened with such severe snow and frosts that no
hackney cabs could ply in London. For the first time in history a
minister of the Crown, in the person of Lord Hartington, was driven

to a Cabinet meeting by sleigh. Regy Brett held the reins.

On 25 March he delivered his maiden speech in the House of Commons, on Kandahar. He agreed with Lord Ripon that the British withdrawal from Kandahar had been right. He saw no danger of Russian invading India, were she to occupy the vacated city. He doubted too that we should forfeit prestige in the eyes of native Indians by the voluntary retreat from a place we had mistakenly captured. To retain it would cost us a garrison of 20,000 troops, to no purpose. The Tories' description of Kandahar as the great citadel and granary of central Asia derived from some oriental tale; it was simply untrue. The pertinent question was whether or not we should allow Russia to occupy Herat, a far more serious issue. 'There is a limit', he said, 'beyond which the strain of Empire cannot be borne,' a financial as well as a moral strain. These high-sounding words did little to relieve the Foreign and India Offices of anxiety about Russia's intentions regarding the Russo-Persian boundaries and Asia in general.[23] Anxiety turned to apprehension when Russia annexed the Akhal country in August. Lord Hartington pointed out these dangers to the Viceroy. Whereas Lord Ripon thought an understanding must be reached with Russia that her annexation of Afghanistan could not be tolerated, he suggested that she might be allowed to take Merv, a fertile oasis and stepping-stone between north-east Persia and the states of Bokhara and Samarkand. Regy agreed with Ripon's proposal. In spite of St Petersburg's solemn assurances to the British Ambassador that she had no designs on Merv, Russia was to occupy it early in February 1884.

It was in the summer of 1880 that Regy made the acquaintance of a man whom he was to get to know intimately – though their meetings were infrequent – until his death four years later. General (Chinese) Charles Gordon belonged to the mystic type of soldier-proconsul such as T.E. Lawrence and George Lloyd of the first half of the twentieth century. He was totally unworldly, incorruptible and fervently patriotic. Since 1877, when with the consent of the British Government he had been made Governor of the Sudan by the Egyptian Khedive, in order to put an end to the slave trade – which he achieved totally – Gordon had been out of England. In May he agreed to become the new Indian Viceroy's secretary. His introduction to Regy came from Lord Ripon. Together with Eugene Brett the viceregal party sailed for India, but on 3 June Gordon, realizing his unsuitability for the post, resigned.

Gordon was far too independent, anti-social and eccentric. At this date he was verging on fifty. With his short stature, brown, curly hair and grey-tinged moustache he made an insignificant figure, apt to be unnoticed wherever he went. Only his steel-blue eyes were remarkable. He loathed pomp and ceremony and was extremely badly dressed: he wore an old hat on the back of his head, an old muffler round his neck, and usually had a cigarette dangling from his lower lip. He abhorred parties and fashionable people, but was blissfully happy walking round the bazaars hand in hand with scruffy little Arab boys. This gave rise to rumours about his morals which were totally unfounded. Another was that he was a brandy addict; in a letter to Sir Philip Sassoon Regy was to write, 'It is an absolute lie that Gordon drank!'[24] Yet he was full of humorous sallies, often at the expense of illustrious personages. If his frailties were few, his idiosyncrasies could tax the patience of his friends. Regy, however, who was never a stickler for etiquette except in royal circles, took to him at once. Gordon became

> a very constant visitor to no. 1 Tilney Street. He would drop in, usually in the morning, smoking his cigarette, and remain sometimes for hours. When Nellie was laid up on the last occasion on which he came, he went up to see her in her room, and Oliver was brought in (he was little more than a baby) and he took him in his arms.[25]

Regy referred to his conversation as 'always refreshing, full of humour and simple as the Book of Genesis. . . . He saw with wonderful clearness, although sometimes not very far.'[26] His religion never obtruded upon his friends, but was as much part of his life as his smoking. He told Regy one day that he believed in the God of Abraham, 'and as I came to your house he walked with me arm in arm up South Audley Street'. Their conversations usually began with India. Gordon was a rigid economist and it was mainly on financial grounds that he favoured the retirement from Kandahar.

Gordon's correspondence with Brett began in January 1881 with a letter[27] in which he advocated the appointment of a Russian envoy at the court of the Indian Viceroy. It was followed by another, three days later, on the necessity for stopping the importation of opium from India to China.[28] On 1 March he wrote him a long letter in his quaint, small hand, railing at Regy about his addiction to social life.

> Since I have had the pleasure of your acquaintance I have seen a desire on your part, to go into things which concern the welfare of our country, and with that desire, a sentiment of not consulting expediency, why do you not with those of the rising generation, the successors of Gladstone, etc., etc., form some sort of community, and acquainting yourselves with all the ins and outs of our relations with our colonies and Foreign Powers, prepare yourselves for the mouths of those now in office?. . . I think if you and some of the younger men were to abandon your fearful treats, your dinner parties, you would come to some definite platform and work on it.

He suggested that in the vacations such young men should visit India, China and the Cape, collect information and see for themselves what was going on in the East and Africa and what needed reforming. They must give up Scotland and grouse shooting in the long recess, and instead 'go to the colonies'. Regy excused himself with the rather weak retort that Gordon did not understand how the social functions which he pooh-poohed were part and parcel of the job of a Cabinet minister's private secretary. He never travelled to China or visited the far-flung Empire.

Far from abandoning his social activities, Regy, with his friend Lord Durham, rented a house in Newmarket for a year. Racing had had its appeal since the summer before his marriage when he went to the Derby and Newmarket. It was soon to become a mania, as well as a relief from the tedium of domestic life; devoted though he already was to Nellie, the excitement of the tea kettle was not enough. He realized from the start of his marriage that communion with the great world had no appeal for her. She did not make a good London hostess. She did not care for his smart racing friends. They both understood at an early stage that she preferred to stay at home with her piano and her babies. Already Regy had horses in training; his colours were light blue with rose hoops. In the nineties he was persuaded to be his own trainer, but he was never very successful. He was too fastidious a man to cope with the rude, rough ways of the racecourse; besides, he was not rich enough. He lost money. By the turn of the century he had completely lost interest in the turf.

John George, 3rd Earl of Durham, was a rich, raffish, patrician Old Etonian, and like most of Regy's intimates slightly younger than himself. His interest in horses and racing was paramount, and he was an inveterate gambler. He made a disastrous marriage to a young woman who had certainly been unbalanced before the event, and became raving mad after it. There were no chores Regy would not undertake for Jacko. He staunchly supported him when he was involved, innocently, in a racing scandal, and helped sort out the dreadful tangles in which he became involved with his mistresses. The chief of these was a popular musical comedy actress, Letty Lind, sweet and gentle, who bore him a son, known as John Harraton, who himself was to become a mental case.[29] It was Regy who got the boy taken by the headmaster of a private school who at first balked over his illegitimacy. Jack Durham was spoilt, wayward, imprudent, generous and attractive, and his life was blighted by the tragedy of his marriage. Regy adored him. He kept all his friend's letters, which were invariably written off the cuff, usualy in staccato explosions of indignation. 'This accursed place!'; 'The weather damnable'; 'Rosslyn is a damned conceited advertising swine' were exclamations which amused Regy and he allowed to pass. But when his friend inveighed in intemperate terms against the erection of the Albert Memorial and a museum ('That damned snobbish fuss over the old woman's jubilee excites my wrath. . . . There is an awful lot of destitution in the country and yet they want us to put up a brazen image of a German hog (dead) & build a huge Institute to the self-glorification of another live pig – No one will use the place.')[30] Regy reproved him, not for *lèse-majesté*, but for philistinism.

There were two political questions that chiefly concerned Brett in 1882. They were Egypt and Sir Charles Dilke. Under a decree of 1876, Disraeli's Tory Government and the French Government had nominated Controllers-General whose functions were to investigate the large funds that had been expended on Egypt, then a tributary of the Turkish Empire under the rule of Khedive Tewfik Pasha. The two European powers were to have no administrative or executive authority. In 1880 the Controllers revealed that the Egyptian national debt was in the utmost confusion. The following year witnessed a serious military revolt under Ahmed Arabi against the foreign interference. By 1882 the turmoil in Egypt was so great that Lord Granville, the Foreign Secretary, entertained the use of force, although by international agreement Great Britain had no pre-emptive interests in Egypt. Britain invited France and Italy to co-operate in an invasion of Egypt. Both refused. Britain therefore felt obliged to act alone.

Great Britain's unilateral action was gravely resented on the continent and by critics at home. As early as January General Gordon had written to Regy, 'Why do you want to touch Egypt? I sent you a Memo which I think showed clearly that Egypt is only a secondary route to India. The Cape is the grand route. Egypt would be much more trouble to govern than India.' But Gordon had got hold of the wrong end of the stick; it was not the intention of the British Government to interfere with Egypt's internal regime. Bismarck likewise was attempting to make mischief between France and England over the issue, even trying to get the Turks to oppose Britain. Throughout the summer and autumn Regy was busily drawing up almost daily memoranda on the crisis for the benefit of his chief. As usual Gladstone was at loggerheads with the majority of his Cabinet. Regy had devised various methods of settling the anarchy in Egypt, but Gladstone firmly insisted that Arabi Pasha had always treated this country with good faith and should not be removed from Egypt. Meanwhile Lord Dufferin, Ambassador at Constantinople, was informed by the Cabinet that strong measures ought to be taken by Turkey.The Sultan's mild reaction was that he could not ask Moslem troops to put down Arabi's Moslem rebels to oblige Christian forces in Egypt.

After further massacres at Alexandria in July and a threat to the Suez Canal, Britain took steps on her own. In September Sir Garnet Wolseley was sent to suppress the Arabi revolt at Tel-el-Kebir. This was followed by the occupation of both Egypt and the Sudan. Regy felt that Britain had got into a mess by putting Arabi on trial; that she should have left it to the Egyptian authorities, so as not to be held responsible for the rebel's execution if he were found guilty. Arabi was indeed found guilty and condemned to death, but the sentence was commuted to exile in Ceylon. In 1901 he was pardoned. Dilke, rather surprisingly, objected that he had not been shot a month ago.

Charles Dilke was a stormy petrel. Before Gladstone was returned to power in 1880 he was the acknowledged leader of the radical section of the Liberal party. On 8 May 1882 Regy informed Lord Hartington that, 'After the House rose, there was a Cabinet in Mr Gladstone's room, and they decided to offer the Irish Secretaryship to Dilke. . . . He refused it, unless he was put in the Cabinet. Mr Gladstone and Lord Granville were very much annoyed, and Lord Granville said, "We will not be dictated to in this way." ' Dilke made another condition which was considered impertinent. It was that Chamberlain should join the Cabinet with him. The two men hunted as a team, being united in the harassment of the Government on the Irish question. As it happened, Chamberlain entered the Cabinet alone as President of the Board of Trade. Dilke remained outside as Under-Secretary of State for Foreign Affairs, under Granville. In fact he was to enjoy extraordinary power. In December he joined the Cabinet as President of the Local Government Board, the Queen having objected to his being made Chancellor of the Duchy of Lancaster on the ground that it would be unsuitable for a man who had criticized the monarchy in public to have control of so large a part of her revenue.

As Under-Secretary at the Foreign Office Dilke had exerted considerable influence on Regy, who, greatly impressed by Dilke's extremely quick and perceptive mind, was inclined to adopt his principles over the Egyptian business. For his part Dilke had come to hold Brett in high esteem. He put forward his name for one of the two under-secretaryships yet to be filled. 'I had an interesting talk with Brett,' Dilke recorded in his diary.[31] 'Knowing his great influence with Hartington, I complained to him of his Chief's folly in always acting as the leader of a Whig section instead of as deputy-leader of the whole party,' and of his complete detachment from politics and want of interest in them. There was, of course, truth in these charges. The lethargic Hartington spent the minimum of time demanded of him at Westminster, preferring to hunt and play bridge far into the night in the company of his mistress, the German-born Duchess of Manchester, at Kimbolton Castle. Brett touched on this in a letter to Lord

Ripon: 'You know how disinclined he is to examine thoroughly any question unless forced to do so by the necessities of the case,' adding that it was very difficult to get the India Office moving at all.[32] Dilke, a shrewd judge of character though inept at conducting his own affairs, thought the Duchess of Manchester a bad influence on her lover. 'Her strong Conservative prejudices and her want of clearness of head made her by no means a useful guide,' he wrote. One of the great beauties of her time, at receptions and balls she dazzled people by her stature, her clothes and her gems. Disraeli, in describing Lady Londonderry as 'staggering under the jewels of the three united families of Stewart, Vane and Tempest', gave the palm to Duchess Louise who had everything on fire, even the neighbouring Thames. He also found her a 'very clever woman', though 'noisy'.

Hartington treated Regy with the utmost politeness, without ever tendering a word of praise. He appeared not to mind advice which many veteran statesmen would resent from a young man. Regy was against the proposal that his chief should be moved from the India Office to the War Office.

> I sincerely hope that you will think twice before you will allow yourself to be made the victim of an intrigue on the part of the Court [meaning the Duke of Cambridge through the Queen] because they think you would be more amenable to their reason than any other member of the govt. . . . . It is amazing that the offer – which I can only look upon as an impertinence – should have been made to you.[33]

His chief would hate the War Office 'with all its pettifogging questions, and its perpetual conflicts with the Royal family'. He supposed that Lord Granville could only be wishing to weaken his influence in the House of Commons and the party. Anything that weakened his position in the party would be the greatest disappointment to his admirers and well-wishers, for he ought to succeed Gladstone. No one else could rally the drifting allegiances of the two most powerful sections of the party, Regy said. If he had to leave the India Office, then nothing less than the Exchequer or Foreign Office was worthy of him.

For reasons best known to himself Lord Hartington disregarded this passionate plea and accepted the War Office. Gladstone made Hugh Childers, a benevolent lacky, Chancellor of the Exchequer. As Nellie Brett remarked tartly, 'They might just as well ask him to be a messenger.'

In December Regy suffered a blow which affected him badly. After a short period with Lord Ripon in India his brother, Eugene Brett was called by his regiment to the Transvaal War. In May 1881, however, he was back in Simla, much to the Viceroy's pleasure. But again he was to be on the move. Regy was instrumental in getting General Roberts to take him as his ADC to the Cape, and Eugene left India. It was always his wish to be involved in the fighting. On his way home from the Egyptian campaign he became ill with typhoid fever, and a few weeks after his return died, at the age of twenty-seven. A popular young man of determination and courage, he had had a promising career in the Army ahead of him.

Regy's progress in the House of Commons was not made easy by the nature of his work for Hartington. He records a 'curious' talk he had in June 1883 with his chief, who had heard that Regy had been discussing with Rosebery the possibility of giving up the private secretaryship.[34] Regy admitted that his position prevented him from taking part in debates, and practice in speaking was what he needed. It also restricted his writing letters to *The Times*, a habit to which he was much addicted. Hartington cautioned delay, because he did not think that he would remain in politics for long. He was finding his sympathies more and more with the Conservatives than with the Liberals, especially over Ireland, the most urgent issue of the day; and sooner than join the Tory party he would leave the House of Commons altogether. So Regy agreed to wait. However, he was soon impatiently badgering Lord Hartington again on the subject of his retirement. In January 1884 Regy told his chief that he had been of little use him since his move to the War Office. He would like to be released from the secretaryship in order to speak freely in the Commons, yet he would also like to continue looking after his chief's papers at Devonshire House. Regy's old friend Harcourt advised him to wait until the end of the parliamentary session; to go now would merely give rise to unfounded comments that he had had a disagreement with Hartington.

In fact his chief's move to the War Office had involved Regy in far more important affairs, international as well as national, than the India Office. With his delight in intrigue, his strong imperialistic views and his friendship with Gordon, the Egypt-Sudan crisis fairly enveloped him. After Gordon's recall from the Sudan as Governor-General in 1879, corruption and anarchy broke loose in that country. The Mahdi (or Moslem Messiah), in the person of Mohammed Ahmed, tried to drive the Egyptians out of the Sudan just as Ahmed Arabi had sought to drive the Europeans out of Egypt. The Khedive was in despair. Sir Evelyn Baring, British Agent and Consul-General in Egypt, compelled him to agree to abandon the Sudan when the Egyptian garrisons, now threatened by the victorious Mahdi in Khartoum, should be withdrawn. In January 1884 Lord Granville, in view of Britain's interest in the area and the vacillation of the

European powers over the ugly situation, sent Gordon back to the Sudan to supervise the withdrawal of the Egyptian garrisons. The choice of Gordon was strongly opposed by a section of the Liberal party as well as by Sir Evelyn Baring, with some reason. After all, Gordon was not as other men. He was by nature a mystic, impulsive and insubordinate. On his arrival in Khartoum on 18 February he immediately resolved, contrary to instructions, not to withdraw the garrisons but to establish a settled government and smash the Mahdi. The British Government at home weakly refrained from either recalling Gordon for disobedience or sending him the troops he badly needed to complete his task. The fact was that ministers and people of authority at home were divided between intense distrust of Gordon as a mischievous meddler and veneration of one divinely inspired and moulded on heroic proportions. Robert Hobart, Brett's colleague and co-secretary to Hartington, told him in January that Gordon had threatened to resign from the Army if he were not sent to the Sudan. When he actually sailed on the 19th of that month, his last words were 'Remember me to Brett.' The War Office was hesitant, but Lord Wolseley backed Gordon up to the hilt.

The long drawn-out story of the siege of Khartoum by the Mahdi, Gordon's piteous appeals for relief, his refusal to withdraw and the home government's tardy decision to send Wolseley in September up the Nile, and not across the desert as some advised, the arrival of the relief forces too late, and the death of Gordon are too well known to need repetition. On 1 April Regy received from Gordon a letter of uncompromising determination to smite what he called the 'Pasha tribe'. Nothing would induce him to leave Khartoum. He repeatedly begged for the appointment of Zebhr Pasha as Governor to succeed him. Zebhr was the only man for the job; he needed him at once for at least four months. But the 'humanitarians' in England would not consider this man who, although of immense influence in the Sudan, had once been a slave dealer, and the Government did not dare to flout them. Gordon's last letter to Brett from Khartoum, dated 3 March, contained these words: 'I am sorry you worry about me, for D.V. [*deo volente*] I am all right. I am comforted that if I try to do my best, one cannot fail. As for Zebhr, I wish with all my heart, he was here, he alone can ride the Soudan horse, and if they do not send him I am sentenced to penal servitude for life up here.' Regy forwarded this letter to the Queen, whose reply through Sir Henry Ponsonby was that Gordon must not be abandoned, although Ponsonby himself was against the despatch of troops. Regy was of course all for supporting his friend whom he, like the Queen, regarded in a romantic light.

A new friend and ally, one who remained a political sympathiser until his death on the *Titanic* in 1912, was W.T. Stead, now Editor of the *Pall Mall Gazette*. This son of a Congregational minister of Yorkshire stock, a man of deep religious convictions and high principles, was one of the most influential journalists ever. He took up causes that were usually unpopular, and ventilated them with such violence and virulence that ministers feared the *Gazette*, hitherto an insignificant publication. Stead initiated new programmes and movements. He first won high praise for his support of Gladstone's anti-Turkey agitation over the Bulgarian atrocities. Gordon was a man after Stead's heart. It was as a direct consequence of an interview with Gordon, which he published in the *Pall Mall Gazette*, that the General was sent on the fateful mission to Khartoum. Throughout the year in which they first met, Brett constantly primed Stead from confidential War Office sources with information and advice about the Sudan campaign. On 27 March he wrote to Stead that, unless prevented by some unforeseen event, he would leave next Saturday morning for Brussels to beg the King of the Belgians (who had tried to enlist Gordon's services as manager of his new Congo state) to telegraph to Gordon on his own responsibility not to abandon Khartoum, but to hold it for the African International Association.[35] He thought no one should know about his trip – which is hardly surprising.[36] Already Regy was taking upon himself responsibilities and actions unauthorized by his chief, who might well have disapproved had he been aware of them.[37] However, on 1 April Regy was blandly assuring the Minister of War that he was convinced nothing would induce Gordon to leave Khartoum until all the people who had been faithful to him could accompany him.

Stead was making himself feared by the Government because he was drawing attention to the likelihood of war with Russia following the Egyptian campaign, and to the degree to which the British Navy had been reduced. The First and Second Sea Lords actually expressed serious alarm, asking him, 'What can be done?' To this the imperturbable Editor replied, 'Give me the facts and I will make them [the Government] listen.' Regy in consequence begged Herbert Gladstone to ask his father to grant Stead occasional interviews, without taking him wholly into his confidence, and exercise his spell upon him without letting him suppose he was trying to 'square' him. Stead must be given time to withdraw from his unpleasant state of hostility to the Government.'[38] At the same time Regy and Herbert Gladstone attempted to persuade Stead to cease his regular evening assaults on the Government. Regy beseeched him not to establish himself in a position of permanent antagonism, which would ruin his future authority.'[39]

One of the causes of the Government's vacillation over the Sudan imbroglio was its preoccupation with the Franchise and Redistribution of Seats Bill. Regy was much involved with his Tory friend, Arthur Balfour, trying to seek a possible compromise between Gladstone and Lord Salisbury. The Government's Bill aimed to extend the county franchise, like the borough franchise, to all occupiers and lodgers paying at least £10 a year rent, thus giving the agricultural labourers political rights. Here again Regy was working with a leading member of the Opposition without Lord Hartington's knowledge. Two years previously he had boldly reproved his chief for expressing in Cabinet his natural objection to the county franchise, after having made a speech in June 1877 approving it. The passing of a Bill to this effect was, after all, only a matter of time after the pledges given by the Government at the last election. Regy had been right. In vain the anti-reformers objected, and the Tory Lords threw the Bill out. In October a compromise was effected, largely owing to the direct efforts of the Queen and indirect efforts of Regy Brett in persuading Salisbury and Sir Stafford Northcote, Opposition leader in the Commons, to have tea with Gladstone in Downing Street. Agreement was reached over the tea tray to bring in a Redistribution Bill, the provisions of which were to be drawn up by the leaders of the Government and Opposition jointly.

Regy Brett was undoubtedly behaving as though he were an absolutely independent Member of Parliament, even independent of party. It was no wonder that he once again expressed his desire to leave his chief. To a letter of 9 December Lord Hartington wrote on the 12th a charming reply. He reluctantly agreed to release Regy so that he might be free to express and act upon his own principles – as though he had not already been doing so. Regy was relieved, but not wholly satisfied with the Marquess's letter. He wanted a public statement made, he wrote to the doubtless bored Hartington,

> to let it appear to the curious world, first, that I give up my position near you because I find it difficult to combine it with the exigencies of parliamentary life on the eve of a general election; and secondly, that my relation with you has on the whole been satisfactory to you. . . . The following proposal would meet the difficulty, if you do not disapprove it.
>
> I would suggest that you should give me – as your predecessors have done in similar cases – a CB [Companion of the Order of the Bath], and that the announcement should be made as follows.

Whereupon he outlined the statement to be issued, which amounted almost to a dictation of terms.

> The only importance I attach to the 'honour' is as a public recognition of your satisfaction. I think that such a recognition, accompanied by the

notice I have suggested, would effectually prevent any insinuations of a kind which would be painful to you, as they undoubtedly would be to me, although so absolutely devoid of any foundation in fact.[40]

The bland Marquess, who was so totally indifferent to honours and recognitions of any sort, must have smiled over the references to the CB. In fact Regy did not get his CB for another thirteen years.

The correspondence between Regy Brett and Lord Wolseley (he was raised to viscount in 1885) is of considerable interest and importance in connection with the Sudan campaign and Gordon's death. Wolseley repeatedly acknowledged that Regy's letters were the most informative he received from home for political news, foreign and domestic. He was grateful, too, to Lord Hartington for not pressing him for details of his strategy. Wolseley's communications to Regy abounded in the usual complaints of the military man on the spot repeatedly sending Whitehall advice which is misunderstood or unheeded. As soldiers go, he was rather more resentful of interference from the War Office than most. He objected to the gloomy forebodings of the press about the outcome of the campaign. As for Gladstone, Wolseley held him in the utmost contempt and blamed him for not allowing the commander of his expeditionary force to make preparations for the relief of Khartoum at least four months earlier than he did. The cost would have been less. He would have had time to assess the situation in Khartoum, and the appalling heat would have been avoided. Regy for his part advised Wolseley not to set up a government in the Sudan hastily, without an order from the Minister for War. At the request of the Editor of *The Times*, George Buckle, he suggested that Wolseley should inspire rather than silence the war correspondents. Wolseley's faults were an unshakeable conviction that he was always right, a quick temper and impatience with any opposition. A deeply religious man, he fervently believed all his life that he was God's instrument. In this respect he was not unlike Gordon, who had been his close friend for thirty years. He was a man of the strictest honour. From the first he was determined that the organization of the Army must be reformed; hence his bitter opposition to the Duke of Cambridge, whose views were totally antiquated and who would have gone back to the crossbow if he could have had his way. As for the Duke of Connaught being the successor of that royal dunderhead, 'you might just as well appoint any amiable young lady of your acquaintance to the post'.[41]

On 17 January 1885 Regy was forwarding Tute cheerful news from Wolseley. The General meant to get to Khartoum from Suakin on the Red Sea, via Berber, and thence up the Nile. He did not need more troops. He had telegraphed for 2000 umbrellas against the torrid sun.

On the 30th Regy wrote to congratulate the General on his brilliant advance.

Alas, by the time Wolseley received this pat on the back events in the Sudan were not going according to plan. On 5 February a telegram reached the War Office at 1.30 in the morning. Khartoum had fallen. Wolseley wanted urgent instructions. Regy Brett, ever vigilant, was at once informed. Parliament was in recess. He went straight to Downing Street. No one there had heard the news. He was told that Gladstone was in the country, staying with Lord Hartington. He went to Lord Granville's house and woke up his valet, who told him that his master was at Walmer Castle. He telegraphed to Lord Northbrook, the First Lord of the Admiralty, to come to London at once. The only minister in London was Dilke, to whom at three o'clock he sent an urgent note that there ought to be a Cabinet meeting immediately. He wrote to Lord Hartington that there was no possibility of the Cabinet being assembled before the following day and offered his advice on the military tactics now needed in the Sudan. He wrote to Wolseley that in his opinion the Cabinet ought to leave the military situation entirely to him on the spot. Regy, furious with *The Times* for its consistent spite against Wolseley, sent that paper an indignant rebuttal of its criticism of the plan of campaign. When a few days later confirmation of the murder of Gordon reached London – on the 26th Regy wrote to Wolseley that his death must now be presumed – the nation's consternation and distress were overwhelming. Lady Ponsonby was sitting at breakfast with her two daughters in the Ponsonbys' cottage at Osborne when the door opened. Unannounced and unattended, the Queen entered. 'Khartoum has fallen! Gordon is dead!' she managed to gasp and, too distraught to add another word, walked out. The disaster made her quite ill. She spent hours in tears, murmuring, 'Always too late.'[42] Her anger against Gladstone was uncontrolled, but he remained totally unmoved.

A day of national mourning was declared for 13 March. Gordon was apotheosized as one of England's greatest heroes and the country clamoured for an expedition to annihilate the Mahdi, who in actual fact lamented Gordon's death. Fortunately for the Government and for Gladstone, whose unpopularity now plumbed the depths, Russian entry into Afghanistan drew attention away from the Sudan crisis. It enabled the quiet withdrawal of troops from Africa to proceed practically unnoticed. Nevertheless, in consequence of the wave of emotion which swept the country Gladstone's Liberalism and his Irish policies suffered severe, if temporary, eclipse.

Regy Brett was much affected by Gordon's death, and he wrote a poem on it.

Cities and battles may be won or lost,
The nation now has ceased to count the cost.
  Regardless who may snatch the prize
  Since, alas, that noble head,
So great and greatly fallen, lies
  Among the nameless and ignoble dead.

He had refused to join the Government's vote of censure on Gordon before his death was announced; now total lack of sympathy with his party over the issue clinched his resignation. In February he sent to Devonshire House all Lord Hartington's political papers which had been in his custody.

Lord Wolseley continued to unburden his heart and soul to Regy. He wrote of his grief and agony over Gordon's fate and deplored the Government's spineless inactivity. Regy assured him that their hero's death had had a beneficial effect on the nation's morale.[43] His friend replied:

The nation seems to be rising up from the comatose state into which it had been lulled by a number of vestrymen, Whigs and Tories, who diverted all public attention from all affairs of Empire, to those of paving and lighting. . . . We can dance and fiddle; laugh at vulgar, half immoral plays, enjoy novels of all sorts, solemn and gay, religious and disgustingly immoral; we struggle at all hazards to grow rich; we swagger about Trafalgar and Waterloo, but we lack the wisdom and the public spirit to spend enough money on works to protect our foreign coaling stations or to create an army in any way adequate to our wants.[44]

Wolseley advocated that Britain should get out of Egypt, invite the Turks to take over the Sudan, and go to war with Russia. Regy was shocked. He told Lord Hartington, with whom he remained in close and amicable touch, that he was astonished by the intemperance of some of Wolseley's letters. Regy's opinion was that the Government should merely abandon the Sudan, concentrate on defending Egypt against an advance by the Mahdi, but at all costs retain the port of Suakin with the railway to Berber. To hold the trade routes from the Upper Nile from falling into the hands of the French or Germans was essential. Hartington himself was highly critical of Wolseley's despatches, which seemed deliberately intended to make a target of the Duke of Cambridge, whom he hated and despised.

There is no doubt that Regy Brett had by now created for himself the reputation of an extremely astute, far-seeing and wise politician. His speeches in the House, although not brilliant, were commended.

It was his diplomacy that distinguished him. Having left Hartington, he was now acting as postman between the Russian Ambassador and Gladstone, using his utmost endeavours to avoid hostilities with Russia. The historian and Member of Parliament John Morley considered that he ought to be appointed ambassador to some country where a first-class diplomatist was needed.[45] Regy disagreed.

In June Lord Salisbury formed a Cabinet, and in November a general election took place. Regy was not re-elected. This is not wholly surprising in feudal Cornwall, where he had revealed to a constituent that his principles would permit large estates to be broken up and the influence of the squire and parson to be curtailed.[46] He was in favour of severing the connections between Chuch and State. He told his old constituency chairman that he was not enamoured enough of Parliament to compromise his opinions in order to be re-elected.[47] In a letter headed 'Private' to an unknown addressee he admitted that he was not very anxious to stand elsewhere for Parliament and was taking no active steps. 'There are reasons of a public and private nature for this disinclination on my part, which I need not trouble you with.'[48] One reason may have been that he did not want to be under an obligation to the Cavendish family by accepting the Barrow-in-Furness constituency which Lord Hartington had offered him. Another may have been his old father's acceptance of a barony this year, and the not distant prospect of his succeeding him in the House of Lords. He had been very anxious for the barony to be hereditary, and pressed Sir William Harcourt to consult Gladstone about it. In any case he turned down several offers of safe seats within the next few months.

On 25 July he attended the marriage of Princess Beatrice to Prince Henry Maurice of Battenberg. He was troubled by the wording of the priest's admonition, printed in large characters on the service sheet, that the state of matrimony was 'not by any to be enterprised, nor taken in hand, unadvisedly, lightly or wantonly, to satisfy men's carnal lusts and appetites, like brute beasts that have no understanding . . .' and that, 'It was ordained as a remedy against sin, and to avoid fornication; that such persons as have not the gift of continency might marry, and keep themselves undefiled. . . .' There in front of him sat Queen Victoria and the whole royal family solemnly and reverently endorsing advocacy of acts by husbands upon wives of gross indecency made licit by the Almighty. Was not matrimony often an obscene relationship? This year there were to be some serious sex scandals which opened men's eyes and made sensitive persons ponder. In one such scandal the oblique implication of a member of the royal family allowed the pious press to ventilate its righteous indignation. Regy felt constrained to remonstrate with his friend Stead against the assumption of the *Pall Mall Gazette* that the upper classes were the chief offenders in seducing girls under age, and that princes of the blood had greater propensity to vice than ordinary people; and for withholding the names of the latter while blazoning those of the former.[49]

In other respects he had no quarrel with the *Gazette*, as yet. That paper had quoted Brett's speech to his constituents in which he deplored the misery of people who lived in crowded dwellings, and attributed the evil in great part to the accumulation of land in the hands of a few. The land laws of England would have to be amended or repealed.[50] Regy was echoing the sentiments of Joseph Chamberlain, who cynically threatened to ally with the Tories in order to help pass Liberal measures. Until his career in the House of Commons came to an end, Regy's sympathies lay with the radical section of the Liberal Party. Thereafter his loyalties were to be thrown into great confusion by a series of unfortunate incidents – Dilke's divorce scandal, Parnell's large number of Irish supporters in the next Government, and the return of Gladstone.

In the November General Election Regy stood for Plymouth. But his heart was not in the contest, and he was defeated. It was a relief to him not to be answerable to a constituency, and he swore he would never go through a parliamentary campaign again. He would instead concentrate his energies on beautifying his new house in the country.

5

ORCHARD LEA
1886–1894

Soon after settling into No.1 Tilney Street the Bretts decided they wanted a house in the country. Their son Oliver was born in March 1881, to be followed by Maurice in April 1882. Then came two daughters, Dorothy Eugénie in 1883 and Sylvia Leonora in February 1885. The family was complete.

In spite of his love of old houses Regy decided to build one to his own design. A brand-new house would be a monument to his forceful personality and impeccable taste. So he bought a parcel of land on the property of his brother-in-law, Victor Van de Weyer, on the westernmost edge of Windsor Great Park, at Winkfield. It was a mere mile from Nellie's old home, New Lodge, and three to four miles from Windsor Castle. Although Regy Brett was all his life regarded as a man of sound aesthetic judgement, Orchard Lea, which was finished in 1884, cannot by present-day standards (for it still survives, although much altered by the various institutions which have recently occupied it) be accounted beautiful. Of nondescript Tudoresque style, it has walls of scalloped tile-hanging, unconvincing half-timbered gables, oriels and latticed windows. Nevertheless the rooms of Orchard Lea, panelled with oak and cedarwood, hung with tapestries and family portraits and filled with some excellent pieces of furniture, struck contemporaries as tasteful and cosy. The garden, transformed from a wilderness of scrub and tangled undergrowth into a bower of rose beds, divided by red-brick paths and adorned with wrought-iron gates, stone well heads and a statue of Pan playing his pipes, was considered idyllic. The future King George V, who motored from Windsor on Easter Sunday of 1907 to tea at Orchard Lea, pronounced it, 'quite charming with lovely things in it'.[1] Even the Kaiser, who did not care for Regy, was to admire Orchard Lea so much that he wanted red-brick houses of the kind built in Germany, and asked Regy to send him some sketches for the purpose. The Crown Prince's house, the Cecilienhof at Potsdam, with its twisted Elizabethan chimneys and profusion of black and white gables, may owe some of its inspiration to the future Lord Esher's residence.

Regy's nephew, writing after his uncle's death, recorded that:

> The furniture belonged mostly to the elegant French periods, but had nothing about it formal or stiff – his were rooms to live in, from which modern contrivance and bits of nonsense were not banished. He was not a collector of furniture or bibelots, but he acquired a number of objects of historic interest: rapiers, miniatures, snuff-boxes, rings, a lock of hair, watches, shoes, clocks, a parchment, a drinking-cup; and all these things were incorporated in the general arrangement of the rooms. His library was large and comprehensive.[2]

In other words Regy Brett was not, strictly speaking, a connoisseur, but a hoarder of objects of family and historical interest. He was intensely proud of his possessions and may, like most reverential owners, have attached an inflated value to some of them. In a bound inventory which he was to have prepared in 1913 he noted in pencil against each item his own opinion: 'Absolutely perfect'; 'very good'; 'Of the very finest quality'; 'Magnificent Louis XV clock; very best period and style'; 'Bas-relief, a real Greek piece, worthy of the British Museum.' And against his elder son's question, 'What is the small statuette?' was the succinct and rather tart 'Answer. Beautiful.' The furniture included an Empire writing-chair 'from Napoleon's suite at Fontainebleau', which was probably correct, judging from photographs of it. Another large writing-chair had belonged to George IV. The gallery chimneypiece, bought by his father in Florence, was sixteenth-century Italian. The stained glass coats of arms in the stair hall windows were given by King Edward VII and Queen Alexandra in memory of repeated visits to Orchard Lea; and among the royal souvenirs was, within a glass frame, the wreath placed on Queen Victoria's coffin by King Edward and given to Regy by the King.

Regy Brett was a highly domesticated man. His home, first at Orchard Lea, and later in his life at the Roman Camp, Callander, was undoubtedly the pivotal centre of his existence. Politics, the royal family and his public duties were secondary. He loved adding to his treasures, rearranging them and planting the garden. At Orchard Lea he saw himself as a simple country gentleman with intellectual preoccupations, who made occasional incursions into the great and rarefied world. Undoubtedly the closeness of his new home to Windsor Castle helped to admit him into the Queen's private circle.

Although no longer a Member of Parliament, Regy's concern with politics was not a whit abated. On the contrary, freedom from constituency obligations and the necessity for strict party loyalty allowed him to spend even more time than before in pursuing that political philosophy in which he was interested. His natural aptitude for intrigue and his connections with influential people enabled him to exert pressure on Liberal and Conservative ministers alike, because they regarded him as an extremely astute and, on the whole, wise monitor, and to feed his friend G.E. Buckle, Editor of *The Times*, with information gleaned from these associations.

Indeed in 1886 Regy's allegiance to the Liberals was tenuous. He was at this time much under the influence of the dissident Radical-imperialist Joseph Chamberlain, who had written to Regy that his policy was to do everything and anything that was disagreeable to the Whigs. They were the enemy. Until they were out of the way, or at least penitent, no good could be achieved. What Chamberlain had in mind was the first Home Rule Bill and its intemperate sponsorship by Gladstone. Regy shared these sentiments without making any secret of the fact. On 16 January he noted in his journal a conversation with Joe, who was very displeased with Gladstone for not adopting his political programme or consulting him about the future of the party of which the Grand Old Man was to resume power on 1 February.[3] Chamberlain favoured giving Ireland self-government on municipal lines. Regy assured his friend that in a great national crisis he would prefer to see the direction of affairs in his hands because of his courage and plain dealing; moreover he had never heard him say a malevolent word about a class or person.

With Gladstone once again at the helm in February, Regy found himself consulted by his closest political friends on whether they should accept the posts offered to them by the Prime Minister. John Morley sought his advice about whether he should become Chief Secretary for Ireland; William Harcourt whether he should take the India Office; Rosebery the Foreign Office. Harcourt said he would have liked Regy, had he still got a seat, to be his Under-Secretary. Henry Labouchere called to ask if he would undertake the editorship of *The Daily News*. Regy declined. Rosebery, of whom he saw a great deal and with whose attitude to the Empire and foreign affairs he was in sympathy, consulted him, while they went for long walks round Hyde Park, as to who would make suitable private secretaries. 'Rosebery called here after breakfast, and we walked to Millais's studio, where we found him with a stalking-cap on his head and a short pipe in his mouth, painting from a model dressed as a kind of nun,'[4] he wrote in a memorandum. Rosebery was convinced that the story about Dilke was true.

Dilke's story was tragic. It was yet another case of a friend in trouble inducing Regy to help all he could. In 1885 Donald Crawford, a Liberal MP, filed a petition for divorce, quoting Dilke as co-respondent. On the public announcement of the charge Dilke denied it in an open letter to the Liberal Association of Chelsea, his constituency. In December he stood again for Chelsea and was re-elected. In 1886 Crawford obtained a decree on his wife's admission of adultery. In February Dilke, on Regy's advice, did not enter the witness box to deny the charge a second time. The case against him was dismissed, but Mrs Crawford's guilt was proven. As a result Dilke was not admitted into Gladstone's ministry, although he continued to sit in Parliament. He was united with Chamberlain over Ireland, resisting most of the Government's proposals. The public, however, regarded him as guilty, and in the next election he was not returned to Parliament.

Chamberlain begged Regy not to abandon Dilke in his need. But Regy never withheld support from his friends, however much their reputations stank in the nostrils of the masses. He visited Lady Dilke, consoled her, explained how her husband was loath to flee abroad and persuaded her to take him away to their cottage in Surrey. Dilke confided in Regy that Stead was persecuting him in the *Pall Mall Gazette*, and appealed to him to stop Stead from interviewing and publishing the statements of the witnesses. It speaks well for Regy not only that his acquiescence was beneficial to Dilke but that he did not forfeit his friendship with the rabid, puritanical Editor. Mrs Crawford, however, withdrew none of her charges, and during the second hearing of the divorce case added gross details which were dismissed by all Dilke's supporters as fiction. Dilke regarded himself as an injured man, and although he returned to Parliament in 1892 never recovered his old impetuosity and dash.

In April Gladstone introduced the first Home Rule Bill, which provided for an upper and a lower House of Parliament to be established in Dublin, and for a Land Bill by which the State was to be empowered to purchase land from landlords and resell it to tenants. On the 21st a letter from Brett appeared in *The Times*, strongly condemning Gladstone's hasty and ill-conceived policy. Practically everyone in the Liberal party except Morley was opposed to it, and in June both Bills were thrown out. In July the Government's defeat brought in Lord Salisbury's second ministry; the Tories' new allies, the Liberal Unionists under the leadership of Lord Hartington, held the balance of power.

Regy Brett was deeply involved behind the scenes in the grotesque resignation of Lord Randolph Churchill, Chancellor of the Exchequer, through pique and a hubristic notion that he was indispensable to the Government. The ostensible reason was his refusal to accept the Cabinet's proposals to increase the naval and military estimates, in the belief that Chamberlain, dissatisfied with the Government's local government scheme, would support him through thick and thin. Both men wrote of their own accord to Regy, begging to discuss the situation with him. On 23 December 1886 Regy sent a telegram to Harcourt that Churchill had resigned through 'freak of temper'. He went to Lord Randolph and found him lying on a sofa in his large library, smoking cigarette after cigarette, pouches under his protuberant eyes and utterly prostrated. Lord Randolph complained that he was shunned like the pest by friends and foes, which was not far from the truth. Chamberlain told Regy he was sure that, if only Gladstone were out of the way, he, Chamberlain, could come to terms with the party.[5] Regy took it upon himself to write on Christmas Day to Gladstone that

> the state of affairs is so grave abroad[6] and in Ireland that I hope you will pardon an old supporter who entreats you to break the silence you have latterly maintained. The present Government has hopelessly collapsed, and Lord R. Churchill's retirement indicates that we are back again into the old grooves of 1874.[7]

He informed his leader that Chamberlain was now demanding a Land Act. If he succeeded he might after all be prepared to discuss a scheme of Home Rule. Morley, Parnell and Hartington would agree that 'the decision remains with you. I pray you may not look with suspicion upon this appeal from one who to some extent has been identified with opposition to your Bills.' In other words he was suggesting that Gladstone should not oppose Chamberlain's innocuous proposals since the future of the Liberal Party was securely in his (Gladstone's) hands. 'A word from you will decide whether England is to have a strong government capable of steering a regulated course through the storm of European conflict.'[8] He ended by saying he had never doubted the ultimate triumph of Home Rule – a strange contradiction of his recent views against that measure. To this rather perky letter Gladstone replied in a friendly, non-commital way, fearing that no practical steps could be taken before he knew when a new government would come to power, or what its intentions might be.[9]

Over Christmas Lord Randolph seemed to have revised his attitude towards his former colleagues. He also confessed to Rosebery that his resignation had been made in a state of dudgeon and he felt sure that Lord Salisbury would ask him to reconsider it. Lord Salisbury did nothing of the sort. He was delighted to be relieved of an awkward and unreliable colleague, and appointed Goschen in his stead. Lord

Randolph's comment to Regy was, 'This is shooting at the pigeon and killing the crow.'[10] On New Year's Eve Regy told Lord Hartington, who violently disagreed with Gladstone's feeble Irish policy, that Morley hoped he would not coalesce with the Tories. By abandoning the Liberal Party he would leave the destiny of the country in the hands of those in whom Morley had no confidence. Morley said, 'I look upon him as the strongest bulwark we have against all the socialist doctrines I hate.' Regy endorsed this view. If Hartington joined the Tory camp the Liberal remnants would gradually drift over to Rosebery or somebody else, because they were not strong enough to hold their own against Chamberlain and Churchill.

In politics, as opposed to normal life, loyalty to friends is nothing. As it happened, Hartington would sooner have died than ally with the Tories, with whom he was traditionally and congenitally out of sympathy.

On 5 January 1887 *The Times* published a letter from Regy in which he argued that Britain was within a short distance of a second measure of Home Rule for Ireland under the auspices of a united Liberal party and with the assent of the majority of educated English people. Chamberlain had been holding the balance between Gladstone's Bills and Lord Salisbury's coercion. Although Buckle published the letter, he told Regy he did not understand his game. 'You are neither Unionist nor Gladstonian. I don't see what you are driving at.'[11] Other friends were equally perplexed. This provoked a private letter from Regy to Buckle explaining his political position. He was a Unionist. He had removed his name from the Liberal Association when he found that its funds were being used for Gladstonian purposes.

> It is true that I have joined no other society, but I have reasons for not doing so, which I consider adequate. To mention one of them, I think it dangerous to crystallize the sections of the old Liberal Party round Gladstone and Hartington, for fear that the legitimate opposition, in whom lies the reversion of government, should be wholly separatist.[12]

Why should he be more specific, since he no longer had a seat in the Commons and never would again? What he sincerely strove for was that Gladstone should never return to office and that the Liberal party should retain the services of Hartington. On the Irish question he sympathised with Hartington and Chamberlain. Regy called Buckle 'a fat-headed ass' who did not know his own business.[13] He was particularly angry with him for having had a fifteen-minute interview with Lord Hartington and coming away without any idea of Hartington's views on any subject. On the other hand *The Times*'s Editor might be forgiven for not wholly grasping his correspondent's cryptic

machinations. The very next day Regy was compiling a memorandum, for his own eyes alone, of conditions in which he might consider
standing again for Penryn and Falmouth! These concerned a wide
extension of popular control over the government of the counties,
without class privilege of any kind; and his absolute freedom to
support any measure which might commend itself to his judgement.
What indeed was he up to?

Sir William Harcourt received a letter from Horace Seymour[14]
warning him against Regy Brett, who carried everything he heard
straight to *The Times* and the *Pall Mall Gazette*. Morley, too, told Sir
William that Buckle received a letter from him every day on the
situation until at last he asked him what he was playing at. Morley
said, 'His game at present is Randolph.'[15] The truth was not sinister:
Regy was a natural busybody. He revelled in being free to manipulate
whomever happened to be the operative and influential instrument of
the moment. Buckle, and to a lesser extent Stead, were his most useful
instruments. His genuine aim was to prevent political combinations
which would be dangerous to the State and, as he expressed himself to
Buckle, to promote the calm and dispassionate consideration of
questions which must be solved, and not by men whom experience
had taught him to suspect.

Apart from political intrigue Regy's time was spent in fairly lavish
entertainment at Orchard Lea, and racing. Frequent visitors were
Johnnie Oswald, Lord Arthur Somerset (known as Podge), George
Binning and Lewis (Loulou) Harcourt, Sir William's son and devoted
confidant. Regy's journal temporarily ceased this year and his engagement book contained only the briefest entries. In any event, since his
marriage in 1879 the journals had become guarded on his private life;
from that point assumptions have to be made and conclusions drawn.
It is impossible to believe that a man who was to tell a friend that he
could never recollect the day when he did not care passionately for
someone – 'I suppose it will come, but life will then be very near the
end'[16] – was without a favourite for a whole decade of his early
married life. But no proof exists. In his correspondence book for 1887
and 1888 Regy wrote that he destroyed some letters from those years
in 1892 and again in 1894.

Newmarket brought about a crisis in Regy's finances. With an
overdraft of £1000 and debts amounting to £2000,[17] he was obliged to
appeal to his father for help. The retired Master of the Rolls nobly
offered him £3000 as a gift, saying he would never refer to the matter
again on the condition that his son no longer ran horses and gave up
betting, which was anathema to him. Lord Esher pointed out that
Regy ought to manage on £4150 a year. He calculated that from his
property at Ranelagh and what he hoped to leave him in his will Regy

would inherit about £130,000. Regy, deeply touched by his father's magnanimity, abandoned racing and betting and merely bred horses. There was, too, a more positive consequence of this domestic crisis in his life. From now on he was to devote his energies exclusively to building up a private influence on national affairs.

W.T. Stead was never very far from Regy's elbow, for Regy was continually feeding him with particulars of ministerial deliberations which he meant to find their way into the pages of the *Pall Mall Gazette*. On 18 April 1888 *The Times* published a series of forged letters purporting to associate Parnell with Irish outrages. It was suggested that Stead was the forger; in fact a man called Richard Pigott was subsequently convicted. But such was his persecution mania since his imprisonment in 1885 that Stead believed he would be made the scapegoat. Some documents were planted on him. He begged Brett and Cardinal Manning to advise him what to do. Regy advised a discreet silence. The Cardinal told him that he was under no obligation to say all he knew if interrogated by the police. In November Stead told Brett that a mysterious offer would be put to him – conclusive evidence of the close connection between the Irish Members of Parliament and the Physical Force Party in America[18] – on condition that the interview was cloaked in the utmost secrecy. Albert Grey offered the use of his room in his father-in-law's Dorchester House while the owners were away. Stead agreed to meet the informer, and on the appointed evening went first to Tilney Street, where he chatted with Regy, until a servant from Dorchester House called to announce the arrival of the stranger. Stead went off with the servant, expecting a plot to murder him. After a while he returned to Tilney Street to report that the whole thing had been a hoax.

Such offers of information were very frequent in late Victorian times. Regy's first task on becoming Lord Hartington's secretary had been to deal with a letter from a lady's maid, offering to inform the Marquess of Cabinet secrets which she had overhead told by a drunken husband to her mistress, whose hair she was brushing. Regy was instructed to have no dealings with the woman.

The year 1889 was largely concerned with a public scandal which far transcended that of the seduction of girls below the age of consent in 1885. The Cleveland Street homosexual brothel scandal caused a furore. Certain noblemen and other persons in society were accused of making assignations with poor youths in an establishment kept for that purpose in Cleveland Street, between the Euston Road and Mortimer Street. Most of the accused fled the country or were acquitted, whereas the procurer and some telegraph boys were convicted.[19] Regy Brett was in no sense implicated, and there is no reason to suppose that he ever patronized the scene of the scandal. On the other hand he spent a lot of time helping a friend who was involved. As he expressed it in his resumed journal, on 5 November 1890,

> From June 1889 onwards, certain events in connection with a great sorrow to a personal friend and his family, occupied nearly all my time. They ended disastrously for all concerned in the closing months of last year. The worry of them was maintained through the first half of the present year.

In the bound volume of correspondence entitled by Brett *The Case of Lord Arthur Somerset* the first letter, undated but probably written in August 1889, is from George Binning to Regy in answer to one Regy must have written to him. By 'settling the affair without scandal', Binning asked if Regy meant there was any hope of the thing being quashed. He had been told that the police had strong evidence on some point against Arthur Somerset. What? He did not care to enquire. 'It is lucky he has such a pal as you to stand by him all this time.' A second letter from Binning referred to 'this awful news. A bitter pill. Old Podge of all people, my pal in the desert marches, one of the best hearted friends. I suppose it is true? Or why should he have left the country? To think of him wandering an outcast for everyone to throw a stone at.' Podge and George were intimate friends, and had in their extreme youth been on many an unspecified debauch together. They had also been on campaign in the Sudan in 1885 under trying conditions.

In 1889 Lord Arthur was thirty-eight and Superintendent of the Stables and Extra-Equerry to the Prince of Wales. With his receding hair, sandy moustache and bushy whiskers he did not present an appetizing appearance. He was inclined to fat; his small eyes were on the watch. In a photograph of the period he has a sensual mouth and a haunted look. His connection with the Royal Household and close friendship with Edward, Prince of Wales, must have caused him great anxiety and embarrassment. On 21 August he wrote to Regy that he was off to Homburg in Germany, mentioning that the impending case might cost him another £1000 which he hadn't got. The Prince of Wales was staying there at the Hotel Imperial. Podge sat next to the Prince's sister, Princess Christian, at dinner and behaved as though unaware of his situation. Meanwhile, at home, Regy was in close touch with Podge's solicitor, Arthur Newton.[20]

In September Podge admitted to his friend that he was in mortal dread of the Prince getting to hear of the story. As might be expected, the *Pall Mall Gazette* and *The Times* had published it in garbled fashion. On the 16th a friend, Hugh Weguelin, raised and paid £1200 to Newton on Podge's behalf. On the 21st Lord Arthur was back in England on a flying visit to his parents, the Duke and Duchess of Beaufort, at Badminton in Gloucestershire. As yet they knew nothing of his trouble. They were good but simple country people.

On the 27th a warrant went out for Lord Arthur's arrest, but he had already crossed the Channel to Dieppe. From there he telegraphed to the Prince of Wales, who had demanded to see him, that he was unable to obey. On 1 October he risked another return to Badminton, this time to see his dying grandmother, the Dowager Duchess, to whom he was devoted and with whom he was accustomed to stay in London when not in barracks. Still his father did not know. Yet Podge was sure his brother, Lord Worcester, did know and was spreading ugly rumours about him. The following day the Dowager died. Lord Arthur was present at the funeral, where a police sergeant was poised ready to receive orders from the Home Office – which by some chance never came – to arrest him at the graveside. On the 3rd he was writing on Marlborough House paper to friends, reassuring them about his circumstances. On the 10th Newton, the solicitor, wrote to Regy that more money was needed to buy off an informer in Paris. He warned him that it was the police's intention to apply for a warrant for arrest unless Lord Arthur resigned his appointments and went away. The same day Podge received a very nice letter from the Prince of Wales, asking why he had gone to Dieppe when he particularly wished to see him. On the 13th, the Prince and Princess being abroad, Lord Arthur went to Sandringham to work as though nothing were the matter. On the 15th he was at the Marlborough Club in Pall Mall where his friends rallied to him. But the situation was becoming uncomfortable. From the Marlborough he wrote to Lord Cranbrook, the Lord President of the Council, accusing him of spreading 'rumours of a most disgusting nature' about him at Gordon Castle. And on the 19th he went to see Sir Francis Knollys, the Prince of Wales's secretary, to whom presumably he disclosed the trouble he was in.

By 21 October he was writing to Regy from Rouen and signing the letter 'Arthur Short'. He asked what he should do. Teach English in France? Or go to Turkey as Master of the Horse to the Sultan? He begged Regy to attend to his furniture and servants. He told him that he had informed his father, who had replied, 'I know not what to say to you – God help you – what will you do? I must go to Badn. tomorrow and tell your mother,' ending the letter, 'Poor dears, and they have both always been so good to me.' His youngest brother, Lord Edward, wrote thanking Regy. He said his father dared not tell his mother because her heart was in such a weak state (in fact she lived until 1906) and was devastated. The Duke would not have Podge's clothes removed from his room until he had broken the news to the Duchess. Then the Duke wrote Regy a letter of thanks for his kindness and help. He would wait for Podge to write to his mother and then would withhold the letter until she recovered from a chill she had caught. The Duke begged Regy to tell Podge he must return and face trial. He wrote again on 4 November that he had pretended to the Duchess that some men enticed their son to a house of ill fame and there threatened to blackmail him. On 8 November Blanche Waterford, Arthur's sister, told Regy she was going to join Podge at Monte Carlo to comfort him. By the end of the month the poor fugitive had arrived at Constantinople, where he was advised by the British Embassy to leave Turkey for fear of arrest by the Turks. So he moved to Budapest, having got Lady Waterford to persuade Lord Salisbury to have the threat of arrest in Turkey withdrawn. Podge told Regy that he was learning Hungarian, had grown a long beard as a disguise and now wanted to go to the East where no one would point at him.

In December Podge wrote that he was hurt that the Prince of Wales would not recommend him for a job and yet had accepted his horse as a present. In fact the Prince, on learning the true nature of Podge's trouble, returned the horse. 'My dear old Redge,' Podge wrote on the 10th, 'I can quite understand the P. of W. being much annoyed at his son's name being coupled with the thing but that was the case before I left – in fact in June or July.'[21] He was of course referring to Prince Eddy, Duke of Clarence, the elder Wales son, who was likewise implicated in the Cleveland Street business.

> It had no more to do with me than the fact that we (that is Prince & I) must both perform bodily functions which we cannot do for each other. In the same way we were both accused of going to this place but not together; and different people were supposed to have gone there to meet us. . . . Nothing will ever make me divulge anything I know even if I were arrested. . . . It has very often, I may say constantly occurred to me that it rests with me to clear up this business, but what can I do? A great many people would never speak to me again as it is; but if I went into Court, and told all I knew, *no one* who called himself a man, would *ever* speak to me again. Hence my infernal position. . . . At all events you and Newton can bear me witness that I have sat absolutely tight in the matter & have not even told my father anything.

On the 20th he begged Regy to get him a passport in the name of A. Short.

On 21 December an interview with Arthur Newton took place at Tilney Street in the presence of Regy and John Oswald. They vindicated Mr Newton from police charges that he had endeavoured to obtain false evidence from telegraph boys who had frequented the Cleveland Street brothel. The same day Lord Arthur wrote from Vienna of his distress to read in *The Times* of the trouble Newton had got into; and the Duchess of Beaufort from Badminton, thanking Regy for all he had done. 'It is all hopeless and miserable, my poor, poor child! May God bless you for your unceasing kindness to the best and dearest of children.' Colonel Oliver Montagu,[22] Somerset's commanding officer in the Blues, also wrote to Regy, denying the *canard* that the Prince of Wales had begged Henry Labouchere[23] not to bring the matter forward and drag his family's name through the mire. On the contrary the Prince was most anxious for an enquiry and was pressing the Government to that end. Montagu accused 'Labby' of lying.

On Christmas Day Lord Arthur wrote again to Regy complaining of the intense cold in Vienna. Besides, whenever he went out, he was followed by police and boys and insulted by the latter.[24] He must get to a warmer climate. Would Regy recommend Italy for him? But Knollys's plan that he should manage his cousin's estate in Lombardy was untenable. The Duke of Beaufort asked Regy if there was no place near Menton where his son could go and be warm; he could then run up to Henry in Monaco. Lord Henry Somerset was the Duke's second son, who for a similar misdemeanour to Arthur's had been obliged to take flight from England ten years previously and was also living in exile.

Meanwhile rumours that Prince Eddy, the Duke of Clarence, was under grave suspicion were running like wildfire through London society. Colonel Montagu, who seems to have been spokesman for the Prince of Wales, wrote to Lady Waterford assuring her that neither parent of the Prince suggested for a moment that she was responsible for the rumours, although he feared that some female members of her family had implicated him. Montagu nevertheless thought Arthur had behaved wickedly in implying by his silence that he was sheltering someone else whom people claimed to be the Prince. Lady Waterford then implored Regy to tell Podge to write a letter to the Prince of Wales's Comptroller, Sir Dighton Probyn, to the effect that he believed Prince Eddy to be perfectly innocent and that a man had threatened to blackmail him.

On 2 February Regy wrote to Labouchere, imploring him to be kind to Lord Arthur's wretched mother and sister by not mentioning their names in *Truth*. He hoped that he would hit out at the Government instead, for all the oral evidence was tainted and none was written; nor was there any police evidence. He felt convinced that had Lord Arthur not gone abroad in the first instance, no warrant would have been issued. Labouchere replied on the 21st: 'My officer tells me that he has written to some of his friends (officers I presume) telling them that he [Lord Arthur] did not commit sodomy, but only engaged in gentle dalliance with the boys. This is confirmed by the credence of the boys at Marlborough Street.' But he affirmed that Lord Salisbury did not tell Probyn they intended to prosecute.[25]

The unfortunate Newton was sentenced to six weeks' imprisonment, having pleaded guilty. His father weighed in with an appeal to Regy, as a friend of Lord Arthur, to plead for mitigation. In effect the Law Institution decided not to take any action at all. Newton complained to Regy that the Duke of Beaufort was refusing to pay more than his previous £1000 towards the case, and he was sadly in debt; and the Duke informed Regy in a long letter, interspersed with an account of the day's hunting, that he was arranging to have money paid quarterly to Podge through his bank.

The Beauforts continued to keep in touch with Regy. In 1895 the Duke wrote that he hoped to go to Calais on Lady Waterford's yacht to meet his son; and two years later that Arthur corresponded regularly with his mother. The Duchess told Regy that her son had considered returning to face trial, being quite sure of acquittal.

> He wrote to his sister the other day, 'If you will try to live long enough, I will come over – stand my trial and go to prison, but I must be sure to find you afterwards,' but that way is not what I could bear. . . . Do you think me troublesome, dear Mr Brett, nor wonder that at such a time as this I can think of anything but my Blanche. He does so feel the prospect of never seeing her again, and if there was a chance of his dear name being cleared it would so cheer whatever time we may hope to keep her.

In fact Blanche Waterford died, probably of cancer, in February 1897, and the devoted brother and sister did not meet again.

Podge's punishment was permanent exile for thirty-six years. By the end of 1890 he had settled in Hyères. At the Villa Sophie he lived out his days, attended by a French cook and a few servants. The warrant for his arrest was never withdrawn. He died, aged seventy-four, in 1926 and was buried in the English section of the Hyères town cemetery. His tombstone bears the epitaph: 'The Memory of the Just Is Blessed.'

Howard Sturgis had written to Regy, 'Podge is queer too. His little domestic arrangements must become expensive! And Chat and the Marco's! What *orageuse* middle ages all our friends have! I am glad that I have settled down into respectable stuffiness.'[26]

Suddenly at the end of 1890 the Parnell-O'Shea divorce case dropped like a thunderbolt. Charles Stewart Parnell, the frigid, haughty, fanatical fighter for Ireland's cause, who condoned and even organized violence and assassination, and who personally raised American funds with which to subsidize disorder and terror, was cited for adultery. It was the Dilke case all over again, only worse for Ireland, in that the English Liberals headed by Gladstone – hitherto Parnell's sympathizers – now dissociated themselves from him. Home Rule seemed doomed. As Jack Durham wrote to Regy: 'Parnell's *amours* were undignified, but not nearly so discreditable as some of mine! But he has been exposed, so must pay the penalty in this most hypocritical and *virtuous* land.'[27]

Regy was no hypocrite. He told Lord Rosebery, the former Foreign Secretary, that he much respected the courage and skill which Parnell exhibited in his tremendous ordeal.[28] He lamented that, owing to the Parnell scandal, Ireland should be sacrificed to the demands of party spirit and English prejudices. He was disgusted that Gladstone, the protagonist of Home Rule, should positively abort his own creation on account of the Irish leader's adultery. On 30 December *The Times* published a long letter from Regy, with an accompanying leader praising him for his honourable conduct (only the previous year Buckle had rebuked him for his disloyalty in speaking against his paper)[29] in acknowledging the rightness of *The Times*'s policy on Irish affairs. Regy agreed with the paper in drawing no distinction between the public moralities or immoralities of Parnell and those of his present or late associates. The leader went on to claim that Regy's arguments confirmed *The Times*'s thesis that the founders of the Land League and National League, the authors of boycotting and the Plan of Campaign, were not to be entrusted with the welfare of a kingdom containing five million British citizens.[30] It intimated that Regy foresaw that Home Rule must survive the present reverses, but would be tolerated by Great Britain only so long as the supreme authority of the imperial Parliament were maintained, and that the Protestant minority, being the sole party acting in unison, must hold the balance of power, for Ulster would yield only to reason. At the same time Regy, in sending a copy of his *Times* letter to Gladstone, begged him not to allow Home Rule, which the majority of Irish people wanted, to be relegated to second place in the Liberal programme.[31] Regy was all for Home Rule, but on reasonable conditions.

At the beginning of February 1892 Regy met Cecil Rhodes for the first time at Stead's house. Rhodes, who had just arrived in London from South Africa, had for the past six months been Prime Minister of the Cape. For three hours he talked of his great schemes. He boasted that all South Africa was behind him – Kruger, Hofmeyer, the Dutch – and also the British, including Lord Salisbury. His ideal was a federation of all English-speaking peoples, to which end he proposed to organize a secret body of the Elect, or helpers, and looked to Stead for assistance. He had made a will leaving his entire wealth to Lord Rothschild for this purpose, he said, but he now thought him deficient in brains and might therefore alter his will in Stead's favour. The Rhodes Society would resemble the Society of Jesus but without attributes; the Elect would bind themselves to work for the Empire just as the Jesuits worked for the Church of Rome. Stead enthusiastically proposed that the society should comprise a junta of three: himself, Milner and Regy, with Rhodes as General. Regy considered Rhodes a splendid enthusiast, but had slight reservations. Rhodes looked on men as machines, which was callous and not very penetrating.[32]

A fortnight later Regy took a long walk with Rhodes at Tring Park, Lord Rothschild's Hertfordshire house. 'He has vast ideas. Imperial notions. He seems disinterested. But he is very *rusé* and I suspect quite unscrupulous as to the means he employs.'[33] In the end the Rhodes Society came to nothing. Rhodes's will omitted Stead on account of his 'extraordinary eccentricity', his pro-Boer sentiments and his spiritualism. Instead the Rhodes Scholarship Trust developed.

During the spring and summer of 1891 Regy saw much of Rosebery. He would lunch with him upstairs in the nursery of Rosebery's house in Berkeley Square with the four children, governess and tutor. Then the two men would descend to talk. Regy implored him, now Lord Granville was dead, to enter the fray, in spite of his hatred of the House of Lords. He must lead the Liberal party in that House. His absence would take the heart out of those who cared for matters besides Home Rule and parliamentary reform, namely the part the Empire had to play in the modern world. Regy's concern was disinterested, for he had no intention of securing a seat for himself in the Commons.

John Morley was another close confederate. They dined together, and Howard Sturgis remarked to Regy: 'His mind is so essentially of the religious type; he seems to have come out of Christianity as Mrs Lot did out of Sodom. He hankers after St Paul. His necessity for making all his judgements fit in with a code of morality and right thinking ("*bien-pensantism*") reminds me of Lady Harcourt.'[34] In truth Morley's brand of agnosticism was of the fervid, proselytizing sort. Regy was intrigued by the way Morley allowed his prejudices to contradict his principles. He was amused by his fondness for and admiration of Rosebery, whose succession to Gladstone he favoured, in spite of his intense disapproval of the Liberal imperialist group which Rosebery so positively represented.

Army reorganization was a matter which had absorbed Regy Brett ever since he became Lord Hartington's secretary and had written in his journal: 'The most perfect expression of our military wants is a small army in times of peace, a large army in times of war, and yet a larger army for purposes of defence; and yet what are wanted are not three armies, but one army. As to conscription for defensive purposes, if it is forced on us by circumstances, we must accept it. . . .'[35] These were sentiments from which he never swerved. In 1891 the Anglo-Italian agreements over Abyssinia, the visit of the French squadron to Kronstadt and the Franco-Russian Alliance turned Regy's thoughts to Britain's unpreparedness for war, should it come. They prompted him to write in November three letters to *The Times*, headed 'The Unpreparedness of England'. He observed that Lord Salisbury might indeed see no cloud on the horizon, but war clouds loomed with terrible suddenness. He recognized that discussions about war preparedness bored people to tears, yet every European country was better prepared than Britain. He pointed out that there was no Permanent Under-Secretary of State for War, and no body of advisers or committee to discuss defence. These timely warnings, hotly defended by Lord Wolseley, are an interesting forecast of the army reforms which were to come early in King Edward's reign, largely owing to Regy's alarms and premonitions.

A new friendship made in 1891 and one which was to mean a great deal to him throughout his life, was with a woman of twenty-four at the height of her beauty and social success. Millicent, then Marchioness of Stafford, received her first letter from Regy on 21 July. He delivered himself of a slightly patronizing homily about the conservation of youth and beauty, typical of his predilection for directing those younger than himself. The two met in a bookshop where he gave her a copy of Tute's *Ionica*, though in after years Regy frequently referred to having first encountered her in the garden of Lady Cardross's house near Newmarket. Regy's journal does not reveal his first impressions, but his letters went on to proffer advice, criticism and sometimes approval. She must read *Daniel Deronda*, Charlotte Brontë and Marie Corelli's *Barabbas*. Dutifully she obeyed. 'I have dinner on a tray,' she wrote, 'in between mouthfuls of fried sole and partridge, read *Sesame and Lilies* and *Barabbas* by turn.'

Milly Sutherland – her husband became the 4th Duke in 1892 – had been married for nearly eight years. She came of raffish stock, being the sister of the libertine Earl of Rosslyn and the 'fast' Lady Angela Forbes and half-sister to the notorious Daisy, Countess of Warwick; she shared the looks, intelligence, wit and charm of her siblings. Everyone she met, from royalty to peasantry, was treated with a sweetness that melted the heart. When she and Regy met she had reached that stage in a loveless marriage to a much older man when a young wife will look for romance. She was to find plenty of it in due course, and some of the passionless sort with Regy Brett. Their affair was platonic, though not because Regy extolled the virtues of self-denial.

From the first she was mystified by this strange, well-informed yet reticent man. 'I suppose in time you will let me find out something about yourself!' she wrote. 'But you're quite right not to give me your "frank confidence" at least, not yet.'[36] He was peremptory as well as bossy. 'Do not pose to me,' he wrote in November 1892, 'and will you please oblige me by dropping the formal style in which you generally write. It is not necessary or friendly.' But the Duchess was not the ingénue he liked to suppose, and was wary of him. She did not know what Regy wanted from her, nor could she understand why her self-constituted mentor did not take a more active part in the world's game. 'Many thanks for sending me the little verses reminding me of my marital duties! I take the hint humbly, though feeling it rather uncalled for. . .,' she wrote. 'As for my dignity, thanks very much. I've got plenty of it when impudence calls it out, but it's better to keep one's claws sheathed till one's frightened.'

Regy could not keep away from her. Around six o'clock of an evening he would walk across Mayfair to Berkeley Square to talk alone in her boudoir. Nellie must have known, but she showed no signs of minding. After two years the nature of Regy's and Milly's friendship had changed, and he could write, 'Heaven knows, you are endowed with all the qualities which any woman could desire; and seem to me to be going beyond the range of comparison.'[37] Two years later still he told her:

> I feel that our understanding is more complete than ever. I hope you have the same feeling. Isn't it a pleasure to you to have someone to speak quite frankly with who is a friend in the sense that he *knows* he cannot be anything more, and therefore never tries to be, but who nevertheless is attracted all the more thereby than the less? I suppose such a relation is hardly credible to most people, and would be difficult except under the peculiar circumstances of this case, in which your character and its influence over me are the main factors.[38]

She now knew, if she had not already guessed before, that he could never be her lover because he was incapable of loving a woman in the way she needed. Yet there was no pretence in his protestation made thirteen years after they first met, 'My sweet friend, I think of you every day.'[39] That was the language of a partner in an *amitié amoureuse*.

Milly Sutherland had a serious rival in Regy's affections which for a time she little suspected. In 1892 an Etonian of fifteen bewitched the forty-year-old man of the world and was to remain an infatuation for three years. Edward, or Teddie, was the son of Colonel Leopold Seymour and his wife Mary, daughter of Russell Sturgis and sister of Howard. Teddie was fair-haired and handsome, with bright blue eyes and a laughing face. Of average intelligence and not cultivated, he was perfectly normal. By the autumn Regy actually admitted to Chat Williamson that Teddie was *au fond* a young barbarian, quite unlike what they were at his age.[40] Teddie would tease Regy to his heart's content. In February Regy was seeing him perpetually either at Eton or Orchard Lea, where Nellie in her wisdom accepted the boy as a son. Regy, once again in close touch with Chat, wrote to him of the boy's gentle and caressing manner, of their 'absolute and adorable intimacy, altogether without reserves or secrets. I suppose it is the culminating point of a perfect passion tempered by the most enchanting romance.'[41]. Two days later he wrote that Teddie was occupying Chat's room at Orchard Lea. 'When he was in bed, I sent him to sleep by combing his hair with my hand – a thing he adores.'[42] The journal for this month and March teams with references to Teddie.

Chat was slightly jealous, and never liked Teddie. A visitor to Orchard Lea this spring and summer, he was undergoing a period of grave doubts as to whether he had been right to enter the priesthood. Howard Sturgis wrote to Regy in April that he was not surprised, and attributed the blame to Regy's influence upon his old lover.

I think that in Chat you have tried to combine the incombinable, the cultivation of the love of beauty, the sensuous enjoyment of life, colour, nature, music, and love, with the priestly vocation. You have had a dream of Renaissance cardinals, not sufficiently considering the differences between Italy in the 15th and England in the 19th century. It has amused you after the dull agnosticism of commonplace friends like L.V.H. or J.O.[43] or me, to have a tame Catholic ecclesiastic tethered on your lawn among the apes and peacocks; not to mention the joy of finding one of your dearest & oldest friends still so much in tune with you, and with a heart open to all influences of love and beauty, in spite of all the years of 'walls grey and monastic' that lay between your old friendship and its latest development. You will be inclined to protest against my laying all the responsibility of our friend's present crisis on *your* shoulders, and justly. No doubt the warring elements were in himself: but it would be idle to pretend that all those enchanting talks and readings of each other's poems over the fire in the room from which I write this to you,[44] have not had their effect. . . . Your responsibility must often frighten you: it is a terrible thing to be a pope. And you *are* 'Pope come Pope' to so many people. Where did you get the gift of such enduring ascendancy over the minds of your friends? You must often wish to get rid of it.[45]

The crash, Howdie ended his letter, was bound to come. Was it better to put it off or hasten it? No matter: it came within a few months, when Chat ceased to be an Oratorian. He found his way, like others of his kind, to Venice where he fell for a gondolier.

In August Lord Salisbury's Government fell and Gladstone embarked upon his fourth ministry. Lord Rosebery, with whom Regy had been pleading in January not to sacrifice parliamentary work to his duties as Chairman of the recently constituted London County Council, but to hand over what he had started to others less gifted than himself, became Foreign Secretary. He accepted the post only after extremely heavy pressure from his friend and the urgent appeal of the Prince of Wales and Buckle, *The Times* Editor, among others. Finally Gladstone submitted his name to the Queen. That clinched the matter. 'So be it,' Rosebery telegraphed to Osborne.[46] On the 16th his old Chief, Lord Hartington, now 8th Duke of Devonshire, married his mistress, Louise, Duchess of Manchester, after a decent two-year widowhood. Regy considered that it would make life easier and tidier for him, since in any case the Marquess saw her every day and never took the smallest step without her advice and sanction. 'I suppose the world will think it foolish. Therefore it is an act of wisdom,' he wrote cynically.[47]

At this time Chat was about to leave Orchard Lea and Regy contemplated taking a long journey abroad. On learning this news Teddie wrote:

> I think your plan of going abroad would be simply unbearable; just think how I should get on; no talks, no advice, no nothing. . . . No. It would be too horrible. Do try and see if you couldn't find something nicer to do; all this seems awfully selfish as if I was only thinking of myself but I don't think you would enjoy it yourself very much. Do you?

The boy of fifteen knew that he had Reginald Brett fairly hooked. At all events Regy did not go abroad; he was far too interested in awaiting the publication of his first book, *Footprints of Statesmen*, just before Christmas. On the whole the popular papers received the book graciously; the intellectual journals found it superficial and sometimes inaccurate. Regy dedicated the book to 'Teddy Seymour, aet. xv.', a fact commented on by Sir William Harcourt and remarked knowingly by others. In the preface he explained that his essays on distinguished statesmen – Godolphin, Bolingbroke, Pitt – were 'written for the entertainment of a friend in the hope that they might stimulate, not satisfy, curiosity'.

The relationship between Regy and Teddie must have been common gossip among the masters and some of the older boys at Eton, for Regy could not keep away from the place. Howdie was well aware of the situation. 'Dear Mr Brett,' he wrote mockingly, 'how *very* kind of you to offer to take my little godson for a change of air; It is *too* good of you, & I am very grateful. I *do* hope he won't trouble you, or be in your way. Haw, haw!'[48]

At the end of the month he dined with his old house tutor Ainger at Eton. Afterwards they walked to Huntercombe with Arthur Benson and H.E. Luxmoore to discuss printing privately a selection of Tute's letters and journals. Unfortunately Tute's brother, Canon C.W. Furse, insisted on editing them, deploring what he called 'the sentimental' in his brother. The project was postponed. When the work eventually appeared in 1897 it was not in fact edited by the brother, but by Francis Warre Cornish. It proved to have shocking lacunae in both letters and journals.[49]

The year 1892 involved Regy in yet another of his friends' scrapes. In the previous November George Binning had announced that he was engaged to be married. The bride was to be Katharine, only daughter and heiress of William Severin Salting of 49 Berkeley Square, owner of a fabulous art collection, part of which he subsequently bequeathed to the Victoria and Albert Museum. Before long George was battling against some very unsavoury rumours concerning his past and present debaucheries, which, although he strenuously denied them, had unfortunately reached the ears of Mr and Mrs Salting. Worse still, the suspicious couple and their daughter were receiving a spate of anonymous and vitriolic letters warning them that their future son-in-law, in addition to being a libertine, was an inveterate gambler. In short, they implied, George Binning was out only for Katie's money. On George's behalf Regy consented to vouch for his character to Mrs Salting. He ascertained that all the letters might have been written by one woman with whom George had once had an affair – a Mrs Bourke. Regy managed to mollify Mrs Salting, and the possible misuse of Katie's inheritance was pre-empted by having Mr Salting nominate two trustees of the marriage settlement.

The next task was to extract a confession from Emmie Bourke, but she had an influential ally in Lady Granby, the former Violet Lindsay, who stoutly maintained that Emmie had not written the anonymous letters. On 23 August 1892 a memorandum was signed by Lord Granby and Reginald Brett to the effect that they had heard all that Lord Binning had to say in his defence and Mrs Bourke in her denials. They felt obliged to concur that Lord Binning had not proved his case to their complete satisfaction although he had a *prima facie* cause for grave suspicion of Mrs Bourke. In the circumstances they recommended that Lord Binning should apologise, which he did. Even so, the anonymous letters did not cease. In September Mrs Salting forwarded to Regy one claiming that Binning was suffering from an incurable venereal disease, and was incapable of fathering children.

George Binning and Katie Salting were eventually married on 21 September. There seems to be little doubt that Mrs Bourke behaved in a contemptible manner. Lady Granby, however, was not of that opinion: in November she wrote to Regy that, since he clearly did not believe her dearest friend's innocence, their friendship must be considered at an end. Regy never wavered in his affection for George, and when his friend died of pneumonia in 1917 he was heartbroken. He was a perfect horseman, a charming musician and a lover of poetry and gardens. Though passionate and restless he was gentle with women and animals, all of whom loved him. He was a fine soldier too, and brave. George Binning was a romantic who fluttered against the bars of life's cage, which never proved strong enough to hold him.[50]

Regy's indifference to public and private opinion meant that he did not curb his infatuation for Teddie. He had done nothing morally reprehensible, so nobody had any right to administer criticism. No longer in Parliament, he felt free to do as he liked. Besides, Nellie raised no objections; on the contrary, she was devoted to Teddie. So he continued to visit the boy at Eton during term time. Teddie realized that there were no limits to the liberties he might take with his elderly worshipper. During the Christmas holidays of 1893 he called without warning at Tilney Street at eleven o'clock one bitter morning, walked into Regy's sanctum and flung himself into a chair before the fire. He announced that he was going to a fancy dress ball that night and needed something to wear. Regy who was writing letters, got up and took the youth to a shop where he bought him an eighteenth-century costume.[51] Before the holidays were over Teddie had influenza, and his parents allowed Regy to move him to Orchard Lea to be nursed. In the middle of August Regy and Nellie took Teddie on a short excursion to Scotland. They stayed in a hotel at Callander, and it was then that Regy fell in love with the place. Before the century was out he was to acquire a house there which was to mean more to him than any home he had hitherto lived in.

He saw a good deal of Gladstone during this last year of his premiership. On 21 February he returned to Windsor from London in the same railway carriage as the Gladstones, who were bound for the Castle. The Prime Minister complained that he could no longer do a good day's work. 'Only five hours today,' he said. 'I am unfit for my place; drawing pay on false pretences.' But whereas his wife drove from the station in a royal carriage, he walked.[52] In August Regy spent three days in the company of the Gladstones at Tring with Nathaniel Rothschild. Gladstone and Regy drove for two hours through

Ashridge Park, talking about Eton and Oxford with ardent affection. He spoke with hurt feelings of the Queen's unkind letters to him, for she had never liked him. He spoke with admiration of Henry Chaplin,[53] an old-fashioned sporting squire, recalling that when a boy he lived next door to Chaplin's grandmother. When she held receptions Gladstone and his brother would squirt water over the footmen and coachmen and listen to them discussing whether or not it was raining. In September Gladstone's Home Rule Bill passed its third reading, but a week later the Lords rejected it.

Chat had now become a worry to his friend. Regy feared for him. Chat had no clear views of the future. He flitted from one place to another, and from the strict dogmas of the Christian faith to the transitory delights of paganism. Regy's journals referred obliquely to his friend's stolen joys and hours of pleasure while he was still at the Oratory and hinted that a fellow priest, Father Stanislas McCall, had fallen in love with him. With his propensity to relish flattery Chat certainly did not spurn his platonic advances, and when Chat left the Oratory Father McCall accompanied him; like Chat he remained a lay priest in orders. He became a sort of background dependent at Orchard Lea, doing odd jobs and spending most Christmases there. The Brett family were fond of him because of his good nature and reliability. He acted as occasional chaperon to the boys, Oliver and Maurice, and he remained a faithful watchdog over Chat's future escapades.

In July 1893 Regy advised Chat firmly to stop flitting from Taormina to Ravello, to stay put in Sicily with his fifteen-year-old gondolier, Salvatore, and to cease worrying about having deserted the Oratorians. 'Vocation is not necessarily constant. It is not your faith, but your vocation, which has been shaken. How simple it would be if you were an Italian or a Frenchman. Here the Puritan movement has leavened the Catholic Church.'[54]

Towards the end of 1893, in a letter to Milly, Regy referred to his achievements over the past twelve months.

> Nothing that I could do cannot be as efficiently done by others, if indeed anything is worth doing! And as for 'popularity' and 'fame' they are *tastes*, like any other, racing or gambling, and they are not my tastes. There are things which I do think worth having, and I try to get them, and this past year I have succeeded oddly enough, wonderfully succeeded. So much so that I am frightened. *Voilà.*[55]

After the initial modest disclaimer, did he mean by the things worth having the flowering of his passion for Teddie and, perhaps, the consolidation of his platonic attachment to Milly? He made no mention to Milly or even in his journal of the publication of his only volume of poems, *Foam*, issued anonymously by Macmillan in an expensive white cloth binding. Nearly all of the poems are dedicated to adolescent boys or to Regy's heroes of the past – Cory, Chat and even General Gordon. Few rise above a rather sugary mediocrity, although some are touching in their simplicity and naïveté of both syntax and sentiment.

At the beginning of 1894 it was apparent to everyone that Gladstone, who had suffered the rejection of his Home Rule Bill the previous autumn and was feeling the onslaught of decrepitude, must shortly retire. Loulou Harcourt, who for ten years had been his father's faithful secretary and confidant and had used every device to get him made Prime Minister, stayed a night at Orchard Lea. His purpose was to persuade Regy to support his father's efforts for the premiership against the only other serious rival, Lord Rosebery. Regy owed much to Sir William Harcourt's past friendship and patronage – without sharing his radical view that Britain ought to withdraw from Uganda and Egypt – but he was also a close friend and admirer of Rosebery, with whose imperialistic attitude he was in total sympathy. Regy admitted that it was a 'painful personal question. Harcourt is 66 and for 30 years has been in the thick of the political mêlée. Powerful forces arrayed against him. (1) The Queen; (2) his colleagues; (3) the sort of interest roused by Rosebery. I am sorry for Loulou.'[56] The host told Loulou that, having discussed the matter with Rosebery, he felt sure the latter would undertake the job if called upon. Loulou retorted that he would sooner his father retired than serve under Rosebery, and in his journal recorded that Rosebery ought to give way to Chex (a nickname for the Chancellor of the Exchequer), who was twenty years his senior. He begged Regy to be abroad when the crisis arose so as to avoid personal embarrassment over the tussle. In his letter of thanks to his host he confirmed their agreement that Regy would tell Rosebery that he ought to stand down.[57] It does not appear that Regy did anything of the sort. When Rosebery went to No. 10 the blow for Loulou was cruel, even crueller than for his father. On the 9th Regy and Nellie took the new Premier to a play and dinner at Willis's Rooms. Rosebery was in tearing form, though grieved at having left the Foreign Office. He would not say goodbye to anyone there and crept unnoticed down the back staircase. From Willis's Rooms Regy accompanied Rosebery to his house in Berkeley Square, where he had further talk – '*very intime* with him'.[58]

Sir William did not take his defeat well. He behaved petulantly, demonstrating his grievance to all and sundry. Rosebery feared he might even organize a *coup d'état*. Regy had his misgivings too. He believed that Rosebery in the Lords and Harcourt as Leader of the

Commons would not make a durable arrangement. He predicted a short government, and he was right. Had the situation of the two men been reversed the alliance might have had a better chance of survival. Meanwhile, though sorry for Loulou, Regy was pleased that Rosebery had got the job.

On 6 June the Prime Minister's cup of happiness was filled to the brim when his horse Ladas II won the Derby. Public acclaim was tremendous. After the race the proud owner, drinking champagne, was so moved that all he could utter was, 'At last!' To Rosebery it was the greatest triumph of his life, for no previous Premier had won the Derby. In the morning he had seen a hedgehog run across his path in the garden. He took it as a good omen, because twenty-five years previously while an undergraduate at Oxford, he had bought a horse which he named Ladas after a mighty courier and wrestler in the service of Alexander the Great. The Dean of Christ Church made him choose between Ladas I and Christ Church. He chose the horse. It too ran in the Derby. On the morning of the race the eager owner, who was staying in Henry Chaplin's London house, found a dead hedgehog in the garden. He was told at the time that it was a bad omen. Sure enough, Ladas I came in last.

It also marked the climax of his career. Immediately he was assailed by anti-gambling, anti-sport, Nonconformist voters. Thereafter his fortunes declined. *The Times* launched a vicious offensive against him for his criticism of Harcourt's death-duty budget – the first time this tax had been imposed – and his proposed lease to the King of the Belgians of territory on the Upper Nile. Regy leaped to his defence and wrote to Buckle, loyally vindicating the Premier:

> Think of the difficulties of his position! Think of his Cabinet and the 'programme' he has inherited! All these shackles are not to be thrown off in a moment. It takes time and patience and much skill and tact to free himself from the burden left by his predecessor. What he has *done* is to be singularly firm (under difficulties which you hardly realise) upon questions of imperial policy, which are vital to us.[59]

He much deprecated the way the press had lowered the Prime Minister's prestige in the Liberal party.

In August Regy was staying at Cowes where, he recorded, 'Teddie and I have a cold sea bath in my room every day.'[60] He wrote to Chat begging him to be nice to Teddie if he overlapped him on a forthcoming visit to Orchard Lea. 'Remember how nice I should be to Salvatore and how little I *really* understand any of your feelings about Teddie.' And as though to enlist sympathy with his infatuation he recounted some of Teddie's most engaging ways.

He does such unexpected things; and the sort of things which would charm you, in intimacy, such as pulling off his clothes in the drawing-room and sitting in the airiest of costumes, complaining of the heat! Altogether, in many ways, he is very much what you were at his age. He is fonder of *me* than you ever were![61]

It is most unlikely that these paeans did much to alter Chat's opinion, any more than did his old friend's reminder of the cavalier treatment he had received from Chat in the days when he was head over heels in love with him. Regy was beginning to throw discretion to the winds. One wonders what Balfour thought when, invited to a *tête-à-tête* luncheon with Regy to talk about his interview with Gladstone, he found another guest in the person of the eighteen-year-old Teddie Seymour. No wonder society was beginning to chatter.

In September Regy was at Dunrobin Castle, the great grey bastioned house built by Charles Barry overlooking the cold North Sea off Inverness. When he got there he and Milly quarrelled, but made it up again, as old friends do, several times. He admitted to himself that the cause of his discontent was 'in the bustle of this great house . . . I get only occasional hours with her'. And he felt tossed about by the vagaries of her temper. He finished the summer by a visit to Castle Malwood in the New Forest, where Sir William Harcourt denied that he was piqued and said that Rosebery behaved disgracefully, keeping secrets from his colleagues, and knowing nothing of the art of politics to boot. He had no patience with his old maidish complaints, his migraines and his insomnia.

During Rosebery's short term as Premier he was in constant touch with Regy, summoning him to Downing Street for discussions that lasted far into the night or for walks in Hyde Park. Walking was Rosebery's favourite relaxation. On one occasion while Foreign Secretary, having lunched at Windsor Castle, he walked with Regy to Slough to catch a train to London. He became so engaged in retailing the Queen's memories of Sir Walter Scott and Mrs Siddons that the two men relaxed their pace. Then they were obliged to run in their frock coats and top hats for a quarter of a mile, reaching the station hot and out of breath. Even so, they missed the train.

Rosebery could talk to his fellow Old Etonian more frankly than to any of his colleagues because Regy held no office under the Crown and had no axe to grind. Moreover they shared an indifference to public applause and an assumed indifference to public criticism. In Rosebery's case there were no honours to covet that he was not already endowed with by birth; in Regy's no honours that he had the least desire for that would not now come to him on his father's death.

On Sunday night, 4 November, occurred what came to be called the

Tilney Street Outrage. Regy and Nellie had been out to dinner in London. Nellie went home in a cab to No. 2, their town house (No. 1 was let), while Regy followed on foot. She let herself in with a latch-key and walked into the hall, shutting the door behind her. In half a minute a bomb went off on the doorstep, blowing the front door off its hinges, hurling the topmost stone step across the street, twisting the iron railings and breaking all the windows. Luckily the blast went outwards. A certain amount of debris followed the door into the hall where Nellie, having quietly shed her cloak and one of her gloves, was eating a grape. No one was hurt, and the servants were safely in the basement and attics. Luckily Nellie had not noticed the bomb on the doorstep as she passed it by, or she would doubtless have bent down to examine it. She had escaped injury and possible death by half a minute. The perpetrators were not discovered and it was thought that they had meant to plant the device on the steps of No. 5, the house of the Bretts' neighbour, Mr Justice Hawkins, who had recently sentenced some anarchists. The London posters next day were splashed with headlines such as: 'Mayfair Bomb. Mrs Brett's narrow escape.' The Prime Minister sent a brief communication. 'Why did you not come on Tuesday as you said you would? You have become an unknown quantity; absent, absorbed, transient. Nothing short of a bomb brings you out of your shell, Yours, R.[62]

6

THE OFFICE OF WORKS AND QUEEN VICTORIA

1895–1901

Before he was midway in his term as Prime Minister Rosebery had worked himself into a state bordering on hysteria. W.T. Stead, so Regy informed Milly Sutherland[1] in February 1895, was dismayed on calling at Downing Street by his host's condition. Rosebery spoke of being 'crucified to his post as PM', describing in detail the 'nails' and 'crown of thorns' which encompassed him. Stead pointed out that after all leadership of a great country and his status were not entirely unenviable. 'It is damnable,' Rosebery replied. Regy was inclined to be impatient with these melodramatic exclamations. Milly thought Regy unsympathetic, but, being at his old friend's constant beck and call, he had had a surfeit of Rosebery's self-pity. Not that he did not relish being in the Prime Minister's confidence nor that he did not like him – in fact he hero-worshipped him, and had done so ever since Eton. He was attracted by his perennial youthfulness, physical charm and patrician hauteur. Rosebery was five years his senior. The gap was too wide for them to have been friends at school, but Regy had listened with awe and wonder to his praises by Tute. 'One of my earliest recollections', he wrote to Rosebery,

> is the stress laid upon your name by one who had the greatest influence over my youth. From that time onward you have always been more to me than anyone else in public life, representing something which every other man lacked. For this reason, if no other, I desired to be beholden to you, and to feel this tie in addition to those of private friendship. All this may be very sentimental, *mais voilà comme je suis*.[2]

Tute had been intoxicated with him. He considered Dalmeny, as he then was, the wisest and wittiest boy that ever lived, and full of fun too.[3] And he summed up the man's attitude to public life in a letter to Francis Warre Cornish with the famous phrase, 'He is one of those who like the palm without the dust.'[4]

Without altogether deprecating Regy's hero-worship Rosebery, one senses, treated his adorer with an amused tolerance bordering on disdain. Regy was always pressing him to call him by his Christian name; it was in vain. The nearest he received by way of familiar address in a letter was 'My dear R.'; then it would lapse again to 'Dear Brett'. Persistently Regy retorted, 'I wish you would regard me as your Sir Horace Mann or your Madame de Grignan and exercise on my appreciative receptivity your great epistolary talents.'[5] All he received were the curtest notes, often containing words of sharp rebuke, and demands for long letters in return. But it must not be supposed that Regy always wrote deferentially. He sometimes reproved the great man for his indolence, urging him to resume active politics and telling him outright that his attitude was at times that of a prima donna. On the whole they had a fine understanding, although Regy doubted Rosebery's capacity for true friendship: 'His sentiment seems so seldom directed towards human beings.'[6] His friendships were abstract conceptions. 'He is rather of the oyster tribe, don't you think?' he lamented to Chat.[7] And Regy relished confidences.

A few days after Stead had given his bewildered report on the Prime Minister's condition, Rosebery telegraphed to Regy peremptorily ordering him to come that night to his Epsom house, The Durdans. Regy found no one staying there but Dr Broadbent, Rosebery's physician, who confided that his patient was almost desperate through sleeplessness. He was on the verge of mental collapse. Walking with a stick and leaning on Regy's arm, Rosebery descended to the dining room where he was not uncheerful on account of his friend's immediate response to his call.

The accepted cause of Rosebery's discomfiture during his brief premiership is ceaseless opposition within the Cabinet to his campaigns for reform of the House of Lords, and disestablishment of the Welsh and Scottish Churches, chiefly fomented by his bitter rival, William Harcourt. These worries were intensified by a severe attack of influenza, and his wife's death in 1890 had been a blow from which he was still suffering. But there may in addition have been psychological apprehensions and anxieties. That he unburdened himself to Regy during his long talk far into the night of 13 March is unlikely; Regy would surely have said something in his private journal. The ostensible reason for the summons was to ask Regy if he still wished for the Office of Woods and Forests. Regy recorded:

He thinks the Office of Works secretaryship more suitable – I said that I had often felt that I had missed my vocation in not going into the Civil Service. He said, 'No, you have missed your vocation in not going into the Diplomatic Service – *that* is the tragedy – as you would inevitably (and he repeated the word twice) have gone to the head of it.' I wonder; and I doubt! Anyway I don't regret it, and I said so. It would have cost me many happy years. But as time passes one wants a tie. It is wholesome.[8]

At last he was feeling the lack of specific duty and position.

The following morning the two went for a drive, and Rosebery admitted his extreme sensitivity to press criticism. He complained of loneliness, saying how much he required companionship. 'You think me a spoilt child.' Regy did not deny it. He thought how ill-fitted Rosebery was for democratic leadership. 'Oligarchic rule was what he understood. He was curiously inexperienced in the subtler forms of happiness which come from giving more than one gets. He has been satiated with the sweets of life; and the long process has left him longing for affection, universal approval, omnipotent authority.'[9]

On his return home Regy wrote Rosebery one of his effusive dissertations, beginning: 'Pascal said the happiest life – which he would choose if he could – began with love and ended with ambition. You reversed the order, and hence the feeling of loneliness. It has sometimes struck me – watching your management of colleagues and of those around you – that you have ceased to value the personal equation in politics as highly as you did ten years ago.'[10] His hand had lost some of its cunning. To Milly Regy admitted that Rosebery's sleeplessness certainly amounted to serious illness of a sort. Here was a man who had been blessed with everything he could desire – intellectual, physical and material. Unfortunately he began life at the wrong end.[11] On the 21st Regy was summoned again by Rosebery, whom he found still more depressed and still suffering from relentless insomnia and worry all night.

This month Oscar Wilde rashly brought an unsuccessful action for criminal libel against Lord Queensberry, and in April and May society was enthralled and appalled by the poet's arrest, trial and sentence to two years' imprisonment with hard labour. Regy's references to the affair were cursory: in his journal he wrote, 'A man of genius behaving like a fool,'[12] and to Rosebery, 'What a fool was Wilde!'[13] In a letter to Milly he was a little more expansive.[14] He told her the scandal was too sordid for words; and that a dirtier scoundrel than Queensberry could not easily be found if it were necessary to produce a champion of public morals. Wilde may have been known to Rosebery, for Jack Durham told Regy, 'The Newmarket scum [the racing lot] say that R.

never had the influenza, and that his insomnia was caused by terror of being in the Wilde scandal. Very charitable!'[15] It is not improbable that Rosebery lived in terror of allegations being disclosed about his private life. In 1893 he went through the disagreeable experience of being pursued to Bad Homburg by Lord Queensberry, who threatened to horsewhip him and was prevented only by the Prince of Wales's intervention. The Marquess is supposed to have been furious because Rosebery had acquired for his eldest son, Lord Drumlanrig, the Prime Minister's secretary, a handsome young man of twenty-six, a peerage enabling him to sit in the House of Lords during his father's lifetime.[16] Drumlanrig committed suicide in mysterious circumstances the following year. In 1898 Raymond Asquith was provoked by the good looks of one of Rosebery's secretaries, by name Waterfield, to exclaim, 'He inclines one to believe the worst of his illustrious master.'[17]

On the 27th May Regy wrote to the Prime Minister that, having said originally that he did not want Woods and Forests, he would now accept the post if it were still going. 'Motives are very complex things, and mine are no exception, but perhaps some day I may be able to throw light on those which govern this decision. Now it is impossible for me to *thoroughly* explain them.'[18] The ambiguity of the dithering is not lessened by the fact that Regy was writing from Paris, where he was staying for the carnival. The eve of Lent witnessed wild scenes; the streets were thick with confetti. 'Terrific romps, but really very amusing when you indulge in them with total strangers, all of whom are good-tempered, and none of whom use bad language. . . . The opera ball was a huge pandemonium,' he told Milly.[19] But two days previously Rosebery had sent him a letter, now waiting for him in Tilney Street: 'It is one of the bitterest drops in a cup that is none too sweet that I have not been able to give you the place you desired,'[20] meaning Woods and Forests. Nevertheless on 2 June he wrote again, offering his friend the secretaryship to the Office of Works made vacant by his cousin, Henry Primrose. Next day Regy told Milly that he had accepted. 'The historical association, the Labour question, and the artistic side of the Office ultimately converted me,' he said.[21] And to Chat he wrote that the new appointment would not 'hamper' him. In some ways it would strengthen his hand in regard to all the things and persons he most cared for. It had always been his wish to work for the Crown without being in politics.[22]

To the many offers of more exalted posts made to Regy Brett already and later – the vast majority of which he turned down – he raised the same guarded objection that they would hamper his private life and be an obstacle to his personal freedom. What was this personal freedom which he so valued that he was prepared to deprive himself of honour and fame? It was not Nellie and the children; his wife never claimed his exclusive attention, but merely gave occasional luncheon parties for his political and social friends, usually with their wives. Like most Victorian statesmen, Regy saw people such as Rosebery, Balfour, Harcourt, father and son, W.T. Stead and his multifarious associates in public life alone at his clubs, the Turf, Buck's, the Marlborough or Brooks's. His children – with the single exception of Maurice – did not mean much to him. As for his non-social friends of the stage and the arts, he preferred to entertain them at the Savoy if he were in London, or at home in the country. Nellie liked most of them, too. As for his boy-friends, like Chat in earlier times, now Teddie, and in years to come others, it is true he often wanted to have them to himself when he would take them alone to plays, and on expeditions, but he also enjoyed having them to stay. Again, Nellie not only made herself agreeable but became extremely fond of most of them. She probably resented Milly Sutherland more than the youths, for, being a simple woman, she saw in her a more likely or more lasting danger.

The fact that he readily accepted the secretaryship of the Office of Works, a comparatively humble post, proves that he was not ambitious for public prominence. On the contrary, he had an aversion to shining in the public eye. His ambitions were private ones. He loved power, and he enjoyed exercising it from behind the scenes.

There had in fact been much intriguing on the part of Loulou Harcourt from his father, the Chancellor of the Exchequer's residence, No. 11 Downing Street, to get the job for Regy. At first Rosebery was frightened of appearing to show favouritism by giving it to a friend. As it was, Tom Ellis, Rosebery's Welsh Chief Whip, was indignant. 'Brett's appointment is simply *execrable* . . . a man with about £6000 a year with five houses in town and country "who has always left his party in the lurch". . . . It will be looked upon as Whiggery with a vengeance. Ugh!'[23] The post was in fact a permanent appointment not a political one, a feature which met with Regy's approval for it meant he would not be dependent upon changes of Government. Regy's boss, the First Commissioner of Works, was for a few months Herbert Gladstone, the Grand Old Man's youngest son. Regy wrote to him at once, asking what his wishes were and when he wanted to see him.[24] In welcoming him, Herbert Gladstone reminded him that the Office's momentous task was the Parliament Street development scheme. Gladstone was succeeded later in the year by Aretas Akers-Douglas, the owner of Chilston Park, once the seat of Regy's grandmother Dora Best's family.

Regy received several half-hearted congratulations. In proffering his, W.T. Stead expressed surprise that Regy should have accepted the post at all. He was sure he would be of use to it, but would the job be of use to him? E.T. Cook of the *Westminster Gazette* was likewise surprised, deeming him worthy of a better place. But Regy was satisfied. He was beholden to no Government. Within limitations he could do what he liked. He could not be turned out; and he could leave when it suited him. His love of ceremonial, his sense of history and his reverence for the monarchy made him a most suitable choice.

Hardly was he installed in his new job than his benefactor lost his. The Liberal Government was defeated over a paltry issue. On 25 June, when Regy lunched at No. 10 Downing Street, he found his host packing up all his family portraits and making claret cup. On 8 October Rosebery resigned the leadership of the Liberal party on the excuse that he found himself out of sympathy with the majority of his colleagues over the Armenian Massacres. To Regy he listed his grievances and the lack of support he received.[25] After making a farewell speech to a crowded audience he wrote in his diary, 'Home to supper. What a relief.' The Conservatives were to hold office for the next ten years.

Regy's new job brought him into closer touch than before with the royal family and the Queen. One of his first duties was to install a lift for her in Windsor Castle. Repairs and alterations to the royal palaces were a recurrent responsibility, and during his term of office the royal palaces were overhauled, the Mall was transformed, the South Kensington Museum rehoused and a series of new Government buildings were planned and begun. For instance, the new War Office, designed by William Young (to be completed in 1907) and the Ministry of Health by J.M. Brydon (completed in 1900) were both begun in 1898. The site of the former was chosen by Regy opposite the Admiralty and the Horse Guards. During his first year of office he was dealing with numerous important if small-scale matters: the layout of the east end of the Mall where it opened into Charing Cross; the complaints from Henry Labouchere of the architect Yates Thompson's plans to demolish buildings in the Westminster precincts; the erection of a telephone kiosk in Kensington Gardens (in the Italian style with a glass verandah on light iron columns); the disturbance of the heronry in Richmond Park; the row over a hideous new lamp-post just erected in front of the Military Knights' houses in Windsor Castle; the serious injury to the Windsor Park keeper, Perkins, through the bite of a mad dog; the avoidance at all costs of protests from 'the anti-scrape people' – the familiar term for members of William Morris's recently founded Society for the Protection of Ancient Buildings – over the renovations of the rooms in Kensington Palace; and even examination with the beefeaters of the vaults of the House of Commons in search of Guy Fawkes, which he thought pretty childish. His duties reached overseas. Among them were the installation of electric light in the Paris Embassy, where Lord Dufferin begged him to allow improvements to the staff quarters. In all these tasks Regy revelled. He was able to exercise his considerable ability for organization and getting his way.

Meanwhile, in the larger world, in December 1895 Dr Leander Starr Jameson carried out an ill-conceived raid from Cape Colony over the Transvaal border in the interests of the British-born 'Uitlanders' – the residents of the Transvaal and Orange Free State. Ever since the British government had recognized in 1852 the independence of the Boers living on the north side of the River Vaal, the Uitlanders had been bitterly complaining of their lack of citizens' rights in spite of the fact that they contributed nine-tenths of the Transvaal state revenue. Nevertheless the precipitate action of the truculent Jameson, who was agent and adviser to the Prime Minister of the Cape Colony, Cecil Rhodes, had not been authorized by the British Government. Jameson's raid was repulsed by the Boers at the beginning of 1896.

Because of his secret confederacy with Alfred Milner and Rhodes, Regy Brett felt very concerned and perturbed. Milner, then chairman of the Board of Inland Revenue, at once wrote to him that, severe as the disaster was, it might be considered better than what would have happened had Jameson been successful in defiance of the Government. Still, the position was critical. 'We may have to give up for years the hope of bringing the Transvaal effectively within the South African 'dominion'. What if the Boers were to place themselves under German protection?' he wrote.[26] Regy was not an admirer of Jameson's action. It was badly mismanaged and most unheroic. It had undoubtedly caused incalculable harm. It had divided the Dutch and the Imperialists in Cape Colony. It had united the Boers and opened the way for outside powers to intrude upon British preserves in Africa. The only good to have come out of it was the extraordinary 'oneness' of the English-speaking world when brought face to face with foreign hostility.[27]

Regy was furthermore embarrassed by Rhodes's public denial of implication in the actual raid. Stead called on Regy to inform him that Rhodes had in fact confessed to him his full complicity in the plot to bring about a rising of the Uitlanders in Johannesburg, and had begged Stead to enlist Regy as an intermediary between him and Joseph Chamberlain, now Dominions Secretary in Salisbury's Cabinet. Regy consented to become go-between, believing that in this way he might improve relations between the Uitlanders and the Government. But Chamberlain was not impressed by Rhodes's conduct; he thought it intolerable that a pro-consul should take it upon himself to make war. He interpreted Rhodes's fostering of a revolutionary movement as being in the financial interests of his Chartered

Company. Regy confessed what had transpired between him and Rhodes regarding the secret society, but Chamberlain was not particularly interested and even rebuked Regy for disclosing to him these confidences. He advised Regy that Rhodes should consult a legal adviser before appearing before him, so Regy took Rhodes to the eminent solicitor Sir George Lewis. Rhodes was impressed by Regy's point made at this meeting, that it was now clear it would take an army of at least 20,000 men to subdue the Boers. Rhodes maintained that it was nevertheless essential to subdue them. The Uitlanders must be convinced that the British Government meant to protect them. Lewis advised Rhodes to address no public meetings but to return to Cape Colony – from which he had resigned the premiership – to improve the fruit and wine industries and to develop the great tract of country called after him.

In the midst of this trouble Nellie's adored terrier, Griz, died in Regy's arms. Nellie was miserable and cried all night. Her husband understood her anguish. To Chat he wrote, 'It is parting with a faithful unquestioning friend and companion of thirteen years' standing. She was a really great factor in Nellie's life. I wish all friendships were as simple and as absolutely untarnished. . . .' His with Teddie was just about to wilt. Regy was beginning to see his beloved without his tinted spectacles. In November 1895, when the boy was still eighteen, Regy endeavoured to get him a job as honorary attaché at the Berlin Embassy, referring to his protégé a trifle rashly as his 'cousin'. But Teddie was considered to lack the aptitude. Through George Binning, Regy tried to get him elected a member of the Turf Club. George wrote that he did not recollect saying he would second him. The committee wanted to know all sorts of things about Teddie which he was unable to impart. He advised Regy to withdraw his name for the present.

Regy continued pulling strings in all directions to advance him. He tried for a clerkship in the War Office and was disturbed to hear from the boy's doctor that he had pronounced 'your nephew' unfit for the job. He enclosed his report, which indicated that Teddie had contracted syphilis. Regy, an extremely fastidious man, was shocked. Nevertheless he tried again. If successful in his examination, Teddie might go to India. But confirmation of his complaint by a second specialist deferred his departure. Finally, the impending trouble in South Africa offered a solution. In 1897 Teddie joined the First Battalion the Grenadier Guards, bound for Gibraltar before continuing to the Cape. 'He drifts out upon the waters,' Regy wrote.[28] These disappointments and the rise of another youth in Regy's affections brought about the end of the romance.

In December 1896 Regy published his second book, *The Yoke of*

Empire, sub-titled *Sketches of the Queen's Prime Ministers*, of which
several of the sketches had appeared previously in *The Nineteenth
Century*. Apart from occasional affectations of style it was a neatly
written book. By treading delicately the author managed to avoid
causing offence to the aged Queen Victoria, who was still very much
alert to presumption and impertinence. Yet he touched upon matters
about which she was unduly sensitive. He gave a résumé of the Prince
Consort's unpopularity, obliquely criticizing him for his assumption
of the role of 'Permanent Minister'. He referred to the Queen's
differences with Lord Palmerston, and her unfortunate relationship
with Gladstone. 'Certain it is that his relation to the Queen, although
it may have been that of a trusted Minister, was not that of a friend.'
By reversing the responsibility he managed to absolve Her Majesty
from all blame. He even dared to refer to Disraeli's hold over the
Queen by his deference to her sex and personal charm. But in all
respects Regy paid unstinted praise to Victoria's character and
greatness.

The last section, that dealing with Gladstone, was the least good,
perhaps because he was still alive, but evidently the old man did not
think so. He wrote to Regy congratulating him, saying that he had
done him too much credit. He particularly liked the way he dealt with
the relations of Queen Victoria with Lord Melbourne, who had long
been to him a figure of singular historical interest. Regy had shown
good taste. Gladstone's sole criticism was that he had 'reprinted the
now exploded error in declaring the Queen to be Head of the Church.
Queen Mary abolished the title which has never been revived.'[29]
Other friends, including Evelyn Ashley, once Palmerston's private
secretary, and the critic Edmund Gosse were loud in praise. Howdie
too did not let the occasion pass without a tongue-in-cheek remark:
'What pleases me most in the book is its high moral and religious tone.
"There is nothing I admire like a man of sentiment." '[30] *The Pall Mall
Gazette* called it a 'brilliant and thoughtful little volume'. Queen
Victoria approved the book, which suggests that – considering the
delicacy of the subjects – she gave not merely her consent but her
assistance in its composition. *The Yoke of Empire* sold out at once, the
author told Milly, admitting that Christmas had something to do with
it. He added, à propos of that festivity, 'I saw a most charming present
yesterday, which I would like to give you! 3 sets of stay laces in a silver
box, white, blue, pink, with gold tags inlaid with diamonds, tur-
quoises and pink pearls respectively. May I?'[31]

The Yoke of Empire certainly did nothing to lessen Regy's position at
court, unofficial though it was. The first weekend of January 1897 saw
Nellie and Regy staying at Sandringham with the Prince and Princess
of Wales. Regy was impressed by the Prince being at the front door on

their arrival. He was impressed by the bevy of servants in red coats and medals. He was impressed by the band playing throughout dinner. He did not so much care for the billiard-playing, which went on till two o'clock in the morning. The Prince inquired whether he would sit on a committee to organize the Queen's Diamond Jubilee celebrations that summer, and to help with arrangements for the service to be held outside St Paul's Cathedral. Other members were to include the Archbishop of Canterbury, the Bishop of London and the Dean of St Paul's, with the Duke of Portland as president. Regy accepted with alacrity.

When the celebrations drew near the Prince had to be consulted on the minutest particulars, such as the siting of the stands to be provided for thousands of children on Constitution Hill, provision of seats for members of the previous Government, and three special seats for the Queen's favourite Indian servant, the Munshi, and his friends. Not surprisingly, most of the work fell on the broad shoulders of the Secretary of the Office of Works. At the same time he was of course fully engaged with his normal tasks: completion of the Temperate House at Kew Gardens, the supply of electric light to the National Gallery and National Portrait Gallery – lack of which had hitherto prevented them from being open to the public on Saturday afternoons in winter – and finding a suitable site in Hyde Park for Watts's sculpture *Energy*.

In June the Office of Works put up a large marquee in the garden of Buckingham Palace for the reception of the suites attached to visiting heads of state. Nobody had considered the necessity of ventilation, and when the tent was full the heat became stifling. One by one people fainted. An urgent appeal was made to Regy to do something instantly. His court dress included a rapier; he drew it and deftly thrust the blade through the canvas flaps of the tent to make window openings. A piercing yell revealed that he had stabbed a housemaid on the far side. However, she was not seriously harmed, and the assembled company was saved from asphyxiation. At midnight Regy organized a huge torchlight military tattoo in front of the Palace; there were 40,000 soldiers in London for the day. On the Prince of Wales's behalf Francis Knollys, his secretary, congratulated Regy on the arrangements at St Paul's which passed without a hitch. For these pains he was made a Companion of the Order of the Bath, which many friends considered rather a meagre decoration for so much effort.

Among the festivities was the famous Devonshire House fancy-dress ball in July. Both Regy and Nellie, who hated that sort of entertainment, attended. Regy's costume was that of 'a gentleman of France of the year 1628 in which', he told Milly, 'I suppose I shall look as big a tom fool as everybody else'.[32] What he did look, with his bald head and drooping moustache, was not a gentleman of Louis XIII's reign, but one of Queen Victoria's. Nellie went as an ample Manon Lescaut. Rosebery, who went as an eighteenth-century gentleman, was much put out by the newspapers proclaiming that he was impersonating Horace Walpole, 'that effeminate gossip and poseur'.

The Diamond Jubilee summer was a riot of social entertainments. The Bretts had the Queen's daughter Princess Louise and her husband Lord Lorne to dinner at Orchard Lea. The occasion was a success in spite of one terrible gaffe – at dessert there were finger bowls, which were still taboo when members of the Hanoverian royal family were being entertained.[33] But the royal guests graciously overlooked them. At a great reception given by the Joseph Chamberlains for the colonial Premiers, the guests exceeded the accommodation and many were unable even to get inside the building. The Princess of Wales had to drive away without leaving her carriage and Princess Maud was almost torn in pieces. 'The footmen were the greatest offenders – ragging all the guests and using most filthy language – especially to respectable elderly ladies.'[34]

At the end of this season it was a relief to get away to Scotland. Regy and Nellie, with their younger son Maurice, slept for the first time at the Roman Camp, Callander, on 9 August. For several years now the Bretts had regularly gone to Callander in Perthshire, the little town known as the gateway to the Highlands. Regy had fallen for the place and managed to buy the old hunting lodge of the Dukes of Perth, which derived its name from the Roman earthen ramparts which enclosed a field bounded by the River Teith. The house, approached direct from the main street, lay between the town and the wide river which flowed in full spate within a few yards of it. When the Bretts acquired it the house was a simple farmstead, roughcast (or harled as it is called in Scotland) and washed pink – hence the family nickname for it, Pinkie. The central porch, bearing an inset plaque inscribed 'Gang warily' and the dàte 1625, was probably built of old materials before 1914, because during the seventeen years before the outbreak of the First World War Regy made several additions, improvements and alterations. These were carried out in stages, mostly by a young architect called Gerald Dunnage. All the changes evinced remarkably conservative taste, with careful regard for the unpretentious style of the original block. The downstairs rooms of the house were low and mostly wainscoted, with the exception of the drawing room facing the Teith upstream, and the library,[35] both additions designed on a more generous scale.

Regy and Nellie together planned the sweeping green lawns and herbaceous borders. Facing the front door a seat on a mound of beech trees overlooked the river. At the rear, a small enclosed garden of yews had a sundial on a stone pillar in the centre. A large walled garden to the east still contains a noble Roman marble well-head acquired by Regy. On a greenhouse a frieze, carved by Howard Sturgis's companion the Babe, bore the Horatian tag, 'Ille Terrarum mihi praeter Omnes Angulus ridet' – That corner of the world smiles for me more than anywhere else. Westwards, beyond the Teith, the solemn summit of Ben Ledi, where John Millais and Effie Ruskin fell in love, broods over the scene. In 1903 Regy bought the adjoining Ben Ledi estate because Maurice wanted it. Regy grew to love the Roman Camp as he had never loved Orchard Lea, and it eventually became his only home. By some happy chance Pinkie, fifty years after the family disposed of it, still preserves that air of love and care bestowed upon it by the Bretts.

Regy rented some 20,000 acres of contiguous forest from his neighbour Lord Moray. He built a little chapel in a ravine overlooking Loch Lubnaig where he intended his ashes to be buried, though as it happened they were deposited in 1940, to be joined by Nellie's and Maurice's, under the canopied Gothic monument to the 1st Viscount Esher outside the entrance to Esher parish church. Regy loved the house and garden, the river, the hills with the rough shooting they afforded, the tranquillity and the local people of this part of Scotland. 'The calmness of the north and its *justesse d'esprit* are so health-giving,' he told his younger son, adding characteristically, 'yet there is no lack of romantic passion in the hills, you know.'[36]

In this first September at Pinkie Chat, who was now living at Comrie near his old home, Lawers, on the far side of Glen Artney, was a frequent guest. He threw himself heart and soul into beautifying the place, drawing up plans and plotting garden beds which were usually altered in his absence by Dunnage and Nellie. Regy told Chat that if anything happened to him all his private papers and letters were to be examined by Chat before anyone else might see them. All 'rubbish, etc.' was to be destroyed and the rest sealed up and handed over to Nellie for Oliver, his elder son, to have afterwards. But events made him alter these instructions.

Not only in his own house but also in the royal residences Regy showed much practical ability and imagination in making improvements. He also drew up a scheme to be submitted to the Queen for opening some of the state rooms at Windsor Castle to the public. In preparing apartments in Kensington Palace for Princess Christian and Princess Beatrice, his patience and tact with these royal daughters endeared him to them. The Prince of Wales's confidence in Brett's good sense and taste moved him to persuade Regy to replant Constitution Hill under the wall of Buckingham Palace with 'lilacs, evergreens and suchlike plants'. The Queen appealed to him through her Secretary, Arthur Bigge, to find out who was to pay for the Jubilee medals to be awarded to those Park Keepers deemed worthy recipients.

Then the Duchess of Teck's death necessitated an inspection of the royal vaults at Windsor. Regy found the vault in which George III's descendants were reposing to be in a deplorable condition, and requested Her Majesty's permission to have it renovated. During his inspection he met an old man who had been present when George IV had the coffin of Charles I opened. The man said that when the lid was removed the King's head looked like that of a living person, absolutely intact, but within a minute it fell to dust. A piece of black ribbon had been tied at the neck to conceal the severance of head from body.

Regy was the following year to make a similar descent upon the vaults in Edinburgh. He found the remains of the Scottish kings lying in confused heaps since the desecration of their coffins by the mob on the expulsion of James II in 1688. When he informed the Queen she was deeply shocked and agreed that he should have them collected and placed together in a decent manner. Care of royal vaults had not entered the minds of previous officials of the Office of Works.

On 27 November the Bretts dined with the Queen at Windsor Castle. Regy's journal entry of this date gives the only detailed description of an occasion which was frequently to be repeated.

Arrived at 8.45. Drove to the entrance in the NE corner of the quadrangle. Shown into the Corridor, where we waited. A few chairs before the fire at the north end. Sir Fleetwood [Keeper of the Privy Purse] and Lady Edwards, Pelham Clinton, Lady Downe, Lord Denbigh, the latter a Lord in Waiting. Other members of the Household passed through the Corridor on their way to their separate dinner. After a while, at a sign from a page, we moved to the southern end of the Corridor, near the staircase across the top of which are the Queen's rooms. The Queen walked in, supported by her youngest Indian – a beautiful[37] youth. She bowed to the company and Nellie kissed her hand. We went straight to dinner. Previously we had been shown our places upon a card by the Master of the Household, which card was placed near the Queen for reference. (Princess Beatrice on her right, Lady Downe on her left).

Gold plate and beautiful Sèvres. Indian servants behind the Queen. A Highlander to pour out the wine. The Queen ate of everything, even cheese and a pear after dinner. No 'courses'.[38] Dinner is served straight on, and when you finish one dish you get the next, without a pause for breath. Everyone talked, as at any other dinner, only in subdued tones. The Queen was in excellent humour. After dinner the Queen rose, and we stood back against the wall. She went out, and we followed. Immediately to the left of the doorway in the Corridor was placed a chair, and in front of it a little table. There the Queen seated herself.

We stood in a circle at a considerable distance away from her. Coffee was brought and liqueurs. The Queen sipped her coffee while the page held the saucer on a small waiter. Then the Princess spoke to the Queen for a few moments and afterwards moved to Nellie. The Queen talked awhile to Lady Downe, who was then sent to fetch Nellie. Meanwhile the circle discreetly whispered. Then the Queen sent for me, and she talked to me for half an hour about her affairs and her family. Finally, she bowed and I retired. By that time it was nearly eleven. In a few moments she rose. Nellie kissed her hand, and she went away. We remained a few moments, had some lemonade and departed.[39]

In a separate paper Regy added that when Nellie rose from her curtsey her dress gave a loud crack like a pistol shot, much to the sovereign's amusement.

He was fascinated by the old Queen – her dignity, absolute faithfulness to tradition and ceremonial, her interest in the past and pleasure in talking, if stimulated by a little audacity and tact; and by her fundamental kindliness and power and empathy. He enjoyed too the almost medieval atmosphere of the court.[40] In *Today and Tomorrow* he described the

> hushed reverence surrounding the Queen, hard to describe and difficult to suggest. It is no exaggeration to say that eminent statesmen and humbler folk alike moved through the corridors of Windsor as through a shrine. It was not the atmosphere of sycophancy or adulation. It was the atmosphere of deep memories. . . . It was an atmosphere of queenly piety, of intrepid courage, of personal sorrows, and of duties simply performed through long years. . . . In spite of its grandeur, there was a solitude, an aloofness, about the life of the Queen which made men half afraid to speak above a whisper.

Regy had learnt instinctively where to draw the line at audacity and how to lay on tact with a trowel. The Queen liked him and responded to his cautious advances. Had he come into her circle when she was a middle-aged woman he might well have assumed a position of authority in her counsels, as he was to do with her son and heir. As it was, during the Boer War there was no recognized liaison between the War Office and the monarch, and the old Queen was being constantly appealed to by soldiers and their relations, so Regy stepped into the vacuum. In this way he gained access to all the secret telegrams received at the War Office. He saw that, because of the Queen's age, her ministers were inclined to take decisions over her head. For example, she was not even told about the appointment of Lord Roberts to the command of the troops in South Africa, much less consulted. With his jealous concern for the monarch's position Regy remonstrated with the Queen's secretariat and those ministers whom he knew. In the next reign he saw to it that such oversights did not recur by informing King Edward, who did not hesitate to rap offending ministers over the knuckles.

Old Lord Esher's life was now reaching its close. In July Regy took his two sons to see their grandfather at the Law Courts for the last time. In November the retiring Master of the Rolls was made a viscount and said goodbye to the Bar. Regy estimated that the only immediate difference made by his father's elevation in the peerage was that he would go into dinner in front of the barons. But the new viscount was not satisfied. He felt that his career had been a failure because he had not reached the highest ambition of a lawyer, to be created an Earl like Lords Mansfield and Ellenborough; he disregarded the fact that they had both been Lord Chancellor.

Regy's two sons, sixteen-year-old Oliver and fifteen-year-old Maurice, were now at Eton; the two daughters, Dorothy or Doll, and Sylvia or Syv, were still in the schoolroom. Until the girls came out they were treated by Regy with mild indifference, but the boys were another matter. From the first his father never cared for Oliver, who was clever, sharp, unmanageable and unsusceptible to Regy's famous charm. But he could not disregard him. Maurice, on the other hand, was not clever, looked upon his father as a person of singular authority and power, was affectionate, weak and easily malleable. In later years Oliver recalled Maurice at the age of fifteen as 'an unattractive & ugly boy with a surly temper & of only average intelligence'. His sister Sylvia remembered him in a less unfavourable light as 'just a plump little boy with rosy cheeks, lamentably spoilt by my father who worshipped him. . . . My brother Maurice could bring out the best and worst in him, and how much suffering and sweetness between these two no-one will ever know.'[41] Certainly from his photographs as boy and man Maurice was singularly plain: dark, with a pug-like countenance, broad cleft chin, and, when he was grown up, a bushy, black moustache. By 1894 he began to be recognized by his father as the most responsive of his children, and by 1896 he had become the main object of his attention. Regy was by nature a monogamous man. He always had to have one person – and that a youth – on whom he could lavish his exclusive fund of affection. Teddie's days were virtually over. When he was about to leave for Gibraltar Regy wrote to the schoolboy Maurice, 'This will make a change in my life – and I shall have to turn more than ever to you, Maurice, will you go on filling up chinks?'[42]

Regy had bound and secreted in the library at Pinkie – to which no members of the family were ever admitted – every single letter that passed between him and Maurice. They amount to thirty-five volumes. The earliest, addressed by the father to 'Dearest Maurice' and 'Dearest Fatty', who was then only thirteen, contain curiously premature interrogations. 'Anybody captured your heart, my Fatty? George [Vesey] perhaps?'[43] And again, 'Have you fallen in love with anybody?'[44] He seemed surprised to learn that the boy had not. As it happened, Maurice, or Molly as he came to be called, was congenitally normal, although to please or keep in with his father he feigned to be interested in boys of his own age. In fact he was already mad about actresses and induced his father to take him to *The Belle of New York* and a new play by Anthony Hope, *The Adventures of Lady Ursula*. He nourished a calf love for Regy's friend and Lord Durham's mistress, the actress Letty Lind, and for Edna May. Oddly enough, Regy encouraged Letty to pay Maurice visits at Eton; he did not take the crush very seriously.

More interesting to him were his son's boy loves. These included the sixteen-year-old Caryl Annesley,[45] 'with eyes like those of a young stag. No photograph could ever quite do him justice,' Regy told Maurice. 'Altogether I don't know when it is that I last saw any human being of either sex, so better worth while loving, and your attachment is a feather in your cap.'[46] The father did everything to encourage this Eton romance by giving Caryl presents of cufflinks, a gold pencil, cheques and cigarettes galore. In fact Regy was in danger of losing his heart to this feather-brained lad, admitting that he too was under his spell. 'If I were not so hopelessly absorbed elsewhere I might be yet more completely subjugated' by his singular charm that was 'not feminine and yet not wholly male.' And he admitted that Caryl might be a good successor to Molly when Molly was tired of his father. The romance between Caryl and Maurice, if it ever properly started, did not prosper. Caryl felt obliged to beg Regy to stop Maurice sending him any more poems, for he really had no time to read them. This is hardly surprising, for Maurice had no talent for writing poetry. Nor was his taste for other people's poetry fully developed: he even dared to announce that he did not care for his father's *Foam*.

Nevertheless Regy was as ambitious for his son in the cultural sphere as the famous Lord Chesterfield had been for his. The ultimate result was about the same. He wanted him to become a man of the world. He must not be bored by grave talk. He must learn the art of conversation while eschewing tittle-tattle. Above all he must improve his mind. Yet his father was anxious that Molly should win his rowing colours and excel at football.

By 1897 Regy was frequenting Eton just as often as he had during Teddie's reign. It was not always possible to have intimate chats on full working days. 'However we did get a walk up High Street with your dear arm in mine,' he wrote in May.[47] Nothing was to be withheld from each other; every trivial circumstance must be disclosed and shared. Moreover, Maurice was enjoined to abstract confidences from his friends such as Neil Primrose, and pass them on to Regy. Maurice was made to record in his diary incidents which schoolboys usually keep to themselves. A prying curiosity, an unnatural sort of voyeurism, overtook the father. He imagined that the disclosure of his son's intimacies with his friends would somehow help protect their own peculiar relationship. He kept asking Maurice when he would tire of him, and complained that he was being 'snubby'. It is amazing that the boy remained so indulgent of the parental prurience. When he was being positively stand-offish Regy, aggrieved, rebuked him. 'I am conscious that I have taught you something in the *"ars amantis"* for which you ought to be grateful to me hereafter! I suppose others will benefit by the lessons.'

By 1898 Regy Brett's passion for Maurice was at its height. He was furious with his friends Loulou Harcourt and the effeminate Gogo (George) Maquay, whom he had asked to visit his son at Eton, for having made a pass at him. As though to console him, he wrote to Maurice on 10 February, 'I would give something to find your hand in mine, or your dear cheek close to my lips.' On the other hand, when Maurice wrote that his tutor, Ainger, 'came into my room on Sunday night and began cuddling, laying his head on mine and putting his arms round me,'[48] his father's reply was, 'What fun his making love to you in his elephantine way.'[49] The danger of his son's affections being stolen from him by the stuffy house-master was presumably less likely than by those sophisticated and worldly harpies, Loulou and Gogo. Regy came to the conclusion that it would be easier and more convenient to have a place where they could meet during the Eton halves. Orchard Lea was too far for Maurice to walk, so Regy managed to acquire a room in Windsor Castle in which to write letters and transact business concerned with his royal duties. When Maurice was a little older, but still a schoolboy, his father gave him a key to the room, which they termed 'The Nest', so that he could take his special friends there on half-holidays and weekends, for Windsor Castle was not out of school bounds. He even left cigarettes for the boys. He told Maurice to keep the blinds of the room down on a Sunday if he did not wish to be disturbed; if he was alone, the blinds were to be left up. Regy got vicarious satisfaction out of imagining the love-making that went on during his absence. Yet he was always a trifle nervous in case tell-tale evidence should be detected by members of the Royal Household or servants.

Although Regy never deliberately concealed his infatuations from the world in general – he was far too proud, and professed himself indifferent to its opinion – he actually confided in few. Chat was the exceptional confidant, and to him he disclosed his feelings for Molly. As though failing to grasp the exact nature of his friend's feelings for his younger son, Chat ventured to put in a good word for Oliver, to which he received the immediate rejoinder:

> I know Oliver much better than you think. He is not reserved with me. The feeling for the other one is altogether different. How can one explain? Who knows better than you how impossible explanations are. Why do you prefer 'M' to some cultivated and mysterious personality? That is the summary of the whole philosophy of love. There is the question – and the reply.

The 'M' referred to was the successor to Salvatore, another gondolier, Marco, on whose account Chat had taken a floor of a palazzo near the station in Venice.

'I am infatuated, and I know it,' Regy wrote to Maurice. 'If you could quite realise how horribly I suffer.' There were times when he found the boy hopelessly indifferent, even positively cold. Trying to reason with him was like pumping a dry well. Only monosyllables were extracted. In any event, Maurice had little of interest to impart. From the pleading Regy moved to the piteous and back again. One dark March evening, after a tiff, in spite of a sore throat and his promise not to be a hanger-on, he bicycled to Eton. He stood under Ainger's house, concealed by the shadows of the elms, softly calling Maurice by the old whistle which was their signal.

> I saw your dear figure pass down the passage after a long wait. You were not in your room before supper, when I first got there. Then I got a good glimpse of your face. When you opened the window I thought I would show myself for a moment, but decided I wouldn't. My tutor had been dining out, and brushed past me, an inch off without finding me out. Then when you went to prayers I went gloomily home. Still I have seen you, Molly. Will you remember years hence how passionately you were beloved?[50]

He was constantly, and in the most grovelling terms, expressing regret for writing too often and hoping he didn't bore Maurice. 'I rely upon you not to make fun of me. . . . I am very unhappy. . . .' It was as well he had not chosen Oliver before whom to throw his pearls – Oliver with his acute sense of the absurd and his mocking laugh. And Regy ended with a cry of almost desperate alarm. 'I am only trying to see how I can save the situation in the eyes of the world.' This was the first time he had ever admitted that the world's eyes might count against him.

Whatever society might be thinking and even saying – Edwardian society's ability to retain scandal within its own perimeter was very pronounced – there are no signs that people held back from him. Regy's advice was no less sought and his company no less requested than before the unorthodox relationship with his son had developed. Princess Louise invited him and Nellie to luncheon at Kensington Palace, and the Duchess of Devonshire to dinner at Devonshire House. No hostesses' doors were closed upon him. John Morley, the historian-statesman, called at Tilney Street on behalf of Macmillan, the publishers, to ask if he would write Disraeli's biography.[51] 'Very flattering,' he recorded. 'But I pointed out that my whole time was absorbed.' It would have involved him in three or four years' work, and his friend Natty Rothschild,[52] one of Disraeli's executors, told him there were fifteen boxes of papers in wild confusion. Also he was not sure whether Natty, or Monty Corry,[53] Disraeli's private secretary, really wished the book to be written at all. Having consulted Joe Chamberlain, who advised that in no event must he leave the Civil Service, Regy refused.[54]

Regy's plans for opening Kensington Palace were going ahead. He asked the Queen's Secretary, Arthur Bigge, if she would allow him to destroy a lot of broken rubbish in the Palace, except some old toys of hers which he hoped she would allow him to put in a glass case for the enjoyment of the public. Bigge subsequently told Regy that she wanted to see her old rooms in the Palace before they were restored. She would be carried upstairs and wheeled in her chair; she hoped the floorboards would be safe, since she did not wish to fall through a ceiling.[55] A week later, on going to the Castle to attend to some jobs for the Queen, Regy wrote: 'I did not see her, but I saw her tea – such a queer little meal – being carried in. Just one cup and a plate of sandwiches. An old "personal attendant" like Lord Palmerston in a white tie, and three gorgeous scarlet footmen, to carry in this Belshazzar's Feast.'[56]

When Gladstone died, all the onus of his funeral fell on the Office of Works and on Regy in particular. One vexed question was the request of the Prince of Wales to be a pall-bearer, for which there was no precedent. The scene at Westminster Hall on 28 May was impressive as the Liberal delegates marched past the coffin in solemn file.

> Men and women really felt the parting; not sight-seers. A last farewell to their old chief. Then the midnight watching. The silence of the great Hall. The kneeling figures. The simple dais and coffin. I fetched Rosebery down at 12 o'clock, knowing he would appreciate. He said, 'May I kneel for a minute?' He is such an enigma.[57]

Regy received fulsome thanks from the Prince of Wales for the success of the arrangements; also from the Gladstone family, grateful for his personal attentions. The Queen, however, would not be dictated to by the press and refused to issue a public appreciation of Gladstone – in which she was supported by Lord Salisbury – although she wrote a message to the widow in her own hand. 'I am sorry for Mrs Gladstone,' she said; 'as for him, I never liked him, and I will say nothing about him.'[58] She was displeased by the Prince of Wales being a pall-bearer and kissing Mrs Gladstone's hand. When Regy next dined with the Queen he was gently rebuked for misdirected enthusiasm over the ceremonial.

He was already recognized as an expert on parliamentary history as well as constitutional precedent, and his advice was sought by statesmen as well as princes. Just as his political sympathies now veered between the right and Liberalism, and the left and Conservatism, so his friendships transcended party boundaries. At Cambridge he had been intimate with Gerald and Frank Balfour. Now he was the friend and rapidly becoming the confidant of their elder brother Arthur, Conservative leader in the House of Commons and First Lord of the Treasury. Regy had long observed from a discreet distance his progress through the Commons. On Balfour's publication in 1895 of *The Foundations of Belief* he was deeply impressed by the author's philosophical justification of his abiding Christian faith. He found the book interesting and powerful, although difficult; it proved its author to be a rationalist of profound intellect. In 1898 he was writing to Balfour to remind him that all the disasters of the Liberal administration of 1880–5 derived from the Government of the day allowing themselves to be swayed by the newspapers. Never once did they hold faith with the policy which (right or wrong in its conception) they had adopted. And he advised Balfour that the British public had absolutely no notions about the Far East; they never looked at maps. 'You can do exactly what you believe to be right with impunity.'[59]

The Prince of Wales's opinion of the Secretary to the Office of Works had been strengthened by Regy's handling of the Diamond Jubilee celebrations and Gladstone's funeral. He was favourably impressed, too, by the confidence he had inspired in the old Queen, his mother. The Prince was constantly sending for him on matters outside the scope of his official position. On the morning of 16 May the Prince commanded his presence at Marlborough House. 'We discussed family business as usual,' Regy noted as a matter of course. 'The Duke of York[60] was there for a while, frank and charming. Finally two messages came from the Princess to say she was waiting, the second so peremptory that the Prince left hastily.'

On 28 October Regy attended a very enjoyable Eton dinner given by George Curzon to celebrate his appointment as Viceroy of India. After dinner Rosebery walked Regy up and down the streets till 1.30 a.m., talking politics, in particular the consequences of the French Major Marchand's occupation of Fashoda in the Sudan with its threat to Britain's control of the upper Nile. The incident was the cause of much concern to the Government. Rosebery was inclined to think that a war with France would simplify difficulties with that country in the future; fortunately this irresponsible opinion by a member of the Opposition was of no account. Owing to Lord Salisbury's firmness the French Government directed Marchand to withdraw on 4 November, and the danger of war between the two powers was averted.

On 25 November Regy was present at a party given by the Queen in the Waterloo Chamber. There was a huge orchestra and a very tiny audience, which had been given instructions to applaud loudly. The Queen wore an unusually low-cut gown, and looked very well. Mulled port, which she liked exceedingly, was handed round. Regy found it curious to watch the old Queen of England giving preference to her daughter, Victoria, the Dowager Empress of Germany. He had a high opinion of the Empress's intelligence and sharpness and saw a good deal of her during her visit to Windsor. She always abounded in pertinent criticism and advice: in scanning plans of the new South Kensington museum she at once spotted faults and made alternative suggestions. The Dowager Empress was far and away the cleverest of Queen Victoria's children.

On 26 January 1899 Regy and Nellie went to stay at Osborne on the Isle of Wight. They were met at Cowes by one of the Queen's carriages, drawn by grey ponies. On arrival they were shown straight to their suite – a sitting room, bedroom and dining room, but no bathroom. They found it pleasant although ordinary – the walls were hung with a rather common paper and dull engravings. At nine they descended to dinner. Prince Henry of Battenberg[61] sat on the Queen's right, and the Duchess of Roxburghe, Lady of the Bedchamber and Mistress of the Robes, on her left. Regy sat next to Princess Henry. When dinner was over they all went straight to the drawing room, where Her Majesty sat down but the men stood. Regy was detained for a long time by the Queen, who talked about her family, as she generally did with him. There was not the stiffness of Windsor, yet Osborne was royal enough. Next morning there was hockey in the garden, the Prince and the Battenberg children 'and the elderly people in-waiting rushing about like boys at football'. In the afternoon Nellie and Regy drove to Carisbrooke Castle, of which Princess Henry was Governor and which came under the guardianship of the Office of Works; there was much to discuss. When they got back to Osborne the Queen sent for Regy. She was sitting, wearing spectacles, very upright at a round table in a queer little room of nondescript character. Once more they entered into minute family affairs, amongst others the improvement to the vaults of St George's Chapel at Windsor. Regy wanted gates to be erected across the coffin niches, through which the coffins would be plainly visible. This was the sort of subject which interested her. Regy informed his son Oliver that the Queen had read to her, or read herself, every dispatch in draft before it was approved and sent abroad. She signed endless warrants and commissions every day, requiring first of all to know what they were about. He wondered who else of eighty worked so hard.[62] She also had a perfect understanding of what was fitting on public occasions. She had some months previously been to Netley to award the VC to two wounded soldiers, both sitting in chairs. 'They were ordered to rise, but the Queen said, "Most certainly not," and raised herself without help (a very unusual thing) and stood over them while she decorated them with the cross.'[63]

Regy experienced at this time a taste of Joseph Chamberlain's irritability which may have influenced his refusal at the end of the year to work under him. The Secretary of State for the Colonies demanded to have the ceiling panels of the great hall in the Colonial Office picked out in gold leaf. Regy was obliged to veto the request because the Treasury could afford gilding only in the Foreign Office and the Speaker's House, which were used for entertainment. Chamberlain worked himself into a tantrum and threatened to have the gilding done at his own expense while putting up a tablet to record the Treasury's illiberality. Regy decided that he was not an attractive personality and called him hairy-heeled. Gilding was then all the rage, and Curzon wrote from India begging to be allowed, at his expense, to have similarly treated the name and dates on Lord Randolph Churchill's bust in the passage leading from the Members' staircase to the Lobby of the House of Commons. At the same time Alice Balfour asked if she could spend £150 on buying a few more chairs to be covered like those in her uncle Lord Salisbury's drawing room at No. 10 Downing Street. She preferred good cretonnes to poor, pretentious stuffs. These were the kind of irksome requests with which Regy was perpetually dealing. No wonder that by May he thought of resigning. He was prevented from doing so by Rosebery, who told him the Queen could not spare him and that he would be doing her a great disservice by deserting the ship. 'You have made the Office what it has never been before & in the midst of all our schemes your absence from the help would be a public calamity.'[64]

In the sphere of personal relationships, Regy's platonic affair with Milly Sutherland was this year at its height. His letters to her now began, 'My sweet friend,' and ended, 'Ever yours, dear', 'Always yours', and even 'Yours devotedly.' For the first time she addressed him by one of his diminutives, Reggie. He told her he always had known their friendship would last. 'No one has ever come between me and you; and to no one has my allegiance been more true.'[65] No one ever had a greater gift than her for bringing out in a few sentences all that was best in a man. Her miniature was always beside him on his writing table. 'How odd that so many sage people have denied the possibility of friendship between man and woman.' He assured her that he never spoke about her to a soul. This was true with the single exception of Maurice, to whom he mentioned her constantly under the unflattering term, the Ninny. He allowed her to suppose that Maurice was in love with her. 'There is no higher education for a boy than to fall in love with you.'[66] Milly replied that the idea frightened her, as well it might; at her age she could not undertake the responsibility. She liked the boy, and would mother him instead if that would be any help. Regy's almost incestuous proposition was a reflection of his insensitivity where women were concerned and an indication that his love for Milly, in spite of his protestations, had never been exactly physical.

On 3 March she gave a ball at Stafford House, standing at the top of the famous staircase all in black, wearing the dazzling diamond necklace that had belonged to Marie Antoinette, a sight which Regy never forgot. In October she had a novel published. He did not find it interesting, but full of acute observation and deep reflection. Then she had a play, *The Conqueror*, performed at the Scala Theatre in which Forbes-Robertson and Henry Ainley had parts. Regy, usually so critical, wrote her a gushing letter of congratulation. After fewer than a dozen performances the play was withdrawn.

In May Queen Victoria made her promised visit to Kensington Palace, giving strict orders that no one but Regy was to receive her. Her escort were not admitted into the quadrangle because she objected to being seen getting laboriously out of her carriage.[67] From what she described as 'my old entrance' she was carried upstairs in her chair, where Regy received her at the door of the state rooms. They passed through a number of narrow rooms which she said she had not seen before, and wrote in her journal:

> Pictures of my life and reign have been hung. . . . The rooms are to be open to the public. . . . I also went down to the lower floor, into the two large rooms, in the first of which I held my First Council, and then also into the one in which I was born. This used to be used as Mama's writing-room and then as a visitor's room. . . . Mr Brett explained everything. He has the merit of the whole arrangement.[68]

She spoke to Regy of her early days and confided that she had no happy recollections of her youth except her dogs. She showed him where her bed had stood when her mother woke her from sleep to announce that King William IV was dead. They looked at some old dolls' houses of hers which were still in the nursery. As a child, she said, she was never allowed to walk downstairs unless someone held her hand.[69]

The same afternoon Regy was obliged to take the Duke and Duchess of York round the palace. He was regaled with more reminiscences from the Duchess,[70] who as Princess May of Teck had likewise spent her childhood in the Palace; but she took a more lively interest than the Queen in the history of the building and its contents. 'She is educating herself carefully and with her exceptional memory and intelligence will be a woman of much importance one of these days. The Prince is just a jolly sailor.'[71] In later years she was to become Regy's most intimate friend in the royal family.

On the 22nd the Bretts dined again at Windsor Castle, where the Grand Duke and Duchess of Hesse were present.[72] Regy sat between the Duchess of Connaught and the young Duchess of Hesse, who was called 'Duckie' and answered to the name. Regy was entranced by her. She was a daughter of the Duke of Coburg (born Duke of Edinburgh) and so a grand-daughter of the Queen. Her husband, a grandson of the Queen through his mother, Princess Alice, was very good-looking, 'but of the Loulou, Gogo type', Regy added in a letter to Maurice,[73] 'and without the skill or good taste to conceal it from Duckie, so that there have been endless troubles. If you saw Duckie you would have no sympathy for him.' Indeed the troubles were to end in divorce two and a half years later. However, Regy had never seen a royal dinner party go with such a swing as on this occasion. The Queen's vivacity aroused Regy's sense of pathos, for it showed how much fun she had missed and still was missing from life.[74] He recalled how the Queen had told him that the fifteen-year-old Queen of Holland, while staying at Windsor four years previously, had asked her. 'Did you ever go in a hansom?' To which her hostess was obliged 'regretfully' to admit that she had not. The child Queen replied, 'I have been in lots, and they are awfully jolly.' The poignancy was in the word 'regretfully'.[75]

On 23 May Lord Esher died of congestion of the lungs at the ripe age of eighty-three. His life had been a progressive triumph of perseverance and hard work over all obstacles. He was buried in the graveyard of Esher parish church, under an altar tomb with an elaborately carved canopy of marble. Beneath the canopy lay the recumbent effigies of himself and Eugénie, who was to follow him in 1904, aged nearly ninety, put there during their lifetimes. Regy lamented his father's death and professed that it was a bore bearing a new name. The Queen sent him a long telegram of sympathy. Henceforth he was the 2nd Viscount Esher, by which title he is best remembered.

With this new dignity came anxieties and worry about the situation in South Africa. The aggrieved and discontented Uitlanders, who had long been pressing for reforms in the Transvaal which would bring them the same rights as the Afrikaaners, were now clamouring to retain the autonomy of their republic. Chamberlain was eager for President Kruger to come to terms with the Uitlanders and bring about a settlement. But the Governor of the Cape of Good Hope, Alfred Milner, adopted a wholly uncompromising attitude. He positively wanted war in order once and for all to subdue the Boers and annex the Transvaal. The jingoistic press and the powerful diamond capitalists Wernher and Beit, whose vested interests in South Africa were immense, were all behind Milner, who was appalled when in July Chamberlain and Kruger seemed on the point of coming to terms. But by August Chamberlain was finally beaten down. The British Cabinet and the Prime Minister, Salisbury, surmised that if British troops were sent out Kruger would surrender. He did nothing of the sort. On the contrary, the Boers declared war on Great Britain on 11 October.

While events were still brewing in the summer Kitchener came to see Regy Esher.[76] He wanted to build and furnish a 'Gordon Palace' for himself, as Governor-General of the Sudan, on the very site where Gordon had fallen. He spoke of his reverence for Gordon and his love of the art of building. Kitchener was at the zenith of his popularity; when Regy had taken him to the Gaiety Theatre the previous year the whole house had risen and cheered him. But Regy did not find him attractive. 'None of the men who served with him were attached to him. I should doubt anyone loving him,' he wrote.[77] Regy had the perspicacity to add that, although Kitchener did not ask to be loved, none the less he may have wanted to be loved; and his severity with the Sudanese troops certainly made him feared and hated by them. Regy wrote to Maurice that he had a hard and rather common face. It showed power, and in the coarseness of his fibre there was strength. His eyes were good; but the mouth and jaw and skin were those of a rough and coarse private soldier.[78] Milner, who knew him well, told Regy in the train to Windsor that Kitchener was a man who summed you up to see what use you might be to him in the order of things, and discarded you if he decided you could do nothing for him. He was always looking to the next move, ignoring everything he had already accomplished. Like Rhodes he was artful.[79] This ruthless man was, however, abounding in ambition and a great organizer.

In November 1899 Regy came for the first time in contact with Kaiser William II of Germany. The strange, ambivalent monarch at once attracted and repelled him. Regy was commanded by the Prince of Wales to meet the Kaiser in the Memorial Chapel of St George's Chapel in order to discuss the Duchess of Teck's tomb. The second meeting was at dinner in the Castle on the 23rd, when the Kaiser was in high spirits. Regy was struck by his lack of hidebound convention and his clever conversation, 'so unlike other royalties . . . with their green parrot talk'. Indeed he saw much talent in him. He was an odd mixture of elements – autocratic, vulgar, half genius, half *gamin*. His Empress was dignified, jolly and plain. She was tall and moved well, but being stout she was dieting and the process was turning her hair grey. Across the table the Emperor was abusing fat women, which seemed tactless, to say the least, and not uncharacteristic. It was strange to see him ragging the Princess of Wales in a rather common way, pirouetting and dancing before her backwards, in order to make her laugh. He had chosen the wrong person, because the Princess of Wales, like all Danes, loathed the Germans. Otherwise the Kaiser, while being extremely cocky, was behaving himself fairly well at this delicate stage of the war. He merely irritated his grandmother by criticizing British operations in South Africa and telling her that the War Office had miscalculated the number of British troops engaged by counting the men twice over. During a luncheon at Brooks's Club, the Kaiser confided in Lord Wolseley that the Germans had worked out a plan of campaign which they would have carried out had they been in our shoes. The Kaiser graciously offered to pass their plan on if it would be any help, adding that his Government knew all the British plans, which it thought indifferent and full of mistakes.[80]

That month Sir Francis Mowatt, Permanent Secretary to the Treasury, sent for Regy and asked him to go to the Colonial Office as Permanent Under-Secretary of State in place of Edward Wingfield.[81] Regy took twenty-four hours to consider the offer before giving an unequivocal refusal. To his friends he made it quite clear that he would have no influence over Chamberlain and would merely be his devil.[82] Sir William Harcourt wrote, 'It shows the high estimate which has been formed of your capacity and sense, that you should have placed at your disposal what may be regarded at the moment as the first place in the profession.'[83] However, both he and Rosebery approved of Regy's rejection of the post when the reasons were revealed.

By the end of the year the news from South Africa was very disquieting. December was a month of disasters: the British were defeated at Stormberg and Magersfontein, and General Sir George White, chosen to command in Natal by Sir Redvers Buller against the advice of Lord Wolseley, was obliged to retreat from Glencoe, where the Guards were decimated. Sir Redvers Buller suffered a reverse at Colenso. Regy had a poor opinion of this general, who was much given to bombast and over-indulgence in whisky and the pleasures of the table. The War Office was furious with White and Buller for not doing what they were ordered. Buller was superseded as Commander-in-Chief by Lord Roberts, and Kitchener made Chief of Staff. In January 1900 the two new appointees reached the Cape. Kitchener immediately ordered the British Army to clear the veldt of pockets of resistance. Buller was deeply affronted by the fact that Kitchener, whom he hated, was now over him; they were not even on speaking terms. Matters were made more ominous for Great Britain by the European powers ganging up against her. The French actually moved a big fleet into the Mediterranean, and the Spaniards seized on the occasion to talk about that recurrent vexation, Gibraltar.

On 28 February Buller somewhat redeemed his defeat by relieving the siege of Ladysmith. In England Regy's younger friends were enlisting fast. George Binning was appointed Colonel of the Blues. Teddie Seymour – whose 'secretive moods' used to make Regy miserable, and now left him 'as cold as ice' – set sail for the second time to South Africa. On the eve of his departure, after a prolonged dinner and conversation, they had a final farewell in Teddie's rooms. Regy felt a temporary renewal of his anguished affection. 'He showed me all his kit with great pride, and the pleasure of displaying was a prelude to the poor darling's tears which followed. I think perhaps I am more to him than anyone in the world,' he wrote to Maurice.[84] Yet their intimacy was never again to be on the same footing.

Henceforth Regy was to pour out in daily letters to his son everything he did, saw and heard. As the years went by, his correspondence with Maurice was largely to take the place of his hitherto jealously guarded and locked journals. The boy of eighteen became the repository of every problem and anxiety, personal or political, that came his father's way. Many snippets of information were highly confidential, and had Maurice not been trustworthy some damaging disclosures might have come to light and got Regy into serious trouble.

No one in England could think of anything but the war. Regy was extremely agitated by its conduct. There was little he could do actively since he held no political post and, because of his Civil Service job, had given an undertaking to Lord Salisbury not to participate in House of Lords debates. So at first his help was ostensibly limited: he merely assisted the old Queen in the choice and dispatch of gifts to her Tommies, a job which could have been fulfilled by any lady-in-waiting. Then he persuaded her to offer Bushy House, adjacent to

Hampton Court, for the temporary care of the sick and wounded, and to allow public access to the property once a week; this was something, even if not much. In addition he was obliged to deal with such futile matters as Princess Louise's repeated protests against tents for bazaars being erected in view of her apartments at Kensington Palace, and the water rising under her floorboards; or providing a bolt for the Prime Minister's door which he might fasten when he wanted to keep out his colleagues – ordinary keys being no use because he lost them.

Being the busybody he was, Regy took up minor causes which the position he had established for himself at court, rather than his post as Secretary of the Office of Works, enabled him to pursue with success. He asked Lord Knollys to suggest to the Prince of Wales that civilians who had given long, faithful service to the Crown, and at present enjoyed no awards, should be granted orders just as were soldiers and sailors who could receive the Distinguished Service Order. As a result the Imperial Service Order was instituted and, in the next reign, the Order of Merit. Furthermore Regy was eager to eliminate the expenses incurred by recipients of the Order of the Garter: the list of institutions and dignitaries who had to be given gratuities was prodigious, and a new knight could be ruined if he were not a rich man. 'If a man has earned an "honour",' Regy wrote to Knollys, 'he should not be called upon to pay for it. If he has not earned it, he should not receive it.'[85] It was as simple as that.

In this second year of the war there was much discussion over some desirable Cabinet changes, and the retirement of older men to allow for new blood. Among the changes effected was St John Brodrick[86] in place of Lord Lansdowne as Secretary of State for War. Four years younger than Regy and a fellow Etonian, Brodrick never won his esteem; he himself came to regard Regy with suspicion and dislike. Balfour asked Sir Francis Mowatt to ask Regy whether he would go to the War Office as Permanent Under-Secretary. On 19 October Regy wrote to Oliver, who was in Germany learning the language, that the offer had not yet been made; it was all very private. He was flattered to be asked to help in the great work of reorganization of the War Office with Roberts and Kitchener. 'What shall I say? I don't see how I can refuse. It is not on a par with the Colonial Office at all. Perhaps the Queen will object. I am sure she will personally be a loser!'[87] The last sentence was not meant to be a boast, it was a heavy little joke. But did he ever really contemplate accepting? St John Brodrick not only thought he did but at the end of his life claimed that immediately after his appointment as Secretary for War was announced Lord Esher had written him a most pressing letter offering himself as Permanent Under-Secretary, while 'assuring me of his best support in inaugurating a new system'.[88] Brodrick professed to be amazed ('I was staggered at the proposal') that to a man of Esher's powers and ambitions the post should have attractions. Here was his senior in age, experience and rank, a man having the run of Buckingham Palace and Downing Street, 'who would not relish having to answer my bell 3 or 4 times a day, while not being admitted to secret conclaves with the military chiefs'. On receiving an urgent protest from the Adjutant-General in the name of the military chiefs, Brodrick turned down the offer. He told Regy that the War Office had decided to appoint a soldier as Permanent Under-Secretary. He recorded that he knew Regy would never forgive him and one day would have his revenge in getting rid of him through his Palace contacts. This, he maintained, is what happened in August 1903.

Brodrick's memory was playing him tricks. Regy did not have the run of Buckingham Palace and Downing Street while Queen Victoria was still on the throne; and although he hesitated before rejecting the post there are no indications among his voluminous papers that he ever solicited Brodrick for it. As it turned out, Regy was spared having to make his usual excuses because the Queen objected strongly to the idea of his ceasing to be Secretary to the Office of Works. However, Balfour renewed the invitation, and Regy wrote to Oliver again:

> I saw Arthur Bigge this week about the WO. I told him that there were two conditions on which I would go there: 1. that the Queen approves; 2. that I got an assurance (a) that I might have a free hand in reforming the administration of the Office, (b) that the Government meant a large reform. If they mean to patch, I had rather stay where I am. . . . I daresay they will think it rather cool, but after all I *don't want* the place. If they wish me to go there I can make terms.[89]

He knew now that he never would have it. A fortnight before, during a long talk with Rosebery about Government changes, his friend had strongly disapproved of his accepting, telling him that he 'should make no sacrifices for "these people", meaning the Government. That point of view never occurred to me. I never thought of ministers. My reasons for refusing these offers are quite personal and private, and I never give them. Never, never will I harness myself to a "political" office.'[90] Certainly he never did. It is difficult to tell which of the two, Rosebery or Esher, was the more recalcitrant. Arthur Bigge had earnestly pleaded with Regy to persuade Rosebery to come out of his shell and assume the leadership of the Liberal party again, for if Campbell-Bannerman continued to lead it there would be small future for it. But Regy had failed.

Before the year was out Mowatt sounded him about yet another appointment. He told him that Chamberlain was anxious for him to go to the Cape as Governor on Milner's retirement. A categorical refusal at once quashed this proposal, which was not pursued further. But Regy confided in his journal: 'Were it not for Maurice I would go at once. As it is, I cannot.'[91] In other words, the private reasons for refusal which he so often kept to himself were a reluctance to be separated from the person with whom he was at the time infatuated.

Maurice had left Eton at the end of the summer half, and his father had decided that the boy should go into the Army. Through Lord Wolseley and other influential contacts he made every endeavour to get him a commission in the Grenadiers or the Household Cavalry, but to no avail; Maurice was turned down for having no qualifications.[92] Plaintively Regy pointed out to Lord Wolseley that Lord Warwick's son Brooke had, at the age of nineteen, been recommended for one of these crack regiments. Wolseley retorted that Lord Brooke had served in South Africa as ADC to Lord Roberts, which afforded him a recommendation.

At the beginning of the year Regy noticed sadly that the Queen was looking depressed.[93] Whenever handed a telegram she went pale. She confessed to him that she dreaded the receipt of those buff envelopes She had lost confidence in her Tory ministers and relied upon Rosebery which, strictly speaking, was unconstitutional. Regy was not surprised that she should be disillusioned with Lord Salisbury's capacity to carry on with the war as both Prime Minister and Foreign Secretary, for he was showing weariness and a misunderstanding of the temper of the public. She was anxious that he should give up being Foreign Secretary, for she disapproved of cumulative offices. She was also hurt that Lord Salisbury, of whom she was fond, did not consult her. He had appointed Lord Roberts Commander-in-Chief in South Africa, whereas she wanted that position for the Duke of Connaught. Lord Salisbury had demurred, and then sent Roberts without even informing her. She could not bring herself to tell the Duke and made Arthur Bigge do it. The Duke, to his credit, did not mind in the least.

On 28 November Regy noted that, although the Queen appeared well, she ate less than formerly: 'Not a good sign.'[94] She was also easily agitated. When Lord Roberts last had an audience at Windsor he sat down in talking to her; and actually fidgeted with her fan, pulling out the ostrich feathers one by one. 'It is the sort of thing that always upsets her, more from fear of a "scene" than any other reason.'[95] On 1 December Professor Osler,[96] who had been sent to the Cape by the Queen to investigate the medical arrangements, came to talk to her. His account of conditions was very unfavourable – antiquated equipment, too few doctors and too much red tape. The whole organization was thirty years out of date, and the Queen was extremely upset that her wounded soldiers had to endure such conditions. She was unwell, and felt deeply the death of her grandson, the son of Prince and Princess Christian, on active service at Pretoria. Nevertheless she had Canadian officers to dine with her that evening. She talked to them all, and on leaving, the adjutant remarked with emotion, 'I could die for her.'[97]

This month the Queen appointed Regy a Knight Commander of the Victorian Order, the last honour she was to bestow on any subject. He immediately wrote her the following letter:

> Lord Esher presents his humble duty to your Majesty and hardly knows how adequately to convey his deep sense of gratitude for the high honour which your Majesty has been graciously pleased to confer on him.
>
> He can only say that as his prayers have always been for the long continuance and happiness of your Majesty's reign, and for the support of Almighty God in your Majesty's many cares and troubles, so his own humble efforts will always be directed loyally to ensure, so far as in him lies, your Majesty's comfort and ease as well as those of the royal family. . . .

He received a charming reply from the Duke of Connaught, telling him that the Queen was ill and tired or she would have written herself, and sending him the insignia of a KCVO, with her appreciation of the manner in which he had at all times striven to meet her wishes and comfort, and those of other members of the royal family.[98] So touched was she that she twice made Princess Christian read Regy's letter to her, saying that no one had ever been more kind to her and attended more thoroughly to her wishes. Quite clearly Regy had made a mark on the affections of his old sovereign. In her will she left him 'rather a quaint ring', of twisted serpents and coloured stones.

There is no doubt that towards the very end of her life the Queen was harassed and made unhappy by the Boers' successful resistance. She was inclined to attribute British reverses to interference by her ministers and requested Regy to express his views (which were hers) on the maintenance of the Commander-in-Chief's authority, which ministers were calling in question. Regy submitted a memorandum in which he cautiously reaffirmed the Commander-in-Chief's personal responsibility to the Secretary of State and the Queen for the efficiency of the Army; and advocated the creation under him of a general staff which should become the authority in matters of army organization and reform.[99] This view conflicted not only with that of the Hartington Commission of 1890 but also with the recommendations of his own committee of 1903–4, which were to do away with the office of Commander-in-Chief. There is every reason to presume that the task imposed on him at this stage by his venerated sovereign was an embarrassment. He was certainly worried that the Opposition might press for the appointment of a committee to inquire into the conduct of the war. It would lead to endless recriminations among the generals, and would upset the Queen still further. He confided his fears to Arthur Bigge, a soldier through and through. The two friends agreed that conscription, which Lord Roberts urged, would never be acceptable to the British people, who were too full of religious scruples and traditionally distrustful of a standing army. A well-paid, small army enlisted for foreign service was what was wanted when peace returned. Great economies could be made in the colonies by the reduction of unnecessary garrisons. And in any case there were too many young men and officers standing about idly.

On 19 January 1901 Regy went to Kensington Palace and saw Princess Louise, who had been summoned to Osborne with the Prince of Wales. 'It is, I fear, the end. What a change!'[100] On the 20th he was at Windsor 'and ordered everything to be got ready for the end and the beginning!'[101] The Royal Household was at sixes and sevens, and Regy was amazed that no one had bothered to consult the Annual Register to see what had happened on the death of King William IV. 'You would think that the English monarchy had been buried since the time of Alfred.'[102]

At half past six on the evening of 22 January the Queen died at Osborne. Princess Louise told Regy that the scene was stately and dramatic. Her mother recognized those around her and spoke their names. She had difficulty in breathing. Dr Reid supported her in his arms. For five hours Princess Louise held her hand. The Prince of Wales knelt at her bedside. The Kaiser stood at the bedhead. When the Prince was obliged to leave for London the Kaiser took charge of everything. 'His tenderness and firmness were extraordinary, so unlike what was expected of him.'[103] He refused to allow the doctors or nurses to take measurements, and took them himself. It was he, the Prince on his return, and the Duke of Connaught who lifted the Queen into her coffin. The new King Edward VII did not attend the Proclamation, because the Queen had left orders that her successor was to be spared this painful ordeal. With about 150 other people Regy was asked to be present at the Council, held in the banqueting room of St James's Palace. The King behaved with great dignity. At first he spoke in a broken voice, but then gathered strength. All the royal dukes kissed his hand. So did the Duke of Devonshire and Lord Salisbury, whom the King raised very tenderly and respectfully. At 10 p.m. the King summoned Regy and Lord Clarendon to discuss the funeral arrangements. The royal dukes attended, talking together and smoking, which they would never have done in the old Queen's presence.

Regy's proposal to bring Queen Victoria's body to London all the way by sea was not adopted. She had given certain instructions which were carried out: there were to be no black trappings, and no hearse, only a gun carriage because – her heart being with her soldiers to the end – she wanted a military funeral. Regy suggested that she should not be buried, but merely placed temporarily near the Prince Consort; King Edward agreed. On 4 February the final obsequies took place. At the Frogmore Mausoleum in Windsor Great Park all the arrangements and the rehearsal were organized by Regy. Teddie Seymour and his guardsmen carried in the coffin. When the royal family and the mourners retired, Regy alone remained behind to watch the stone placed over the coffin. Thus he was the last of her servants to take leave of her. He brought away with him the wreath of bay leaves which had hung over the grave.[104]

A year before she died, Queen Victoria happened to mention to Regy that a recumbent effigy of herself had been sculpted in white marble by Baron Marochetti at the same time as the Prince Consort's. In February Regy asked the Clerk of the Works at the Castle where it was kept. No one had heard of it, and there was much scepticism as to its existence. After detailed inquiries an old workman remembered that in about 1865 the figure had been walled up in the stores at Windsor. When the brickwork was taken out, it was discovered by pure chance – or rather Regy's insistence.[105] On 9 February it was hoisted into place next to that of her husband.

7

EDWARDIAN APOGEE
1901–1907

On the accession of Edward VII Regy Esher was in his forty-ninth year; the new monarch, on the other hand, was in his sixtieth. At last, after being kept strictly in the background he had come into the limelight of majesty. He was his own master, and throughout his remaining years was to prove his worth, despite a deficient education.

Regy was in the full vigour of middle age. His health was sound, only temporarily impaired by occasional manifestations of gout and recurrent colds and influenza. Yet he was the most abstemious of men, a teetotaller to all intents and purposes. He rarely drank even a glass of wine when in company, and when alone contented himself with barley water. He never took a glass of sherry or a cocktail before a meal. It was his abstinence that was probably responsible for his wonderful complexion, which was pink and white and without a blemish. His eyes were grey-blue – not steely – and twinkling, with creases at the corners from smiling. His long nose over a fair moustache hid a full and somewhat sensual mouth. Were it not for his almost total baldness, he would have been accounted extremely handsome. His figure was superb. He moved with an easy grace, never having been seen to run in his life; his walk was not unlike that of Arthur Balfour, unhurried and magisterial. He never lost his temper and his manner was the same towards both the great and the humble, with a gift of drawing people out that made them suppose they were more intelligent than he knew them to be. Although to strangers he might appear arrogant, he was no snob; if anything he preferred the company of his intellectual inferiors. He exhorted his sons to follow his example in being polite to subordinates and friends alike; and even wrote to Oliver when in Rome to be sure on leaving his hotel to shake hands with the manager.[1] In admiring these qualities and his boyish charm the man of letters Arthur Benson wondered 'why people don't like him or trust him more. I suppose he is unscrupulous.'[2] Others who were not beholden to him for favours thought the same, being suspicious of his outstanding affability. Those whose cause he took great pains to advance were amazed by his trustworthiness, diligence and intense loyalty. The truth is that Lord Esher, being half French, had the polished Gallic manners of his mother's compatriots which many English upper-class persons of the Edwardian age considered artificial, disingenuous and sometimes sinister.

Until Queen Victoria's extreme old age Regy had not been particularly intimate with the Prince of Wales. But the latter, having witnessed Regy's attachment to his mother in her decline, had the acuteness to see that in Regy Esher he had an ex officio servant and confidential adviser who was utterly dependable, sympathetic and companionable. As King Edward's reign progressed, their friendship increased. Yet strictly speaking Regy never belonged to the so-called Marlborough House set. He was not raffish enough, and he was too intellectual.

The circumstance of Regy's position as Secretary of the Office of Works threw him into the new King's orbit from the start of his reign. The royal geniality, combined with dignity, impressed Regy. His Majesty would ask him to sit, and even smoke. Regy would sit but he would not smoke in the presence of his sovereign, not even his rose-tinted cigarettes with their aromatic scent. Carefully the King went through every detail of the forthcoming Opening of Parliament, scribbling notes which he then handed to Regy. It was the sort of ceremonial in which both men delighted. At the Opening, on 16 February, Queen Alexandra looked stunningly beautiful in black, wearing a galaxy of jewels and the Koh-i-noor diamond.

Regy wrote to Chat Williamson at the beginning of March that the King and Queen were charming to him. He saw them nearly every day, 'most intimately, fussing about their private affairs'.[3] It was amusing, and not uninteresting, but very different when compared to the great 'silence' that formerly hung about the corridors of Windsor. 'You will understand this. It is a rent veil. Now the Indian servants, in whom Queen Victoria delighted, wander around like uneasy spirits,' he told Maurice, 'no longer immobile and statuesque as of yore. It may be my imagination, but the sanctity of the throne has disappeared.'[4] It took time for Regy to get used to the comparative lack of stiffness in the new court. With his love of formality and reverence for the Crown, he regretted the change. At audiences the King would stand with his back to the fireplace. A person summoned was told to enter the room unannounced, and if he wished to leave the room he might do so, with a bow to the King, and return when he wished. If anything, the King was too kind and debonair, too human.

King Edward loathed the gloom of both Windsor Castle and Buckingham Palace, referring to them as 'Scottish funeral parlours'.[5] One day he made Regy walk with him, the Queen and the Duchess of York through the state rooms and all the private rooms at Windsor. The Queen said she wished to live in the state rooms. The King insisted on occupying Queen Victoria's old suite and using his father's room. 'There was quite a smart difference of opinion. He was very firm and rather cross – to *her*, I mean.'[6] Nothing was left undiscussed. The Queen showed excellent taste, while the Duchess remained very gentle and appreciative. Then Regy lunched with the three of them. After luncheon he drove with the King to the Memorial Chapel at Frogmore. On parting, the King said to him, 'For God's sake, don't give up your appointment. You must never leave my service.' 'He talked over some very private affairs with me, and I shall not venture to write down the conversation. He is certainly a great-hearted King, and when he stood by his Mother's grave, I could see that he inherits her romantic spirit – without display!'[7] The romance showed itself in his sentiment. He also decided to use his father's old rooms in Buckingham Palace – rooms closed since 1861. This could not happen until he was able to get rid of his brothers and sisters, who had been camping in the great barrack which Queen Victoria had disliked and seldom occupied in her widowhood. He told Regy he would compensate each of his royal siblings with a carriage and pair which, by saving perpetual calls on the Buckingham Palace stables, would be cheap at the price. To Regy's astonishment, Queen Alexandra said she had never been into Queen Victoria's rooms at the Palace. She examined everything they contained.And the King admitted that he had never seen Hampton Court properly. The old Queen had been extremely jealous of her possessions as well as her rights. Now her eldest son and his wife were behaving like children, playing with their new inheritance and thrilled by the treasures revealed to them at every corner.

Though he liked the new royal couple, Regy was soon aware of their failings. The Queen could often be tiresome – for instance she refused to meet the King's wishes to move immediately from Marlborough House to Buckingham Palace, and kept putting off the days appointed. Her obstinacy was so great that neither cajolery nor threats would move her.[8] The King, for his part, would give way to repeated demonstrations of schoolboy irritation when in the least thwarted. He was of course irredeemably spoilt, and in this and other respects he reminded Regy very forcibly of the mother. He had the same way of emphasizing his speech, when moved to irritation, by lowering his head. But he spluttered and swore in a way wholly unlike Queen Victoria. Having categorically rejected a suggestion, he could usually be brought round by a compromise. His fundamentally genial nature would do anything to avert a major row. He had a bad memory and was changeable. He could not recollect what he had said a week before, which created difficulties for his ministers; he would agree to something and then deny that he had done so. Consequently Regy feared that his reign would not be nearly so comfortable for his ministers and servants as that of his predecessor. 'There is no doubt,' Regy wrote, 'that kingship is an art or a profession (like any other) which requires years of training. There should be a law that no one is to succeed to the throne after 30! Even that is late!'[9]

Queen Victoria had not been dead for a month when Arthur Bigge discussed with Regy the propriety of having an official life written, as though he had Regy in mind for the author; but Regy persuaded him that it was too soon. He suggested, however, that her papers should now be collected and arranged, and that a selection of her unpublished journals and letters up to a certain date might be printed. So remarkable a personality should be allowed to speak for herself. Already a proposal for a memorial to her was in motion. By 22 February Regy had been appointed to serve on the Committee for the Queen's Memorial and act as honorary secretary. The scheme suggested was to remove the row of trees in the centre of the Mall and transfer the carriageway beneath Carlton House Terrace to a line centralized on Buckingham Palace; to place a statue of Her Majesty seated under a canopy in front of the Palace and to erect an arch at the eastern end of the avenue. Letters were sent to a number of architects inviting them to submit schemes. Aston Webb's architectural layout and Thomas Brock's design for the statue and groups of statuary were approved by the King, and a model of the scheme was erected in St James's Palace, to which the public were admitted. Every member of the royal family, including the Kaiser and the dying Empress Frederick, was consulted. But in spite of Princess Louise's objections to the site – which would, she affirmed, create a meeting place for mobs – and her suggestion of an alternative site in Green Park because of her mother's love of being surrounded by flowers and trees, as well as her hatred of asphalt, the scheme was adopted. The colossal white monument was not to be unveiled until 1911, by King George V.

The King also took the liveliest interest in preparations for his Coronation, which were entrusted to Regy. Whereas His Majesty concerned himself with the minutest details – the Queen's throne must be of the same design as his own, though smaller, and must stand within the canopy to the left of it, and the back of the Prince of Wales's chair must have no feathers and the Princess's must be three steps below her husband's – Regy meticulously studied the Coronation ceremonies of previous monarchs, seeking out printed service sheets from Charles II's time onwards. He vexed himself whether the procession from the Tower to Westminster Abbey should take place the day before the actual Coronation (as had been the case from Richard II's to Charles II's), or the day following. Should the King hold an investiture on the day previous to the procession? Should he hold a banquet at the end of the week in St George's Hall? Regy urged the King to retain all the old traditions that were not positively ridiculous.[10] In this he was supported by Bigge, who even wanted to revive the tradition of the Hereditary Champion riding into the Hall and throwing down his gauntlet. The King balked at this; he took a more prosaic view of archaic customs. At all costs Regy was determined to keep the Heralds away from the arrangements, for they had made unforgivable muddles over the Diamond Jubilee celebrations. They were ignorant of ceremonial, being, in the words of Sir Arthur Ellis, the Comptroller of the Lord Chamberlain's Department, 'ghastly cads, not a gent among them and Cath. hangers-on of the D. of Norfolk'.

During the summer of 1901 Regy actually complained about the number of summonses he received from the King to Windsor, Sandringham and Balmoral; they interfered with the immense amount of office work he had to get through. What he soon found particularly tedious were the everyday dinners he was obliged to endure after he and the King had had discussions. Dinner was at 8.30 sharp. Men and women left the dining room together at 9.30, and bridge ensued till after midnight. Regy seldom got home to Orchard Lea before two in the morning. He noted that the King behaved in a very proprietorial way about his boxes and letters. He opened all the former and did not always send them down to Knollys immediately. He tried opening all the letters, but soon found that four hundred a day were too much for him; so he would merely look over the envelopes himself and sort them unopened.

A dinner party at Windsor was a very different affair altogether. The first under the new regime took place on 8 April, and both Regy and Nellie were invited. The assembly was large because the whole Household in waiting dined with the King and Queen, and not in their private room. The Oak Dining Room being no longer used, the quiet, impressive entrance of Queen Victoria into the Corridor was as obsolete as Queen Elizabeth's might have been. The company assembled in the Green Drawing Room. The King entered unannounced with his daughters and sister, and they dined in the White Room which looked very well. The Indian servants were retained. The dinner was like an ordinary party, with none of the 'hush' of the old

Queen's dinners. Afterwards all left arm in arm, as they had entered, for the Green Drawing Room. The King took Regy into the White Drawing Room, where he talked about the Queen Victoria Memorial. After that interlude there was the inevitable bridge. The Queen would never play for money, pretending that she could not afford it. The Princesses slipped away, and Regy and Nellie were allowed to make their bow and curtsey.

Life at Sandringham was quite different from life at Windsor. The King regarded Sandringham as home, and even referred to it as such. There was no ceremonial at all: it was like staying in an ordinary country house. After dinner the Queen played patience with Gladys de Grey[11] and Nellie. The King sat on a sofa talking to Regy for an hour. Then the women went to bed, at which point the King led the way to the billiard room. While he sat down to bridge with three friends, the rest lounged about gossiping. All the clocks at Sandringham were kept half an hour fast. When Queen Victoria came to stay she had put them back; she called it a ridiculous habit and a 'lie', which was characteristic of her. During a second Sandringham visit the King took Regy alone in his brougham to look at Houghton, the Cholmondeleys' beautiful house, then 'steeped in slumberous neglect, grass-grown court and chilly rooms, even in June'.[12] They were not expected by the old caretaker, and Regy had to explain who they were. On leaving, the King had to borrow a sovereign from Regy with which to tip her. During the return journey he said rather pathetically, 'I was allowed no money as a boy, and got out of the habit of carrying any. But then I had no boyhood.'[13]

Regy, Arthur Ellis and Lionel Cust, Surveyor of the King's Pictures, were formed into a triumvirate to supervise improvements to all the royal palaces. Most of the actual work done was delegated to Joseph Joel and his son, Joseph Duveen, both of whom became friends of Regy's and on his behalf bought and sold paintings and works of art for the rest of his life. Ellis, who had been with the King since 1867, said, and sometimes wrote, amusing and risqué comments about court problems. Cust, Director of the National Portrait Gallery, owed his court job to Regy. They made a happy team, and were kept extremely busy. Regy was inundated with notes and commands about where electric bulbs and house telephones were to be installed in Buckingham Palace. Ellis wrote to him:

We must let these extremely tiresome Gentlemen at Arms have a *gite* with WC. They are all upon my back, clamouring on this subject, and being a decayed body of elderly men (full of bad piss) they insist on opportunity of getting rid of it as they live in the suburbs and arrive an hour before they are wanted, and all want the *retirardo* incessantly.[14]

The King would wander into the half-furnished rooms where Regy was engaged with the workmen. He would sit on a turned-up table in the middle of the ballroom surrounded by piles of bedroom furniture, smoking a cigarette. It was no use asking him to make suggestions, for he had little imagination. On the other hand he had a quick, trained eye and an instinct for what was right and what pleased him. 'I do not know much about Arrt,' he would say with his characteristic rolling of the 'r's, 'but I think I know something about Arr-r-angement.' He certainly did.[15] Often his good sense and taste prevailed over his advisers'. Lord Clarendon's proposal to alter the Buckingham Palace ballroom and redecorate it in the style of Fontainebleau, introducing a throne covered with Bs, was vetoed at once. The King said the proposal showed lack of historical perception and would make him an object of derision to foreigners.

Soon after the King's accession Regy received an honour which was intended to be an acknowledgement of his satisfactory guardianship of the structure of the royal palaces. He was made Deputy Constable and Lieutenant-Governor of Windsor Castle, a subsidiary office to that of Constable and Governor which was traditionally held by a member of the royal family – at this time by Princess Louise's husband, the 9th Duke of Argyll. With the Deputy's post went the offical use of a room in the Castle (which Regy already enjoyed unofficially) overlooking the Long Walk. To the rather empty honour was attached the medieval right of 'pit and gallows', which he felt tempted to exercise upon some of the Windsor and Eton worthies. One of the duties which devolved upon him was care of the military knights and their ever-recurrent problems. Another was the sorting and arrangement of Queen Victoria's papers. If the post brought Regy no extra remuneration at least it was accompanied by a special uniform, which consisted of a dark blue tunic with scarlet facings, a gold sash round the waist and a hat with a straight plume. With the uniform went the coveted privilege, likewise granted to Nellie, of formal entry into His Majesty's court.

A more substantial offer came Regy's way at the end of the year. Sir Ernest Cassel, one of the greatest financial magnates of the day and a close friend of the King, proposed to Regy that, in return for a large share of the business, he should leave the Office of Works and associate himself with the magnate's enterprises in Egypt and America. Regy told Maurice that he was considering the offer and, if he accepted, it would be solely for his sake. Sitting next to the King at dinner two days later Regy broke the news to him; the King strongly objected, but after pressure from Cassel he consented.[16] In June 1902 Regy found himself a partner in Cassel's financial house at a salary of £5000 a year, and 10 per cent of any profits. Although he always remained on friendly terms with Cassel, the association was not a success; Regy hated the City. In 1904 he retired from this, his only venture of the sort. The truth was that money-making did not interest him, a fact which nullified the insinuations of self-interest to be levelled against him by the press in 1907. More serious was his lack of financial sense; Regy was an inveterate spender, constantly overdrawn at the bank. He owed Jack Durham a large sum, for the return of which the Earl was obliged to press him.

The crescendo of Regy's career encompassed the reign of King Edward VII; it began auspiciously with the opening of the twentieth century and lasted for a decade. But coincidentally the tenor of his family life deteriorated, although his relations with his wife remained firm. He treated her with invariable respect and kindness, which she repaid with unremitting devotion. On the whole she accepted his male friends, and was in return accepted with genuine affection by most of them. She practically adopted Teddie Seymour as another son; she wrote friendly letters to Podge Somerset when he fled abroad, and even sent him a small present; she and Howard Sturgis were very close – Howdie frequently begged her to stay with him at Tan-yr-Allt at Tremadoc and bring her dog and maid. There were but rare occasions when she had a dig at one of those whom she considered unworthy favourites. Regy wrote to Maurice, disloyally, 'It was rather amusing last night to hear Nellie say rather spiteful things about R.A.E. Just as she does when she thinks *I* admire anyone. Such are the vagaries of the green-eyed monster. She has evidently seen that you have a fancy for him. It always amuses me these outbursts.'[17]

Whether his relations with Maurice were to the ultimate advantage of his son is open to question.They certainly led to resentment and suspicion on the part of Oliver, Dorothy and Sylvia, to whom Regy showed a corresponding lack of affection that was almost pathological. In January 1902 the King told Regy at dinner that he had just signed the gazette approving a commission for Maurice in the Coldstream Guards. That very morning Regy had to take the King to see the Nest. He looked at the photographs and asked to whom the blazers belonged. 'Fancy,' Regy wrote to Maurice, 'if you and the kids had been there. I should have conveniently lost the key.'[18] He was running risks. Regy's infatuation with his son had in no way decreased; he lived on a knife edge, ever on the watch for the slightest betrayal of coldness or indifference. He was at times afraid to speak in case he annoyed Maurice. His greatest happiness, yet pain, was to indulge in reminiscence. 'It is many days now – how many since you used to drive home with me sitting always by choice, on my knee – and ever since those days – now years ago – no unfaithful thought has ever crossed my mind.' And unwisely, 'I was almost certainly the first human being who kissed you at all, and quite certainly the first who kissed you passionately. I love to linger on these facts. . . .'[19] But how much did Maurice care to linger on them? And how did he respond? He assured his father that 'if you ever refused to help me in any way or to love me I should from that moment begin to hate life and should most probably kill myself.'[20] Yet he begged to be excused his congenital inability to tell those he loved what his feelings were. In return Regy showed his son some of Ernlé's affectionate letters to him, of which Maurice protested that he was jealous – it was of course his father's whole purpose. He also made Maurice read through his old Eton 'Trap' letters, to make the boy say how much he envied those romantic days, and suggest that Chat and Elliot were to Regy what Caryl and Reggie Herbert were to him. 'But both are little in comparison with what you are to me.' What would their relations have been had they been at Eton together? Then, Maurice's natural inclinations getting the better of him, he blurted out that he had had a romantic dream that the actress Ellaline Terriss had asked to sleep with him at Orchard Lea – 'the sweetest night I have ever known in dreams'.[21]

As he grew older so he treated his father peremptorily. During his last half he would summon him to Eton that very day, would order him to get theatre tickets and book tables in London restaurants. He reproved his father for casting sheep's eyes at Milly Sutherland at the Stafford House party. It must have been observed by others. Perhaps it was intended to be. Really it was not at all the thing.

As for Regy's elder son, he perplexed and frightened his father. Oliver's was a baffling character. Very clever, he was in youth sharp and inclined to be selfish. Always a tease, he was in middle and old age greatly beloved. He deeply and not unnaturally resented the knowledge that his father criticized him to his younger brother, whom Oliver knew to be far less intellectual and fascinating than himself. Even Nellie thought her husband was not quite fair to Oliver. Regy would write to Maurice while both boys were still at Eton, 'Oliver looking rather boiled and stuffy. He has taken no exercise lately.' In 1898 he discussed with Maurice Oliver's failings and whether he ought to take him away from Eton. 'I am so desperately afraid of a gradual sinking into disreputable company, and second-rate loafing habits.' Oliver might be indolent at the age of eighteen, but he never ran the risk of falling into bad company. And had he been aware of his father's complaints to his younger brother on this score he would, rightly, have been extremely indignant. 'I am trying to be really nice to Oliver,' Regy wrote patronizingly, and again, 'I often wonder why it is that your life and mine have hitherto run into closer grooves than his and mine.' Then he gave Maurice the answer to his own query. It was that Oliver scoffed. He ridiculed the real affection his father endeavoured to give him. In other words, Oliver was quick to sense that when his father addressed his rare short notes to him beginning 'Dear Nollikins' instead of 'Dear Oliver', the effort to be affectionate was forced. Moreover, he did not care to be asked if he had crushes on other Eton boys – which was not in his line – or to be sent copies of his father's old journals and schoolboy letters written when he was the same age. He found it distasteful to be the vicarious medium of his father's nostalgic desires, and declined to convey to him gossip of Eton boys' affairs, which did not interest him in the least. While Oliver was still at Eton, Regy wrote him a letter which seems incredibly unjust and unkind.

> You and I have drifted a good deal apart of late. You may think this my fault, but I have always told you that I recognize no duty towards you other than to supply your necessities until you are old enough to supply them yourself. Beyond that, it is a matter of attraction only, and I stand exactly in the same relation to you as the rest of the world. You cannot, as a rule, expect affection or devotion unless you take a great deal of trouble to inspire it.[22]

It was not as if Regy were an impoverished parent who had struggled to send his two sons to Eton; and Oliver knew perfectly well that Maurice by no means stood in the same relation to his father as the rest of the world. Evidently Oliver sent a submissive reply to this wounding epistle, for Regy wrote again the following day, graciously: 'You took my letter and some of my cruel remarks "standing up" like a gentleman. I cannot congratulate you sufficiently. It made me like you better than I have done for ages.'[23]

In October, having left Eton, Oliver went to France to learn French in a count's château on the Loire. It was not a success. The count made advances to Oliver, who vigorously repelled them. Oddly for him, Regy took his son's side without hesitation. He expressed himself definitely shocked by 'the little beast'. Yet he reproved Oliver for calling the Count 'Loulouesque', which he said was unfair – presumably to Loulou Harcourt. Henceforward Regy reluctantly accepted the fact that his elder son was perfectly normal, and even exhorted him to cultivate young women. 'It sounds banal, but on the whole, repays you better than longing after boyhood, and the past.'[24] Oliver never hankered after the past, and all his life looked eagerly ahead for the next excitement to which life invariably treated him. By the turn of the century, father and son had reached a temporary state of neutrality in which a certain mutual respect lay dormant. But Regy never understood Oliver, whom he wanted to see as a dreamer, a poet, a sentimentalist and everything that he had been. 'We have so much in common that it is quite terrifying.'[25] It is almost terrifying that a man so intelligent and wise in his dealings with kings and prime ministers could be so obtuse and wrong in his estimate of his elder son's character.

Regy's understanding of his two daughters was no better. Doll, the elder, was at the age of seventeen stage-struck and for a brief moment thought that she would like to become an actress. When Nellie warned her husband of the very real possibility of Doll running away from home in 1899, all he remarked was, 'Queer things are girls. You never know what they are driving at.' And to Maurice he complained, 'She is too conceited and wants snubbing. Girls are very tiresome things until they are grown up. I have always thought so.' Because he never made the slightest effort to win her confidence and affection he was to continue to find this exceedingly forceful and original girl tiresome long after she had grown up. Half Doll's trouble during her adolescence was rivalry with her physically more attractive younger sister, Sylvia; terrible rows ensued between them. Regy's method of dealing with them was to tell Doll that she was like a cook complaining of the housemaid. 'They are a couple of spit cats, and want a real good smacking. I wish you would administer it,' he told Maurice.[26] No wonder that Sylvia came to realize that as the youngest child she had never been wanted.

> My sister Dorothy, 'Doll', and I were aware at an early age that women were only brought into the world to become the slaves of men. Every morning it was our duty to lace up our brothers' boots . . . I felt that nobody loved me and that I was the cuckoo in this illustrious family nest. It even seemed to me that my father's voice altered when he spoke to me, as if he were forcing the words through cubes of ice.[27]

There were no such awkwardnesses between Regy and his sovereign. On the afternoon of 14 February 1902 Regy went to Marlborough House in order to accompany the King to Westminster Abbey. Somebody had proposed removing the screen between the nave and choir. The Prince of Wales, who was to have gone with them, was late and the King would not wait; he was always punctual to the minute. Regy drove with him in what was called the 'French brougham', an incognito carriage with no servant on the box. A service had just finished. The King looked carefully at everything. Within five minutes he pronounced without any hesitation that the screen was not to be removed. Having then examined St Edward's shrine and other features of the Abbey, he drove Regy to Buckingham Palace, dropped him there, and went on to tea with the reigning favourite of his mistresses, Mrs Keppel.

The King was more and more concerned about the Coronation

which was to take place on 26 June, speaking as though he had a premonition that it would be fraught with disaster. He talked to Regy for hours on end about his own robes, the form of service, the procession. Regy persuaded him to return from the Abbey to the Palace by the longer route, having gone by the shorter one – a reversal of the published order. He also had a helpful discussion with the Princess of Wales, who possessed force of character, tact and sound sense. On the 20th the King was taken ill. He had not been well before going to see the Tattoo at Aldershot, where the damp and chill of the Royal Pavilion had induced violent spasms. The Queen, with Princess Victoria and the Prince of Wales, sat up with him all that night. When Dr Laking reached him at four o'clock next morning he realized that something was seriously the matter. Nevertheless the King and Queen drove to Windsor in a travelling carriage with four horses. During the journey the patient was very weak but slept. Regy watched him arrive, looking feverish and feeble. Next day the Portuguese Minister, the Marquis de Soveral, sat with him while the others went to Ascot races. The day after that his temperature rose to 102; he sent for Regy, receiving him in bed overlooking the East Terrace. Although flushed, he was very bright and cheerful. Jack, his terrier, was lying on the bed and when Regy kissed hands growled at him, just as Teddie Seymour's dog used to do when he took a more intimate liberty with his young master. Having been warned by the doctors not to talk business, Regy gossiped. The King told him to make Milly Sutherland arrange her hair differently and criticized Lady Granby, a thing he was fond of doing. He said it was absurd of her in giving a ball to make her daughter Marjorie dance a *pas seul*. Also that she painted Marjorie's cheeks, which was sinful. After a quarter of an hour Regy rose, kissed hands again and left. When the suggestion was put to the King that the Coronation should be postponed, he said he would prefer to die in the Abbey. Regy discussed the situation with the Bishop of Winchester and they agreed that, unless the King rallied, the ceremony must be cancelled.[28] On the 24th the King was operated on for appendicitis.

Already flocks of crowned heads, royalties of all sorts, presidents and other important figureheads from Europe and beyond had assembled in London. The shock to them of the last-minute announcement of the King's illness and the cancellation of the Coronation was overwhelming. Thunderstruck, Prince Danilo of Montenegro went for a drive with Sir Lionel Cust in Hyde Park to recover his senses; halfway round he suddenly burst into tears, laid his head on Sir Lionel's shoulder and declared between sobs that he was '*fortement émotionné*'. The general public were stupefied.

By one of those inopportune freaks of fortune, in June Regy was gazetted a Knight Commander of the Order of the Bath for his work on preparations for the Coronation which had not taken place. The award was, however, fully deserved. At the end of June his secret-aryship of the Office of Works terminated, and on 7 July he was launched into Sir Ernest Cassel's office in the City. The first matters with which he was concerned were a shipping combine about which Cassel was to see Joe Chamberlain, and Curzon's proposal to open great steel works in India. The King nevertheless insisted, when he was better, that Regy should resume his Coronation work. Nor was Regy's City business allowed to interfere with his constant summonses by and attendances on the sovereign. He was obliged to join him on the royal yacht *Victoria and Albert*, where His Majesty recuperated, sitting on deck in a specially constructed chair. Since his operation he had lost two stone, and eight inches round the waist. While the Queen and the Marquis de Soveral, a favourite guest, went to Osborne, the King presented Regy with the insignia of the Bath on deck. Although a very difficult patient, who would barely allow his wound to be dressed, the King made a lightning recovery and the Coronation took place on 9 August. No sooner did he resume his normal life than he again began to eat and smoke too much, as Regy noticed while staying at Balmoral in September. He also never went to bed before 12.30 in the morning.

Before the South African War had ended, on 29 May, Regy was appointed chairman of a small committee of three to inquire into the construction of military barracks. The terms of reference were to consider the present system of construction and maintenance of barracks and to report whether, in view of the large and increasing scope of the duties devolving on the officers of the Royal Engineers, they should not be relieved of this work; and to suggest how the construction and maintenance of barracks could be carried out by alternative means. Many distinguished soldiers gave evidence, and Regy established for himself the reputation of an extremely competent committee man.

The following October the important South African War Commission was set up to investigate the causes of the muddles which had nearly brought about Britain's defeat by the Boers, and certainly a long drawn-out war by a great power against what amounted to a small army of Dutch settlers. Lord Elgin, ex-Viceroy of India, was appointed chairman and Regy a member. The instructions conveyed to the members, though comprehensive and far-reaching, were somewhat wanting in precision. So the Commission took the line that they must investigate the inefficiency and defects of army administration at home as well as on the field throughout the war, and suggest remedies to meet future contingencies. As Regy was to write to the King on the

12th of the month, 'The condition of the defences of Your Majesty's Empire (in December 1899) – fortresses, guns, ammunition, were in a state which made it almost a crime to embark on any course of policy which might have involved the nation in war.'[29]

The Commission sat for 55 days, heard 114 evidences and answered altogether 22,200 questions. It concluded its business in June 1903. The King took a profound interest in the progress of the sittings and, at his request, Regy wrote him a daily detailed account of the witnesses' evidence. He also passed on to the King the views of the leaders of both political parties, with whom he was in constant contact. Nor did he hesitate to give the King his own opinions, even when they conflicted with those of the other members of the Commission. The result was that his influence over the monarch became entrenched and very formidable. It is hardly surprising that St John Brodrick, the Minister of War, was extremely suspicious of this influence over the Crown, coming from a single individual with no post in the Government.[30] In his eyes – and he was by no means the sole critical minister or army general – the role which Regy had adopted for himself was more unconstitutional than that of the sovereign who acted on his advice. He deprecated the subterranean activities of this man, which were to affect vital questions of military policy and appointments throughout the remaining years of the King's reign.

Indeed, Regy did not merely confine his contacts with the King to correspondence. He was at the Palace or Windsor Castle at all hours. Knollys told Brodrick that he was often with him three or four times a day. He was also, in view of his past work at the War Office under Hartington, continually walking into that building and gleaning information from permanent officials who were old associates. Often before a decision had been reached by the Cabinet, Brodrick complained, 'the issue had been largely pre-judged on the incomplete premises of an observer who had no official status'.[31]

On the whole, the personal views and opinions that Regy imparted to the King were wholesome. They were in a nutshell that the War Office was inefficient, obfuscated and interfering; that the Army was never given its head; and that the situation of the Commander-in-Chief was nebulous and anachronistic. 'As Your Majesty can well imagine, it is difficult to thread the way through the mazes of the War Office system. At every turn the road appears blocked by some Board or Committee, designed apparently to conceal the place where such responsibility should lie.'[32] So runs the passage in one letter to the King. On the other hand, 'The tendency [of the War Office] is nevertheless to treat the generals in command as children still tied to the apron strings of the war departments.'[33] And finally Regy explained to the King that Lord Roberts, the present Commander-in-Chief, 'is morally weakened in dealing with service reforms by the conviction that his responsibility is unreal, and that he is absolved by another authority. This Lord Esher ventures humbly to suggest is the greatest question connected with the organization of Your Majesty's Army.'[34]

The findings of the Elgin Commission were a terrible indictment of the relations that existed between the Army in South Africa and the Government, particularly the War Office at home. A summary of these findings, as defined by Regy, could be reduced to three main points. These were (1) a reorganization of the War Office Council, and a clearer definition of its functions as an Advisory and Executive Board (as at the Admiralty), to be presided over by the Secretary of State, in whom final responsibility to Parliament must be reserved; (2) internal decentralization of the War Department, by a rearrangement of duties under the respective members of the Board, abolishing the existing cross-jurisdiction; and (3) the investment of the Commander-in-Chief's post in the sovereign, and the appointment of an Inspector-General of the Army responsible to the Secretary of State for the efficiency of the military forces of the Crown.[35]

The integration was purely a constitutional manoeuvre. The old Commander-in-Chief's power was in reality to be merged in the new Army Board. The idea was Regy's. When E.F. Benson wrote in *The Spectator* in 1934 that Lord Esher, in his posthumous *Journals and Letters*, was revealed to posterity as the controlling influence behind the South African War, he was anticipating events. It was in fact as a member of the Commission set up to inquire into its shortcomings after hostilities that he revealed himself as a power behind the throne.

Several members of the Commission, including Lord Elgin, disagreed with the proposal to make the sovereign the Commander-in-Chief. The King himself objected, at first rather strongly; he was extremely sensitive about this supreme post, and all Regy's tact and persuasiveness were required to explain how archaic the post was in a modern context. A letter he wrote to the King on 21 May reveals his remarkable historical knowledge.[36] He prefaced his argument by emphasis on the dual control within the War Office, with its accompanying jealousies and mismanagement, and told the monarch that the C-in-C's post was of comparatively recent creation. If George III had retained his reason, the Duke of York would not have been made C-in-C. As it was, on the Duke's death the Army was for years without one. The title was not borne by Lord Hill or Lord Amherst, and until the death of the Duke of Wellington it remained in abeyance. Then came the long rule of the 1st Duke of Cambridge, a man of extremely limited intellect behind his round, wrinkled pumpkin face. Although he was a member of the royal house, his views often clashed with Queen Victoria's. The danger to the monarchy in the office being held by a subject of headstrong temper, such as the Duke, who had the backing and loyalty of the Army behind him, was clear. Certain sections of the War Office, Regy went on, sought to augment the powers of the C-in-C, whereas the King was anyway head of the Army all over the world – a point often lost sight of. He reminded King Edward that the Hartington Commission of 1888 sought to abolish the title, but Queen Victoria towards the end of her reign was unable to face so momentous a change. The creation of an Army Board or Council, which he was advocating, must, he urged, involve the abolition of the Commander-in-Chief. In his view the authority of the monarch would thereby not be minimized, but enhanced. In a subsequent letter to King Edward Regy wrote that during the rule of Wolseley, and now of Roberts, there had been no complete loyalty to the C-in-C. All the more reason and urgency, therefore, to vest the office in the monarch, with the Secretary of State for War as his constitutional adviser.[37] Finally, Regy's advocacy of an Army Board to be appointed by His Majesty's order persuaded the King to accept his arguments.

Although the King could be won round by very careful, preconcerted pleading, he by no means invariably agreed with his mentor. There were occasions when he flatly contradicted him, and even snubbed him. For instance, he abruptly ordered Regy by telegram not to reply under his own name to a letter in *The Times* by a critical correspondent, signing himself 'Civilian';[38] it was unwise and unbecoming for a member of a royal commission to do so. To the disappointment of the editor of *The Times*, Regy replied anonymously. Again the King was to disagree emphatically with Regy that the new Secretary of State for War, Arnold-Forster, should be excluded from attendance at meetings of the War Office Reconstitution Committee about to be set up. Regy gave way like a shame-faced schoolboy. Sometimes the King's opposition to his adviser was prompted by his Secretary, Francis Knollys, or the Prince of Wales's Secretary, Arthur Bigge, himself an old soldier who was critical of the fact that the forthcoming Committee did not include an army representative.

The appointment to the War Office of Hugh Oakley Arnold-Forster, a grandson of Dr Arnold, formerly a publisher, an ardent supporter of tariff reform, fluent speaker and writer, and at the time Secretary of the Admiralty, was due in a negative sense to Regy. On arriving to stay at Balmoral in September Regy was immediately sent for by the King. He had no sooner kissed hands than the King told him he wanted him to become one of his ministers, and proposed the War Office. Regy was completely taken aback but had the presence of mind to say he must think about it. He had every intention of refusing, he wrote to his son Maurice.

It is not in my line to go back into politics. . . . I can do more good outside and, heavens, how much happier the life. Just imagine what the tie would be, night and day at the WO. I am purely selfish in the matter, and I really do not think that I can bring myself to sacrifice all independence, all liberty of action, all my *'intime'* life, for a position, which adds nothing to that which I now occupy.[39]

These were the same old reasons trotted out, not omitting the most cogent of all, reluctance to sacrifice his *'intime* life'. Another reason was more valid: he did not want to join a Tory Government. Regy found his opposition made more awkward by the fact that the Prime Minister, Arthur Balfour, who was also staying at Balmoral, strongly supported the King. Regy was being pressurized. Balfour pointed out that, by declining, Regy, as author of the proposals for army reform, was failing to take the very action which he had so ardently proclaimed necessary. Regy begged that Akers-Douglas should be made Minister and that he, with Admiral Fisher, might be left to reorganize the War Office from outside. Balfour pointed out that this would hardly be suitable. The Balmoral visit was spent in meetings with the Prime Minister and audiences with the King, while notes were dispatched to Balfour's room. Surely, the latter replied, his friend must understand that he would fail lamentably in the double capacity of servant to the King and colleague of the Prime Minister by saying no. Finally Regy summoned up his courage and categorically refused under any circumstances to become Secretary of State. 'Political office is abhorrent to me, and I have not the qualifications for it.'[40] Arthur Balfour soon relented, but at first the King was very angry. Regy felt humiliated and highly embarrassed to be disobliging his host, especially when the host happened to be his sovereign. Never, he told Maurice, did he remember having a nastier time. Finally the King's good nature reasserted itself and he was kind, even forgiving. Yet Regy learned later that he had made himself unpopular at Balmoral. The King's attitude was that Regy wished to take all the credit and none of the risk of reform.

The press got hold of the rumour that Regy was going to the War Office and Rosebery immediately wrote to him, hoping, without specifying reasons, that it was not true.[41] Howard Sturgis was more forthright: the thought of his old friend taking office in a Tory Government, and especially the present one, made him feel sick.[42]

Although Regy had been a close friend of Balfour's brothers Frank and Gerald at Cambridge, it was not until middle age that he became intimate with Arthur, who was four years older than himself. Their link was the subject of army reform, about which both men felt much the same despite their political differences. Regy's work to this end during King Edward's reign brought them in close sympathy. The younger man was mesmerized by the Prime Minister's extraordinary power of getting things done with the minimum apparent effort and maximum insouciance, and was greatly attracted by his affability, even during periods of crisis, which would have made another leader of his country abstracted and withdrawn. 'The Prime Minister was charming, so unpriggish, and outspoken. No silly mystery, such as I remember Rosebery to be guilty of when speaking to his friends,' he wrote.[43] A.J.B. for his part enjoyed Regy's company and conversation. When dining with Admiral Sir John Fisher he always asked to have Regy on his right 'as being the most to his taste'.

The findings of the South African War Commission received much publicity. The prominent part played in their definition by Regy earned him high praise from the press and the public. As a result Balfour, with the King's approval, appointed in November a committee of three to advise on the creation of an Army Board for the administration business of the War Office. It was called the War Office Reconstitution Committee, better known as the Esher Committee. Its members, dubbed 'the dauntless three', were Lord Esher, chairman, Admiral Fisher and Sir George Clarke, the Governor of Victoria, who was brought home for the purpose.

The Committee acted with great speed. By December, on Clarke's return from Australia, the report had virtually been formulated by Esher and Fisher, whom Sir Frederick Ponsonby saw as a devious, Machiavellian pair getting their way by backstairs intrigue. Clarke agreed with every detail, and became a sort of battering ram on Regy's behalf. He was an insensitive, clumsy, uncouth and infinitely boring man, but a staunch upholder of Regy's principles which he promulgated hammer and tongs. The report made three recommendations: the appointment of a general staff, which later became known as the Army Council, framed on the model of the Board of Admiralty; the separation of military from administrative duties, and the decentralization of the latter; and the abolition of the rank of Commander-in-Chief, with the appointment of a new post, that of Inspector-General, responsible to the Secretary of State for War. The report was published at the end of February 1904, and the Committee lingered on for several weeks, giving advice and generally dictating directions to the War Office. Regy had a struggle to get it adopted by the Cabinet, even with the Prime Minister on his side and the King approving.

'The dauntless three' had caused considerable upheaval and much resentment amongst the old guard. Officials, some distinguished, were dismissed. Go-ahead young officers such as Douglas Haig congratulated Esher on weeding out the superannuated fogies from the War Office. So too did Joe Chamberlain, who shook his hand and said that it seldom fell to the lot of any man to be able to do such great service to his country.[44] Arnold-Forster, who in default of Regy had succeeded Brodrick as Secretary of State, was more guarded in his praise. Fully aware of Lord Esher's treatment of his predecessor, he was at first querulous and on the defensive, particularly after being rebuked for disloyalty in criticizing in Parliament the report's second recommendation. Regy managed to pacify him with the emollient methods which he well knew how to administer. 'I find it difficult to reply, in adequate terms, to your letter, which has touched me deeply,' was Regy's method of deflecting the Minister's not unjustifiable resentment.[45] He went on.

> It is very rare (indeed I know of no instance) that a private citizen obtains from a Minister of the Crown so warm a recognition of efforts to assist in an act of government. We realize all the difficulties of the task before you, and the high merits of the schemes which you have fashioned to deal with the enormously difficult problems left unsolved by your predecessors.

The truth is that while the Esher Committee was at work the Minister for War was desperately trying to implement his own ideas of War Office reform. The two schemes were not basically incompatible, but differed in particulars. Regy had doubts about the practicability of some of Arnold-Forster's, and he had the ear of the court, who had a poor opinion of the Minister.[46] The King could not make him out and Knollys thought his evasiveness amounted to mendacity. Regy, on the other hand, genuinely liked him; he admired his knowledge, honesty and lack of self-seeking. But his liking was not untinged with patronage: in accepting the Minister's friendship he recorded that 'the poor little brute has some sense of gratitude'.[47] But then Knollys confided in Balfour that Arnold-Forster was not quite a gentleman. Arnold-Forster for his part believed Regy to be genuinely friendly towards him, 'though of course he very much likes to gossip and to know as much as he can of other people's business. I think he is to a large extent, "all things to all men".'[48]

Perhaps the most important consequence of the acceptance by Parliament of the Esher Committee's report was the rebirth of the Committee of Imperial Defence (CID). When the Esher Committee's findings were forwarded to the Prime Minister in March before they reached Parliament, Balfour immediately effected one of its most vital recommendations, the setting up of a permanent secretariat for defence purposes. Previous attempts to set up such a body had been made by Salisbury and Balfour in 1895, and again by Brodrick in December 1902; but all had been spasmodic and ineffectual. There were no regular meetings and no minutes were kept. To Balfour must be given the credit for establishing a permanent Committee of Imperial Defence on a new basis. It was to be consultative, not executive; it was to have no administrative functions; it could not prescribe a policy to the Cabinet, nor give directions to the Army and Navy; its sole duties were to collect and collate information, and advise. Balfour's original idea was that the committee should meet only when summoned by the Prime Minister, who was its permanent member, but further changes were to be made by Campbell-Bannerman and Asquith. The latter realized that in preparation for war every department of state was involved. He made the CID into a standing committee, which indeed it had virtually, although not constitutionally, been from the very beginning, at the instigation too of Lord Esher – who joined as a permanent member in 1905 – through his introduction of sub-committees whenever he found them needed for specific issues or crises. The chairman of the CID was the Prime Minister. Ex officio representatives were the Minister for War, the First Lord of the Admiralty, the First Sea Lord, the Director of Naval Intelligence, the Director-General of Military Intelligence, the Chief of General Staff and the Director of Military Operations at the War Office. The secretary was Sir George Clarke, Regy's faithful creature and ally. The question why the CID was formed in 1904 finds an answer in *Today and Tomorrow*[49] (1910):

> Every variation in the balance of World-power, every acre added to the Dominions of King Edward, and every change, either by Treaty or understanding with a Great Foreign Power, alters the conditions and purposes for which an Army is required. That these alterations should be constantly and scientifically stated, was one of the main objects for which the Imperial Defence Committee was constituted, and for which it is retained in its present shape.

Regy's activities in financial affairs were not progressing smoothly. By July he was writing to Maurice that he hated the City and did not think he could stand it much longer. He could not grasp the intricacies of high finance; his only reason for continuing was that Maurice should benefit from the money he earned. But even this spur was not enough and in August he left the job, though without making more than a slight dent in his friendship with Cassel. His ambitions for Maurice's career were touching. Regy believed his son to be endowed with limitless capacities for success in his career, and he continued to pull every string for his advancement. By 1905, through the King's strenuous pressure on the young soldier's reluctant colonel, he had got Maurice seconded from his regiment to the staff of General Sir John French, who consented to take him out of gratitude for all that Regy had done for the Army. In vain the colonel pointed out that, although he had a favourable opinion of Maurice's abilities and considered him a promising officer, he was totally inexperienced and untried; and that the consequence of premature promotion would mean his regimental duties having to be performed by fellow officers. Fritz Ponsonby, then Assistant Secretary to the King, agreed with the colonel. None of these arguments deflected Regy once he had made up his mind. Maurice's subsequent unpopularity with his fellow officers was accentuated by his failure to visit them while on French's staff.

By 1904 Maurice's crush on Ellaline Terriss was over, and another star in the theatrical firmament was dazzling him. On 1 September Regy wrote to Maurice, 'How did you like Zena Dare? Is she at all attractive?' The answer was that he did, and she was. When he met her, Regy too found her very much to his liking. For seven years before Maurice was able to marry Zena he loved her distantly and despairingly. Regy loved her with an emotion which perhaps he had only once before expended upon a woman – Milly Sutherland – though with a different objective in view. He may in his way have been 'in love' with Zena. Certainly he saw in her the perfect partner for the son he worshipped – someone tractable whom he could guide and to a certain extent dominate, someone of whom he need not feel unduly jealous, and someone who might not, like a society girl, resent and reject Regy's inevitable omnipresence. And thus began what Oliver Brett mischievously called the second incest.

Zena Dare, unlike most actresses of the Edwardian age, came from a respectable middle-class background and had been well brought up. Not a classical actress or a great beauty, she was an extremely competent actress in light comedies, pretty and seductive, with a sweet personality. Within a few years of being on the stage she was sought after by all the rich young gentlemen in society. In her old age she told a friend how lines of hansom cabs drew up outside the stage door when first she became a star. But, being what was called a 'nice' girl, she gave back to her suitors the diamond bracelets and other tantalizing presents they thrust upon her.[50] Regy saw at once that Zena had to be wooed and won with caution and care. She was not going to fall into Maurice's lap like a ripe plum. It is doubtful how far she was ever to be in love with Maurice; at first she was probably more attracted by the charm and sophistication of his father.

The courtship was a long and slow affair, for Maurice was a clumsy and nervous wooer. He was dependent upon his father's guidance as to what to do, and Regy sent him countless letters of advice and suggestions. 'Ask her to go for a motor drive with you next Saturday, and arrange when to pick her up. Suggest Hampton Court and luncheon.' By way of encouragement to Maurice he stressed how like a boy she was, 'and that is the secret of your excellent relations with her'.[51] He advised him to take her not to a box at the theatre but to the stalls, because it was better not always to put her in the limelight. On Maurice's behalf he sent Zena telegrams about arrangements and even opened her letters to his son. He told Maurice when it was high time that he kissed her. He asked him when he was going to take her into his full confidence. And finally, when Maurice was on his way home from the East in 1910 he exhorted him, rather impatiently one feels, to take her, when he got back, into his arms 'vigorously and passionately', when she would not resist.

Whenever an opportunity arose, Regy would do a good turn to his old school. In June he persuaded the King and Queen to make a special visit to Eton. The headmaster delivered an address to Their Majesties in School Yard. Unfortunately there was a muddle about the script of the King's reply, which could not be found. So the Provost, the Captain of the School and the Captain of the Oppidans handed their own addresses, adorned with light blue silk, to the King, who smiled, bowed but said nothing. The occasion was a huge success notwithstanding, and the boys were bowled over by Their Majesties' affability.

King Edward's reliance on Regy was almost total. He regarded him as an infallible oracle, steeped in nineteenth-century politics, whose knowledge of the constitution and all that pertained to the precedents, prerogatives and protocols of the Crown was beyond compare. He esteemed him because, not being a paid servant, he never danced attendance. They either met or corresponded every day, the King sending short, sharp little notes in his crabbed, indecipherable, Germanic hand. Every missive began 'My dear Esher,' and ended 'Yours very sincerely, Edward R.' Regy's to his master were of course scrupulously formal, phrased in the third person throughout: 'Viscount Esher presents his humble duty and begs to suggest to Your Majesty,' etc. The King kept all Regy's letters locked up in a drawer and would not even hand them over to Knollys. It was firmly understood that Regy would never disclose the confidential discussions which the King had with his ministers at audiences and passed on to him. After 1904 all appointments to the War Office, which had to be approved by the King, were first agreed to and often suggested by Regy.

Regy for his part was extremely protective of the King's authority and dignity. He kept up a long correspondence with Knollys over the way ministers tended to overlook the sovereign's constitutional status. He strongly deprecated those ministers who failed to keep the King informed of executive acts which they were contemplating and for which they did not seek the King's authority before implementing them. He considered that such behaviour amounted to an infringe- ment of the Privy Councillor's oath. Arnold-Forster was one of these offenders, and even had the impertinence to let his secretary write on his behalf to the King on an important constitutional matter. During Queen Victoria's youth and middle age, every dispatch in a treaty with a foreign power, and every item on a forthcoming Cabinet agenda, was discussed in detail with her. Her ministers recognized that the monarch was allegedly unbiased in all political affairs and trained to avoid conflicts over Cabinet decisions. In fact her discretion often forestalled a minister's impetuous move when such a move involved risks and perils to the state. Queen Victoria's advanced age and the urgent actions called for by the South African War were eventually the cause of dispatches sometimes not being submitted to her. Regy Esher was determined that in the interests of the monarchy these lapses must not recur.

Regy made allowance for King Edward's shortcomings, which were personal rather than public. He kept them to himself, his diary and his letters to Maurice, which amounted to the same thing. 'He has one great fault for me,' he told Maurice, 'which is his commonplace personality. I cannot find in him any trace of original thought or feeling. So unlike the Queen [Victoria] who was unique.' He never read a book; he talked all day and allowed no time for thought.[52] More regrettable was the fact that, although naturally intelligent, he was hopelessly unable to concentrate and to adopt a definitive view. His judgement was over-hasty. He was of course a stickler for etiquette, and once sent to Maurice through an equerry a reproof for referring to the Russian Emperor instead of the Emperor of Russia.

In spite of his daily contacts with the King Regy complained that the only times he was able to have intimate and leisurely conversations with him were during the annual visits to Balmoral. This September of 1904 there were no guests staying beyond the immediate family. One of these was Prince Arthur of Connaught, whom Regy described as a 'very amiable but silly goose', and 'very chancy in his kilt – sits in odd positions – and shows everthing he has to show, which is not much'.[53] More to his taste was old Donald Stewart, who had been the Prince Consort's stalker and lived in a sort of lodge called Cantzig. He had been at Balmoral before Queen Victoria went there in 1848 and he had accompanied the Prince Consort on his first expedition to the hills. He called John Brown every name under the sun, describing him as an 'abominable mon'. One day the King and Regy had tea in his lodge. The King was wet through when he arrived and said, ' "Donald, lend me a pair of your shoes and stockings at once." And presently he appeared in them looking very queer.'[54]

As principal author of the War Office Reconstitution Committee's recommendations, Regy kept a wary eye on the War Office and strove to see that its policies were subordinated to the CID. But he failed to move the Tory Government to reorganize the military forces in accordance with the recommendations of his Committee. The Liberal party was divided over the issue, and Arnold-Forster had his own ideas which did not always coincide with those of 'the dauntless three'. In January 1905 a secret sub-committee of the CID was appointed, with Balfour in the chair, which it was hoped would hasten the Government's Army scheme through Parliament. The secret committee won the backing of Joe Chamberlain, now a convinced imperialist. This was the outcome of several clandestine dinners arranged by Regy for Chamberlain and the Prime Minister to get together, talk and reach agreement. Briefly, the terms of reference of the secret committee were acceptance in principle of Arnold-Forster's scheme for the reorganization of the Army, but to work out for his benefit what its purpose, size and strength ought to be.

Regy confided to the King that whereas the Reconstitution Committee never intended promotions of major-generals to lieutenant-generals to be made by the Secretary of State except on the recommendation of a selection board, the War Office had failed to put this recommendation into effect.[55] He reproved Arnold-Forster in no uncertain terms for failure to understand that the Prime Minister had laid down fundamental principles which were meant to guide all future Army reformers. And he did not share the Minister's opinion on certain matters, such as the reduction of several battalions of long-service troops and the retention of two militias – short-service army plus militia. 'I know', he ended, 'that you will not misunderstand this plain speaking.'[56] It was a bold stance for an independent peer to take up against the accredited Secretary of State for War. Regy was engaged in much correspondence this year about army matters with such diverse people as Kitchener, Repington, Amery, Maxse, Roberts, Fleetwood-Wilson, Rawlinson and Haig.[57] He made it his business to convey to Balfour that the King was greatly disturbed by the debate in the House of Lords in August on the falling off of officers in the Army and auxiliary forces, and the fact that no steps were yet being taken to implement the recommendations of the Esher Committee to organize a general staff. It was a further instance of his methods of bringing pressure on the Tory Government from behind the scenes.

Meanwhile Regy's infatuation for Maurice had by no means

subsided. In January he wrote to his son, 'Never think there is any inflexion of your voice, or passing glance of your eyes, which fails to find a response in me. . . . I send you some lines written, while you fell asleep last night, and I sat, as I always love to do, on your bed, watching your dear eyes closing, and listening to your quiet breathing.' Already he was bracing himself to face the inevitable parting, which actually was still several years ahead. He added, 'All your strenuous ambition to live an honourable life, and your extraordinary pure love for what is best in woman and man, are adorable to me.'[58] Zena – there was no disregarding the fact – was now getting a firm hold of his adored Maurice. He could not prevent himself from giving vent to dire apprehensions. 'I suppose our great and profound intimacy must come to an end some day. . . . Indifference would be a terrible punishment for me, even if I could survive it.'[59] It was more than he could bear to contemplate, but he was unwise to communicate these fears to the object of his love. The reaction was more moderate, and more forbearing than might have been the case from a less tolerant and kindly son. It was a marvel that Maurice, a very ordinary young man of twenty-three, put up with the emotional outbursts. After experiencing another of these jeremiads Maurice wrote:

> You made me extremely miserable last night and I have been ill all day today. Cannot you have a little faith? Is love such a doubtful quantity to you that you must be for ever watching and trying to anticipate its flight? . . . Have you and I anything in common with the rest of the world? Are we so like other people and has our love any resemblance of their loves? . . . You say to yourself that love *must* grow weaker and in that belief you make yourself and those you love unhappy.[60]

Then he added a phrase which does not entirely absolve him of guile. He protested that his love for Zena and his life in the Army were both to give his father pleasure. He told Regy that he had just had Zena to lunch with him. 'She is a most charming companion to pass the day with, much more of a boy than a girl and I was delighted.' There is something disingenuous in this statement.

Regy's indifference to his other children was correspondingly marked, though it is true that he recommended Oliver as assistant secretary to his friend John Morley on his appointment as Secretary of State for India.

> He is *very* intelligent. He has been – since Eton – to Berlin and Paris, and he has worked with Spender on *The Westminster*, and of late has been electioneering with Haddo in E. Berkshire. I am sure you would like him. . . . You would find him very trustworthy, and a most excellent arranger and compiler of papers, etc., for which he has both taste and talent. I hope you will forgive me for asking.[61]

The application was successful. At least he had done his duty by his elder son.

Doll, by now of age, a natural rebel against society and convention and as yet uncertain what her bent was to be, was left at Orchard Lea, with Sylvia, to her own devices. These amounted to a crush on a neighbour, Margaret Brooke, the estranged wife of the White Rajah of Sarawak.[62] Doll could not keep away from Grey Friars, Ascot, where the Ranee lived, having first been welcomed by that distinguished lady as a possible bride for her elder son, Vyner Brooke, the Rajah Muda. The Ranee had a commanding presence, was highly intelligent and extremely musical. Liberal in outlook, she had a large circle of intellectual friends and was full of vitality and gaiety. When it became evident to her that Vyner was not interested – he was in due course to marry Sylvia – the Ranee endeavoured to end the relationship. But Doll would not keep away and continued to try to insinuate herself back into the Ranee's good graces by the most extraordinary devices, like ensconcing herself in the hatch between the kitchen and the dining room of Grey Friars, and popping out like the good fairy expecting to be rapturously received. Regy loathed the Ranee, whom he charged incorrectly with cheapness and less unjustifiably with intrigue. The fact was that he was jealous, on his own and Nellie's behalf, of the affection which the Ranee had given, and he and his wife had withheld, from their two daughters. He felt obliged to end his elder daughter's escapades, so having taken the minimum notice of the poor girl's education and interests he had the matter out with her. He told her she was degrading herself and humiliating her family. 'All the servants know of these back-door escapes, and probably all the village by now.'[63] And she had alienated her mother. As a result without a word of warning Doll left Orchard Lea for the Ranee, who out of pity consented to receive her. Even so the Ranee would not keep her for ever, and Doll moved elsewhere. 'The Grey Friars' intrigue is getting on my nerves,' Regy wrote to Maurice, in whom he confided his perpetual irritation with the rest of his children. 'Doll is almost suicidal because that beast of an old woman will not reply to her letters. . . . It is hard on that wretched ass Doll, who has put all her eggs into one basket.'[64]

The year 1905 brought Regy more unpaid duties and further responsibilities. The King appointed him the sovereign's representative trustee of the British Museum. He also made him take the chairmanship of the Executive Committee of the King Edward VII Sanatorium at Midhurst. He was made a Commander of the Legion of Honour by the French President. One June day at Buckingham Palace the King turned his grandson, little Prince Edward, out of the room and told Regy he thought the Government had behaved badly in criticizing the work he had done voluntarily for army reform, and that he would make him a Knight Grand Cross of the Royal Victorian Order. Certainly there was considerable ill-feeling towards him in ministerial quarters, and the King was well aware of it. The new Lord Salisbury, then Lord Privy Seal, writing in April to his cousin, the Prime Minister, from *Britannia* where he was Minister in Attendance, complained, 'I think Esher's relations with the King are in the highest degree unsatisfactory. He ought either to be a responsible minister and defend his views in Parliament or (at the very most) he should confine himself to intensely confidential communications with yourself.'[65]

Regy told the King he would far rather receive an honour from him personally than from the Government. The King replied, 'It is very nice of you to say that.' He was touched and gratified, and when Regy left him repeated their conversation to Knollys. Nothing further was said about the honour. But when the secret Esher committee was wound up the King urged the Government to recommend that Regy should be created a Knight Grand Cross of the Order of the Bath. The Government retorted that it would create a bad precedent – were they to give Lord Esher the honour, they would automatically have to reward the chairmen of all commissions and committees. To Maurice Regy wrote, 'There is something in this and I think the PM was right.'[66] However, in December Balfour on his enforced retirement from the premiership, did offer him the GCB. This time Regy declined it, giving the same valid reason that the Government had previously given to the King. He did not want the new Liberal Government to regard him as a spy in their midst left over by the Conservatives. Such an interpretation would not put him in good stead with the CID. Finally the King awarded him the GCVO, an honour given personally by the sovereign.

By the autumn of 1905 it was clear to everyone that the Conservative rule which had endured for nearly ten years was doomed. As early as July Regy told Maurice that if the Government survived a month there would be a War Office crisis and Arnold-Forster would retire. 'Then the question will arise whether I shall take his place or not. I am rather inclined to do so.'[67] The Government, as it happened, lasted until the end of the year. In October, when a General Election was in the offing, the King sent for him to Balmoral and said he wanted him to be Secretary of War. Regy evaded the predicament by pointing out that the period would be far too short for him to achieve anything before the new Government took over. The King accepted his point. He was, Regy remarked, 'almost affectionate in his manner'.[68] Instead Regy pressed the King, should the Liberals come to power, to make Haldane Minister of War.

Far more to Regy's taste and inclination was the status he was establishing for himself as Royal Archivist. A small ex officio committee was set up consisting of Knollys, Sir John Fortescue, the Royal Librarian, and himself as chairman; they were to look into the whole question of the royal papers at Windsor and report to the King. At the same time his brother-in-law, Victor Van de Weyer, handed over to Regy all his father's boxes of letters from Queen Victoria concerning the foundation of the kingdom of Belgium, in which he had played a major role. Regy offered them to the King. It is true that they were beginning to suffer from damp, and he wished to be relieved of them.

Regy's association with Balfour had by now become extremely close. He was in constant touch with the Prime Minister. He would send him, either direct or through his Secretary, Jack Sandars, notes of suggestions on every conceivable matter of topical importance. He warned Balfour of Kitchener's dissatisfaction over the treatment he was receiving in India from the Viceroy, Lord Curzon. Regy was regularly corresponding with both Kitchener and Curzon.

On 16 November Regy was waiting in No. 10 Downing Street to see Jack Sandars when the Secretary was summoned by the Prime Minister to discuss the date of the Government's resignation. On learning that his old friend was downstairs, Arthur Balfour sent for him to join the discussion. Balfour asked Regy what he should do, and Regy advised him to dissolve Parliament himself rather than let in the Opposition for them to go to the country. And so the Conservative Prime Minister took the advice of the public figure looked upon as a member of the Liberal party. Balfour went to Windsor that evening. On the 20th Regy spent several hours with Balfour, his brother Gerald and Sandars. Together they went through the 'Change of Government' papers of 1873–4 when Gladstone was succeeded by Disraeli, which the King had told Regy to show the Prime Minister. For at an audience on the 17th the King had failed to get any decisive recommendations from Balfour on how to act – at the best of times he found conversation with him difficult. He asked Regy if he could understand what Balfour was driving at. Regy reported the King's bewilderment to his friend outright, whereupon the Prime Minister had another long talk with the King, explaining to him the difficulties with which he was confronted.

On the 28th Regy saw Balfour, who told him he had decided to resign and that the King was opposed. Francis Knollys came up for a conclave at Downing Street, being admitted secretly through the garden entrance, after which he persuaded the King to accept Balfour's resignation.[69] The following day Regy reported to the King that in a speech at Bodmin Rosebery had created the impression that he would accept office in a new Liberal Government; then had withdrawn his consent and was in consequence plunged in depression. On the last day of the month Regy begged Spender, on behalf of the King, to persuade Campbell-Bannerman to leave Scotland for London owing to the political crisis.

On 1 December Regy had a long talk at Downing Street with Balfour while he was dressing. Balfour was in high spirits, delighted to be free of the responsibility of his office. On the 4th Morley asked Regy if he would accept the War Office in the new Liberal Government. Regy commented on the absurdity of politicians of both parties offering him the same post. That day Balfour saw the King at Buckingham Palace and handed over the seals of office. Afterwards he came into Knollys's room and seemed a little moved. He then drove back to Downing Street with Regy. In the evening the King received Campbell-Bannerman.

Regy barely knew Campbell-Bannerman, a Glasgow wholesale draper's son who had, in spite of succeeding Hartington as leader of the Liberal party in 1899, remained a nebulous figure in politics. The man who had opposed Chamberlain's South African policy, describing Britain's methods of warfare in South Africa as 'methods of barbarism', belonged to the Radical, anti-imperial wing of Regy's party with which he did not feel at all sympathetic. But now that the man was about to become Prime Minister Regy felt he ought to make his acquaintance. On 5 December he got his friend Loulou to introduce him to Campbell-Bannerman's Secretary, Captain Sinclair, whom he liked and in return introduced to Francis Knollys. The same day Regy handed the King a memorandum outlining the procedure customarily adopted by the monarch on a change of Government. He sent a copy to Campbell-Bannerman, who acquitted himself satisfactorily at his audience except that out of shyness he forgot to kiss hands. The next day Regy called on George Curzon in Carlton Gardens, at his request. Here he heard from Curzon's own lips what Curzon had been telling the King about the famous row he had had with Kitchener when he was Viceroy of India and Kitchener Commander-in-Chief in that country.

Having engineered Haldane's appointment to the War Office, Regy immediately persuaded Gerald Ellison, who had been secretary to the Esher Committee, to become Secretary to the new Minister for War. The two men took to each other at once and Ellison became Haldane's confidant and adviser. Regy then brought Haldane down to Windsor Castle, where the King was delighted with him.

Richard Burdon Haldane, eminent statesman, lawyer and philosopher, was a new friend whom Regy first got to know well while staying at Balmoral the preceding October. Regy wrote to Rosebery that he liked him with few reservations. He found him shrewd, adroit and exceedingly clever. He foresaw that he would prove an ally and supporter of the Defence Committee, for Haldane made it clear that he was determined to create a perfectly equipped military machine, believing 'in force as the foundation of Empire'.[70] Having been educated at Göttingen University and speaking fluent German, Haldane made a special study of German military organization. He straightway realized that England must build two ships to every one of Germany's. He was a man after Regy's heart. Haldane's sole weakness, which was yet to become evident, lay in a wish to please everybody and propitiate outlying sections of his party not worthy of propitiation.[71] The Haldane army reforms were to be as much Esher's and Balfour's as his own.[72]

On the 11th Regy saw the King, who made him stay to luncheon. His Majesty was very satisfied that Campbell-Bannerman had assured Haldane he would give him a free hand at the War Office. In the evening Regy and Nellie dined with Ernest Cassel to meet the King, who was far from well and severely oppressed by the weather. The political to-ing and fro-ing of this December week was made horribly complicated by one of London's worst recorded fogs which, owing to every house chimney belching forth coal fumes, enveloped Westminster with an impenetrable pall. At night the King's carriage was preceded and followed by a dozen running footmen with flaring torches, a thing never witnessed before. Moreover the fog did not suit the King's weak throat and chest; it affected his breathing and obliged him to escape to Windsor until conditions in the capital improved.

On the 13th Captain Sinclair arranged for Regy to go to No. 10. Regy thought fit to assure the new Prime Minister that he had always been absolutely loyal to Arthur Balfour, and so he would be to him. 'I explained my relation to the King, and the confidence with which I was honoured.'[73] He then rushed back to Tilney Street in order to write to the sovereign all about the interview. Campbell-Bannerman had admitted to him that, whereas formerly he had been prejudiced against the Defence Committee as an institution, he was now determined to accept it and work with it. He admitted that it was 'his weakness to poke fun at people, although he should not be taken seriously!'[74] Regy considered this a charming *amende honorable* and felt sure future relations between him and the King would be cordial. Campbell-Bannerman had spoken to him very confidentially about his colleagues and their characteristics, all with humour and shrewdness. He referred to Haldane's high-pitched voice and 'rather feminine and old-maidish sensitiveness', which led him to dub him 'Priscilla'. Regy was particularly gratified by the Prime Minister's total lack of resentment of his confidence with the King. Altogether he foresaw no difficulties in working with the genial draper's son from Glasgow.

Campbell-Bannerman's brief premiership was made hideous for him by the rapid deterioration of international relationships and his declining health. The possibility of war with Germany had been mooted by politicians over the past ten years, chiefly on account of Kaiser William II's aggrandizement of his fleet to match the number of Great Britain's warships. Then the Morocco affair nearly brought matters to a head. Britain's recognition of France's predominant interest in Morocco, in return for certain concessions in Egypt, was a principle of the entente cordiale of 1904. Without any warning the Kaiser, deciding that his country had a stake in Mediterranean matters, landed at Tangier on 31 March 1905. He immediately made advances to the Sultan, who was resentful of French 'pacific penetration' of his country, and posed as the champion of his sovereignty. Germany's aggressive interference caused such dismay in France that it brought about the downfall of Théophile Delcassé, the Foreign Minister and principal creator of the entente.

Nearly a year later the three powers involved agreed to a conference on the whole question at Algeciras. The French were frightened, and anxious to know how Britain would act in the event of war with Germany. Fisher, the First Sea Lord, would not commit himself. King Edward was furious with his nephew William. Regy, not surprisingly, was deeply involved. On 18 January 1906 he called upon Mr Alfred Beit of Wernher, Beit & Co., the intimate friend and adviser of Rhodes and ardent imperialist. Regy sent the King a full account of the interview. Mr Beit talked uncommonly well and was extremely intelligent. He explained how, as a result of his gift of an important Van Dyck painting to the Berlin Gallery, he had just returned from Potsdam where he received the thanks of the Kaiser. William had then talked very freely to Mr Beit on politics. He had complained that the press of France, Belgium and America were bribed by English individuals with the connivance of the British Government. He wanted to come to a friendly understanding with France about Morocco. There would be no war with France unless the British continued to arouse anti-German feeling among the French. He knew that some very influential people, such as Admiral Fisher, wished for war; and that Fisher was confident that the strength of his fleet was paramount. Beit deprecated the innuendo that Britain's Navy was spoiling for a conflict with Germany. The Kaiser went on that he had no objection to the entente cordiale, for he had his entente with Russia – the Treaty of Bjoerkoe, made between himself and Tsar Nicholas II in July of the previous year. Beit made it clear that if the Algeciras Conference did not turn out satisfactorily, England was bound to assist France. He observed that, whereas in Germany the people thought Britain wanted war, in Britain the people thought the

Kaiser wanted war. To this the Kaiser retorted that for eighteen years he had done his best to preserve peace.[75] On the other hand – so Regy confided in Lord Knollys – the Kaiser complained that his uncle Bertie had been most rude to the German Ambassador in Paris, saying to him, 'You won't and shan't have this conference.' And now the conference was about to take place.[76] Indeed, while the conference was in session Jackie Fisher wrote to Regy in strict confidence that the British Navy was fully armed and prepared for war at a moment's notice.[77] All the while Regy was regularly sending King Edward CID reports asking for the royal advice, while deftly putting forward his own recommendations. 'At half past five', Regy wrote to Maurice on 21 January,

> I met the King by appointment in the corridor [at Windsor]. . . . He came out of his room with a pot hat on, and his stick and his dog, and we wandered about the Castle for two hours, as if we were out for a walk. We went to the Library and ransacked every kind of bookcase and picture cupboard. He got rid of an enormous number of rubbishy old coloured photographs and things.

At least Regy salvaged Queen Victoria's paintbox and sketch bag, which the King allowed him to send to the Royal Academy.

On the 24th Maurice went to his father's room in the Castle where three of the royal grandchildren were having tea with him, a thing they did nearly every evening when at Windsor. Regy was greatly taken with Prince Edward[78] who 'develops every day fresh qualities, and is a most charming boy; very direct, dignified, and clever. His memory is remarkable – a family tradition – but the look of *Weltschmerz* in his eyes I cannot trace to any ancestor of the House of Hanover.'[79]

King Edward, whose own handwriting was abominable, complained to Regy that his was indecipherable and ordered him to get himself some new spectacles. Obediently the courtier complied. 'They are rather strange to him,' he wrote to the King, 'but Lord Esher reflects often that it is his duty to wear them, however inconvenient, in obedience to Your Majesty, and he ventures to hope in the interests of Your Majesty and the State.'[80] One wonders whether His Majesty ever smiled over the apparent subservience of his faithful, self-appointed, unpaid servant, or whether he took these deferential little notes for granted without a tremor of the eyelid or lip. A few months later, in spite of the new spectacles, Regy took to having his letters typewritten, 'as he thinks Your Majesty will find it so much easier to read than his bad handwriting'.[81]

It was at about this time that Regy wrote to Maurice, 'I told you that in parting the King said to me, "Although you are not exactly a public servant, yet I always think you are the most valuable public servant I have," and then I kissed his hand, as I sometimes do.' The passage has been extensively quoted as indicating what a toady the 2nd Viscount Esher was. Certainly the spontaneous kissing of the royal hand was not common even eighty years ago. Yet Regy was definitely and unquestionably devoted to his master. Otherwise why should he have slaved for him for so little material reward? Moreover, the passage just quoted from the published *Journals and Letters* does not end as abruptly as the readers of those bowdlerized four volumes are led to suppose. In fact Regy continued: 'But in doing it I only thought how little all this meant including the kiss, compared with a kiss upon another hand, and a few words of affection or appreciation from other lips.'[82] Presumably kisses were still vouchsafed to Maurice's hands as well as to the King's.

Regy was at this time feeling his way cautiously with Zena. He gave her little presents. In January she wrote in her childish hand a letter of thanks for a clock as well as a hat, which did not suit her and which she had changed. Maurice told his father that he would not be jealous were he to overhear their conversation. And as though to make the situation better he added:

> There is very little of the woman about her and much more of the boy as I have often told you, and it is the youthful companionship I like now and again. After all I spend more hours in a week with you than I should in a whole lifetime with her. . . . To me she has got a great charm. But there it ends, and how can there be any sort of analogy between you and her. Jealous! Why, I might as well be jealous of Sir George Clarke.[83]

Maurice's naïveté was very transparent. He knew that Zena's so-called boyishness constituted an important element of her charm for Regy, who had remarked upon her part as a boy in *The Gay Gordons* suiting her intelligence as well as her physique. If a proper role were offered her she would, Regy felt, make a real actress.

Then in March Maurice made it plain to his father that the days of their close dependence on one another were passing. Regy was at once thrown into paroxysms of distress. Again he reproached his son for drifting away from him. 'I cannot face such a future,' he wrote to him, 'and you must help me, for both our sakes, to plan out a future which will not make the recollection of the past wholly one of regret.'[84] Maurice was sometimes driven almost to distraction by these repeated protestations. He reminded his father that when he was at Aldershot he was continually seeking pretexts to get leave to see him in London.

And when he got there he was frequently kept waiting until Regy was free – at the Palace, the Defence Committee office, Tilney Street or the India Office. 'And yet once because I wound my own clock and a second time because I tell a servant to fill a bath, you say you "cannot face the future" and that we are "drifting".'[85] These are the words of a young man fed up with an old love when engaged upon a new one.

There were signs by midsummer that Zena was getting bored by her suitor's attentions, to judge by the excuses she made not to meet him. It was Regy who was ultimately to bring them together as man and wife. Meanwhile his depression and elation were still fluctuating, but by December the latter was in the ascendant. He was telling Maurice that in all their years of happiness together he had never felt his goodness to him more deeply than in the present.[86] And when he sensed that his son's affections were secured he dared to scold him for his failings. On New Year's Eve he reproved the silly young man for questioning the usefulness of knowledge. He reminded him that in his profession he was the superior of all his contemporaries. And why? Because of his knowledge, inculcated by his father. The years that lay ahead would bring him still further knowledge and accordingly further advancement in his profession. He ended by a resumption of the tragical note, 'Very soon you will marry. It is better so. I should like to live so long. Then nunc dimittis. . . . And Nellie feels exactly as I do.'

The stage still held Regy in thrall. He was always at the theatre, and with few exceptions preferred the relaxed friendship of actors and actresses to that of politicians. May Yohé was now a particular friend. 'Dear thing, she was perfectly sweet – dressed as a middy and jockey,' he wrote to Chat Williamson.[87]

One of the political friends was Haldane, of whom Regy was seeing much during the first half of 1906. At the beginning of their friendship they did not always see eye to eye. Regy was critical of the War Minister's plan to place the Territorial Army in the hands of local bodies, and also of his too low estimate of the number of men required to be sent abroad on outbreak of war.[88] These points conflicted with Regy's Note on *Military Requirements of the Empire*, which was printed for the CID in March. It is not difficult to see how Regy's opinions brushed off on the King, who made his go-between remonstrate with Haldane for allowing the Army Council to appoint a new GOC in London without previously consulting him. He also strongly objected to the new War Office ruling that no lieutenant-general might hold a command hitherto held by a major-general. In fact at Sandringham the monarch was soon letting off a salvo of strong language about his Secretary for War, calling him a 'damned radical lawyer and a German professor', and declaring that all his confidence in him was gone.[89]

Regy said what he could for Haldane until the latter fell foul of him too. In May he was reproving the Secretary of State for not laying his reduction schemes before the King. He opposed the plan to reduce the battalions of the Coldstream Guards, telling him that no major war could be won by naval action alone. With the Empire Britain was no longer an island people. It was no use relying upon volunteer forces. He felt certain that every sensible Englishman believed war was bound to come, an opinion which he also passed on to Kitchener, to whom he wrote that the public should be warned of the probable dangers Britain would have to face.[90]

By the autumn, although Regy considered Haldane to be very uncertain in his own mind, he was working in great harmony on Army reforms with him. He was much impressed by Haldane's having attended the annual manoeuvres of the German Army in the summer. He had come to realize that the Minister was a man who refused to be pushed and took his time in assessing situations; and that his final assessments were extraordinarily sound.

In a not dissimilar fashion Regy was already dictating to the Prime Minister. In March he sent him a long memorandum requesting that distribution of the military forces of the Crown throughout the Empire should be brought up to date.[91] As things stood they were just as they had been in the Napoleonic Wars. By April he was telling the King that the Prime Minister was ageing and finding it increasingly difficult to fix his attention on details. Government work was being carried out in the departments practically without reference to him. The King might shortly be faced with a change of leader. His Majesty took this information seriously.

The authority Regy exercised in Army matters, small as well as great, is exemplified by the Guards Ragging Case. After a mock trial, a young probationer called A.R. Clark-Kennedy was set upon by four brother officers of the Scots Guards on the pretext that he had dirty habits and suffered from the itch. They tore off his clothes, smeared him with motor oil and covered his hair with jam and feathers. In desperation he jumped out of a window and spent the rest of the night in an Aldershot hotel. The experience was followed by a nervous breakdown. The brutality of the case was made worse by the fact that the commanding officer had told the officers to deal with Clark-Kennedy in their own way.[92]

A question was raised in the House of Commons; Sir John French was furious about it and Haldane considered dismissing the officers from the army. The offending four were arrested and all other Scots Guards officers were recalled from leave and confined to barracks. The gutter press made all kinds of inaccurate and injurious insinuations against the Brigade of Guards. Regy described the case as a disgusting one of simple bullying and brutality,[93] but he described the wretched victim as 'a dirty, immoral, unsatisfactory young man', which he conceded, however, was no excuse.[94]

A Board of Inquiry revealed that the senior subaltern among the bullies, or raggers as the commanding officer and adjutant preferred to call them, was one N.V.C. Dalrymple-Hamilton. When the King learned the name he expressed to Regy the hope that the young offender would not be dismissed from the service, for that would be a devastating blow to his father. He thought he should be transferred to another regiment. 'Please write to me fully and undisguisedly when you think anything will interest me; and I think you know of old that I take indeed in most things,' the King wrote somewhat cryptically to Regy.[95] Regy felt obliged to say that Sir Arthur Morton had pronounced that Clark-Kennedy, the probationer, seemed after all not a bad boy, and intimated that the medical officer had made all the mischief. Finally, on the express wish of the King, Regy saw that the penalties imposed on the young raggers were relaxed.[96] The only person in the case to come out well was the ill-used probationer, who was very reluctant to speak up against his bullies.

The better Regy got to know Haldane the more fond of him he became, and more appreciative of his great gifts. He endeavoured, not without ultimate success, to convince the King that he was an exceptionally brilliant individual, as well as a lovable man. In August he drove from the Roman Camp to visit Haldane at his family home at Auchterader. He wrote the King an account of the visit, telling him first of the remarkable journey he had made from Orchard Lea to Callander. He drove there in three days in the Daimler that formerly belonged to the King, covering 130 miles each day very comfortably.[97] As for Cloan, it was a nice little property of wood and moorland near Gleneagles. The semi-modern house in the Scottish baronial style – a small laird's house much added to by Haldane – stood on a hill. It was cosy and comfortable but the rooms were chock-a-block with scientific instruments and electrical contrivances, all the work of Haldane's brother who had a laboratory in the house. Regy described the house party for the King, who loved to know how people lived outside royal palaces. There was an old mother, aged eighty, capable and clever; a sister with a degree in law, the very counterpart of Mr Haldane in petticoats; and a Scottish professor. They were all cultivated, intelligent people, and eminently Scottish. Regy dared to predict that His Majesty would grow to get on well with Haldane.

King Edward did eventually become much attached to Haldane, who reciprocated his friendliness. The King showed his favour by putting him on the list of those whom he wished to meet at other people's dinner tables and invite to his own house parties at Sandringham. Once, while both were staying at Marienbad for a cure, the King took Haldane for a motor trip into the country. They stopped at a little roadside inn with a rickety wooden table in front of it. 'Here I will stand treat,' the King said. He ordered coffee for two and then said, 'Now I am going to pay. I shall take care to give only a small tip to the woman who serves the coffee, in case she suspects who I am.' The woman, of course, knew at a glance, and was presumably disappointed by the meagre gratuity. They then drove on to a place of which the King was very fond, a monastery inhabited by the Abbot of Tepel, where they were given a large tea. The King enjoyed himself very much, gossiping with the monks and teasing them.[98]

In September Regy accompanied Douglas Haig, then a major-general who had just finished service as Inspector-General of Cavalry to Kitchener in India, on army manoeuvres. It was a tough experience for a civilian of fifty-three, up and about from 6 a.m. till dusk. They camped in the grandstand at Goodwood, sleeping on the ground; Haig snored heavily on the palliasse next to his guest.[99] Three years previously Regy had commended Haig to the King as a most capable cavalry leader who regretted the abolition of the lance.[100] In giving evidence to the South African War Commission, Haig had stressed the paramount importance of cavalry in modern warfare. It was through Regy's influence that Haldane now gave him the job of Director of Military Training at home. Haig wrote numerous letters to Regy during the first decade of the century; they are extremely dull and give the impression of a highly competent officer, dutiful and unimaginative, who treated soldiers as expendable automata. They also exhale an aroma of self-righteousness. Undoubtedly clever, Haig had absolutely no small talk and little humour. When entertaining strangers to luncheon during the Great War he would maintain a monastic silence that was disconcerting. Aloof in mind, he could be nobly censorious. Sir John French claimed him as his greatest soldier friend; and Regy admired his single-mindedness and reliability. At first he thought he had in Haig an impressionable pupil and never ceased dinning into impervious ears the conviction that his and Haldane's scheme was the best way of leading to comprehensive military service. The whole youth of the country must gradually but surely be trained to defence, just as compulsory education had been accepted in the previous century, not by destroying the voluntary schools but by encouraging them. Regy later found that Haig's strength and weakness lay in a totally unresponsive attitude to discussion and advice.

In August Regy suggested to the King that some officer of authority, sound judgement and high rank should be put in command of the Mediterranean forces, with the defence of Egypt as a primary objective. He nominated the Duke of Connaught.[101] Regy had long maintained that the Duke, though far from clever, was sensible and capable of grasping points; and that if he were an ordinary officer he would easily hold his own and prove an able administrator. Accepting this premise, the King succeeded in convincing Haldane and the Foreign Secretary, Sir Edward Grey, of the immense importance of having at Malta a military governor such as Regy had described, in order to indicate to the world that Britain had not abdicated her paramount position in the Mediterranean.

> On the 16th November the King sent for me about 11 and read me a correspondence with the Duke of Connaught about the new Mediterranean Command. The Duke's letter, in reply to the King, who had used some very complimentary language, was not very gracious, and the King was evidently hurt. He replied very sternly, and told the Duke quite straight, that he would have that or nothing, and he could not believe that he wished to become a mere London loafer![102]

At the very end of 1906 Regy spent a day with John Morley at his Wimbledon house. He had become fond of the distinguished historian, biographer and reluctant Secretary of State for India. Since 1877 they had kept up a correspondence without ever reaching Christian name terms. The chief difference between them amounted to their respective opinions of Disraeli. Whereas Regy venerated him, Morley pronounced him a bombastic jingoist. But then he was deeply shocked by Kitchener's imperialist views. Regy also disliked Morley's Irish policy, which amounted to acceptance of Parnell's extreme demands. Otherwise their views were in such accord that Morley made Regy his literary executor. Morley was a somewhat sad figure, prickly and jealous of Lord Rosebery's position, wealth and effortless advantages. He had been greatly put out by the Kitchener-Curzon dispute, being slightly in awe of the former and socially ill at ease with the latter.

In one of his gossipy letters in which the King delighted, Regy described Morley's house, called Flowermead, as being 'externally rather a commonplace villa, on the edge of the Common; but it contains an exceedingly fine room added by Mr Morley, entirely filled with books, many of them left to him by Lord Acton. There are over 11,000 volumes in the room, and the lighting and arrangements are excellent.'[103] To Maurice he wrote that the household consisted of

> two servant maids and a plain wrinkled old wife. Memories of some Lancashire village in which he was born, hovering about him still. . . . What then is the secret? Why has power been given by his fellow-countrymen to this man, who has inherited neither position nor wealth? He is decidedly no flatterer of the democracy, and no demagogue. So what is the cause? I do not pretend to explain – but it is certainly *not* that he remained content with half-knowledge or low standards.[104]

It was an admirable answer to Maurice's stupid questioning of his father as to the usefulness of knowledge. Haldane, who was on Morley's mental level, maintained that his intellectual range was so wide that he always saw beyond what one was saying to him. Morley was then sixty-eight and anxious to be relieved of his government post. But the Prime Minister pressed him to remain, pointing out that difficulties which no one but he could resolve were likely to arise.

Regy's long experience of the Army made him increasingly worried by young officers' lack of education. As a result, most of them between the ages of twenty and thirty succumbed to idleness, sport and having a good time. He believed that incentives should be offered for serious and intensive study of special subjects of benefit to their careers. On reaching the rank of lieutenant a young officer might commence a three-year course of reading and lectures on military history, topography, geography, strategy and foreign languages. In January 1907, on the invitation of Sir John French, Regy delivered a lecture at Aldershot entitled *The Study of Modern History*, which was subsequently published in pamphlet form. He received congratulations from many authorities, including the influential J.A. Spender and General Sir Ian Hamilton. Regy told the young officers that every great general had been versed in the history of his own and past times, adding as an exhortation that every young officer worth his salt aspired to become a great general. He urged them to make a careful and reflective study of 'what has happened, and of the like or similar things which in accordance with human nature will probably hereafter happen'. He reminded them that although the British were an island race they were no longer an island state.

In the same month he received a telegram from Francis Knollys asking him to have breakfast with the King at ten the next day. This was a new departure and a privilege which Regy had never had conferred upon him before. They were together *tête-à-tête*.

A page asked me if I would take tea or coffee! At 10 precisely the King's door opened, and he came in with his terrier. We went into the room overlooking the Mall. There was a small table. Two places laid. All the breakfast on the table in front of the King. His tea near him, my coffee near me. He served, and the pages and footmen left the room. He asked me if I would have some fish. There were 3 dishes. Fish, omelette and bacon. When we had finished fish, he rang his bell, and the servants changed the plates.

Same ceremony repeated after omelette.

Then marmalade – and he asked me if I would smoke. We sat there till just before 11.

He talked all the time – Army. Government reconstruction. Gossip. . . .

At 11 the King said au revoir till Windsor.[105]

In March an attack on Regy's influence on and interference in political affairs was made by *The Standard*. A leader writer complained:

> The trouble is that he [Esher] now occupies an undefined and therefore, irresponsible position. He is neither a permanent official accountable to the Secretary of State, nor liable to the criticism of Parliament. . . . 'Lord Esher,' writes one of the correspondents, 'has considerable influence, and even, to some extent, an executive power without any sort of responsibility. . .'. Parliamentary government is being set aside if the functions of Ministers are being discharged, with whatever zeal and efficiency, by a person who holds no office and draws no salary.

The attack aroused considerable controversy and delighted Regy's enemies, of whom there were many. Lord Mersey, for instance, affirmed that Lord Esher was not popular at the Foreign Office because he was supposed to repeat things to the King, which Edward Grey much resented.[106] It was spread abroad that the attack had been instigated by Arnold-Forster, which, whether true or false, unloosed the vials of royal wrath on that retired minister. Regy instantly wrote to Knollys, professing that he did not mind the attack except for the lie that he had promised promotions in the Army. 'Any influence which it is assumed I may have, is only what we all have, and is every Englishman's right, i.e. to express his opinions to whomsoever he pleases.' A second point to which he took exception was that his position was 'unconstitutional'. 'The point interests me, as you know I am fond of such speculations. But can you imagine anything more absurd than to label as "unconstitutional" the action of a Minister who employs me or any other person to "assist" him in work for which the Minister only is responsible.' He much objected to being dragged into temporary notoriety. 'However, so long as the King, and you, and a few others, do not mind, and that neither Haldane nor C.-B. flinches, I shall remain unruffled.' He added somewhat plaintively that he had little wealth and got paid nothing for all the help he could give to the country.[107] The letter was meant to be shown to the King; and of course it was. Knollys replied at once that no friend of Regy's could possibly pay attention to *The Standard*'s mean attack.

Colonel Charles à Court Repington, then military correspondent of *The Times*, a great busybody and bore who throughout the decade wrote interminable letters to Regy on Army matters, assured him that his editor, Buckle, considered *The Standard* attack absurd, and no credence could be given it. He thought that Regy's sole vulnerable point was his financial association with Sir Ernest Cassel. Regy at once retorted that he had severed that connection by leaving the City in 1904 before he joined the CID; that his only City connections now were four rather unremunerative directorships. One was the Royal Opera Syndicate Ltd, which meant voluntary work; the others the Central London Railway Co., the Egyptian Daira Co. and the Agricultural Bank of Egypt.[108] Buckle and Repington agreed that politics and finance could be said to meet in the last two. The Prime Minister and Frederick Ponsonby advised Regy to give them up to be on the safe side in the event of any future criticism. Regy complied at once, and informed the Palace.

On 25 March questions were raised in the House of Commons by Mr Thomas Gibson Bowles and two other Members, and quickly dispatched by the Secretary for War. Mr Haldane denied that Lord Esher had any official position or authority in the War Office. He stated that he was merely a member of the Defence Committee, a body quite distinct from the War Office; and he had no say in the appointments made by the War Office. This last statement was strictly correct if one discounts the advice the accused gave gratuitously to the King, who was the source of all appointments. Asked by Sir R. Hobart in a friendly spirit whether this unique national service rendered to the Army and Admiralty by Lord Esher would be rewarded, Haldane replied generously, to the accompaniment of 'Hear! Hear!', 'Lord Esher has rendered to imperial services greater benefits than the public yet appreciates. I wish I could hold out any hope that they will be adequately rewarded.'

These parliamentary replies and written testimonials from Balfour, Campbell-Bannerman and Morley ought to have been sufficient reassurance. But Regy felt very hurt, in spite of what he may have said, by *The Standard*'s attack, and brooded over it. This intrusion into his carefully guarded privacy had not the slightest effect on his intimacy with the King, nor did it lessen the King's confidence in his unofficial servant and adviser. During the fracas Regy was writing to Lord Knollys that, in deference to His Majesty's wishes, the committee of the Cabinet, meeting on the House of Lords issue, did not propose to touch upon the hereditary principle, much to the chagrin of Mr Lloyd George. It was merely limiting its inquiries into the possibility of a serious deadlock between the two Houses at some future time. Representatives of both Houses were to meet and deliberate. These representatives would be selected in such a manner as to ensure predominance of a majority from the Commons. Knollys told Regy that the King would be much annoyed if not kept informed about a grave constitutional question such as reform of the Lords. As it was, he regretted the Lord Chancellor's speech about Home Rule, which the Government assured the electorate they would not be raising in the current session of Parliament.

In May Regy was again doing the very thing to which *The Standard* would have objected, had it known. He warned Lord Knollys that Haldane was about to ask the King to approve General Sir William Nicholson's appointment as Chief of the General Staff. He hoped the King would not approve, because Nicholson was unpopular with the officers and was not a leader who commanded the confidence of the Army. In September Regy was intriguing with Haldane to persuade the King to send Lord Grenfell from Dublin, with a field-marshal's baton, to the London County Council in order to get rid of him. The following year Lord Grenfell's term as Commander-in-Chief in Ireland was duly concluded, he was made a field-marshal, and, even though he did not join the LCC, he devoted the remainder of his life to the Church Lads' Brigade. In October Regy advised the King to put the office of Warden of the Cinque Ports temporarily into commission in order to snub those busybodies who had impertinently hinted that the Prince of Wales was not worthy to fill it. Even the Great Seal has not been exempt from this treatment, he wrote to Knollys.[109] The King accepted his advice. In November, with Campbell-Bannerman showing signs of increasing ill health, Regy, at Morley's request discussed with the King the rival claims of Asquith and Grey. He then told Morley that the King would consult no one, and would exercise his own prerogative.

Campbell-Bannerman understood the King no more than Gladstone did Queen Victoria; and too often he neglected to communicate Cabinet proceedings to him. Knollys informed Regy of the King's dissatisfaction with the Prime Minister, and suggested that he might endeavour to put matters on a more easy footing; he feared the King was being made a fool of. Regy, with that wisdom which dictated to him when he could and should not proffer advice, told Knollys that he thought Campbell-Bannerman was too old to be cured. The indolence of age was upon him. Writing letters bored him. He lacked experience, and besides complained that he never heard direct from the King. The result was sad in the interests of the monarchy. In the Queen's time the practice of regular communication between sovereign and Premier was maintained because the constitutional position of the sovereign was regarded as independent of personality. Today the King's personality was a great factor and thus a stumbling block in the way of his successors. His office should be as sacred as his person. The matter was one of extreme delicacy, and no one was able to tackle C.-B., Regy said. As things were going, Cabinet decisions would soon be taken before full statements were put before the monarch. The authority of the Crown would be weakened and the standard of safety in foreign and home affairs, especially the former, would be lowered. Knollys necessarily looked at the problem from the King's point of view, and Regy from that of the constitution – which was, he claimed, the same thing. In the circumstances the only solution in his view was that the King should write regularly and openly to the Prime Minister, so arousing in him an understanding of his reciprocal duties.[110]

In November a clutch of European crowned heads were staying at Windsor Castle; Regy and the unwilling Nellie, who more and more disliked pompous functions, were called upon to help entertain them. On the 15th a banquet was held – finer, Regy averred, than the Russian Winter Palace gala feasts which were renowned for their extravagance and splendour. It was the combination of medievalism and twentiety-century finesse which impressed the historical sensibilities of both Eshers. He was aware, too, that the ancient castle with 'the line of beefeaters in their gorgeous dresses, and the luxury of gold plate, flowers and diamonds', together with the comfort and convenience of the suites apportioned to the guests, greatly struck Kaiser William and his Empress. 'Our King makes a better show than William II,' he noted. 'He has more graciousness and dignity. William is ungraceful, nervous and plain. There is no "atmosphere" about him. He has not impressed Grey nor Morley.'[111] To Sir Edward Grey, the Foreign Secretary, he inveighed against the Jews, saying, 'There are far too many of them in my country. They want stamping out. If I did not restrain my people, there would be a Jew-baiting.' These ominous words deeply shocked the Foreign Secretary and, if overheard by Cassel, himself a Jew and who was staying at the Castle, would have struck him as highly distasteful. That perspicacious financier considered the Kaiser's knowledge superficial and his views unreliable. He agreed with Regy that Germany was going to contest with Britain command of the seas and commercial supremacy; her geographical grievance had got to be redressed. She must have outlets for her teeming population, and these outlets could only exist within the confines of the British Empire. In other words Germany was Britain's enemy.[112]

As for Morley, he closely scrutinized the Kaiser at dinner. Similar doubts about his character to those which Regy had expressed were germinating in his mind. Morley observed William's convulsive movements. His energy, said Morley, was a great factor, as it was in Napoleon. Regy admitted that this was the case and said he had, like Napoleon, 'the courage of his desires'. The Empress again found favour. She was 'a dignified figure, admirable *tournure*, and well dressed'.[113]

Two days later the King and Queen of Spain arrived by car from

London. Though only twenty, the Queen of Spain had already grown matronly. In the State Dining Room twenty-four persons sat down for luncheon. They included the King and Queen, the Kaiser and Empress of Germany, the King and Queen of Spain, the King and Queen of Norway and the Queen of Portugal.[114] Regy found the King of Spain a particularly charming, good-humoured and intelligent boy, quite unchanged since he met him two years ago. On that occasion Regy was much interested in the fact that one of the courtiers slept in his bedroom every night to guard him, like the early Valois French kings.[115] Alfonso was given to whimsical behaviour. On running into Regy in the quadrangle he said to him, ' "I want to give you something," and took a Malmaison carnation out of his buttonhole and placed it in mine.' Regy did not say whether he was disappointed or merely surprised.[116]

During this round of official entertainments Regy was impressed by the Prince of Wales's attitude towards India. The Prince showed much concern about the problem of the Indian princes and upper classes being educated in England and then returning to India to become what he termed 'slaves' to a distant monarch and white overseers.[117] He told him, 'Personally I think we have now come to the parting of the ways, we cannot let things rest as they are. We must either trust the natives more and give them a greater share in the government or anyhow allow them to express their views.'[118] Kenneth Rose has remarked about this sentiment that the future King George V revealed more vision than the brilliant Viceroy Curzon.[119]

In December Regy was staying at Sandringham where he drafted for the King a long memorandum to the Prime Minister, expressing His Majesty's concern that the Cabinet had decided to withdraw some 8000 men from the garrisons of South Africa. He asked that careful consideration should be given to it in consultation with Lord Selborne, the High Commissioner, and the General Officer Commanding in South Africa. The King was so suspicious of the War Office that he would not sign any document it sent to him without its first being certified by Regy.[120] The most trivial decision on Army matters made without his first being consulted he regarded as a slight, including an alteration of the shape of the bayonet, which Regy admitted to be 'puerile'.[121]

The party was made merry by the company of the Marquis de Soveral, an intimate friend of the King and great admirer of the Queen. The singularly astute Portuguese diplomat was the most delightful companion and enjoyed nothing more than playing the fool, unless it was talking seriously. He was a splendid conversationalist, and when he did talk seriously his friends realized how clever he was. He had a supreme contempt for his own Government. Known as the

Blue Monkey, this ugly but fascinating man broke many susceptible female hearts in Edwardian society. He was such a favourite with both King Edward and Queen Alexandra that he was allowed liberties which would not have been tolerated in their own subjects. At dinner on this occasion Soveral, who was sitting on the Queen's right, told Regy, across her, that Lord Clarendon, who became rather senile towards the end of his life, asked Queen Victoria, 'Ma'am, can you tell me the secret of your eternal youth?' Without blanching the old Queen replied at once, 'Beecham's pills.'

For Christmas 1907 the King sent Regy the latest of the Windsor Castle catalogues with a personal inscription; and the Queen a gold cigarette case with her monogram. The Eshers spent the festive season at Orchard Lea, with Chat Williamson as their guest.

8

EDWARDIAN DECLINE
1908–1910

The year 1908 opened at the height of Edwardian splendour and glamour – at least on the surface. But the pleasure-loving and pleasure-giving monarch's health was on the wane, and the menace of war on a scale never before experienced was hovering over the heads of men like Regy Esher, aware that the power of peace-keeping amongst the European sovereigns was rapidly declining.

On 4 January Regy went for the twenty-first time to see *The Merry Widow*, 'one of the most charming plays with music ever put on the stage'.[1] His twenty-second attendance may have been in March, when he took Bernard Shaw. The operetta had captivated the whole of Europe. The King had first seen it in Vienna and urged the producer to bring it to London. He did so, but with misgivings and against the advice of friends, putting an unknown, untried girl called Lily Elsie[2] in the title role of Sonia. London was instantly at her feet. Whenever Regy was smitten by an actor or actress – and it was usually the latter – he immediately went backstage, introducing himself to the cast and making friends. He would take the leading lady to supper at the Savoy, and if he liked her very much would invite her to stay. Among his favourites were May Yohé (Maysie), the star of *Florodora*, Edna May, Lydia Flopp (for whom Maurice fell), Fan Danys, Elsa Levy, a popular visitor at the Roman Camp, Maud Allan, who danced in *Salomé* practically naked before King Edward at Marienbad, and of course Ellaline Terriss, Seymour Hicks's wife, to whom he was devoted. Seymour, a talented playwright and author of *The Man in Dress Clothes*, *Bluebell in Fairyland* and *The Earl and the Girl*, became a close friend. It was Regy who was largely responsible for getting Seymour Hicks a knighthood, and honours for Arthur Wing Pinero and Beerbohm Tree. It is hardly surprising, therefore, that in October he was invited to be chairman of a sub-committee of the Shakespeare Memorial Committee, including Granville Barker, Pinero, Bernard Shaw and Beerbohm Tree, to examine the proposals for a National Theatre. It was Granville Barker's aim that a National Theatre should benefit less well-off audiences, and reform Britain's theatrical system. At the first meeting the sub-committee estimated that the enterprise would cost at least £500,000. Not until 1963 did the National Theatre come into being, and then largely through the activities of Regy's son Oliver when chairman of the London Theatre Council and President of the British Drama League.

Chat Williamson, always a great favourite of Nellie's, spent three weeks at Orchard Lea over Christmas and the New Year and then left on 8 January for Vienna. Chat had enjoyed the visit enormously, so Howard Sturgis told the Eshers, having 'wallowed in a sea of caress and tender thought – Isn't that Chatian?'[3] The Eshers were much impressed by the way their visitor had retained his youth and skittishness. Regy told Maurice that Chat

> chose the route of hedonism – the direct pursuit of his own whims and pleasures and he has resolutely stuck to his choice. His path has never been deflected to the right or left. Refined self-indulgence. Luckily he has found friends to help him pursue it. But the man like Napoleon who chooses the nobler life, cannot afford to make excursions up bypaths. If he does he runs enormous risks.[4]

For his part Chat was much impressed by the Brett family. He considered that Nellie had improved socially. Oliver he found 'very clever (against which adjective Regy pencilled, 'I wonder') but shifty!' As for Doll, her emancipation had not yet been totally achieved. Her escapades with the Ranee were simply the fruit of her parents' neglect. Regy, however, was so alarmed by her eccentricities that he called in a certain Dr W.N. Barron, who specialized in what today we would call psychoanalysis. This sensible man wrote Regy a forthright report on his patient's condition, which, he affirmed, was not hysterical; it was mentally morbid. He bluntly attributed it to lack of parental love and sympathy, and said it was the result of Doll's environment, which her parents could modify. 'She has an obsession, unhealthy, and of pseudo-sexual manner,' namely for the Ranee. Her parents were proposing to remove the only enthusiasm the poor young woman had. 'Your lordship will no doubt forgive me for calling a spade a spade, and candidly your daughter's interests are not centred in home life. At present they are centred in S. Ascot.'[5] He advised Regy to send her abroad, to travel, but in the autumn Regy was making inquiries of the

Secretary of the Slade School. Doll went there to study painting, and in this way her career was established for seventy years.

In fact at the age of twenty-five Doll went through an experience which probably disturbed her emotional life and affected her attitude to men permanently. It was her first sexual encounter. Regy wrote to Maurice on 20 September,

> Here is something I am not supposed to know. . . . Doll a year ago, at Olea, was kissed by Loulou, unexpectedly, and kicked him on the shins! A picture for you! He tried again and failed. At Nuneham he took her into a dark grotto, and asked her to sit on his knee. This handsome offer she rejected. These were his old games, played with both sexes for years. Curious in a Cabinet Minister, because so risky! She told Chat, and yesterday was talking about it, quite naturally to Syv and Eve (Brand) and Oliver (the latter told me). Note all the aspects. Loulou *still* not to be trusted with his *friends*! For of course, he did not mean to stop at kissing. Then Doll of course told the Ranee, and everyone else, except me.
>
> By this proceeding she puts it in the power of Henry Brooke, or anyone else who hears of it, to insinuate that I tolerate and condone. It never occurs to her that only two right courses are open. To say nothing, or to tell me. The former was defensible. The course she takes indefensible. However, I am to know nothing, and in this I acquiesce.

The old satyr Loulou Harcourt's advances went far beyond kissing, as Sean Hignett explains in *Brett*.[6] To Doll they were horrifying and traumatic. Had Regy been more in tune with Doll's predicaments and ambitions, his daughter would probably have sought his advice and comfort. It must be conceded that the way her father told his younger son of the incident is callous and lacking in sympathy; and Regy barely criticized Loulou for disloyal and brutish behaviour towards a friend's daughter.

The Slade led to Doll's introduction to the Morrells at Garsington Manor, and their Bloomsbury friends. Lady Ottoline Morrell, for whom she developed an infatuation, took her under her wing. Doll, known to her new world as Brett, cut her blonde hair short and dressed like a boy, becoming first the intimate companion of Lytton Strachey, Carrington and Mark Gertler, before moving on to Katherine Mansfield, Middleton Murry and D.H. Lawrence.

Sylvia had published her first book, *A Story with a Purpose*, in 1906 and was sitting at the feet of J.M. Barrie, now welcomed by the whole Brett family under the nickname of 'The Furry Beast'. She was engaged on an article for *The Westminster Gazette*, assailing the current method of bringing up girls, of which she had some experience. Regy, whose liberal reactions could be unpredictable, considered it quite admirably composed. He even went so far as to draft a letter to the editor of that journal, signing himself 'Ancien Régime'. He refuted Syv's theme that well-bred and carefully brought-up young girls of the day could not hold their own in life's treacherous passage with young men of the same kind against the more experienced young ladies of the theatrical profession. He referred disparagingly to 'the very small class of white-waistcoated and possibly eye-glassed youths who haunt stage doors of theatres and drift from Covent Garden balls to the Trocodero'. It is not quite clear to whose side Sylvia's father was allying himself.

At the very end of 1907 *Queen Victoria's Letters and Journals* were published in three volumes. As long ago as 1901 King Edward had given Regy permission to start arranging his mother's correspondence, which amounted to millions of words; it was this task which had brought him the keepership of the Royal Archives. As he read through the voluminous material Regy concluded that the early papers up to the death of the Prince Consort in 1861 ought to be carefully collated, vetted and made public, subject to judicious omissions; he obtained King Edward's consent. Regy realized that, with all his other interests, the task of editing required assistance. During his frequent visits to Eton in the 1890s he had made friends with Arthur Benson, then a house-master. Benson was a hypochondriac and, though there was little physically wrong with him, in 1903 he concluded that being a school house-master was too much for him in spite of the fact that he was only forty-one. Benson was delighted when Regy asked him to become his assistant – at this time he was a great admirer of Regy, and his letters to him are almost deferential. But as time passed Benson stood up to him. He did not approve of all levity being eliminated from the Queen's correspondence, wishing to retain its spontaneity and colour. Yet both men were scrupulous and accurate, and worked together in apparent harmony, Benson conceding to Regy, 'I do not honestly think you need ever be afraid of being too frank with me on any point.' Regy allowed Benson the whole of the joint share of payment from their publisher John Murray up to £1200, and beyond that a two-thirds share of profits, leaving a mere third for himself.

Notwithstanding this ostensibly happy relationship, Regy looked on Benson as an over-credulous old woman. Benson's attitude at the time can be gauged by a sentence in his journals: 'I feel E is always a little contemptuous of me.'[7] Later sentences indicate that he was a little resentful of Regy's role in reading through selected letters while leaving to him all the spadework. In years to come he became more critical still, calling him 'essentially secret and indolent, with a touch of decadence, greedy of reputation, wealth & power, but afraid of real responsibility'.[8]

At the express wish of the King, the two editors agreed that it would not be suitable to publish letters written after Prince Albert's death, when the Queen's loss of power in dealing with political matters was most marked, and showed her in an hysterical and somewhat selfish light. The joint intention was that the papers should illustrate the early training of the Queen by Melbourne and then Peel; the coming of the Prince Consort; the influence over him of Uncle Leopold, King of the Belgians; the growth of the Prince's powers; the change in the relation between the Crown and the ministers after the retirement of Lord Aberdeen in 1855; and the culmination of the Prince Consort's rule between 1859 and 1861. 'Of course with regard to the last much could be said, but we are hardly the people to say it.'[9] The Esher and Benson three volumes were such a success that the editors were pressed by many people to continue with further volumes, but Regy announced that it was not yet feasible because so many subsequent delicate events, such as the unification of Germany, the Franco-Prussian War, the Russo-Turkish struggle in the Near East and the German-Danish differences still rankled in the minds of contemporaries, and also because many public figures concerned in them – not excluding the King – were still living. He knew it was a pity, because of the interesting development of the Queen's character, but felt obliged to counsel the King that it would be best to postpone publication of four subsequent volumes for a generation at least. King Edward, as usual with Regy, concurred.[10] Only in 1922, on the intercession of Regy, did King George V reluctantly give his consent to further volumes of the Queen's papers being published. By then Regy was too old to act as editor, and the task fell to George Buckle.

King Edward had to admit that the Prince Consort had been a bad judge of English boys and English life. He made Regy sit down with him in his room and go through two volumes of old letters concerning his early upbringing. The King told him how much he had hated being given a house of his own at Oxford, and thought it had impeded his education there. He also detested being made a lieutenant-colonel in the Army too soon, protesting that he should have begun at the bottom and worked his way up.[11] A month later Regy sat with him for an hour and a half listening to further reminiscences of his early life and particulars of his and his sisters' financial affairs, the substance of which Regy did not disclose to a living soul, or even to his journal. It was on this occasion that, speaking of Regy's success with his Territorial campaign, the King said, 'You are a wonderful man, everything you touch succeeds.' Whereupon Regy kissed his hand when he parted from him.[12]

In spite of the fact that, owing to excessive caution, scarcely a single letter of the Queen's was published in its entirety, the volumes were faultlessly edited and the explanatory notes all that could be desired. The only thing to mar their unanimously favourable reception was the blazing row that ensued between *The Times* and John Murray. *The Times* was vitriolic in its criticism of the form of publication, maintaining that it should have been a biography, that the books were too expensive and that the publishers, against whom they began to wage a vendetta, were trading on the name of Queen Victoria. Murray threatened legal action unless *The Times* retracted, and the only reason they did not pursue it was the King's close concern with the book. The so-called Book War was ended by Regy, who brought about agreements between the litigants to the ultimate satisfaction of both parties. *The Times* behaved shabbily throughout. In October a new cheap edition was published by Murray in conjunction with *The Times*.

A more unfortunate – because lasting – consequence of the publication, and one unknown to the public, was the destruction of many of the original, unbowdlerized manuscripts. King Edward burnt several packets of private letters from the Queen about family concerns, letters relating to Princess Frederick of Prussia's marriage and letters from the Queen (lent, incidentally, by Lord Rothschild, who was their owner) to Disraeli. The King also burnt all the letters concerning the Lady Flora Hastings case and the Granville correspondence.[13] Regy was permitted to read these papers, and it is a pity that he did not think fit to suggest that they should be kept, for the King nearly always accepted his advice. On the contrary, in some instances Regy encouraged his royal master to destroy them. On top of this holocaust must be mentioned Princess Beatrice's systematic destruction of some thirty volumes of letters to Prince Alfred, Duke of Edinburgh, and the Grand Duchess of Hesse, besides her industrious manipulation of the scissors on her mother's diaries.

Defence was still one of Regy's principal concerns. Work on the Committee of Imperial Defence took up a great deal of his time. After Balfour's resignation the CID had turned into a secret conclave and had failed to become the focus of military opinion. During the nine years before the First World War its offices were at No. 2 Whitehall Gardens, a house with a peaceful outlook on the river, and Regy's room had once been occupied by Disraeli. The recollection brought home to Regy that the CID was undoing the work of Dizzy and Bismarck at the Congress of Berlin in 1878, at which they imagined they had curtailed Russian encroachments on eastern Europe and brought enduring peace to the Near East.

In January and February 1908 the CID were occupied in prolonged discussion of invasion and the forces which Britain needed to repel an assault by a potential enemy such as Germany. Dissension over opposing policies within the Admiralty was becoming acute: Sir John Fisher, the First Sea Lord, was attacked by Lord Charles Beresford, in charge of the Channel Fleet, for weakening the Navy; and by the Government for wishing to make it unduly powerful.[14] Relations between the two admirals were becoming increasingly strained. Politicians, in defiance of party loyalties, were taking sides; Regy was a strong partisan of the First Sea Lord. He had prepared a note on the invasion question, printed for the CID,[15] in which he pointed out that the country might be ill prepared to resist a raiding force of 12,000 men, particularly if the Regular Army was abroad at the time. In such circumstances the King would be empowered to call on the Territorial Force. But commerce would be badly disrupted if the staff of major firms were suddenly enlisted. Therefore he advised that the number of regular troops sent abroad at any given time should be limited.

The King, on the other hand, ever sensitive about the state of national and imperial defence and the condition of the forces, was much put out by an article by J.L. Garvin, editor of the *Observer*, criticizing the unsatisfactory state of the Army. Regy begged the King not to pay undue attention, and denied the truth of Garvin's alarmist remarks. 'How can any of these excellent quill-driving gentlemen know?' he wrote caustically but fatuously. 'Your Majesty has had experience of them. The man who writes that kind of article is a clever, half-educated, long-haired, seedy-looking person who hangs about public offices, and would black Sir John Fisher's boots or write anything he could pick up from the private secretary of a minister.' Regy can hardly be excused if he did not know at the time who the writer was; and if he did know, he was being very foolish indeed, for Garvin was one of the most astute political journalists of all time, and when he issued a warning he was motivated solely by conviction and patriotic concern. Regy was convinced that all the generals would deny the charge. 'Your Majesty can *never*, under a voluntary system, have an army on the lines of a continental army.' Haldane, he persisted, had in fact done more for the Regular Army than any minister since Cardwell.[16] But the King was not reassured. Frederick Ponsonby told Regy that the King had disagreed with a great deal of what he had said. He feared that Regy paid too much attention to the opinions of serving officers, who naturally had no alternative but to obey the Secretary of State's changes. The King said the British were the laughing stock of Europe; that efficiency had given way to economy. It would have been wiser to create a Territorial Army before reducing the Regular Army.[17] But Regy was not going to be put down so lightly. He told Knollys that the King was wrong in his assertion that the British were a laughing stock; he doubted whether at any time since Palmerston's day had Britain loomed so large in the European hegemony.[18] And to the King he wrote that the condition of the Army was far superior to what it had been in 1899.[19]

It was probably in 1891 that Regy and Fisher first met; they took to each other at once. Fisher's reasons for their mutual admiration are well expressed in his *Recollections*. They had the same sort of Machiavellian mind. As Sir Frederick Ponsonby wrote,

> Both preferred to come in at the back door instead of the front. There was something tortuous about both of them, but while Fisher loved a fight and was prepared to stand or fall by his measures, Esher was very susceptible to public opinion and shrank from any responsibility. I always think that Esher's strong point was that he never minded who got credit for any measure he devised so long as it was adopted by the authorities.[20]

At the same time Jackie Fisher was extraordinarily forthright; he never minced his words before the rawest subaltern or the mightiest monarch, and never paused to reflect before he spoke. He was a contradiction of ruthless toughness and almost feminine sensitivity. His day began at four o'clock in the morning. Deeply religious, when in London he would go into Westminster Abbey before dawn to meditate. He was also passionately fond of dancing. Staying at Windsor, he rolled back the carpet in the drawing room, seized a lady-in-waiting and, to the surprise of the King and Queen, began to waltz. At sea he would dance with his officers. While on board the royal yacht during a visit by the Tsar and Tsarina of Russia, he made the imperial and royal families spin round the deck. Some of them said afterwards it was the happiest and most carefree fortnight they had ever spent. He became the devoted crony of King Edward, who allowed him to take personal liberties denied to others but was once overheard to remonstrate with Jackie, 'Will you kindly leave off shaking your fist in my face!'

Since 1904 Fisher had been absolutely convinced that war with Germany was inevitable, and had been largely responsible for the ensuing arms race. His naval reforms involved the wholesale destruction of small ships; instead of them he introduced the immense dreadnought and encouraged the building of destroyers. By this means he reduced the Navy estimates in 1904–5. Old-fashioned sailors were highly critical of these drastic measures. Yet he was always supported by the King – and Regy.

After this date his rambling, often un-coordinated missives – which Regy termed his 'nautical love letters' – invariably began, 'My beloved Friend', and would end, 'Yours to a cinder', or 'Yours till Hell freezes'. Jackie, as he was known to all ranks, was tremendously popular on the lower deck and an inspiration to young officers, who admired his flouting of routine and contempt for custom and rigid precedent.

Lord Charles Beresford was of a different mould. A dashing sportsman, prominent figure in smart society and friend of the King since childhood, he had none of the originality of Fisher. Courageous, conventional and devoted to the Navy, he was a difficult man, impatient of control, and from the very first he was out of sympathy with Fisher's changes. Whereas he allowed his personal antagonism to Fisher to cloud the later years of his career, the other merely brushed aside his rival as a brainless nonentity who had only 'the low cunning and power of repartee of an Irish car driver; and he understands the limelight'. When the Admiralty Board was asked by the Government, supported by Lord Charles, to reduce the naval estimates by a further £1½ million, Fisher threatened to resign. Lloyd George and Churchill argued with him in vain, but Campbell-Bannerman, who did not really esteem him, ordered Asquith, the Chancellor of the Exchequer, to give way. Jackie maintained that Beresford wanted to decimate the Fleet. Enraged, Lord Charles feigned illness and so enveigled to his bedside those ministers opposed to Fisher – which, Regy declared, 'was worthy of Pepys'.[21] Jackie, Knollys and Regy, dubbed 'The Triumvirate' by *The National Review*, dined at the Carlton, drank champagne and rejoiced. So deep was the mutual hatred of Fisher and Beresford that Regy suggested to Knollys that the King ought to summon the two and make them shake hands in his presence.[22]

Regy did not, however, approve of Jackie's autocratic tendencies, and did not hesitate to tell him so. 'Your pitfall is that you want to carry your one man rule from war into peace, and all history shows the fatal track along which *One Man* has walked to disaster.'[23] This was the true Liberal reiterating his party's basic philosophy. He also urged Fisher to range himself with the CID against Beresford, instead of mistrusting it and treating the members as though they were idiots. The King likewise took him to task when he had behaved particularly outrageously. Fisher admitted to Regy that the King had sent for him and told him that he was Jekyll and Hyde – Jekyll in being successful in his work at the Admiralty, Hyde as a failure in society; also that he talked too freely and was reported to have said that the King would see him through anything. It was bad for both of them because, if the Prime Minister should decide to dismiss Fisher, the King, being a constitutional monarch, could not prevent it.[24]

On 29 May Regy informed the King that Balfour had attended a meeting of the CID that morning, at the request of the Prime Minister. It was an occasion unique in the history of political administration for a Prime Minister to call into counsel the Leader of

Reginald Baliol Brett at Eton, 1868, at the age of 17, wearing his rowing blazer and 'Britannia' boater.

Staying at Studley Royal, Yorkshire, with the Ripons, in the 1870s.
Back row: Charles Williamson (Chat), Lord Ripon, Reginald Brett.
Front row: Eleanor (Nellie) Brett, Loulou Harcourt, Lady Ripon (Hat), Sir William Harcourt, Lady Harcourt.

Chat (Charles Williamson), Reginald Brett's lifelong friend from Eton days, at Orchard Lea, Windsor Forest, about 1887.

The Gallery at Orchard Lea, Winkfield, about 1887, the Bretts' first house in the country, which they built in 1883.

Eleanor (Reginald's wife, Nellie Brett),
Lady Esher, about 1900.

Oliver Brett (the elder son, later 3rd Viscount Esher), aged about 25 in 1906.

Dorothy (Doll) Brett, the elder daughter, an artist in Bloomsbury circles, who painted this self portrait in oils, 1920.

Sylvia (Syv) Brett, when Ranee Muda of Sarawak, about 1912. She was married to the last White Rajah, Vyner Brooke.

Maurice Brett, the younger son, when Assistant Provost Marshal in his Paris office during the First World War.

Lord Esher confronting Britannia. Caricature by Max Beerbohm, 1911, entitled *Pertness Rebuked*. Lord Esher: 'Never mind who I am. Just go and do what I tell you.'

Zena Dare, a well-known and popular actress, a few years before her marriage to Maurice Brett in 1911.

The Roman Camp, Callander, Perthshire. It was acquired by Lord Esher in 1897, and remained his favourite house until his death.

the Opposition over deliberations of a most secret sort, connected with the defence of the realm. A.J.B. excelled himself: he gave a masterly exposition of most carefully formulated views. He was listened to in reverent silence. Regy considered that the luncheon party which Balfour gave at the Carlton on 3 July for Asquith, French, Knollys and Sir Charles Ottley, Secretary of the CID, was no less a triumph, the host's object being to bring the leaders of the Government and Opposition together on the highest questions of peace strategy.

By the beginning of November Regy was able to tell the King that the CID report on invasion had been considered. The Committee had endorsed the opinion of the sub-committee presided over by Balfour that, assuming the Navy to be maintained at a second-class power standard, the British Isles were safe from invasion. There was a novel rider attached, which was that an expedition fitted out secretly in German ports could not effect a landing by evading the British Fleet; nevertheless at all times an army must be kept in Britain of such strength that no hostile force of less than 70,000 would have a chance of success. The CID's decision had naturally strengthened the hand of the Secretary of State for War against those who had been anxious to reduce Army numbers. Furthermore, at least six dreadnoughts must be laid down every year for the next four years.[25] At the same time A.J.B., in a long talk with Regy, said he had assured Asquith that he did not want a debate in Parliament which might increase the risk of war by speaking about it in public in this way. At the request of the Government, also, the King asked Lord Roberts not to raise the question of a German invasion in debate in the Lords.

The French were appealing for a pledge of military intervention from Britain if Germany declared war upon them. Auguste Huguet, the French Military Attaché in London, lunched at Orchard Lea on 11 November in order to sound Regy on this point, since the Quai d'Orsay regarded him as the King's mouthpiece. Huguet had been instructed to convey the information that, if the answer were favourable, British troops should be put under the command of their generalissimo. On 14 December a note by Lord Esher[26] on this very matter was printed for the CID. The author's view was that Britain could not commit herself to the amount of help she might offer France, bearing in mind circumstances attending the crisis, conditions in India and the Empire, and public feeling generally.

How real was the danger of war in the last months of 1908? To answer that question it is necessary to take a view of the events leading up to November of that year. In a sense Regy was indirectly responsible for triggering off a war of offensive words between Great Britain and Germany, as represented by the Kaiser. On 22 January he had written a letter to the Navy League, enclosing a copy of another

from him to the Imperial Maritime League, refusing to join the
Council of that League on the grounds that its primary aim was to get
rid of Fisher, the First Sea Lord. Rather unwisely he gave the Navy
League permission to publicize his enclosure addressed to the Imperial Maritime League, which also referred to the fact that some
quarters were minimizing the German building programme while
pressing Parliament to insist upon a reduction of British naval
estimates. The Navy League forwarded the letter to *The Times*, which
published it on 6 February. At this the Kaiser, always sensitive to the
Navy League's opinions, did an unprecedented thing by writing a
personal letter to Lord Tweedmouth, then First Lord of the Admiralty. The rumours in the British papers, he averred, of 'German danger'
and 'the German challenge to British naval supremacy', which were
being dinned into British ears, 'might in the end create most
deplorable results'. He strenuously denied the truth of these rumours.
'The German Fleet is built *against* nobody at all,' he insisted. 'Our
actual programme in course of execution is practically only an
exchange of old material for new, but *not* an *addition* to the number of
units originally laid down by the [Naval] Bill ten years ago.' Britain
had an absolute right to build as many ships as she wanted. 'It is very
galling to the Germans to see their country continually held up as the
sole danger & menace to Britain.' And he went on:

> In the letter Lord Esher caused to be published a short time ago he
> wrote: 'that every German from the Emperor down to the last man
> wished for the downfall of Sir John Fisher.' Now I am at a loss to tell
> whether the supervision of the foundations & drains of the Royal
> Palaces is apt to qualify somebody for the judgement of naval affairs in
> general. . . . The phrase is a piece of unmitigated balderdash, and has
> created intense merriment in the circles of those 'who know here'.
> Actually the British Navy is 5 times stronger than the German.[27]

On the same day the German Emperor wrote to King Edward from
Berlin on a postcard, enclosed in an envelope:

> Dearest Uncle, the very animated discussion in the British press about
> naval matters have [*sic*] interested me very much. But I have detected
> some uneasiness about the German Naval Programme, which is
> unfounded, arising as it does from misconceptions. I therefore took the
> liberty to write to Lord Tweedmouth & to give him the information
> necessary to enable him to see clearly. With best love to Aunt and
> cousins, ever your devoted nephew, Willy.

In the envelope he enclosed a copy of his letter to the First Lord. King
Edward was enraged. He was anyway feeling very distressed by the

assassination in Lisbon of the King of Portugal, with whom he had much in common, and his elder son. 'The excellent, brave King, and that nice amiable Duke of Braganza,' Regy wrote in his journal, 'such a jolly boy, whom I took over the Castle a year or so since.'[28]

Lord Tweedmouth, a foolish man, flattered to be the recipient of a personal letter from the Kaiser, replied over-politely that of course England bore no unfriendly feelings towards his country, but 'as Your Majesty is already aware, the press in Great Britain does not admit any official control, especially on the subject of the Navy'.[29] A memorandum answering His Imperial Majesty's letter point by point was being despatched by the Foreign Office to the British Ambassador in Berlin. Lord Tweedmouth then proceeded to boast to all and sundry of the honour that had been bestowed upon him. King Edward, on the other hand, sent an icy reply to his bumptious nephew: 'Your writing to my First Lord of the Admiralty is a "new departure" and I do not see how he can prevent our Press from calling attention to the great increase in the building of German ships of war which necessitates our also increasing our Navy. Believe me, your affectionate Uncle.'[30]

Lord Tweedmouth's inability to keep his mouth shut enabled the British press to get hold of the story and make the most of it. Colonel Repington was not slow in publishing a very mischievous and indiscreet article in *The Times*, disclosing what had happened and exacerbating feelings both in Germany and at home.

At a levée on the 19th Fisher rushed up to his 'beloved friend' jubilantly. In telling Regy that he had received the greatest compliment ever paid to man by being in the Kaiser's bad books, he disclosed that the King was very cross with him. 'He began in violence against you,' he wrote, 'but I pointed out to him that *I* was the culprit because *I* it was who showed you all the plans at Portsmouth, and also it was out of *pure friendship* to *me* that you wrote the letter. . . . So it was rather lovely, & he is a sweet!'[31] The King agreed with Fisher that admittedly it was a good letter because Esher was a most able man. But it did not prevent His Majesty from writing Regy what he considered a timely and well-merited reproof. He deeply regretted

the publication of the letter which Lord Esher wrote to the Navy League as the remarks about Sir John Fisher were very unfortunate, and though Lord Esher wished to do Sir John a good turn, the King is afraid the reverse is the result.

The allusion also to the German Emperor was likewise very unfortunate, and has, the King knows, caused him great annoyance.

The next time the King sees Lord Esher, he will point out to him how injudicious were the remarks which he made as to Sir John Fisher having told him of the future plans of Sir John when the latter was still Commander in Chief at Portsmouth.

It was not often that Regy received such chastisement from his master, and he was upset. Like a whipped schoolboy, he wrote a grovelling apology for his indiscretion, assuring his royal master somewhat pusillanimously that his letter to the Navy League was not meant for publication, at least not widely in the national press. Nevertheless he was deeply concerned by the crisis in the Navy brought about by the disarmers and the minimizers of the German programme.[32]

The King soon forgave him, as always. Besides, news of Campbell-Bannerman's succession of heart attacks foretold a change of Prime Ministers. John Morley had just visited the old man on his deathbed. He was very cheerful and addressed him in broad Scots as a fellow national. They talked philosophy and religion. C.-B. said, 'You know, I have put politics on one side and never think about them.' Morley's comment to Regy was, 'A curious position for a Prime Minister!'[33] Accordingly, Regy's advice on the constitutional problem about to be faced was badly needed by the monarch. Regy was at once asked to look up papers relating to the precedent that confronted Queen Victoria when calling on Lord John Russell on Palmerston's sudden demise in 1865. Queen Victoria's case had been straightforward; she was quietly at Windsor Castle and readily accessible. King Edward, on the other hand, was going to Biarritz for a holiday, and nothing would stop him. In the circumstances Regy advised that the moment Campbell-Bannerman retired or died the Prime Minister designate, Asquith, would have to go to Biarritz and kiss hands either in the British Consulate or on board a British ship. The King told Regy that he would not be as intimate with Asquith as with C.-B., for whom he had warm feelings. He then turned to the Kaiser business and laughed. 'When next the German Emperor comes over,' he said, 'we must hide you away, or send you on a bicycle tour.' And when Regy said goodbye he kissed his hand. Their relations were as before. On 5 April C.-B. resigned and Asquith had to dash to Biarritz. For the first time in his reign the papers criticized the King for dereliction of duty; he had left the country when he knew his Prime Minister was dying. Regy had known all along that his master's absence would be a mistake, but for once he had not liked to say anything.

Good came out of the Kaiser's letter in that Balfour drew from Asquith a declaration that the Navy would in the next three years lay down ships enough to ensure British superiority. Nor did Regy's royal scolding prevent him writing an important article in the May issue of *The National Review*, entitled 'Today and Tomorrow',[34] on the serious menace to Britain's maritime trade by the enormous growth of the German Navy, and its shift from the Mediterranean to the North Sea.

By October the situation in the Near East was very grave, with a real danger of Bulgaria attacking Turkey on the pretext that Bulgarians were being maltreated in Macedonia. Furthermore, Austria's annexation of Bosnia and Herzegovina came as a great blow and surprise to King Edward. He had just returned from visiting the Emperor Franz Josef, who made no reference whatever to his intentions.

Regy did not waste time before he took steps to make his measure with the new Prime Minister. In May he called on Asquith in Downing Street and was received in the Cabinet Room downstairs. Regy straightaway asked him if he had any special injunctions for him as a member of the CID; Asquith begged him to remain on the Committee. Regy also asked if he might continue publishing articles on the present situation. Asquith counselled him to stick to historical subjects rather than current topics, which Regy did not seem to interpret as a snub.[35] Their relations, though strictly cordial, were never to be more intimate than Asquith's with the King. Regy would never drop in on Asquith as he did on Balfour, to be received in Arthur's bedroom and allowed to sit on the end of his bed and talk about books until noon. Yet Asquith recognized in Regy a valuable intermediary. Within a matter of weeks he was begging him to persuade Winston Churchill, who was pressing for the reduction of the Army estimates, to settle his quarrel with Haldane; and in December chose him as the fittest man to obtain from Balfour his views on the defence schemes. He also acknowledged him to be an expert on Army matters, pronouncing his secret document prepared for the CID 'a most important State paper', and ordering it to be printed.

Regy was somewhat critical of the new regime at Downing Street. When Morley told him that after dinner with the Asquiths to meet Clemenceau they sat down to bridge, implying that there was no conversation, Regy exclaimed how different the atmosphere at No. 10 was from that of Gladstone's time. He thought that the court had much to do with this change, by abandoning the tense atmosphere that had prevailed in Queen Victoria's reign for the laxness of King Edward's. The change at court was reflected in the ministers. When Morley inquired what would happen when the Prince of Wales succeeded, Regy replied simply that everything would change again.[36]

As it was, he was cultivating the friendship and confidence of the Prince and Princess of Wales. He respected the Prince for his sterling qualities, but was under no illusion that he had the mental capacity of the King. Yet he considered the Princess to be more intelligent than Queen Alexandra, though without the latter's charm. He was gratified by her pronounced historical sense and curiosity about the past, which were not shared by her husband.

The morning after Campbell-Bannerman's death the Prince of Wales telephoned, inviting Regy to an early luncheon at Marlborough House; he was very worried about something, and had an admission to make. This was just what Regy relished. On the guest's arrival he was told by the Prince that he had 'put his foot in it' by telling Winston Churchill in the course of conversation that Asquith was not a gentleman. The Princess interrupted with, 'You said it, George, at the top of your voice. Everyone heard you.' Winston of course had repeated it to Rosebery and others. Regy agreed that it was an unfortunate remark to let slip, especially to someone unreliable such as Winston, but there was nothing that could now be done about it. They must hope that no friend would be so mischievous as to pass it on to the object of this criticism. The Prince was very humble and contrite and agreed he was too outspoken at times. Actually he liked Asquith, but not Winston, which made the lapse all the more unfortunate. After luncheon Regy had the first of a series of long talks with the Princess about the education of her children. It went as follows:

> *Princess*: George refuses absolutely to make any distinction between the boys at Osborne and David.
> *E.*: I think he is right.
> *Princess*: But George goes too far. I am most anxious that David should learn German. Captain Sinclair objects, and says he *must* do what all the other boys do, and nothing different. You see how George has suffered from not knowing French and German. The other day in Paris *I* enjoyed everything. But he was not really amused. He knows nothing about pictures or history. He is told something about Francis I, and it conveys nothing to him.[37]

She then begged Regy to speak to the Prince of Wales. Regy exhorted her to tell David everything. 'When my boys were at that age [fourteen], I talked to them on equal terms, as if they were grown up. It is the wisest and safest plan.' She must also explain to him the nature of his future responsibilities.

> *E.*: The danger you all suffer from is that no one tells you the truth, and you have no chances of getting false ideas either about things or people rectified by discussion. Most people are shy and stiff with you, and you are shy and stiff with them. The vast majority think that it is easier to agree with all you say. You hear from malicious people statements adverse to someone, and you have no opportunity of hearing the other side. To convince a young prince of this fact is the highest education. He should be brought up to understand why Haroun al Raschid went about in disguise.[38]

The Princess quite agreed. She had found a friend who was a statesman and yet a man of the world, a man who had the courage not to mince his words, and to be candid with a genuine wish to help and guide.[39]

The Prince of Wales did not talk to his sons on equal terms; he merely bawled at them and did not expect them to answer him back. Yet he told Regy that he dared to stand up to his grandmother. When he was twenty Queen Victoria had sent for him. On his arrival at Windsor she had been charming and talked of all sorts of things. When he reached his room he found a note from her asking him to change his name from George, which she hated because it reminded her of George IV, to Albert. He refused point blank, and she accepted it.[40]

In September Regy was bidden to Balmoral. His Majesty was most kind, and they talked on a wide range of subjects for an hour and a half.

The King: I want very confidentially, to ask your opinion. Can you tell me what you think of Burghclere as [Loulou Harcourt's] successor? [Harcourt was First Commissioner of Works, and did not in fact resign until 1910.] I am brought much into contact with this Minister, as you know. How would Burghclere get on with me and *Pom*?[41]

E.: I think Your Majesty would like him. . . . He has some artistic taste, and knowledge, and he is a man of the world, and a pleasant fellow. He would not interfere much with Pom.

The King: As for Winston, there never has been anything like the self-advertisement of this marriage of his.

E.: Winston is *very* young in some things.[42]

Then they got on to the German Emperor. The King said he was 'impossible', and 'two keels to one' was the only answer.

Sir Edward Grey was one of the guests, and he and Regy went for long walks. Regy was deeply impressed by Grey's singularly fine character: he was honest, dignified and unselfish, with a gentleman's high sense of duty. Someone once remarked in Lloyd George's presence that Grey was the sort of man who, if asked to sign something he shouldn't, or be shot, would say, 'Shoot!', to which Lloyd George interjected, 'Yes, but if you said, "Sign or I'll shoot your pet squirrel," he would sign at once.' Grey told Regy that a man's character was not formed by environment or actions, but by his thoughts when he was alone. He believed Winston to be a genius; his fault was that phrases mastered him, rather than he them. He thought the Kaiser not quite sane, and very superficial, a view which coincided with Regy's own.

That touch of insanity was emphasized by the astonishing interview given by the Kaiser to *The Daily Telegraph* on 28 October, in which he claimed that he alone had prevented France and Russia from humiliating Britain in 1900. He alone had drafted a plan of campaign against the Boers, sent it to the Queen of England and saw it victoriously adopted by Lord Roberts. He and a select few of his countrymen had been Britain's friends, whereas the majority of the German people were anti-British.

The interview, gratuitously sought,[43] infuriated the entire British public. The King told Regy that it had made his visit to Berlin in February very problematical. To the Prince of Wales he said, 'I always suspected that he hated me, and now I know it.' The Prince then reminded his father how nineteen years earlier the Kaiser was to go to Vienna on a state visit. He was furious when he learned that the Prince was on a private visit to Prince Rudolph, and sent the British Military Attaché in Berlin to Vienna to tell Prince George that he ought not to be there. 'I will not have him taking the wind out of my sails,' he shrieked. Prince George, hurt by his rudeness, left for Romania.[44]

The Emperor's reaction at the reception of his interview with a leading British newspaper may be judged from his behaviour at the opera in Berlin a few days later. He flung himself into Mrs Cornwallis West's box, Regy wrote, 'and gesticulating wildly, and shouting loudly, said, "Well, this is the way I am treated in England, when I try to show I am her friend. Just wait a while, and we shall see how the English will live to regret!" '[45] Grey considered that the Kaiser was such a menace to international peace that he ought to be put under restraint. Regy wondered whether he had not inherited some of George III's madness.[46]

On the day of publication of the Kaiser's 'interview' Regy, lunching with Lord Morley, Secretary of State for India, was asked if he would consider succeeding Minto as Viceroy. 'I said decidedly *No*. I should hate it. Besides the Viceroy today is a mere puppet in the hands of the Secretary of State. I did not say this.'[47] Three weeks later he was pressed by Morley to reconsider the proposal. Again Regy protested that he was greatly honoured, but reluctant to give up his work with the King and the CID, which he was confident of doing better, and for which he was better suited, than the other. He wrote in his journal:

> This, I believe, a unique experience, within four years to have been offered the S of S for War by Mr Balfour, and the Viceroyship by his successor in office. I am confident that in going to India, I should be throwing away the substance of power for the shadow. . . . Besides, every day questions arise, of vital importance to our country, when I can have my say, and can sway a decision. India would be for me (it sounds vain, but it isn't) parochial.[48]

On the other hand he did accept the Prime Minister's offer of a Knight Grand Cross of the Order of the Bath, which he valued as a nice commentary on the Kaiser's impertinences of the previous year. It also meant that the King had not only forgiven his indiscreet letter to the Navy League but positively endorsed his contempt for and dislike of his imperial nephew.

Regy was deeply involved in the antipathy between Fisher and Beresford which was to cause a wide division in the Cabinet over naval policy. The sides taken and the rows that ensued almost caused a scandal in political and social circles. Opposition to the First Sea Lord and the new First Lord, Reginald McKenna, in their hastily drawn-up programme to accelerate the building of eight battleships, resulted in the resignation of Beresford from the Channel Command and his being championed by Lloyd George and Winston Churchill within the Cabinet. The Prince of Wales, who unlike his father strongly disapproved of Fisher, wrote a frenzied letter to Regy about men who put party before patriotism and the welfare of their country. 'It makes me absolutely disgusted with politics when these kind of things go on. We must maintain our Navy at the two Power standard plus 10% otherwise we shall cease to be a power in the world at all, & it is also a matter of life & death with us.'[49] These sentiments were those of every Tory in the state who knew what was going on behind closed doors. The Cabinet as a whole supported Fisher. An Admiralty Inquiry reproved both Fisher and Beresford for not working together for the best advancement of Admiralty policy.

Regy spent the first months of 1909 being bashed like a shuttlecock from one side of the political net to the other, intriguing with A.J.B. to threaten the Government if it did not support Fisher, urging the Prime Minister to modify his bias against Fisher, beseeching Fisher to mitigate his venom against his critics, and arguing with Winston and Lloyd George, whom he advised that resignation would ruin them both and do no good to anyone. Lloyd George took the point at once. Winston was stubborn and surly. At the same time Regy urged his friend Jackie to begin building his ships for all he was worth. He also spoke very plainly to the Prince of Wales, deprecating his open criticism of Fisher. He pointed out that the King was acting constitutionally in supporting the Board of Admiralty and his First Sea Lord. It would be a very different matter were it known publicly that the King or the Prince of Wales was trying to pull down a man in high office.[50] This rebuke seemed to have aroused no resentment, for the Prince dined with Regy a few weeks later at the Marlborough Club to meet Balfour, Ottley, Bigge and others, where they sat talking happily till 12.30.

Meanwhile Regy created a society called the Islanders to propagate the 'idea that the British Empire floats on the British Navy, and that *Two Keels to One* is the basis of naval supremacy'.[51] The society, financed by an Australian millionaire, was to be 'perfectly secret and perfectly democratic', and as regenerative as the Jesuits, 'if we are not to go downhill as a nation'. The Islanders became quite a power in the land at the next General Election.

A less controversial matter, because it was only in its infancy, was aerial navigation. Already in 1908 the British had every reason to be apprehensive about Germany's growing air power. At the turn of the century Paul Fauchille, eminent editor of *La Revue Générale du Droit International Public*, was the first to advocate the international freedom of the air. He maintained that the air was too fluid and immense to be detained and appropriated by one country more than another. Great Britain, on the contrary, insisted that each country could claim a right to the air space above its territory in self-preservation; and this was the premise which she rigidly adhered to at the International Aerial Navigation Conference in Paris in spring 1910. It was, too, the cause of the deliberations of that conference coming to naught. In October 1908 the CID set up a sub-committee to consider strategic developments in aviation as they concerned Great Britain. Regy was made chairman of this sub-committee, whose members were Lloyd George, Haldane, McKenna, W.G. Nicholson, J.S. Ewart, C.F. Hadden and Reginald Bacon. The sub-committee 'was distinctly circumspect in its evaluation of the military potential of the aeroplane', writes Keith A. Hamilton. 'Of more concern to its members was the airship, and especially the large rigid type with which [Count] Zeppelin was associated.'[52] Circumspect the Aerial Navigation Sub-committee may have been, notwithstanding the evidence given by the Hon. Charles Rolls, who foresaw that the aeroplane would become a very serious menace in warfare bombing by an enemy. It would bring to an end England's island invulnerability. Bombing would be more effective perhaps from dirigible airships, or balloons: 30,000 feet had been reached in a balloon, with oxygen; the aeroplane had not yet risen higher than 150 feet.

By 1909 the Defence Committee already believed that war was the one certain purpose to which aircraft would be put, and Germany the one potential aggressor furnished with Count Zeppelin's developments. Invasion by airships on a large scale could be dismissed, but a small raiding force might inflict a staggering blow to an arsenal or dockyard. If this were to happen Britain had as yet no means of warding off such an attack. The best means would be an equivalent number of airships to the enemy's, and the Defence Committee recommended that money should be allotted to the Admiralty for this purpose. 'There appears to be no necessity', the Committee went on, forgetful of Rolls's premonition, 'for the Government to continue experiments in aeroplanes, provided that advantage is taken of private enterprise in this form of aviation.' The Aerial Navigation Report of 1910 led to Regy putting forward proposals for a Corps of Aviation, which during the First World War became the Royal Flying Corps. By 1911 the British Army had five aeroplanes of various makes, and two dirigibles of small dimensions.

Winston Churchill was the one Cabinet minister to take the development of the aeroplane seriously. As President of the Board of Trade he wrote on 9 January 1909 to Haldane at the War Office a letter of sufficient interest and importance for the Secretary of State to send Regy a copy. Churchill had just spent one and a half hours with the engineer and inventor, Sir Hiram Maxim, on flying machines.

He declares that Wilbur Wright's successes are due to his brain and nerve more than to the efficiency of his aeroplane; that he is in fact a great artist rather than a great inventor . . . that improved patterns will largely discount the need of personal skill; and that such improvements are at hand. The improvements which he has in mind consist first in a motor which yields double the horse-power of the Wilbur Wright engine; secondly, in a carburettor which automatically secures a steady & uniform supply of gas, irrespective of temperature, speed or other circumstances; thirdly, in a gyrostatic arrangement for balancing. Such a machine which he declares himself capable of constructing within a year, would rise from the ground without extraneous force, would lift and carry half a ton exclusive of the engines, of its own weight & the weight of the driver, would travel at a maximum of 55 miles an hour & at a minimum of 32 miles an hour. Its total cost would be £2,000. . . . Its most obvious military use would be, in conjunction with others, to destroy naval bases by dropping nitro-glycerine bombs upon the docks, lock-gates, vessels in the basins and workshops. Other uses will occur to you. He suggests that the difficulty of hitting the object aimed at will be greatly reduced by lowering the bombs upon a piano wire to within a moderate distance of the ground & trailing them from the aeroplane, which would keep a greater altitude.

Of course I do not touch upon the tactical or strategic aspects, except to say that they appear to me to be very serious, & that I should be very much disinclined to accept reassuring statements from military & naval quarters unless supported by solid argument. But upon the purely mechanical question there can I think be little doubt that a very searching and authoritative investigation is required.[53]

It speaks well for both Haldane's and Regy's acceptance of seemingly preposterous inventions of destruction in the early infancy of the flying machine that they both unhesitatingly endorsed Churchill's enthusiastic proposal that 'a very searching and authoritative investigation' was required. Regy at once invited Churchill to give evidence before the Defence Committee. He was fascinated by the developments of the aeroplane, which he followed with curiosity and enthusiasm. When Louis Blériot flew the Channel on 25 July he was invited to luncheon with him. He refused, with the typical excuse that he hated that sort of hysterical thing; yet he admitted that the airman's feat had ushered in a new era.[54]

Lord Northcliffe wrote to him from Pau, where he was making a study of the machine. He had seen one which could fly perfectly at forty miles an hour at a height of up to about a mile. The German and French officers deemed it to be practically unhittable. Provided with wireless telegraphy, its operator could scout an enemy's positions in a way impossible by any other means. Yet no one from the War Office had been to look at it, whereas the United States, France, Germany, Italy and almost certainly Spain had made arrangements for procuring Wright aeroplanes.[55] Sure enough, Charles Rolls was soon in pursuit; he wrote to Regy offering to go on behalf of the War Office and inspect the Wright machines, ascertain when they could be delivered and the terms Wright would make with the Government. He would be instructed on how to pilot the machines, and arrange for Army officers to be given tuition and organize demonstrations.[56] Within seven months Rolls had got a series of Wright machines made in England ready for the Government's disposal, and was asking the War Office where they had prepared suitable flat landing grounds.[57] The following year this gallant pilot was killed in a flying accident.

In February Regy was offered an honorary colonelcy by the 5th Battalion of Royal Fusiliers; he accepted with alacrity and joy. It was to stand him in good stead when the war came, for it was as a colonel of the regiment that he was able to wear khaki and the badge of that rank to which his critics liked to claim he had no title.

Regy was convinced that Britain's place in the world could not be maintained by sea power alone. Equally he believed in those days of peace that compulsory service, or conscription, would be a method utterly repugnant to the freedom-loving British unless they were hard pressed in warfare. The only way acceptable to the vast section of patriotic youth which he confidently believed to abound in the nation was by joining the Territorial forces. To this end, therefore, he devoted his tireless energies, involving himself in a campaign to raise recruits in London. In a pamphlet entitled *The Dynamic Quality of a Territorial Force* he wrote, 'It is the noblest sacrifice which young men today who cannot afford to be professional soldiers can make of their leisure.' Britain could not rely upon her Regular Army in time of crisis. Regy became chairman of the Territorial Force Association in February 1909, and launched his campaign with the generous gift of

£10,000 from Mr Harold Harmsworth to the London County Regiments, to which the following year Harmsworth contributed a further £5000. In these endeavours Regy had the full backing and support of Haldane, without which the scheme could never have been launched in the first place. But the King and Knollys were lukewarm. To their conservative way of looking at things, compulsory service seemed the only sure way of building up Britain's reserve of strength to withstand the potential enemy, Germany. Other powerful voices were raised in dissent, including Lord Roberts, who still exercised tremendous influence on public opinion. When, in a speech at Callander in May, Regy uttered a serious warning about Britain's parlous position, he used the adjective 'odious' in describing conscription. The speech was widely reported and evoked from Lord Roberts a sharp rejoinder. In deprecating the adjective, the old hero said that compulsion might have to come, like compulsory taxation or education, and would have to be accepted willy-nilly. After all, in other countries compulsory service was the rule. To this Regy replied a little lamely that the voluntary system would in that case have to be abandoned with regret; but in the meantime let it be tried first.

So unavoidable did war seem in the summer of 1909 that on 8 July Regy was writing to Kitchener, asking him to interest himself in the need for mobilizing the 1,200,000 partially trained men and officers throughout the Empire in the event of a crisis. At present there was no such plan in being. The Prime Minister and his principal colleagues in the Cabinet – as well as Balfour – Regy assured his correspondent, were aware of and in agreement with Regy's policy. Would Lord Kitchener accept the post of Commander-in-Chief in the Mediterranean with a seat on the CID and the presidency of the Selection Board? The proposition, he claimed, commended itself to the King.[58] Regy followed up this plea with another letter explaining to Kitchener the underlying idea that in time of war the Mediterranean garrison should form the nucleus of a great imperial concentration of forces, naval and military, drawn from every quarter of the Empire.[59]

It seems an extraordinary assumption of authority on Regy's part until one remembers his assurance to Lord Knollys, after *The Standard* onslaught on him in 1907, that every proposition he made was, if accepted, implemented by a minister of the Crown. And of course Regy's propositions to Kitchener were made at the behest of Haldane, who believed that his friend's influence with the great soldier carried far more weight than his own. As it was, the Minister for War had already written to Kitchener to the same purpose on 8 July, with the additional carrot that he was recommending to the King the offer of a field-marshal's baton, irrespective of Kitchener's acceptance of his propositions.[60] He sent Regy a copy of this letter.

Regy was at this time the most influential member of the CID, and worked with Haldane in close concert. But even he was becoming disillusioned by the Committee's ineffectiveness. At the end of the year he threatened to resign from it unless the Prime Minister made some changes in its status. He complained that it was doing increasingly less work. The Admiralty was obstructive and would not disclose its tactics to the Committee. What decisions the Committee did reach were treated like amiable aberrations of a few well-meaning amateur strategists.[61] He had no wish to be associated with disaster. Stephen Roskill, writing on the importance of the CID before 1914, was doubtless correct in his assumption that 'Esher was probably the only person near the seat of power who appreciated the true significance of this weakness in the constitution of the CID.'[62] C.L. Ottley, the Secretary, was certainly no less concerned than Regy, to whom he wrote that the CID ought to have official recognition. Officially the CID was non-existent. Ottley was tolerated up to date because so far he had been harmless. Come a war there would be differences of opinion. And here was the Government expecting Germany to declare war, and building up a Navy. Yet if war came, who was to direct whom? He thought the CID ought to have this authority.

The offer to Kitchener of the post of Commander-in-Chief in the Mediterranean arose from the Duke of Connaught's sudden resignation in July of the appointment at Malta. The King was so angry that he would hardly speak to his brother. The Duke suggested that his resignation should date from October, but the King insisted that he must leave at once. He told Regy that it was all the fault of the women. Connaught preferred idling around London boudoirs, and all he was good for was to be the leader of cotillions. The King told Haldane and Regy to impress upon the Prime Minister that nothing would induce him to retract from his decision; that the Duke's connection with the Army had ceased forthwith and there was to be no going back on his relinquishing the Mediterranean High Commissionership. The Duke wished to issue a statement on his reasons for resigning. He was heavily sat upon by both the King and the Government, and not allowed to. Had he issued a statement Haldane would have been obliged to answer questions in the House of Commons.

Since Regy had been responsible for Connaught getting the job two years before, his reinvolvement in the Duke's affairs caused him embarrassment. The Duke knew only too well that the King had confided his displeasure to Regy, and he suspected that the confidant may even have been the originator of the draconian measures now taken against him. At all events the next time they met, on manoeuvres at Swindon, he refused even to acknowledge his presence. As for the Duchess, in a letter to her husband she wrote of Regy with an acidity that no other member of the royal family has committed to paper. She said, 'I see Esher has now brought out some of Mama's letters. It makes me hot with indignation to think that that creature had the fingering of them!!'[63] The Duchess had a fretful character and was not clever. In going over Clarence House with the Connaughts in 1906 Regy had been struck by her total ignorance of every domestic detail of that royal palace. Compared with the knowledge of the Duchess of York, hers was abysmal. As it happened, Regy was very reluctant to get mixed up in royal family affairs, especially since the King invariably relented after he had urged Regy to be severe with his relations; which was of course precisely what had happened on this occasion.

The morning after his visit to the Prime Minister Regy breakfasted alone with the King.

> I waited in the little room lined with his Indian armour for a few minutes, when he came in, punctually, with his dog. He looked wonderfully well, thinner and younger. We sat down, each with our small silver coffee pot and boiled egg. Fish was handed to me. Then the servants left the room, and he began at once about the Duke.[64]

He was already remorseful over what he had done, and begged that his brother, the last one left and his mother's favourite, should be allowed to go back to the Selection Board. He said his relations had blamed him for the Duke's removal. Regy protested. He told His Majesty what Haldane's answer would be, and asked him if he had read Kitchener's answer to Haldane about the Mediterranean Command. He had not. 'So he sent for the boxes and we found it. He read it there and then, and saw at once how precipitous and foolish the Duke had been.'[65] The King then dropped the subject and turned to the budget. He was very displeased with Winston Churchill's speech at Leicester, which he pronounced vulgar and 'American'. Churchill, who had just left the Conservatives and joined the Liberal party, referred to the Tories as obliged to fall back on their dukes for support – 'these unfortunate individuals who ought to lead quiet, delicate, sheltered lives . . . have been dragged into the football scrimmage'. It did not come well from one who spent his weekends amid the luxury and splendour of Eaton Hall and Blenheim Palace. It was all very fine for his new associate Lloyd George, sprung from a lower middle-class Welsh dissenting family, to abuse the Duke of Westminster in person – although that was in reprehensible taste and provoked Regy to expostulate, 'I suppose we ought not to expect grapes from thistles and a man who, unfortunately, is not *quite* a gentleman, to fight as if he were one.'[66] Regy was not the only gentleman to consider that

Winston was a traitor to his class. 'If it had not been for me and the Queen, that young man would never have been in existence,' the King said to Regy across the breakfast table. 'How is that, Sir?' his guest asked, surprised. 'The Duke and Duchess [of Marlborough] both objected to Randolph's marriage, and it was entirely owing to us that they gave way,' was the reply. This was not the first time that the King regretted his and Queen Alexandra's powers of persuasion, nor was it the last. Only two days later he was telling Regy how the cheek and conceit of W.C. ('whose initials are so well named!') irked him.[67]

The King then mentioned how he had lunched four times with the actress Maxine Elliott, whom he thought very clever, handsome and charming. Both men agreed that if Rosebery had had any pluck he would have married her. There was a pause. Regy decided that, since women not of the patrician class were being discussed, the moment had arrived for him to raise a subject which had long been on his mind. He asked the King, 'Suppose a young officer in the Guards married an actress, would he have to leave the Army?'

'Certainly not,' the King said. 'The rule is quite clear. If an officer marries anyone whom his brother officers' wives cannot meet, he must go, but there must be a *real* objection. . . . For instance, if she is a woman of bad character, or has lived with the officer as a mistress. But if an actress is respectable, he certainly need not leave the Army.'

In the afternoon Regy met Maurice at Orchard Lea and eagerly imparted the good news – hot, as it were, from the horse's mouth. Suddenly Maurice's situation seemed transformed. Until now his father had assured him that 'the conventions of the aristocratic and monarchical superstitions' were a bar to his marrying an actress, however respectable, and remaining an officer in the Brigade of Guards, which was his profession. Now he would not have to leave his regiment if he married Zena, for she was indubitably not a 'woman of bad character'. For years the courtship had been lingering without Maurice bringing himself to propose. Zena, pursued by numerous unrequited suitors, was almost certainly not in love with the precious 'Molly'; and Regy had been playing a game with the couple, encouraging them one by one and at the same time blackmailing Maurice with threats of breaking off his peculiar relationship with him because of fancied signs that his son was growing tired of the father's overpowering passion. In July Maurice wrote his father a letter of reproach not untinged with fear.

I am not angry, only bitterly hurt and disappointed. I have too many memories of former partings to be unconscious of the difference. Two years ago, a year ago, nothing would have stepped in between, and I feel it. . . . I hoped that the great tragedy, for me, would never

come. . . . . I thought that *you* would remain. Am I wrong? Try and bear
with me a little longer. I have only you and Zena in the world. She, I
have always realised, must go one day, but I am terrified of losing you
for then I should indeed be alone. Remember I have no real friends.
Some people are nice to me because of your position, and partly because
of my own, but they are all ready and waiting to turn and rend. M.[68]

He was full of self-pity and devoid of self-confidence, aware that Zena
was not pledged to him. The only positive assurance in his weak head
was that he deeply loved Zena. Even so, he was frightened of his love's
intensity. He must – he would – rely on his father telling him when to
go ahead and propose. Towards the end of the year the occasion arose.

In November Maurice Brett had to sail for India on duty with Sir
John French. Before sailing he, Zena and Regy had a long and serious
talk together. Everything was thrashed out – the King's words,
Maurice's obligations to his chief, Sir John, their financial situation if
Regy made provision for them and the approximate date when they
might marry. In short, Regy gave his informal consent to their
engagement, and Maurice was allowed to present Zena with a
diamond ring. With what enthusiasm Zena accepted it she did not
record. On 26 November Regy wrote, 'My beloved Maurice left for
Ceylon.'[69] He was away for three months, loathing every moment of
his absence and every place he went to – Colombo, Penang, Singa-
pore, Hong Kong (where he had a row with the General for speaking
out of turn in praise of Fisher). Only Canton did he fairly like. His
letters to his father and his betrothed made an unrelieved catalogue of
homesickness and pining for Zena.

When Maurice was safely sailing across the Indian Ocean Regy had
an intimate two-hour talk with Zena at Orchard Lea. She told him
that until a month or two earlier she had not even known that Maurice
loved her after all these years. Regy put her wise, and told her that she
would find in him the most passionate and ardent of lovers. She was
surprised. 'Of this I am sure,' he wrote to Maurice, 'that you must let
let yourself go absolutely, when next you meet, and crush her to death
in your arms' – advice which he had given his son to little avail several
years before. 'I told her that you were the dearest thing in the world to
me – which she knew – but that I would give you up to her. There, my
Maurice, I have rounded off our sweet life together, by doing all I can
for you.'[70] In a further letter to Maurice he told him to pluck up
courage and tell the General he would be marrying Zena on his return,
and hoped he would keep him on as his ADC. This would make the
world appreciate that Zena was not an ordinary stage girl. 'You see,
my Maurice, I woo her in your absence.'[71] It was only too true. In a
further letter he assured him that he had extracted a promise from

Zena that, when married, she would in no circumstances think of returning to the stage.[72] The reason for this seemingly cruel condition was not snobbish belief that actors and actresses were socially inferior, but fear that if she did return to the career in which she had achieved such renown and glamour she might well take to somebody else.

But there were matters other than domestic ones to occupy Regy's restless mind. The year 1909 was clouded not only by the imminence of war but by the beginning of that constitutional conundrum which made the last months of King Edward's reign a great tribulation and was to darken the first of his son's. The question of the House of Lords' status and the eventual limitation of its powers arose with the introduction of the Chancellor of the Exchequer, Lloyd George's, people's budget. It proposed increases in death duties, the introduction of supertax, children's allowances, and the revision of land taxes, amounting to 20 per cent on unearned increment of land values, to be paid either when the land was sold or when it passed by inheritance on death. It was described by Rosebery as 'a social and political revolution of the first magnitude'.

The land clauses of the Bill, opposed by Rosebery, caused much stir among the landowning Tories, so fully represented in the Lords, and a good deal of irresolution from the cross benches. Regy thought that Balfour should solemnly warn the country of the constitutional crisis which this particular matter portended and of his intention, if returned to power at the next election, to reverse them immediately. It would be a gamble, but preferable to the Lords throwing out the Bill, which would be madness. He told his son that the King thought so, too. The Prince of Wales, on the other hand, took the opposite view – a dangerous one. But then he was a good family man, like Charles I.[73] Regy did not fail to tell Knollys, for the King's information, that Asquith's speech confirmed his opinion that it would be inexpedient to throw out the Bill.[74] To his mind, the whole situation too perilously resembled that of 1640.[75] Jack Sandars, Balfour's secretary, informed him that it was practically certain that the Lords would reject the Bill. Ernest Cassel told him that if the Lords let the Commons get away with the budget, which was anathema to the public, then there was little further use for them, and they had better go under. It was true that there was tremendous excitement in the nation as to whether the budget would pass.

At Balmoral in October the King discussed with Regy his delicate position concerning the Lords. He thought it would be wise for him to intervene before there was a crisis. Regy gave him three precedents: that of 1832, when William IV saw Lord Wharncliffe, who was leader of the waverers and hated the Reform Bill, but finally advised his friends to accept it; that of 1869, when Queen Victoria arranged with the Archbishop of Canterbury and Lord Cairns (without consulting the Tory party) the passage of the Irish Church Bill; and that of 1885, when Cairns and the Duke of Richmond (with the approval of Gladstone) came to Balmoral and settled with the Queen the compromise over reform and redistribution.[76] Regy also endorsed the propriety of the King bringing Asquith and Balfour together in an endeavour to prevent a conflict between the two parties.

Lord Knollys, who was bitterly opposed to the Bill at first, told Regy that he would vote in the Lords against its rejection in order to show that he was acting in the best interests of the monarchy, however much others might think his views to be merely coincident with the King's.[77] But he soon decided against this step after hearing from Regy that Haldane considered it would be a great mistake for anyone connected with the Palace to vote either way.[78] Since the dispute was between the two Houses the King must not be brought into the mêlée, Regy advised Knollys. His prerogatives must not be used by either Lords or Commons. Of course, the Executive Government would try to use the King. 'It now becomes solely a question of drawing a ring round the combatants, and insisting that the Sovereign shall not be used as a catspaw to drag the chestnuts out of the fire,' Regy wrote.[79]

Haldane wanted to know what Regy's views were. He said there were two choices for the King – to surrender his right to create peers to the Prime Minister, or to pledge publicly his support for a Parliamentary Bill by the promise to create a sufficient number of peers to pass the measure. Regy pointed out that

> the former would be an abdication by the Sovereign of his prerogative, not only on his own behalf, but that of his successors, which to his mind was an outrage. With regard to the second, for the King to create the enormous number of peers required to pass a Bill, opposed by the majority, through the present House of Lords would also be an outrage on the common sense of the country.[80]

Once only had peers been so created – a mere twelve by Queen Anne in 1712.

In eliciting a promise from the King before the Election, the Government were proposing to make the King a party to their dissolution programme. This was a monstrous proposition. If put to him before the Election, the King should firmly reject it. The sovereign's freedom of action would thereby be unimpaired, and his ultimate decision would of course be guided largely by the result of the appeal to the country. Regy begged Knollys not to let his views be known to a soul except the King. He earnestly hoped that further reflection by the Cabinet would spare the King from having to discuss either choice of action with his ministers. On 30 November the Budget Bill was rejected by the Lords. Asquith consequently dissolved Parliament after condemning the action of the Lords 'as a breach of the Constitution and a usurpation of the rights of the Commons'.

In acknowledging his memorandum Knollys told Regy that he would not show it to the King because it would put him even more against Mr Asquith's Government than he was already. He agreed that the two proposals were both inadmissible. The first would mean taking away one of the few remaining prerogatives of the sovereign, one of such importance that it would be better for the King to abdicate than to submit to it. The second would be hardly constitutional. Knollys asked Regy to find out from Balfour if he would form a Government in the event of the King refusing to commit himself to Asquith's demand that he should create peers, which was tantamount to destroying the Upper House.[81] Regy accordingly invited himself to stay at Whittingehame, Balfour's house in East Lothian, on his way to Callander. Balfour could hardly believe that Asquith had the impudence to make the King promise to create peers before a Bill had been introduced in the Lower House, and had no hesitation in saying that the King ought not in any circumstances to agree. To do so would be a breach of his Coronation Oath. As to Knolly's question whether he, Balfour, would form a Government if the King held firm, he could not commit himself. It depended on the composition of the House. All he conceded was that the King would be running a greater risk in submitting to Asquith's demand than in refusing it.

As things turned out, the Lords' rejection of Lloyd George's Finance Bill on 30 November was followed by a General Election in January 1910 in which the Liberals were returned, albeit with a small majority and dependent on the Irish Members' vote, which was always unpredictable and unreliable. Oliver, who had stood as Liberal candidate for Huntingdon, was beaten in spite of Sylvia's canvassing and speaking for him. Regy assured his 'dearest Noll' that he was proud of him. Oliver was not unduly upset and resumed dabbling in play-writing, which was hardly more successful than his politics. The King, Regy and Mr Balfour were not unduly depressed, since the Government had not been given a clear mandate for the budget or the destruction of the House of Lords. In February the new Cabinet cautiously decided that it would not be fair to ask the King for guarantees, although these pious sentiments were soon abrogated, as indeed Regy foresaw they would be.[82] Regy busied himself first in improving a badly worded draft of the King's Speech for the Opening of Parliament, and secondly in writing the King a precautionary lecture, urging him not to create a large number of peers in the event of the Cabinet changing its mind. Regy was adamantly against reform of the House of Lords, he told Knollys, adding in a petulant manner not uncommon with him, 'and if I am turned out of the House of Lords, I shall give up *all public* functions, which I now perform for nothing!'[83] Over this issue he was not at one with Balfour, who thought there should be thorough reform, not just mere tinkering. Balfour did not share his friend's pessimistic view that the Lords had failed, or that the future of the monarchy was bound up with the hereditary Upper House. In his view the Crown depended on democracy, not on the Lords. At present the House of Lords was not strong enough to hold its own; it needed strengthening. Sure enough, as soon as Asquith's Government had regained confidence, the Prime Minister went back on his disavowal of February. In April Lord Morley, now Lord President of the Council, urgently called Regy to his house at Wimbledon. He confided in him that if the Government were defeated over the Veto Bill the Prime Minister would 'warn' the King that, were a majority to be returned in favour of the Veto Bill, they would not remain in office, or attempt to pass any measure through the Commons, unless they had obtained the King's assurance that he would create enough peers to pass the Veto through the Lords. In the event of a dissolution of Parliament before the Election, the Prime Minister would communicate this political procedure to the country. Morley told Churchill of his unwillingness to be a party to such a measure. Churchill replied that, if it were rejected by the Cabinet, he would resign. So too would the Chancellor of the Exchequer, Lloyd George. Morley asked Regy how he should act over this dilemma; Regy advised him unhesitatingly to resign from the Cabinet if the measure did pass. He immediately reported this conversation to the King.[84]

Lord Knollys was in despair. Ruefully he wrote that Regy had always been firmly of the opinion that when the crunch came the Cabinet would never demand guarantees from the King, and now they were doing it; 'I think they are treating him extremely badly.'[85] He added that if he were the King, and the Election results went in favour of the Liberals, he would abdicate.[86] This was not much help. Nor was the Prince of Wales's avowal that he too was in utter despair. The situation was undoubtedly very critical and telling on the state of mind of the King, who was determined, notwithstanding his own views, to remain strictly impartial – a thing easier said than done. For whatever step he took, he would be accused by the Government or Opposition of acting against the policy of its party.

At this stage Randall Davidson, the Archbishop of Canterbury, stepped into the fray. Perhaps from his spiritual detachment he could proffer some helpful counsel. He invited Balfour, Lord Knollys and

Regy to attend a conference at Lambeth Palace on the constitutional crisis. After much discussion the outcome was that if the King refused to create peers, which was the course Balfour thought proper, and to dissolve Parliament and call for an Election, A.J.B. would come to His Majesty's assistance. He saw no objection to the King proposing a compromise if any reasonable basis could be found. Balfour's attitude throughout the discussion was strictly constitutional and impartial; he even spoke up for Asquith's rights as Prime Minister. But it was easy to see in which direction his sympathies pointed.[87] The crisis was, however, temporarily relieved by the Lords passing the Finance Bill without a division the next day.

Apart from recurrent attacks of bronchitis and in spite of heavy smoking, over-eating and drinking, King Edward's health had remained fairly static since his operation for appendicitis in 1902 until the spring of 1910. Now, however, his physique was visibly deteriorating. On 7 May Regy recorded in his journal:

> Today is Saturday. This day week the King started at 9 o'clock for Sandringham. I saw him the previous evening and he was in excellent spirits, and apparently in excellent health. He was full of exhilarating courage, and had said to Soveral, '*Pas de cinq cents pains, pas cinq pains, pas un pain.*' To me, without the *jeu de mots*, he said much the same thing. It seems that at Sandringham he stood about in the cold wind, and when he came back on Monday he shivered slightly. On Tuesday and Wednesday he was not well, and coughed a good deal, but he gave many audiences and only missed going to meet the Queen in the evening when she arrived from Italy. That was Thursday. In the course of the day he received three or four dull people. The Queen heard at Calais that he was ill. It was the first time she had heard of it. Yet all that day there was much uneasiness at the Palace, indeed Francis Knollys and a few people who knew him well, and marked the change of colour and the growing weakness, had already given up hope.[88]

Regy, knowing King Edward's wonderful powers of recovery, never lost hope. On Friday the royal patient insisted on rising; being fastidious about his clothes, he rejected what his valet had put out for him. He saw his Extra-Equerry Sir Arthur Davidson early in the morning and discussed business with Knollys, but was feeble in his speech. At midday he saw Ernest Cassel. In the afternoon he walked to the window to look at his canaries. Princess Victoria, his daughter, was with him. He felt faint and she just managed to lead him to a chair. It was the first of a series of alarming fits. The Queen, who had returned, never left his chair. A sort of stupor overcame him.

Regy went to the Palace at five o'clock, then went out to dine and returned. At nine the Archbishop came. He, Knollys, Davidson and

Regy sat in Knollys's room. No one else was present. Several came and went away. Regy was sorry, because he was the only one of the King's great friends to be absent at the end. At 11.30 the Prince of Wales said his father would see the Archbishop. A quarter of an hour later the King died. The Archbiship made the sign of the cross over him, murmuring appropriate words. They all kissed him. At a quarter past midnight the new King and Queen came into Francis Knollys's room, King George V dreadfully moved but dignified. 'I kissed his hand,' Regy wrote, 'and he took both mine and pressed them. I then kissed her hand. She was weeping terribly, and looked a picture of simple grief in an ugly blue dress and hat.' The King and Queen then left for Marlborough House. Regy again kissed their hands, and 'she rather clung, like a child for a moment, and said, "This is going to be a terrible time for us, full of difficulties, I hope you will help us." I could not speak. They seemed to me, not a King and Queen, but two poor storm-battered children.'[89]

Four days later Queen Alexandra sent for Regy to say 'goodbye to our dear King'.

There she was, in a simple black dress with nothing to mark specially her widowhood, and moving gently about his room as if he were a child asleep. And I honestly believe that this is what has been in her mind all these days.

The King was lying on the bed in which he always slept in the room I knew so well – the curtainless simple bed. His head was inclined gently to one side as if in comfortable sleep, and his hands laid on the counterpane, with the pink sleeve of his pink nightdress showing. No appearance of pain or death. There was even a glow on his face, and the usual happy smile of the dead who die peacefully.[90]

The Queen Dowager talked to Regy for about half an hour, 'with only a slight diminution of her natural gaiety, but with a tenderness which betrayed all the love in her soul', and the natural feeling that she had at last got her husband entirely to herself. For Regy felt sure then that he had been the love of her life. She said piteously, 'What is to become of me?' as though she was an orphan waif. Regy was moved to tears. She was sitting on the little chair by the King's bed with all the things in the room just as he had last used them, with his hats hanging on the pegs. To make the situation more poignant Caesar, the King's terrier, would not go near her, as though he held her responsible for his master's silence. He waited all day for the King, wandering disconsolately around the Palace. He slept either on the King's bed or on that of his nurse, a comparative newcomer, in the small room next door to the King's, but never on the Queen's.

On reaching Francis Knollys's room Regy, at his old friend's request, started drafting a message which Queen Alexandra wished to have sent to the Dominions. They were reading it over when a note was brought down from the Queen with a draft of her own. It was far better, Regy allowed, than his effort, coming straight from her heart and written without an erasure of any kind.[91]

Regy was extremely indignant over the account which Mrs Keppel put about, implying that she had been summoned to the King's deathbed by the Queen, who thereon fell upon her neck and wept with her. 'Mrs Keppel has lied about the whole affair ever since, and describes quite falsely, her reception by the Queen,' he wrote, on learning from Knollys later what actually had happened.[92]

> The Queen did *not* kiss her, or say that the Royal Family would 'look after her'. The Queen shook hands, and said something to the effect, 'I am sure you always had a good influence over him', and walked to the window. The nurses remained close to the King, who did not recognize Mrs K. and kept falling forward in his chair. Then she left the room with Princess Victoria almost shrieking, and before the pages and footmen in the passage, kept on repeating, 'I never did any harm, there was nothing wrong between us,' and then, 'What is to become of me?' Princess Victoria tried to quiet her, but she then fell into a wild fit of hysterics, and had to be carried into Freddy's [Sir F. Ponsonby] room, where she remained for some hours. Altogether it was a painful and rather theatrical exhibition, and ought never to have happened. It never would only she sent to the Queen an old letter of the King's written in 1901, in which he said that if he was dying, he felt sure those about him would allow her to come to him. This was written in a moment of weak emotion when he was recovering from appendicitis.[93]

The criticism sounds harsh, for whatever her faults may have been – and one of them was rapacity over money – Mrs Keppel's affection for the King was deep and genuine. And there is no doubt that her advent as *maîtress en titre* did much to humanize her lover. As Milly Sutherland observed to Regy at the beginning of the reign, 'The King is a funny man – a child, such a much pleasanter child since he changed mistresses.'[94] Mrs Keppel was extremely skilful. She never bored the King and was always good-humoured. Her hold over him never relaxed. As for him, his adoration was matched by his admiration. Whenever they were in the same room with others he watched her all the time, furtively, and was never happy when she was talking to anyone else.[95]

Regy found the long drawn-out funeral ceremonies very moving and very taxing, especially on the morning when he had to walk from Buckingham Palace to Westminster between Francis Knollys and Sir

Dighton Probyn behind the coffin. Several days were spent at Windsor making arrangements for the final obsequies in St George's Chapel. When the Friday morning came he had to walk in front of the naval ratings who were carrying their burden up to the Castle. At the foot of the grave he stood with the Prime Minister during the last rites. Regy was so impressed by the conduct of the new King that he wrote to him, receiving in return what he called 'a perfect letter', which showed his charming nature.

A number of people wrote to offer their condolences to Regy on the death of King Edward, as for the loss of a personal friend. They were right to do so. When Queen Victoria died, he had mourned her with profound veneration. With the accession of her son he did not believe he would ever become as fond of him as he had been of the mother; but he did. His veneration may not have been so great, but his affection was deeper. How fond the King became of him we may never know, for kings rarely record their feelings for their subjects on paper. King Edward certainly liked him and depended on him to a very large extent. He should have been extremely grateful, for Regy was not one of his salaried servants and his services were given gratuitously and unstintingly, the only reward he received being an honour or two. Certainly he may be counted among the first ten of the King's intimates, for the raffish and rich companions of the King's youth, the members of the so-called Marlborough House set with whose society he was undoubtedly more at ease at cards, on the turf, out shooting and larking around the billiard table far into the night, had either died or retired from the scene by 1901. In 1913 copies of Thomas Brock's bust of King Edward were ordered and presented to the ten men most honoured by the King's friendship. They were Crewe, Horace Farquhar, Arthur Sassoon, Redesdale, Cassel, Carrington, Rosebery, Devonshire, Soveral and Esher.

Loyalty and modesty were perhaps two qualities which Regy most admired in his master. King Edward always supported his ministers and servants, even when he did not like them. Once he gave his confidence he gave it unreservedly, and he repaid the devotion he inspired with unremitting kindnesses. 'No man knew more truly his own strength and weakness. Experience, not knowledge, instinct, not reflection, made him a statesman,' Regy wrote after his death. He recalled Soveral saying to him, *'Vous êtes un grand diplomate, un homme d'état, et vous l'ignorez.'* The King looked puzzled and smiled. Intellectual statesmen like Balfour, Haldane and Asquith underestimated his unerring judgement of men and women, and his sure instinct to take the right decisions. There was only one man, Regy conceded, who could occasionally deflect his purpose, and that was Francis Knollys. Men of superior intellect do not always appreciate that a man or woman can love life's pleasures and yet also handle serious matters with great success. King Edward was such a one. Jackie Fisher grasped this fact when he wrote, 'I don't mean to urge that King Edward was in any way a clever man. I'm not sure that he could do the rule of three – *but he had the heavenly gift of Proportion and Perspective.*'[96]

Regy Esher's influence on King Edward during his short reign of less than a decade was profound. He was constantly in the royal presence, whispering advice and wise opinions in a manner which neither irked nor embarrassed the King; and when he was not present he kept him informed of day-to-day events and gossip about ministers and everyone of high estate. He supplied him with long memoranda and drafted letters, many unsolicited, for his master to send to heads of foreign states as well as members of his own Cabinet. St John Brodrick complained that Regy took it upon himself to write to the King about everything that transpired at confidential meetings, even private evidence given in the absence of reporters, before the subjects under discussion had been submitted to responsible ministers.[97] To them, no doubt, Esher's ceaseless chattering and relaying of secrets to the sovereign were intensely irritating. But they had to put up with them. Men like Sir Lionel Cust, who were themselves courtiers, recognized that his services to the King were invaluable, especially at the beginning of his reign when he had few friends in society who were reliable or even cultivated. 'Looking back after an interval of twenty-five years,' Cust wrote, 'I give my considered opinion that the remarkable influence which Lord Esher exercised over King Edward VII in the early years of his reign was well applied, of great assistance to the King at a critical moment of his life, and of benefit to the nation at large.'[98]

Regy's influence over King George V was never to be of the same intensity. This King did not inherit his father's appreciation of intellect in other men, which he signally lacked himself. Yet at the beginning of his difficult reign he too was glad to rely on Regy's help and advice. Once he shook down into the saddle, and as Regy with advancing years became less involved and less interested in public affairs, he called less frequently upon his father's old mentor. It was natural and to be expected. On the day of Regy's death the King's diary made no reference to the event, merely confining itself to the state of the weather.

9

GEORGIAN AFTERMATH
1910–1914

Six days after the death of King Edward, Regy, Francis Knollys and Soveral dined together at the Marlborough Club. In place of Jackie Fisher the fourth member of the quartet of friends, who of late had habitually been meeting to talk freely about international affairs, was Charles Hardinge.[1] On this occasion there was no discussion of foreign – or, for that matter, domestic – politics. All four could talk of nothing but the late King. Indeed Fisher, too grief-stricken to attend, had written to Regy, 'I can't shake off the sense of loss in the King's death.' 'I think we four', Regy wrote in his journal, the fourth being Fisher and not Hardinge, 'are those who will never get over our loss.' In five months' time, when the last of the Braganzas, Dom Manoel ('such a nice-looking boy'), was driven from the throne of Portugal, Soveral severed all ties with his own country and made his permanent home in England.

The breath was barely out of King Edward's body before the press were besieging Regy, the recognized great panjandrum of the court, for written appreciations of the new King and Queen (he refused *The Times*'s invitation), and a character sketch of His Late Majesty (he accepted Murray's for *The Quarterly Review*).[2] He restricted himself to childhood anecdotes of the young Prince Edward, which his readers consumed with avidity: the Prince's governess had remarked that as a small boy 'he looked through his large, clear blue eyes full at one with a frequent very sweet smile'; he could become passionate and determined enough for an autocrat; he engaged in occasional 'stampings'; fortunately his 'lovely mildness of expression and calm temper' got the better of him in the intervals. Regy revealed that when an adolescent the Prince was not allowed to read the novels of Sir Walter

Scott; that in later years he found fault with the education imposed on him by the Prince Consort and Queen Victoria, and his isolation from other children; and he even lamented that his mother withheld all discussion of matters of state from him. So he fell back upon the turf, the theatre and society. The article was rather bold but Regy's aim was to suggest what a pity it would be were the present young Prince of Wales made to go through the same limiting experiences. Wide interest was shown in the article by the press, and a few journalists tentatively criticized Queen Victoria's methods of upbringing.

On 3 July the new King sent for Regy to talk about the inevitable memorial to his father, perhaps a statue in the centre of the Broad Walk in Green Park. It was agreed that, so soon after the appeal for his grandmother's memorial, it might be difficult to raise the money. Was the King aware that Queen Alexandra had already requested Mr Brock, the sculptor, to design a figure of her husband to take the place of the group entitled *Maternity* on the Victoria Monument facing the Palace? Queen Alexandra was behaving as though she were still the Queen Consort. She had not got over the fact that, as Princess of Wales, she had never been allowed to do as she chose. 'Now, I do as I like,' she told Regy in 1903, and, in spite of being widowed, intended to go on doing so. Her temperament did not lend itself to widowhood, and she was inclined to deprecate her daughter-in-law, Queen Mary's, authority.

Work on the Victoria Monument was by no means yet finished and Regy found himself clambering all over it alone with the Kaiser, in perfect amity in spite of William's offensive reference to him as the supervisor of the Windsor Castle drains in the Tweedmouth letter. Regy had to admit that 'he was the most genuine *mourner* of all the foreign potentates', which was yet another indication of his Jekyll and Hyde character.

Regy had his own idea for a suitable memorial to the late monarch – the foundation of a professorship of Literature at Cambridge, in spite of the fact that King Edward had scarcely opened a serious book in his whole life. He got Sir Harold Harmsworth to offer £20,000 – a generous sum – to the Vice-Chancellor for that purpose.

Regy found the new King quite unchanged by his apotheosis. He was the same direct, simple Prince he had always been, with his friendly manner and winning smile. But his responsibilities were weighing heavily upon him. He could not sleep, and woke every morning at five to make notes on the matters of the day ahead. Though genuinely attached to his new master, Regy was well aware that he was not as instinctively able as his father. Whereas King Edward would ask for opinions and eventually make up his own mind, King George liked to discuss problems by the hour, afterwards remaining as much at sea as before. Yet Arthur Bigge, his faithful Secretary, told Regy that, 'except for the German Emperor, he is the only royal prince to whom I find I can talk as man to man,' adding, 'he is really clever, perhaps too much so.'[3] King George V certainly cannot be called an intellectual, but he was endowed with down-to-earth common sense, buttressed with instinctive and often sound prejudices. Regy's misgivings were about the new King's uncontrolled vehemence, such as his partisan opposition to Fisher, his outspokenness and lack of reserve. When still Prince of Wales, George dreaded his ultimate succession and was pessimistic about how he would endure kingship. This did not inspire Regy with confidence, and led him to tell Milly Sutherland in 1908 that 'the net result is to make one uneasy at the prospect of the day when P. George succeeds his father. He has all the domestic merit and political demerit of George III.'[4] Whether Regy wanted to relinquish the extraordinary and unconstitutional position he had enjoyed during the past decade under a sovereign whom he had revered may be judged from the letter he wrote to King George immediately after his father's funeral.

Sire, I have been trying to write to Your Majesty since that terrible night, but I have not found courage.

Today, the Queen took me to look at my dear King and Master for the last time; and it was a moment I can never forget, as a seal set upon the kindness and confidence of many years. Up to this day, life seemed at its end for me, and I have been within an ace of praying Your Majesty's leave to go home to Scotland for good – as one whose work in the world is over.

Then, there has come over me the sense of all the kind things Your Majesty has said to me from time to time, and all the uncertain future which lies before you and the Queen, and I feel that the dear King whom I have loved, and served, would have thought it cowardly to shirk one's duty to one's Sovereign and country.

Your Majesty must believe in my deep and respectful affection for your person and that of the Queen. To me you both seem very young and I very old – but such years as yet lie before me, I will try and devote to your service. I know Your Majesty well enough to feel supreme confidence that your people who have so universally lamented your beloved father, will very speedily recognize to the full that the best legacy to them is the Sovereign who by the Grace of God now reigns over them. Please forgive this freedom of speech which is written from the heart, and with fervent prayers for Your Majesty and the Queen, I remain, Your most affectionate and Your Majesty's devoted servant, Esher.[5]

Somehow it is hard to believe that, had the King accepted the professed inclination of his father's mentor to retire to Scotland for good, Regy would not have been much put out. He was a mere fifty-eight, in vigorous health, a slave to work and intrigue who enjoyed the reality of power he had so long wielded. Moreover, he honestly believed he could guide the new King's faltering steps until he acquired the confidence that would surely come to him.

The reply he received was gratifying.

> That last sad ceremony was indeed a terrible ordeal for me and I tried hard not to break down. I have indeed lost in my beloved Father the kindest and best friend I ever had. . . . But I know that God will give me strength to try to follow in his footsteps & to do my duty & to work for the welfare of my people & this great Empire. I am most grateful to you for all you did to make the sad ceremony at Windsor so perfect & so beautiful.[6]

Without positively imploring Regy not to bury himself for all eternity in the wilds of Scotland, King George implied that Regy's future assistance and counsel would be welcome. Nevertheless, when Regy offered to surrender his two rooms at Buckingham Palace which King Edward had given him for his work, most of which was now ended, the new King accepted gratefully. Yet he had the grace to say that he hoped Regy would retain those he had at Windsor. Most of Regy's friends imagined that his links with the court would be as strong as before. Indeed, W.T. Stead predicted that Regy would be more in accord with George V than with Edward VII. He also predicted that Lord Esher's position as a factor in the affairs of the Empire would remain unchanged. And so at first it did. As Kenneth Rose has pointed out, the King, in spite of his profound reverence for his father's superior wisdom, did not feel at home with all the old gang of courtiers. Count Albert Mensdorff and Regy were among the few old cronies of King Edward who continued to find favour at court.[7] The former's claim to close intimacy with the King was through his being a second cousin twice over, rather than the Austrian Ambassador.

Regy's relations with Queen Mary being on a much closer footing, it is very probable that she advised the King not on any account to lose the services of so valuable a counsellor. She certainly was responsible for his continued custody of the royal papers.

Although naturally reticent, Queen Mary was able to communicate very freely, especially with those who shared her interests. While Princess of Wales she frequently came down to Regy's room in the Castle, looked at his things and chatted about Hanoverian papers, furniture and family portraits. They exchanged presents, she giving him a little Stuart jewel, he offering her a portrait of Charles James Fox. When Queen, she consulted him about her rearrangements at

Buckingham Palace, asking him to choose silk hangings for the picture gallery. By 1910 Regy felt he could say almost anything to her. Adept at flattery, he would praise her knowledge of history so that she blushed. He even commented upon her looks. 'Perhaps you will forgive me for saying that all the *women* [at the opera] were enthusiastic about Your Majesty's appearance last night. "So very pretty and so very young" was the usual verdict.'[8] He was extraordinarily frank. 'You know that I have always felt that you would make the most of your great opportunities, and now, at last, the great reserve qualities which have always been there, will begin to be understood and appreciated.'[9] He produced from the Windsor archives papers about her great-grandparents. She was fascinated by the mystery of her great-aunt, the Princess Amelia who was said to have married one of George III's equerries, unknown by name. After her death a man called Garth appeared, claiming to be her son. In his turn Regy told Queen Mary of his scheme for a London equivalent of the Musée Carnavalet, which specializes in historical exhibits relating to Paris. The King was opposed to anything leaving Windsor, but the Queen thought the two of them might bring him round to the idea.

In addition to talking with this sympathetic listener about her forebears who had been dead for a century and more, Queen Mary liked to discuss her immediate family. Over tea at Buckingham Palace she confided the difficulties she encountered with Queen Alexandra. The King did not want to hurt his mother's feelings, but the new Queen Mother simply would not comprehend her changed circumstances. She thought everything in the Palace still belonged to her, and she wanted to keep her old rooms at Windsor. For this attitude the influence of her sister, the Dowager Tsarina of Russia, was largely responsible, because in Russia Empress Dowagers traditionally enjoyed authority superior to that of Empress Consorts. The Queen's complaint was followed a few days later by a letter to Regy from Knollys, begging him to explain to Queen Alexandra that she ought not to dispense King Edward's belongings to various institutions since they were heirlooms. Regy spent an hour with her and was able to put this right. She was very unhappy; her life seemed finished. Even her home country of Denmark, which she had looked forward to visiting, proved a disappointment. She would never get over not receiving 'his' letters while abroad. She would never wear anything but black again.

Regy gave the Prince of Wales, on the day he was confirmed, a little book, which had belonged to General Gordon. The General had passed it on to his brother, Eugene. And Regy wrote to the young Prince 'a short homily on [Gordon] that dear and faithful servant of Christ and the Crown'.[10] Whatever the boy thought of the gift, he wrote a very nice note of thanks. 'The boy is a darling. Backward but sweet,' was the donor's comment. Regy was in his heart of hearts a little in love with the handsome Prince of Wales, now sixteen, the age at which he found youths most appealing. Queen Mary had often spoken to Regy about her eldest son with some apprehension: two years previously she had been worried about his bad spelling; one year ago it had been his sudden shyness and wish to avoid all ceremony and public greetings. She had argued with him in vain, telling him it was his duty to submit to these taxing demands. She thought him very babyish but perfectly innocent up to date, which surprised her. He used not to like his father, who was rather a martinet – he put his sons over his knees and spanked them. But these holidays he had said to his mother, 'You know, I think Father now is quite a nice man.' Yet she had no influence over the Prince who, if she tried to exert it, showed resentment. King George, too, talked to Regy about Prince Edward. He wanted his son to improve his mind. Regy considered that the Prince's childishness was caused by the limitations of his tutor, Henry Hansell, 'a man, however, in whom the King reposes great confidence'.[11] He did not seem to attribute part of the trouble to the King's perpetual snubbing of his son. In front of the King, the Queen showed Regy a charming and sensible letter just received from their son, showing interest in the political situation and announcing that he now read *The Morning Post* and *The Westminster Gazette*; King George, however, instead of commending him promptly wrote telling the boy to read not *The Morning Post* but *The Times*.

Regy may well have been right about Hansell, who was only a semi-educated man without a grain of fun or humour. Nevertheless Regy was not the best person to give advice on the upbringing of children, considering how lamentably he had failed with his own. Besides, he was quite incapable of dissociating a child's qualities and promise from its appearance. Prince Albert (later George VI), the younger son, not being good-looking, was dismissed by Regy as a boy of no account whatsoever. Had Regy had his way with the Prince of Wales, he would have indulged his every whim and thoroughly spoilt him. This was luckily outside his province, and he could do no more than give him presents on every festival occasion and bombard him with letters. To Queen Mary he wrote, 'I feel sure that the Prince of Wales, who is a perfect darling, will, if he goes on as he has begun, showing so much intelligence, and with his wonderful improvement in manner, be a worthy son to you both.'[12] It was very easy to write like this, but he advanced few positive suggestions for the improvement of an untrained and wayward mind.

On the political front, Regy found himself in a slight quandary about Lord Kitchener's future. In July 1909 he had strongly urged King Edward to send him as Viceroy to India on the impending retirement of Lord Minto. He had emphasized to Knollys what a superb administrator he was, although no soldier in the field. Lord Morley and the Cabinet were opposed, the former considering Kitchener idle and caring only for loot. But the King had set his mind on the appointment. On 29 May 1910 Knollys reminded Morley that this had been King Edward's last wish. Kitchener, running into Regy in St James's, told him he wanted it to be clearly understood that if he were not sent to India as Viceroy he would leave Britain altogether. There was no other job he would take. Regy advised him not to threaten Lord Morley, who was a stubborn, proud and obstinate man.

> He talked volubly, and although his strength looms big, especially when he sets his jaw, and shows his overlot of teeth, he is not the strong silent man, but the talkative headstrong man. It is not a pleasant face, and the nose lacking in refinement. He would, I should imagine, walk over the dead body of his best friend.[13]

Kitchener got as far as dining with Morley, Haldane and Regy being the other guests. Regy then corrected his first impression of Kitchener. He now imagined his capacity to be considerable. He guessed he had complete command over himself, and was cunning. 'Feeling, passion, anger, pleasure, all would be subordinated to the business in hand whatever it might be.'[14] On the 25th Morley decided not to send Kitchener to India. He had already asked Hardinge at King Edward's funeral if he would go as Viceroy. On hearing of this King George was angry. He not only thought Kitchener the most fitting candidate, but felt that his father's wishes had been brushed aside. Kitchener sulked.

There were worse tribulations and anxieties in store for the King than the frustration over Kitchener. No sooner had the mourning period passed, and before the new King felt anything like settled into the unaccustomed saddle, the Parliament Bill was back on the agenda. Ever since 1894, when Henry Labouchere's amendment to the Address condemning the hereditary principle was carried by two votes in the Commons, reform of the House of Lords had been raised by successive Liberal Governments. Both Gladstone and Rosebery harnessed the Liberal party to this policy. But when the House of Lords declared itself the safeguard of the electorate's wishes against those of the House of Commons, notably on the Home Rule issue, the subject was deferred for another decade. Under Campbell-Bannerman's Government the question had again become acute. In June 1907 the Prime Minister obtained a large majority in the Commons for a complicated resolution by which the Lords' veto could be over-ridden when the Commons had three times passed a Bill. But on Campbell-Bannerman's death in 1908 the matter was again shelved. A strong

committee of the House of Lord's, under the chairmanship of Rosebery, presented a report in favour of restricting the hereditary element
and adopting a method of selection of peers. So matters stood until the
introduction of Lloyd George's budget of 1909. With the Lords'
rejection of the people's budget the fat was in the fire. The Liberal
leaders contended that the right of the Lords to reject a financial
measure was obsolete and must be positively abolished. In January
1910 they went to the country for a mandate to carry out this measure.
The result for the Liberals was not wholly reassuring: the return of
Liberal and Conservative seats was about equal. Asquith, now Prime
Minister, was obliged to rely on the uncertain alliance with the Irish
Nationalist Members and a sprinkling of Labour Members. Nevertheless, Asquith proceeded to define his intentions in the Commons and
had actually tabled a Bill to be sent up to the Lords when King
Edward died in May. Until the autumn a kind of truce enabled both
parties to take breath and confer in a series of secret meetings on how
to reopen the question with the least damage to the constitution and
least awkwardness for the Crown.

On 9 October Regy, staying at Whittingehame, obtained Balfour's
dictated views, which had been outlined during the Archbishop of
Canterbury's conference at Lambeth Palace in April before the late
King's death. Balfour's strong opposition to Asquith extracting pre-
conditional promises from the King was unequivocal. Asquith might
then well resign. And what would happen? The leader of a minority
party might be called upon. If he refused, the King would be justified
in sending for some outside statesman of repute either to form a
Government or advise a dissolution. Rosebery was such a statesman.
But he might refuse to do anything. Then it would be necessary,
Balfour pronounced, to give the heads of departments some official
rank to enable them legally to secure a dissolution.[15]

Regy, who by now made no bones about having severed his
allegiance to the Liberal party, objected strongly to the Parliament
Bill, which sought to alter the relationship between the two Houses of
Parliament. He told the Leader of the House of Lords, Lord
Lansdowne, that he disliked what he called the 'new-fangled' proposals for the composition of the Upper House. He argued that the Lords
had never once rejected a Finance Bill sent up from the Commons. It
seemed to him worth considering the reduction of future Parliaments'
terms from five to three years. If this were done, some of the most
serious objections to the Veto Bill would be modified.[16] Yet to the
King he had sent a memorandum only a week before making light of
the Bill. If it passed, it would certainly affect the potential strength of
the House of Lords, but would not strike it a mortal blow or diminish
the authority of individual Members. Unless an important Bill were to

be introduced at the beginning of a new session, it would be unlikely to pass the Lords, if objectionable. The hereditary principles were not going to be infringed. In fact, the consequence might conceivably enhance the authority and prestige of the Upper House, for the public at large would believe it to be in closer accord with democratic principles than the Lower.[17] The memorandum seems curiously optimistic compared with the letter to Lord Lansdowne. We can only suppose that Regy wanted to reassure the nervous King, who had written to him deploring the breakdown of the last conference between the parties, that the changes to be brought about by the Bill would have no adverse effect on the standing of the monarchy.

The King had every reason to feel jittery and upset. On the 10th Asquith went to Windsor and left him with the conviction that no guarantees were going to be asked of him. A few days later Asquith returned, accompanied by Lord Crewe, whom he knew to be a personal friend of the King. The Prime Minister, fortified by his henchman, did on this occasion demand guarantees. The King was persuaded to understand that he was obliged to give them; he felt badly let down. The occasion rankled, and for a long time afterwards he looked coldly on Crewe. In fact exactly three years later Regy recorded that:

> The King talked very excitedly to me yesterday, for 1½ hours. He traversed a lot of old ground; still overweighted by the idea that if he had refused the 'guarantees' in November 1910, all present troubles would have been obviated. That is by no means so clear. But what *is* beyond all question is the suppression (accidental I think) of vital information by F.K. [Francis Knollys] of what the Opposition thought in 1910 of the general situation, and of what the King ought to do. F.K. is old – and he was under the recent agitation of the death of his old master. Anyhow, he did *not* give to the King the information which was due to him.[18]

The King was also gravely offended by Knollys's inaction. It was his chief reason for getting rid of him as soon as he decently could.

Francis Knollys belonged to that succession of private secretaries to the sovereign, beginning with Sir Henry Ponsonby, to whom the monarchy owes a considerable debt. Different though the royal secretaries to Victoria, Edward VII and George V were, they were united in putting the interests of the Crown first. The advice they gave was disinterested, intelligent and almost always wise. Francis Knollys had been in the Royal Household since 1862 as assistant to his father, who was Treasurer and Comptroller to the then Prince of Wales. He became devoted to his master as Prince of Wales and King, and could speak to him absolutely freely and tell him the whole truth. 'I can think of few disasters graver than if he were to be separated from the King,' Regy wrote in his journal. 'He is the only man who speaks quite frankly to H.M., and is listened to. Not that he always pleases, by any means.'[19] This relationship made him rather proprietorial about the King, and the equerries often complained of the difficulties he created. He became, however, a very close friend of Regy, whose position was *sui generis*, and not calculated to cause the same jealousy within the Household. The two men were constantly meeting and as constantly writing to each other on every conceivable subject without the slightest reserve. Such was their friendship that Knollys frequently asked Regy to do things he never could do himself, such as urging Fisher to resign as First Sea Lord in September 1909. With Fisher, too, he was very intimate. He was known to have put into the fire a letter to the King from the impulsive Admiral which he felt sure Fisher would regret having written.

The apparently contradictory side of Knollys which made him enemies and was mistrusted by hide-bound Tories was his wholly Whiggish instincts. They induced severe critiscism from men such as L.J. Maxse, who over the Parliament Bill had actually accused him of having sold his sovereign.[20] They were also one cause of Arthur Bigge's dislike, not untinged by jealousy, which rubbed off on his master, King George. Yet Knollys considered the Socialist George Lansbury's election to Parliament in December 1910 to have been an outrage, eclipsed only by Lloyd George, a Cabinet minister, having spoken on his behalf in the constituency. 'By supporting Lansbury he has openly avowed his sympathy with Socialism which in other words is Republicanism, for I suppose all Socialists are Republicans.'[21] A.C. Benson, seeing Knollys and Regy together, remarked that he liked Knollys's 'rather tired, rubicund, simple face. He seemed just a simple-minded, hardworking man, over-worked, but most courteous and kind. C/d with the elegant Esher Knollys much more of the Kingdom of Heaven, I thought.'[22]

Arthur Bigge (created Lord Stamfordham in 1911) was twelve years Knollys's junior. He owed his life service to the royal family to a close friendship with the Prince Imperial, son of the Emperor Napoleon III. While staying at the Empress Eugénie's house after the Prince's lamentable death in the Zulu War he was presented to Queen Victoria, who took a fancy to him, making him her Groom in Waiting and Assistant Private Secretary. On her death he became Private Secretary to the Prince of Wales, whom he accompanied on his tour to India in 1901. Sprung from a north country parsonage, Bigge preserved all his life a certain austerity, always eschewing the fashionable. His impartiality, like his lack of humour, was never questioned. Until his death he served King George with steadfast loyalty and devotion. Regy's relations with him were never quite as intimate as with Francis Knollys: the two men were never on Christian name terms, and even the King called him Bigge, long after his ennoblement. 'Dear Bigge passed peacefully away at 4.30 today . . . I shall miss him terribly,' he wrote in his diary on 31 March 1931. After Knollys's retirement, Regy and Stamfordham corresponded regularly until the outbreak of the First World War. Their letters were always cordial, respectful rather than affectionate, the Secretary's being almost painfully discreet. Stamfordham held Regy in high esteem for his sage advice, knowledge of constitutional affairs and ability to express himself clearly in memoranda. On Regy's death he wrote to Lady Esher that 'he was a man to whom it was a delight to turn for information and help on almost any subject, ever certain of a patient hearing, of advice, wise, kind, charitable, uncensorious and based on that wide experience of the world and his fellow creatures, which was a predominant characteristic of his charming personality'.[23]

When the Veto Bill reached a crisis in the middle of November Bigge was spurring the King on to refuse Asquith permission to dissolve Parliament, so that he would resign and His Majesty might send for Balfour. As soon as he heard of the King's indecision Knollys asked to see him at once at Buckingham Palace. He, on the contrary, beseeched the King to do what Asquith asked. He pointed out that Balfour could form a Government only with the support of the Liberal moderates, which was not to be thought of; even then he would be absolutely powerless. Fortunately the King followed the older Secretary's counsel to abide by the advice of his responsible ministers, thus sparing the monarchy criticism and even danger. But it did not make for a good relationship between Knollys and Bigge, nor between Knollys and the Tories out to defy Asquith.

The King told Regy that he was greatly relieved at having given way; he felt satisfied that the Veto Bill would do less harm than the abolition of the hereditary principle. He also confided in Regy his ideals and aims. He was determined to visit India and all the Dominions in turn, in spite of his ministers' objection to the long absences from the kingdom which these visits would entail. What his father had done for Europe, he would do for the Empire. He understood, which his ministers seemed not to do, how the world had shrunk because of steam power and electricity. Regy implored him not to listen to suggestions for a regency in his absences. 'People here must get accustomed to the idea that there is no difference essentially between Edinburgh and Ottawa.'[24]

The year 1910, which was in effect to witness the decline of Regy's influence over the monarchy and affairs of state, also saw a revival of press attacks on him. To some extent Regy himself provoked them by the publication of his little book of essays, *Today and Tomorrow*. On 27 April an article rather than a critique of the book appeared in the *Daily Express*, entitled 'The Anomalous Position of Lord Esher', and calling him the arch-apostle of outside interference. That was all very fine, the journalist intimated.

> It is however quite another matter when an irresponsible civilian however clever, seems to arrogate to himself a position which becomes practically subversive of departmental control. . . . Amateur interference by irresponsible persons, however high in rank, cannot be for the good of the office in which it is exercised. . . . A basic rule of the British constitution is that influence shall be enjoyed in proportion to responsibility taken. This rule is unhappily violated in the position accorded to Lord Esher.

But what was Lord Esher's position? He had already answered that question in 1907, at the time of a similar attack by the *Standard*, in denying a trifle disingenuously that he had any influence beyond being chairman of several committees and a member of others. Again he pointed out that since he was positionless he never gave orders to anybody, only advice to the Crown and ministers of state, which they sometimes took and often did not. If they took it, it was they who issued the commands. The *Daily Express* journalist went on to condemn his selection of officers for high command in the services. But here again, if Regy made suggestions to the Minister for War, it was that minister who made the promotions, not he. The *Express* accused him of not only being content with chairing the Army Reform Committee without consulting the Army, but also assuming the right to tackle the reform of the War Office. To this last complaint the obvious retort was that the War Office could reject his recommendations if they did not like them.

On 5 August Milly Sutherland wrote to Regy that she had dined with Haldane, 'still murmuring over you – I wonder what you exactly *did*. He seems in such a "O Jonathan, my son, my son" sort of mood (or was it Absalom?) that both he and French in quite different ways are lacking in understanding of *man*, though the former is a perspiring philosopher (2nd class), and the latter full of simple saws.'[25]

What Regy had done was to write, as Chairman of the London County Territorial Association, an article in the September issue of *The National Review*. After declaring his basic principles to be in favour of voluntary service, and praising Lord Haldane for bringing in the Territorial Force and after four years' service the Territorial Reserve, he then announced that the enlistment of recruits was gravely deficient, and advocated compulsion. He got into trouble from all sides. *The World* (a 6d periodical) took up the cudgels in a series of vitriolic articles. They first attacked Regy for being an *éminence grise*, the first time the expression was actually applied to him. It went on to question the competence of the advisers surrounding the King.[26] The second, headed 'The Cabal – Conclusion: The Cabal must go!' began:

> Our first demand is that Lord Esher, whom we regard as the *fons et origo* of the Cabal, should be made directly responsible to Parliament. His position should be defined in a White Paper, and justification for the permission extended to him to have access to confidential War Office papers, a privilege ordinarily allowed to the Secretary of State. He should be obliged to answer questions in the House of Lords. His performance is shrouded in obscurity. All we know is that he is responsible for certain developments in military policy. He conceals his share in events dexterously . . . his position is un-English, undemocratic, unconstitutional; he must come out into the open, be seen or tried, like every other public servant. If he succeeds he will remain; if he fails, he must go.

This was hot stuff, which tailed off into a jumble of angry words about Lord Esher's sedentary life and lack of acquaintance with the rough and tumble of parliamentary warfare.[27]

What Haldane objected to was that Regy had no right, as a member of the CID, to publish in *The National Review* an article that could be interpreted as an attack on the War Office and Admiralty. Furthermore, the Prime Minister agreed with him; Asquith thought that Regy ought to refrain from writing controversial articles on national defence in party magazines. The King was of the same opinion. Regy replied to Haldane, thanking him for letting him know the Prime Minister's views and the King's. He imagined his old friend and ally had not read the article and was merely taking its content from hearsay. Regy showed pique, which he always did when thwarted. He thought there was nothing in his article unbecoming to a member of the CID. After all, he gave much time to the Committee and never revealed its secrets. He said it was no great pleasure to him, nor a very valuable privilege, to be a member of the Defence Committee. The only emolument was abuse from *The World* newspaper and a certain clique of journalists and Members of Parliament.[28] If the Prime Minister really thought he had overstepped the mark, Regy could always retire. 'Nearly all my life I have been independent in the sense that I have been free to say what I please. . . . It is for that reason that I have cut myself off from the advantages (and perhaps some of the drawbacks) of *office* in the ordinary sense of the word.'

Haldane was not entirely mollified. He was still aggrieved. The Prime Minister would see Regy's letter.

But frankly, and speaking as a friend to friend, can you wonder at the feeling your article has caused – even in my own mind? You have not only been a member of the Defence Committee, a position which has given you an official title to be listened to. But there is more. All the world knows that you have worked with me from the beginning of the Territorial Scheme, and that I have laid everything before you, in detail at each turn. . . . But – and here is the substance and sadness of it – you suddenly declare – in the pleasantest language certainly – but that does not make it better – that the underlying hypothesis is unsound and that the scheme will in your opinion fail to secure the necessary numbers, i.e. fail *in toto*.[29]

Was it surprising that there were such bitter and unjust conjectures in the current number of *The Saturday Review*? So that paper, too, was in full cry for his blood.

Knollys also weighed in. The King thought Regy would have done better to send his article to the Prime Minister before publishing it and to ask if he objected to it. 'I entreat you as a very great and warm friend of yours not to put yourself in a false position on this point,'[30] he wrote, and to allow those jealous of him to throw stones. Asquith wrote to Haldane commending him for his letter to Regy, and coldly remarking that he felt sure Esher 'would be sorry to lose his place at the CID'.[31]

Assailed from all angles, by friends as well as foes, Regy reflected. Only Arthur Balfour saw nothing in the article that was unbecoming of him.[32] And truth to tell, Balfour's views always prevailed with him over other people's, as he was not slow to point out to Knollys. None the less Regy apologised to Haldane for hurting him, when he consistently wanted to assist in his splendid tasks. If Haldane thought it desirable he would deny the proposition that 'I am brought by my inside knowledge to the conclusion that I must reluctantly *condemn* the scheme with which I am associated.'[33] This was more a personal regret for having wounded an old and valued comrade than a retraction. In fact Regy stuck to his guns. He even wrote to Knollys standing up for his conduct. He thought the King, on the threshold of his reign, ought to realize that if members of the Defence Committee were not to be allowed to express in public their personal views about matters not before the Committee, because they might differ from those of the Government of the day, then he would not get first-rate men to sit on it.[34] There is no doubt that Regy was not endowed with the team spirit. In this respect he was un-English – and he was, of course, half French. It was perhaps as well that he did not accept the Cabinet posts offered him throughout his career, for he would have had difficulty in getting a team to work under him. No permanent breach of his friendship with Haldane was caused by this correspondence, and on 18 October the Minister of War begged Regy in the friendliest terms to come over from Callander to Cloan for the night.

In 1909 Regy formed an association by correspondence with a man whom most of his friends would have supposed to be well outside the range of his sympathies and beliefs. He had read a little pamphlet called *Europe's Optical Illusion* which made a great impression on him. Finding that no publishers would look at it, the author printed it himself and he distributed copies to prominent men in Britain, France and Germany; Regy was one of them. Out of the blue Regy wrote to the author advising him to leave Paris for London where he, Regy, would find a rich man to set up a foundation to promote the discussion of his ideas. In 1910 the pamphlet in question was amplified and reissued in book form as *The Great Illusion*; it was to become one of the most influential political treatises of the first half of the twentieth century. Ten thousand copies were sold within three years, and the book soon appeared in seventeen different languages. On 30 October Regy received the author's first letter, accompanying a specially bound copy and stating that he would have dedicated it to Regy had he not supposed the recipient would take exception to much that the book contained, more so than the original pamphlet. Regy was, he assured him, the first man who mattered to give him whole-hearted encouragement. The letter was signed Ralph Lane.

Lane was the son of a draper and grocer from Holbeach in Lincolnshire. In early youth he had gone to America where he had worked as a manual labourer, ending up as a newspaper man in San Francisco. He was shortly to use only his two middle names, Norman Angell. *The Great Illusion* was essentially addressed to the Kaiser, its thesis being that successful armed aggression could never benefit the aggressor economically. It was a new, startling and, as it happened, irrefutable proposition. It inevitably made a strong appeal to pacifists and was derided by soldiers and militarists. Marxists of course cashed in on it, although Angell was far from being a Marxist. His belief in democracy was profound, and his dislike of Communism unalterable. Angell's tragedy was that he had so few years for his gospel to sink into the understanding of European statesmen before the First World War broke out. The rest of his career was spent in defending his beliefs in Europe and the United States. He became one of the pioneers of the League of Nations:

Until 1914 Regy was the active supporter of the frail-looking idealist, with his short, spare figure, sharp-cut features, conspicuous brow and pale complexion, thin lips and alert eyes. In 1912 he helped create, with the financial support and endowment of Sir Richard Garton, an industrialist MP, the Garton Foundation for the promotion of the study of international polity. Regy became its chairman and appointed his son Maurice part-time secretary, which until the outbreak of war fulfilled the aims of its organizers. After the war its activities took another direction, but by then Regy had little to do with it. His connection with Angell, for whom he always retained admiration and sympathy, slackened as he, Regy, threw himself unreservedly into the war effort against Germany. In return Angell attributed Regy's change of attitude to

> A sort of casual bitterness and hostility. He became contemptuous of the efforts of [President] Wilson to secure some sort of post-war international organization and occasionally sent me messages . . . which seemed to hint that he looked upon my own line as having degenerated into the naive sentimentality of convenient pacifism.

In fact Regy did not discard Angell's thesis, but merely put it aside until the war had been won and they could reassume it on a new basis improved by experience. Angell never allowed his regard for the slightly precious, insulated statesman, who was his very political opposite, to wane. Years later he acknowledged that, although he had worked closely with Esher for several years, he had failed to realize the vital part he was playing in the affairs of the nation; and how greatly he was influencing the course of events at home, in the Empire, and in Europe. Esher was one of the most influential men of his time.[35]

Regy's whole-hearted support of Norman Angell's ideal, during a period when jingoism was the commonly accepted attitude of the majority of his class, is proof of his readiness to investigate and accept new ideas, especially those which might ensure peace to the pre-1914 world. He was bold in subscribing to what were avowedly Socialist principles. If ever an example were needed why this unusual man steadfastly declined to hold office in Governments which would prohibit him from giving vent to free expression of his views, the association with Norman Angell is a shining one. For not only did he help promote Angell's ideals by his chairmanship of the Garton Foundation, but himself gave several important lectures and addresses on them which received wide publicity.

Regy's interests at this time were by no means confined to politics and political theory. He was consulted about a proposed new site for the Science Museum collections between the existing Natural History Museum and the Imperial College of Science. He pronounced it a bad one because both those institutions might one day wish to expand, and recommended the site where it now stands. After talks with Queen Mary, who greatly encouraged the scheme, Regy and Loulou Harcourt, the First Commissioner of Works, drew up plans for the

London Museum, first established in Stafford House, St James's. Its original purpose was to exhibit relics of Queen Victoria and King Edward. In July Regy launched an appeal for the endowment of a Chair of Genetics and an experimental station at Cambridge, as a testimonial to Arthur Balfour who had read a paper on the subject at the university. Through the generosity of Mr William Watson of Maypole Dairies, dubbed by the Prime Minister 'the munificent milkman', £50,000 was given anonymously. A baronetcy was awarded in return. Regy was made chairman of the Trust and in 1912 he and a posse of dons selected an acre of ground at Storey's Way as a site for the laboratories and Professor's lodge. In spite of damage by suffragettes the following year, the buildings were completed. At Regy's wish the lodge was named Whittingehame.

Throughout this busy year Regy was working himself into a frenzy over the impending marriage of Maurice and Zena, which he felt should be deferred no longer. He was still incapable of thinking about his son in a normal manner, and while awaiting Maurice's return from the East in February he actually made himself ill with anticipation. His passion was not yet spent, nor was his ill temper which he turned on Zena for once again prevaricating. He taxed her with having played with Maurice's affections for six years. 'She wants dominating and her spirit breaking,' he told his son. 'With any other man what risks she would be running.' In August Regy learned with relief that Zena had at last made up her mind. He could not prevent himself from interfering in the young couple's plans: beloved Molly must transfer to the Black Watch; must remain French's ADC; must work in the City. Meanwhile Zena must not work in a hat shop, which was not a chic thing to do, but should work for Milly Sutherland's cripples, which was an acceptable occupation. Zena went on quietly acting until such time as her future father-in-law might stump up enough money for her to leave off doing what was frankly the breath of life to her. In truth, she had few interests beyond the stage, and Regy worried inordinately what she would do once married, for of course she would then have to leave the stage. That, as far as Regy was concerned, was clearly understood.

It was not understood by Zena or Maurice, however. The young couple took the bit between their teeth and on the morning of 23 January 1911 were married in a register office in the Harrow Road to avoid – as Zena afterwards explained – a society wedding, which she dreaded. Furthermore, this clandestine marriage enabled her to continue acting with Seymour Hicks for several months; she was billed at the theatre, and did not wish either to let him down or to be involved in expensive legal actions. Immediately after the ceremony she took off her wedding ring and hung it round her neck on a platinum chain. For a while she did not want Regy to be told, because she knew he would disapprove of a daughter-in-law of his being on tour. But the secret could not be kept. Surprisingly, Regy did not seem to be offended, or even to mind. He seemed to find an elopement rather romantic, and merely hoped she would not remain on the stage longer than necessary. Stage life was so tawdry. Besides, he now observed that she never looked her best on the boards. Before the month was out he went to London to house-hunt on their behalf. He soon bought No. 19 Thurloe Square, South Kensington, telling them that until they could move in they might live at Orchard Lea. That would certainly show the world that he and Nellie did not disapprove of the union.

Maurice had a year's grace from the Coldstream Guards after his marriage and remained as Sir John French's ADC at the Horse Guards. He was very hard up, and practically every month brought requests to his father for money. Repeatedly Regy paid up. With these financial demands Maurice indulged pious fears lest, now he was a married man, Regy would drift away from him. 'I suppose it is jealousy but I cannot prevent the feeling.'[36] It was unreasonable of him, but his father must realize that he was not a very clever man. On 24 April Regy wrote in his journal, 'At present he is so absorbed in Zena that he rarely talks to me: all interest in life, except her, seems to be dead.' He consoled himself by writing a nostalgic poem, which he called 'A Year Ago'.

> Life was full of wonder for my friend and me.
>   Now the days are spent and aching memory turns
> Back to sunny hours that never more may be . . .
> Just a little longer let me wreathe your hair,
>   Just a little longer let me hold your hand.

It is true that during this first year of his son's marriage Regy's letters to Maurice became a trifle less affectionate. The exaggerated sentiment is subdued.

My beloved Molly, your sweet letter was an unexpected find. . . . If I have given you all you wanted in life so far, you have given me years of pride and happiness. It is not only your fidelity to me, but your perfect behaviour to Nellie and your affection for her that I prize. No human relations were ever much more perfect than ours.[37]

There is a slight valedictory note perceptible in this gracious tribute; it is hardly surprising that in the circumstances the old emotional grip should slacken. Besides, Regy had other fish to fry: another minnow had swum into his pool, in the youthful person of Lawrence Franklin Burgis, who was to play a prominent and beneficial role in Regy's domestic life.

As well as Maurice, Regy's other children were about to leave the nest for good, but the vacuum they left behind was barely noticeable. On 21 February Sylvia married His Highness the Rajah of Sarawak, Charles Vyner Brooke. The courtship had been going on for several years. The dowager Ranee, whom Regy called 'a devil' and 'a treacherous beast', had been working up the match ever since Doll and Syv had taken refuge from Orchard Lea at Grey Friars, her house in south Ascot. She had realized from the first that Doll's expectations would meet with no response from her son. Sylvia, who was physically more attractive in a conventional way than her sister, was not particularly interested in her wooer and during the courtship had flung herself at the feet of various men, including those of Regy's past love, George Binning. In 1908 she wrote to her father a rather vulgar letter from the latter's house, Mellerstain in Berwickshire, hinting of her attaction to George and speaking of Katie Binning with much disrespect. 'Katie has some lace collars. I should like to choke her with them.' A year later she addressed her 'Dearest Pupsey', again from Mellerstain, saying that she was very much in love indeed. 'Why will they put me in a double bed, it is so insinuating.' Regy may not have welcomed the marriage to the Rajah or lamented Sylvia's loss, but he managed to establish that as Ranee she took precedence immediately after the Indian princes. She would be treated as the consort of a ruler of a state under British protection. Meanwhile, Oliver was in the United States courting an American girl whom he was to marry the following year.

As a result of the General Election in December 1910 – the second within one calendar year to return the Liberal party under Asquith – Regy was on duty at Windsor most days during the ensuing months. He held himself in readiness for the King's attention when His Majesty was not out shooting, for the House of Lords Veto Bill was approaching its climax and the King could not spare Regy's sympathetic ear and guiding hand. On 10 January 1911 Regy attended a dinner at the Marlborough Club with Knollys and Balfour and, as soon as the servants had left the room, made for the King's benefit a memorandum of the conversation that ensued. 'Let us put our cards on the table,' Balfour said. If the King were asked by the Prime Minister to promise the creation of a mass number of peers in the future, His Majesty should make a strong remonstrance. Unfortunately if he, A.J.B., were called upon by the King, he would not remain in office for more than a few days. He could not call another Election after the two of the previous year. He might ask for his protest to be laid before the whole Cabinet. Further than that he could not go. The King would have to give way. Balfour felt certain, however, that Asquith, Lloyd George and Crewe would safeguard His Majesty's position as far as possible.[38] When the memorandum was submitted to the King His Majesty protested that what he would mind most about creating peers in the mass was damaging an historic institution. At the beginning of February Regy wrote:

> We have had twelve days at Windsor, and a great many guests. The King is hoarse from talking. *She* has not been very well, and is rather frightened at the year's prospects. The King talked to me a good deal about the political situation and read aloud to me Lansdowne's memorandum on the possible course of events. . . . The King sees clearly that he cannot refuse to accept advice from Asquith unless he can find an alternative PM and to dismiss their ministers, *on the chance* of their losing their majority at a new general election, would be a dangerous manoeuvre, and a pure gamble.[39]

Regy was amused by the changes that had come over life at Windsor, he told Milly Sutherland. They were back in Victorian times. Everything was so peaceful and domestic. Dinner was in the old room in which Queen Victoria had dined. Then an hour in the Corridor, where she had always sat – and King Edward never – and bed, or at any rate retirement, at ten o'clock. There were early-morning rides at 8.30. The Queen sat mostly in a tent before the East Terrace; the King in his room all the morning. 'And how does it all affect or influence the lives of millions of drudges? Not a jot, I imagine. That these baubles should . . . interest us, when we think at other moments of the solar system and the insoluble problems of life and death,' struck him as whimsical.[40] It was his recurrent pretence, when in one of his cynical moods, that, although he served kings and wore a coronet, he cared nothing for what they represented beyond the picturesqueness of the symbolism.

Almost the whole of the summer was spent at Windsor. The Queen would come to Regy's room to look at papers. He showed the King the fine 'George' which had belonged to Bonnie Prince Charlie and had been left to him by Aunt Adèle.[41] He saw the King about the service for the Garter Knights in June and other private matters. He sat with the Queen in the garden and walked back with her to the Castle. The Prince of Wales sat with him in his room for a long time, and was as charming, friendly and simple as any ordinary young man. In between these diversions Regy was working on the archives, the keepership of which he had offered to resign, but Stamfordham would not release him.

Regy never disguised the fact that he had to care passionately for someone. In view of Maurice's final and irrevocable commitment to Zena it is not surprising that the following sentences appeared in Regy's journal. On 18 April: 'Thrushy talked to me on the telephone this morning,' and on the 24th: 'Got two letters from Thrushy.' From this time onwards letters between Regy and Thrushy proliferate. Thrushy – Lawrence Burgis – who in 1911 was not yet twenty years old, was the last serious attachment of Lord Esher's private life. The first surviving letter from him is dated 5 September 1909 and begins, 'My dear Chief, it is very good of you to remember me. Having ripping hols and shall be more than ready to return to Town. . . . I can't make out why I am having such long hols. I am sure I don't deserve them.' Already at the age of seventeen the boy had left the King's School, Worcester, and was engaged in secretarial work for Regy. How Regy made his acquaintance is unknown. That he was attracted by his youth there can be little doubt, although Oliver Brett described him as plain and lower middle-class with a cockney accent. In a group photograph of Maurice Hankey's staff, which Burgis joined at the end of the war, he has a handsome, alert face and receding, straight hair. He was unquestionably normal and married at the age of twenty-two. Nevertheless he remained devoted to Regy until the day of his old chief's death, and to his memory ever after. The first message of Regy's death which Maurice dispatched was to Burgis, who was attending a disarmament conference at St James's Palace and was due to meet him for luncheon at Brooks's Club that day.

In many ways Regy's relationship with Thrushy was the most satisfactory of his love affairs, because it is unlikely that it was ever more than Socratic. Certainly Thrushy was devastated by Regy's death, and his mother wrote to Nellie: 'Lawrence has lost one who can never be replaced, father, friend, adviser, and one who guided his life absolutely. The love that Lord Esher gave to Lawrence was wonderful, and I do trust that our boy will in a small measure be a comfort to you in the future. For me I shall always hold the memory of Lord Esher sacred.' Thrushy owed to his patron his promotion in the Army during the war and the success of his subsequent career as a secretary in the Cabinet Office. How else in the first quarter of the century could a man of his standing have achieved what he did? Nellie adored him, and as a token of her affection left him in her will the guard ring to her wedding ring, with a charming note of gratitude.

The other members of the Brett family were not so appreciative. Maurice told his father in the early days of the romance – for that is certainly what it was to Regy's mind – that Zena, 'like all the others, is horribly jealous of Lawrence. . . . She feels the difference.'[42] And again, 'I am afraid you will never get the family to like Lawrence. His chief fault seems to be an insolence of manner, and his attempt to capture Doll, but I suspect jealousy is the underlying cause of it all.'[43] He was right with his last words; and Regy didn't care a damn what any of them thought. At first he pretended to find Lawrence merely useful with his shorthand, being speedier at dictation than poor Stanley Quick who had served him for many years. Then he made no bones about his affection for him. Why should anyone be jealous of Lawrence? Zena of all people! '*You* might,' he told Maurice, 'but then you *know* there is no cause.' He admitted that he had to some extent taken Maurice's place, 'because I am obliged (and always have been) to have a companion. But all those others, who don't care a pin whether I am alive or dead, why should *they* care? Their lives would pursue an even tenour without me. They need not grudge me Lawrence.'[44]

It was wonderful to have once again a very young man to instruct, to enrich with anecdotes of all the famous people he had known, to mould in his ways; someone who was not only responsive but alert, clever and eager to learn. Someone on whom he could lavish the wells of emotion which Maurice and nobody else seemed worthy to plumb. The fact that he came from a more modest station in life than Regy's own made the task not only easier but more rewarding. Such a relationship flattered his not inconsiderable vanity. One of his favourite sayings was: 'A statesman should, above all things, be attractive to young men. Should be able to catch their souls. Gladstone could do this; Sir Robert Peel did it. Certainly Lord Hartington was not of the soul-catching order of men.' Regy relished adoration just as he liked being admired. It was a blow to him when in April John Singer Sargent declined to paint him on the excuse that he had done no portraits over the past two years, and was devoting himself to other work. But he was to be painted twice by Glyn Philpot. His appearance in middle age was very arresting: Anita Leslie had written that when he entered a room people stopped talking and looked round at him.[45] He preserved his slender figure and his flawless complexion, which Sylvia described as that of a young girl. His very presence struck awe, and his cold, critical grey eyes, which missed nothing, announced that their possessor was a man who had the power to create or destroy another at will.[46]

On 6 July Regy, having been seized by sudden and excruciating pains at the Roman Camp, was hurried to an Edinburgh hospital and operated on for appendicitis. With the help of two delightful nurses and Nellie's splendid ministrations – she never left him for five weeks – he pulled through. His mind must have travelled back to the spring of 1902 when Doll had nearly died of peritonitis, to be followed by King Edward himself, and the concern of the royal family lest Regy might have conveyed germs from his daughter – so little was then known of the complaint – and infected the monarch. Regy was cheered by twice receiving letters of condolence from King George and Queen Mary. He regarded his illness as a test of friendship and love. Whereas Oliver and the two daughters showed perfunctory concern, 'My Thrush and Chat wrote to me from home *every day*. Molly was perfectly sweet and came *first* to see me.' Every attention and lack of it was registered. 'My Thrush went up to London on Saturday night and returns tomorrow morning.'[47] He basked in the affection of the few he truly cared for. 'One thing was curious about my illness,' he wrote to Lawrence. 'So many people *kissed* me! I have never been so kissed! Chat kissed my hand and face – so did Howdie, and so did Loulou!!! Was not that curious? Rather touching too. Then the funny old Duke of Argyll held my hand all the time he was with me.'[48]

He returned to the Roman Camp on 10 August. During his absence Regy was missing great excitement at Westminster over the passage of the Parliament Bill. Lord Crawford's insinuation that the appendicitis was feigned in order to keep him away from an awkward situation in the House of Lords was of course absolute rubbish.[49] Throughout the debates at Westminster the heat was overpowering, the temperatures veering between 97 and 100 degrees in the shade. Asquith in the Commons finally revealed that the King was prepared to use his prerogative if the peers persisted in their opposition. The threat was enough, but only just enough, to bring the Upper House to its senses. On the 10th they voted with the Government and submitted, if not gracefully then resignedly, to be shorn of further powers.

On the following day Regy wrote from his sofa at home to congratulate the King on the result of the previous night's division. He assured him he had had plenty of time to consider events dispassionately. He was certain the King could not have acted differently. His Majesty was beyond all praise, he wrote, for not swerving an inch from the role of a constitutional sovereign. His courage in not casting about for advice but in taking his own decision was manifest. He, Lord Esher, must show him one day the paper which Arthur Balfour had drawn up at Whittingehame the previous October. It would console him, if he had any doubts of the wisdom of his action. 'When the history of the past year comes to be written', Regy went on, 'the procedure of Your Majesty's Ministers in November will be very justly criticised. It was not procedure worthy of Ministers who were bound to consider the position of the Sovereign.'[50] In answer to this effusion 'The King wrote me such a sweet little letter,' he told Maurice a few days later. 'He *is* a little dear.'[51] Margot Asquith naturally did not subscribe to Regy's indictment of the Liberal ministers, but to comfort him in his convalescence she wrote him a long letter about the virtues of the Cabinet members. Throughout the proceedings her Henry did not have one moment's anxiety:

> He wrote and wired me always in the same words, 'not one peer will be made.' His only apprehension was lest the King's nerves got shaky. The bulk of the country think the K has shown marvellous dash. . . . You know without snobbishness I love him he is the dearest keenest little man in the world but he has rather silly surroundings.[52]

At the beginning of October Regy was invited to Balmoral, a visit which the King and Queen intended to be a sort of prolonged convalescence. But a stay at Balmoral could never offer total relaxation in spite of the royal kindness. 'Nothing could be more affectionate', he wrote in his journal, 'than the King and Queen. They make me *sit* always in their presence and "fuss" about me. I am walking every day with the Queen, and she talks (as she always does with me) about her children and her amusements *and* politics.'[53]

Regy observed how very much Balmoral, like Windsor, had changed since the late King's reign. Everything was very homely. The Queen sat calmly knitting, having lost her malaise. The two boys kissed their father and went to bed. Compared with what it had been, Balmoral was now purely domestic bourgeois. There was no longer that electric element. 'The Court', he wrote, 'will be like the court of George III.'

He had a confidential talk with the King, who said that

> if he had had to create 400 peers he would never have held up his head again. What he especially resented was the promise exacted from him the previous November that he would tell no one. He said, 'I have never in my life done anything I was ashamed to confess – and I have never been accustomed to conceal things.' He described vividly and with pathetic simplicity his anxiety on the days of the final crisis. He asked Rosebery to dinner with him and the Queen, alone. He reminded Rosebery of his having said that he would render the King any service in his power – and then added, 'I am now going to ask you to fulfil your promise.' 'What can I do?' R. enquired. 'You must speak and vote for the Bill.' R. threw up his hands and said, 'I cannot do that. I should be stultified.' The King said not another word and passed to other topics – and they had a most agreeable evening. Next day he had a short note from R. to say he would do what the King wished.
>
> But the day of the division, after R. had made his speech, he disappeared. Finally Walter Long unearthed him in his club, and carried him off to the H. of L. He then made that second short speech which . . . carried 20 votes with him.

The King sat up until after the Division waiting for the result. When it was announced he sat down and wrote the following: 'My dear Rosebery, I thank you with all my heart, Yours very sincerely, George RI.'[54]

The Archbishop of York and the Prime Minister were fellow guests at Balmoral. Lang went out stalking with the King, which must have been the first time for centuries that an archbishop had done such a thing. Asquith, more communicative and warm than hitherto, came to Regy's room and told him all his secret plans and thoughts for the future. He considered it extraordinary that, whereas the French and British General Staffs had arranged all details in the event of war with Germany, the Cabinet had not even been consulted.[55]

Indeed, the likelihood of war with Germany loomed ever closer. The arrival on 1 July of the Kaiser's gunboat *Panther* at the Atlantic harbour of Agadir in Morocco triggered off alarms that reverberated round Europe.[56] Yet Sir John French, visiting cavalry manoeuvres in Germany in August, told Regy that the Kaiser had been perfectly charming, showed him everything, and trusted him on his honour to reveal nothing to France. He merely warned him that the sword of Germany was 'sharp' and that 'any people who run up against it will find it so'. He could manage France very well, he continued, if the British press did not egg that country on to resist him. He mentioned Harmsworth's *Daily Mail* as a hostile irritant. The impression Sir John received was that Germany was prepared to fight the moment diplomatic negotiations broke down. The Kaiser was undoubtedly worshipped by his Army: he moved among the officers and men more like a father than an emperor, though always maintaining his dignity. Yet Sir John noticed a lack of initiative among the troops and a rigid reliance upon rule.[57]

Regy was of the opinion that current rumours of imminent war were damaging and without proper foundation. He deplored the War Office spending all its time planning advances to Berlin. He thought the Board of Admiralty were making themselves absurd by ostentatiously and provocatively rushing up supplies of coal to the ports. No one in Britain knew what the Germans or the French were doing. Unless a coup occurred in some irresponsible quarter he did not believe that a war would break out yet. It was too big a risk for Germany. By this he did not mean that Britain should not be prepared for what he had long envisaged, the *ultimate* conflict with Germany; but what he saw and feared was precipitation – out of nerves – into a premature war. It did not mean that he was an appeaser. Regy merely believed that Britain had come within an ace of war in August 1911, and so he told C.P. Scott of the *Guardian* nearly three years later. The imminence of it had been unknown to the Cabinet, who were mostly away on holiday at the time. Regy denied that it came about because of action by the Defence Committee – most of the Defence Committee, too, were away. The whole business was carried through by a small junta of Cabinet ministers on the Committee: the Prime Minister, Lloyd George, Churchill, Grey, French, a general and two admirals. But Regy admitted to Scott that the Defence Committee knew that intimate communications, with a view to a potential war with Germany, were being sent between the Army and Navy chiefs of France and England (just as they were at the time of this talk) – in spite of the Government pledge that nothing of the kind would happen again without the whole Cabinet's knowledge.[58]

If in his heart of hearts Regy was pessimistic, in public utterances he advocated the forging of an alliance between Britain, France and Germany which would guarantee the status quo of north and central Europe. 'Think what this would mean! It is surely not an unthinkable proposition,' he had written in an article for the *Deutsche Revue* the previous September. This theme he repeated in several letters to the press, including an important one to *The Nation* of 23 December, praising Sir Edward Grey for keeping the peace of Europe and urging his countrymen to understand, even if they could not condone, Germany's desire for territorial expansion in West Africa and the Orient.

When Arthur Balfour retired from the leadership of the Conservative party on 9 November Regy's misgivings took a deep plunge. He could never forgive those who had caused his retirement, he told his old friend, because he was the only statesman of any party to whom he believed Britain's destiny could be safely entrusted. Not that he would raise a finger to displace Asquith in order to hand over the country to the Tories without A.J.B.[59] In a charming and grateful reply Balfour parried the compliment · by begging him not to despair of the Conservative party. 'I think it quite possible that Bonar Law [his successor] may surprise you.'[60]

As for home affairs, Regy felt a particular concern for the plight of the miners in the coal strike of the late winter of 1912. He was at Callander at the time and made a special journey to the nearest pit, at Bannockburn, to talk to the strikers. He was convinced that they had real grievances, and wrote a letter to the King to tell him of his first-hand experience. The coal miners were thoroughly disillusioned by their leaders. They were not agitators, or revolutionaries – they wanted to work. But they were now starving on eight shillings a week plus a one-shilling allowance for each child.[61] To Chat he wrote that it was a tragic situation. The miners were in the right, fighting for a living wage. In his opinion the men liked work better than their employers. Meanwhile they were hungry and bored. He admitted that one must admire the way this strike was managed: the parliamentary speeches were restrained, and there seemed to be a real effort to come to a friendly understanding. Robert Smillie, the strike leader in Scotland, a man of transparent integrity but over-vehement in speech, had been lunching with Mrs Asquith. The Government and the strikers were all behaving like gentlemen – in no other country would opponents behave like this. Of course there was suffering, but the owners were helping the strikers' wives.

Because of his innate Liberalism Regy nearly always took the side of the underdog. In 1898 he had been violently opposed to the anti-Dreyfusards.[62] He hated religious persecution of all kinds. He had been opposed to the desecration of the tomb of the Mahdi, for instance, because the Mahdi was believed by his followers to be a holy man.[63] When a housemaid in his employ was committed to trial for stealing a few pieces of inexpensive jewellery from his daughter Doll, the magistrates criticized him for saying that his family did not wish to prosecute. It was immaterial, the magistrate declared, what Lord Esher thought or wished. However, Regy had her sent home to her mother with some money. Another maid, who gave birth to an illegitimate baby, he protected from the fury of her self-righteous parents. And when Dr Maunsell Vollins was imprisoned for causing the death of a patient – unfairly, as Regy thought – he raised heaven and earth with the Home Secretary for a remission of the sentence.

Regy was constantly at the King's beck and call. Suddenly sent for at an early hour, he would drive post-haste to Windsor from Orchard Lea, or if the King were at Buckingham Palace take an early train to Paddington. On these occasions the King was invariably charming, simple and natural. The royal secretaries were in constant correspondence with Regy on trivial matters as well as important ones. How, for instance, was His Majesty to reply to a letter from a cardinal informing the King of his elevation to this dignity? Letters written in the King's own hand would arrive, beginning, 'Burn!' or 'Please always burn my letters', lamenting two articles in *The Times* about the Navy – 'absolute rot' – and deprecating Winston Churchill's deplorable speech in June to the effect that the British Fleet was not strong enough to send a detachment from the North Sea to the Mediterranean. The King was strongly opposed to Winston's policy of abandonment of the Mediterranean. He talked to the Prime Minister about it and was able to floor him with his superior knowledge of the ships.

Regy was also at this time in charge of the new front imposed on Buckingham Palace, for which he selected Aston Webb as architect. He was still chairman of the Queen Victoria Memorial Committee, which was paying for the project. He insisted on the drawings being submitted to the King before any work was started; even so, the King was piqued that the plans had first been displayed in the House of Commons tea room.

In April Regy told Maurice that, now he was in his sixtieth year, it was high time for him to cut down his duties, and to undertake new ones only if they were of paramount importance. He declined Loulou Harcourt's pressing demands that he should become chairman of the Advisory Committee of the Imperial Institute, but at the urgent solicitation of the Secretary of State for War, John Seely, he did accept the presidency of the County of London Territorial Army Association – which he resigned only in 1921. On 20 March he delivered to the Royal United Services Institution an important speech on the co-ordination of naval and military services.

The *Titanic* disaster of April 1912 sent a shockwave through the nation. That this superb and luxurious liner should founder on its maiden voyage with such huge loss of life seemed at first incredible. To Regy it brought the death of a friend and colleague in many a social and political battle, W.T. Stead. Nothing had happened to Britain since 1880, Regy declared, which had not been influenced by the personality of this extraordinary fanatic, visionary and philanthropist. Owing to overwork and strain, during the last few years of his life Stead had grown somewhat eccentric: he became an ardent spiritual-ist, conversing with Wellington, Disraeli and Palmerston and seeing himself quite incongruously as Charles II, a man whose temperament was diametrically opposed to Stead's. The most straight-laced of men in public life, he also endowed his women friends with the attributes of that monarch's mistresses. When the *Titanic* went down Stead had been on his way to take part in a peace conference in the United States. Regy wrote a fervent and moving tribute to Stead's widow, calling him 'one of the few very honest, very single minded and really *good* men, I have ever known. There was nothing he ever undertook, which he failed to talk over with me. Often and often we differed in opinion, as you know, but it made no difference to our friendship or intimacy.'[64] Stead, a congenital Roundhead in spite of Charles II, had felt no less fervent admiration for Regy, of whom two years earlier he had written:

Who is Lord Esher? Something bizarre, inexplicable, abnormal, something that does not fit in with our notions. He is a man of original genius who has carved out for himself a unique place in the world of affairs, and who in doing so has discarded almost all the usual steps and stairs by which in this country men ascend to the highest positions. He runs after nothing, but all things seem to run after him.[65]

He went on to say that Regy was an incarnate paradox. Seldom seen on the platform or in the pulpit, nevertheless he was the man who got things done. At bottom he was a man of letters, devoted to Plato, J.S. Mill, Wordsworth and George Eliot, with a strong penchant for the theatre, given to speculation on recondite problems of faith and morals, 'but ever impelled into political affairs by the desire for power and knowledge'. Regy, though immensely flattered by these words, may have cavilled over the attribution of power-seeking, for he protested perhaps too much that he had no wish to be thought of in this way by the public.

Regy prided himself on working behind the scenes. For instance he could never keep away for long from the Prince of Wales's problems and future. In July Queen Mary had a lengthy discussion with him in her audience room at Windsor. 'She is disturbed', Regy wrote, 'because the boy has no one with him in France but the tutor Mr Hansell,' trustworthy and generally unexceptionable, but an old woman. She wanted an equerry to join the boy, and mentioned several names that had been recommended to her; but Regy thought they were all unsuitable. It would be an interesting and rewarding task, he considered, for a young man with imagination.[66] A fortnight later the Queen tackled Regy again on this subject. They sat in the garden at Buckingham Palace, but were interrupted by the King, who wanted to talk about the Navy and the Cabinet's decision on the Mediterranean issue. When he left they were obliged to go through proofs of Regy's forthcoming book, *The Girlhood of Queen Victoria*; Queen Mary was rather drastic with her excisions. The book was intended to show the relationship between the young Queen Victoria and Lord Melbourne before her marriage. The author had already suffered the criticism of Queen Victoria's two daughters, Princess Helena and Princess Beatrice, who wanted him to eliminate all expressions of affection and terms of endearment in her journals. The result would have made the subject of the book appear as stiff and cold as an icicle, and Regy resisted in so far as he was able. Both princesses, however, stressed their mother's underlying humility and modesty, Princess Helena claiming that: 'she was so wonderfully tolerant of others' faults and so broad-minded in her views. . . . She had an intense sense of humour and a wonderful capacity for enjoying things; and an unbounded sympathy for others.' The reviews of this book were uniformly favourable and the sales fairly satisfactory.

After their interrupted tête-à-tête in the garden at Buckingham Palace, the moment Regy arrived at Balmoral in September the Queen walked him up and down the river for nearly two hours to discuss every conceivable detail of the Prince's character, his education and temptations. Regy promised to write her some notes on the subject.

Called *The Education of the Prince*, the memorandum was, oddly enough, published as an article later in the year. It reads tritely and is a guarded speculation on the Prince's character, envisaging the experiences of good and evil to be encountered at Oxford. Regy courageously hinted that the Prince ought to mix with other young people and not be kept too isolated. This freedom he was allowed, unlike his grandfather and namesake.

The Queen encouraged him to win the Prince of Wales's confidence. The boy ('who looks very thin') was now eighteen and, by royal standards, grown up. Regy recorded a very long talk he had with him.

> We walked for about an hour and a half alone. I let him have his say about the Navy; he is devoted to his old profession.[67] How is it possible to have been so long a sailor, and not to have got 'imbued with the spirit of it?' was his question. His memory is excellent and his vocabulary unusual, and above all things he thinks his own thoughts. They are long thoughts too. What is the explanation of that dreamy look of his? It is wonder – the wonder of the world and its riddles – and the mystery of coming manhood that hangs over him. He has opinions and strong ones upon Naval matters – and he aired them all in his grave fashion – views on types of ships, on a sailor's education, on strategy and naval policy. He told me of his friendly relation with the officers and men with whom he had served, how he loved to talk to the men of their homes and their pleasures and their troubles. He was full of the 'responsibility' of midshipmen and young lieutenants, and eloquent on the merits of such a training. And presently we broke away from the past, and I said two things to him. First, that no P. of W. can have the advantages of his birthright, without the disadvantages of a hampered youth. 'More of the latter than the former,' he said.[68]

Two significant points emerge: the Prince of Wales's liking for and interest in ordinary people, which was to lead him into trouble during his own short reign for expressing too overt sympathy with their hardships; and secondly, that innate melancholy, shown through the expression of his eyes, 'that dreamy look' remarked by Regy once before, as though indicative of his destiny, his inability to cope with the dignities and anonymities that run parallel with kingship. Regy continued by asking him

> *how*, if he were charged with the education of *a* P. of W., he would plan it. This riddle he is going to think over. He said, 'I am not clever, not a bit above the average.' I asked him how he knew that. He replied by the test of examination. But he sees that this test is only *half* a test. It is a charming mind, grave, thoughtful, restrained, gentle, kindly, perhaps a trifle obstinate and sombre for so young a lad.[69]

Soon afterwards the Prince went to Magdalen College, Oxford. At last he had escaped the tutelage of the mediocre Henry Hansell, whose one undisputed accomplishment, a past proficiency at games, was matched by a present total inability to impart knowledge. After one term Regy thought he saw an acceleration in his royal protégé's mental development. In December he introduced 'the little P. of Wales' to the Marlborough Club. On his election the Prince chose Regy as his first luncheon guest. Regy told Queen Mary about the success of this initiation of the heir to the throne to man's estate. She still thought him very young for his age, however, and inclined to be too introspective. When Regy suggested that, with the Prince's nature and inclinations, it would be well if he could go back to sea, she disagreed. She told him that after Prince Albert ('quite a commonplace character,' Regy noted) had paid his brother a visit at Oxford he had wished to be at Magdalen rather than at sea. The Queen had told the Prince of Wales, who had merely said, 'I suspect that we both envy each other.' Regy told the Queen that the Prince of Wales possessed atmosphere and personality, and in this respect was the only one of her boys who took after her. 'I said, "If you were not the Queen, and came into a room, everyone would ask who you were." She was evidently pleased with this rather personal observation and said that her mother used to tell her that.'[70]

During the Balmoral visit – the other guests were Balfour, Loulou, Kitchener, Henry Chaplin 'and some odds and ends' – Regy, although he naturally did not say so, seemed to have been the most favoured. The routine at Balmoral was the same as during the two previous autumns. The only variation after the Sunday evening stroll round the gardens was a visit to the mausoleum. 'Queer people,' Regy commented. The only troublesome thing was being given a bedroom on the ground floor, because the royal children would pester him mercilessly through the window; and he couldn't very well complain about them. One day he rowed the monarch on Loch Muick, while His Majesty caught trout for tea. The King, charming as usual, talked to him by the hour. He told him that the Duke of Wellington had just found in the cellars of Apsley House thirty-seven boxes of George IV's papers, marked by the 1st Duke 'To be destroyed unread'. The King wanted Regy and Fortescue to look through them at Windsor, and he also hoped Regy would soon get to work on George III's papers, which Ponsonby would be sending down to Windsor.

Early in October the Esher family learned that Oliver had at last married the American girl he had been courting in New York. The engagement had been protracted and not without its setbacks. As long ago as March 1911 Regy had written to congratulate Oliver, hoping that he was bringing home a sweet girl for a wife, that she was ambitious and not too fond of society, 'which is a weakness of American girls', and that she was neither too worldly nor too rich. Oliver must explain to her parents, his father wrote, that he and Nellie were poor, homely people, not in the smart set. Regy and Nellie sent their future daughter-in-law a jewel that had belonged to George III, and they asked for details of her antecedents because they had no American reference books. Antoinette was the only daughter of August Heckscher, a rich industrialist of German descent. She was pretty, the apple of her parents' eye, clever, well-read and direct. However, before the year was out she had broken off the engagement. Regy thought her conduct unpardonable, and he doubted whether his son could be happy with her even if they patched the thing up. Howard Sturgis took the sensible view that there was no dishonour to anyone; it was sensible of 'the tempestuous creature', as Regy described her, to have jilted Oliver if she was not in love with him. Wretched and chastened, Oliver returned home; but he soon went back to New York, renewed his suit and was accepted. Seldom can any marriage have brought more contentment to two people who were the exact opposite of one another – he witty, mischievous and highly intelligent, she earnest, without much subtlety but of undeviating integrity. After her eventual introduction Regy told Oliver that she had been a great success at the Roman Camp, and he felt sure she would provide his son with that stimulus he so much needed. 'The Queen has been badgering me to describe A. and I have painted a marvellous picture of her charms and virtues.' For the first years of their married life Oliver and Antoinette lived at Orchard Lea.

Unfortunately, however, Regy never forgave Antoinette her first lapse of what he considered good taste by rejecting the hand of his flesh and blood, to whom he was never deeply attached, in order to gain time to ponder the change of scene that would be hers for the rest of her life. The fact was that both Regy and Nellie took a dislike to her from the start. Howdie quickly realized this and, being a kindly man, rebuked Regy. 'Don't be wicked about your daughter-in-law and *encourage* yourself in dislike. *I* mean to like her very much if possible. . . . It isn't given to everyone to have the great gift of charm but one mustn't be *unjust* to them on that account.'[71] He pointed out that 'it's a terrible ordeal being handed round on a fork for your . . . husband's friends and relations to smell at, awfully shy work for a girl'. Sylvia at once perceived her parent's hostility to the shy and occasionally awkward bride from across the Atlantic. Whether to curry favour with Regy and Nellie or merely to satisfy her own malice, she revelled in her sister-in-law's social *faux pas* which she recounted in letters to her parents. When Oliver inherited his father's papers and letters he came upon these references, tore out of their rich bindings as many pages as he could and never spoke to his sister again.

A few thousand miles away from these domestic happenings, on 17 October 1912 the First Balkan War had broken out; Regy was deeply worried that if Great Britain acted with France and Russia she might get dragged into trouble at the heels of Pan-Slavism. He thought that Edward Grey ought to revive the European entente and obtain agreement among the Great Powers.[72] On 2 December he delivered a lecture entitled *Modern War and Peace* to the Cambridge University War and Peace Society. In giving due praise to Norman Angell's sentiments and reasoning, he stressed that unfortunately reason did not always prevail. Economic rivalries sometimes led to conflict. So, during the age of transition towards the attainment of the Angell ideal, England must arm. No responsible minister in present circumstances would disarm. Modern war, he pointed out, would be quite different from wars of the past when fighting was left to the professional soldiers. Today it might lead to complete stoppage of continental and imperial trade, the ruin of manual workers and the closing of the Thames to shipping.[73] The speech roused his old friend Howdie to expostulate that he was running with the hare and hunting with the hounds by giving Norman Angell lectures and simultaneously preparing for war with the CID.

During this week the King complained to Regy of the difficulty in which he was placed between Knollys and Stamfordham. The jealousy of the two men, the King said, was intolerable, and, as Regy confided to his journal, 'now that F.K. considers himself *mal vu* by the Opposition and will hardly speak to the Opposition leaders, the position is *most* embarrassing. It is difficult to know what to do. It is almost impossible to tell F.K. the unpleasant truth, however much it is wrapped up. The King suffers under the dilemma.'[74] The dilemma was that George V had never intended Knollys to remain after his father's death. Needless to say, it fell to Regy to impart to Knollys the King's unpleasant predicament; all his tact was called for, and exercised.

Francis Knollys was seventy-five, and for fifty of those years he had worked in the Royal Household. Like most old men, he did not see the necessity for or take kindly to the idea of resignation. When Regy told him that it was only natural for the new King to want to replace his father's private secretary with the man who had served him during his years as Prince of Wales, Knollys adopted an injured attitude. *They* were not satisfied with his faithful services to the Crown and intended to reject him in favour of a young and comparatively inexperienced junior (Stamfordham was in fact sixty-three and had served Queen Victoria in 1880). On 19 January 1913 Regy wrote Knollys a soothing letter:

My dear Francis, the more I think over our talk, the more I feel pained at the notion of your abandoning the direct service of the King under the stress of a sentiment that you have been 'badly treated'. It would be a shock to those who have admired for so many years those high qualities that have proved over and over again so useful to the country, and who furthermore, are devoted to you personally. It is borne in upon me more strongly than ever, that your comfort and peace of mind – not to mention your personal dignity, which is a smaller matter – would benefit enormously by retirement, and by the severance of official ties, but it would be disastrous if any cause were to be associated with your voluntary action in such a matter, other than your anxiety to be relieved, after so many years service, of onerous duties.

The very natural difficulties of the situation, as you and I know it (the impossible commingling of new and old wine) are not for the public palate, and I can only beseech you, dear Francis, when the break comes, to remember only the brilliant successes of your long career, and bury the difficulties and unpleasantness of recent growth, which no one (as you know) appreciates more keenly than your very affectionate friend, E.[75]

On 15 February Knollys wrote to Regy: 'I am leaving the King's service. I will tell you all about it when we meet. I am going at once.' Knollys was amazed not to find time hanging heavily upon him; on the contrary he read, played golf and was happy. The King, delighted that the situation had been resolved, talked very kindly about Knollys to the Household.

However, he never quite forgave him for the injury which he believed Knollys had done to him. In September the King sent for Regy and again blamed the departed Knollys for not having laid before him, long before November 1910, the whole story of the Parliament Bill. 'It was treating me like a child,' he explained.

I suppose he thought I had not the intellect to deal with a matter of such importance. He was my private secretary, bound to me by every tie, and he never so much as told me a word of what had been happening, and he never showed me that I must accept the Minister's advice. He left me with Asquith and Crewe. Why Crewe? Why did Asquith bring Crewe? Because he was a friend of mine and they thought he could influence me. After Asquith had talked for a quarter of an hour, and argued with me, he turned to Crewe and said, 'I can do no more. You try'; and then Crewe began in his hesitating way and talked about the position in which the Queen and my father had left the Crown, and here was I going to ruin everything. So I gave way. But what ought Francis to have done? Why didn't he insist that I should get *in writing* the views of the Ministers and say that they should have an answer next day at 12? He was in a conspiracy with them. I know it now. . . . Do you suppose that if I had been a little longer on the throne that they would have coerced me as they did? Let them try it again. I shall never forget it, and never forgive any of them.[76]

It is true that the King was coerced by Asquith; but it is not true that Knollys was in conspiracy with Asquith's Cabinet. He was far too loyal a servant of the monarchy. But his instincts, being wholly Liberal, aroused suspicion among the Tories who were the King's friends, and irked the King himself. His impartiality was always acknowledged by Balfour, even after their bitter quarrel when Balfour accused him of inviting him to dine in January 1911 in order to pump him and pass on his views to the Prime Minister. Furthermore, the King forgot that on his father's demise he had begged Knollys to remain with him at all costs.

Regy spent many days with the King and Queen at Windsor in January 1913. Together they would come to his room in the Castle where he was hard at work sorting George III's and George IV's papers. Regy regarded George IV's as so much gunpowder containing dangerous ingredients. He loathed the man, whom he called an unmitigated cad and 'the meanest and vilest of reprobates'.[77] He had difficulty in engaging the King's interest in George III's letters, though the Queen was fascinated. With a wave of the hand the King decided that the bundle of letters to George IV from Georgiana, Duchess of Devonshire, addressed to 'My dearest Brother' as she termed him, and mostly appealing for money, should be burnt. On the other hand Regy persuaded him to spare one letter from 'Perdita' Robinson to the Prince of Wales, sent in 1780 when he was eighteen. It was written with much feeling. 'The rigmarole of Mrs Fitzherbert and "Bessie Pigott" her friend – masses of them,'[78] were all condemned to the flames. Regy was greatly to blame for this wholesale holocaust, the result of an inexplicable prejudice.

While Queen Mary went religiously through the boxes the King would discuss current topics. He was very disturbed by a speech of Bonar Law's in which the Opposition leader stated that a situation might arise in which the Home Rule Bill 'is waiting for the Sovereign to *decide* whether or not it shall become law'; in other words the Bill was dependent on the King's initiative, whatever the advice of his ministers might be. It implied that the King's authority was no longer to be limited to the practice of the last two hundred years of automatically signifying the royal assent to bills after their acceptance by both Houses. This was what Regy called a dangerous new departure in doctrine, raised by the Opposition, as a result of a definition of the Royal Veto in the Parliament Act.[79] In connection with Bonar Law's speech Colonel Repington of *The Times* called on

Regy. He expressed the view that the King should have more competent counsellors than at present, and suggested Rosebery, St Aldwyn and the Archbishop of Canterbury. Regy told him bluntly that the King was perfectly able to ask for advice when he needed it, from first the Prime Minister and secondly the Leader of the Opposition. He added that under a constitutional monarchy the men nearest to the King (including himself) were bound to be obscure and that any other system might engender jealousies, criticism and even revolt. He sent a report of the conversation with Repington to Asquith,[80] which the Prime Minister acknowledged gratefully. He considered Regy's notes important in view of Knollys's departure, and wrote,

> If Messrs Repington and Robinson[81] desire to destroy the Monarchy, they have certainly hit upon the best device for the purpose – the setting up, and getting to work of an irresponsible junta of elder statesmen – composed by the way (as it must be) for the most part, of people whom both the great Parties in the State have tried and (for good or bad) discarded, with of course the inevitable shifty Archbishop thrown in.[82]

The idea was grotesque. He congratulated Regy for blowing it 'completely out of the water'.

Throughout this year the King was extremely worried about his constitutional position. Having weathered the harrowing experience of the Parliament Bill, he was now confronted with a recurrence of that perennial vexation, the Irish question. In June the Commons voted for Home Rule, and in July the Lords rejected it. The King once again saw himself the controversial catalyst in the constitution, on whose action extremely grave consequences would depend. Regy was sincerely sorry for him. He knew the King to be conscientious with a keen sense of his duty, but a man of limited intellect who wavered and prevaricated. One great misfortune was the fact that he did not yet feel at ease with the Prime Minister; he liked him, but was rather afraid of him. Asquith was at first inclined not to consult the King when he should, wishing to avoid whenever possible obstruction from what he construed as a figurehead incapable of proffering him useful advice. As time went on, however, their relationship grew warmer. The King lost his fear and respected Asquith's direct dealing with him. Asquith came to value the King's common sense and was touched when he learned from his wife and daughter of the King's liking for him. But in 1913 King George felt out of sympathy with his Cabinet ministers, although he was kind in manner to them all.[83] Knollys having now gone, Stamfordham and Regy were the two men to whom he looked for sympathy and advice. But neither of them had ministerial authority. Guidance he was not lacking. As Stamfordham wrote to Regy on 15 February, he wished good-intentioned people would not trouble themselves about the King, and leave him to exercise his own judgement over Home Rule and other grave issues.[84] Nevertheless, if the King did not need guidance, he badly needed consultation. This Regy was even better able to provide than Stamfordham since, not being a paid official, his time was his own and his views were disinterested. They were not, however, always accepted.

Staying at Balmoral in September, Regy saw that the King was worrying himself ill about politics. His position was uncomfortable. Loulou Harcourt, then Colonial Secretary, Curzon and Bonar Law were also at the Castle. The first caused disquiet by telling his host and sovereign quite plainly that he would be obliged to oppose him if he did not endorse the Home Rule Bill. So Regy composed for the King a long memorandum, the gist of which was that the King must give way to the recommendations of his ministers even if he disapproved of them. The only prerogative he had was remonstrance. At this period of grave crisis over Ireland he advised the King what questions to put to the Prime Minister before assenting to his recommendations. These questions amounted to whether an appeal ought not to be made to the electorate before risking civil war through arousing the hostility of Ulstermen by passing the proposed Bill. After reading the memorandum, the King sent for Regy and talked for an hour and a half. Regy begged him not to lose time but to put his questions to the Prime Minister before the Cabinet had made up its mind. The King replied that he did not wish to move till the psychological moment arrived. Regy resisted this idea, urging the wisdom of stating at once what he felt. The King rang for Stamfordham, who agreed that he should await the statement of advice promised by Asquith. So Regy's counsel was rejected.

> It was characteristic of the King that he took up a phrase of Bagehot's which I had used to the effect that he would have to sign his own death warrant if sent up to him by Parliament, and he said, with a laugh, 'That's all very well but I would shoot through the head any Minister who brought it to me to sign.' And I believe he would![85]

The rebellion of the Ulstermen, if the Bill were passed, and his troops' obligation to put it down, were an additional worry to the poor King. He complained to Regy that the Government expected his troops to shoot down the disaffected in Ulster. Rather than obey such a command, every officer would throw up his commission. In reply, Regy affirmed that it was better to have fighting in Ireland than that the monarchy should be involved.

'Yes,' the King said, 'I know that. It is all party. They want to *use* me, and to make me pull the chestnuts out of the fire for them.'

Regy said, 'Both parties. They are equally to blame.'[86]

In great desperation Regy wrote to Arthur Balfour from Balmoral asking if he might spend a night at Whittingehame when he left. A second constitutional crisis was revolving round the King. The Government were seeking to make use of the King to pass Home Rule without any further reference to the people. He knew full well that among the Unionists a certain faction was anxious to induce the King to dissolve Parliament, another to induce him to withhold his assent. The greatest service that could be rendered to the King at the present time was to devise some expedient by which he could put himself in the right with the Unionist Party and the other half of his people. The anxiety to do the right thing 'is seriously affecting our dear little King's health'.[87] Only Balfour could help resolve this problem.

Meanwhile Regy had hours of conversation with Curzon. Both men agreed that the contest must be allowed to solve itself in Ireland by battle. Curzon's advice was that the King should immediately prepare a statement of his reasons for wishing to appeal to the nation, and explain in the strongest possible terms his reluctance to giving his assent to the Home Rule Bill at this moment; the document should be presented to the Government, so as to protect him whatever might happen in the future. But Curzon did not advise the King's refusal should the Bill pass the Commons a third time.[88]

As the months went by, Regy saw the situation drifting towards dangerous disorder. He advised the King that the country and the Government were underestimating the likelihood of revolution in Ireland, and that he saw a very real risk of bloodshed ahead. He went so far as to advise the King to act unconstitutionally by positively encouraging the people of Ulster to resist by whatever means was in their power, even if a General Election were to go in favour of the Government's Home Rule policy. This advice from an elder statesman was a very grave matter and its wisdom open to question. Lord Chancellor Haldane, with whom he had discussed the matter, disagreed with him. He believed that by a play of firmness in policy and a rigid maintenance of order not a drop of blood need be shed.[89]

By December Regy was confessing to Stamfordham that his conclusions about Ireland were no longer what they had been at Balmoral in September. After the recent speeches of the Prime Minister, Bonar Law and Carson he doubted whether the sovereign would be thought to have acted properly had he allowed the opposing forces in Ireland to rush into conflict. Instead he now recommended that the King – admittedly at risk to himself – should insist on a dissolution, and if it were refused by Asquith, send for a neutral statesman such as Rosebery to form an interim Government for the purpose of appealing to the country.[90] There was something magnificent in the way Lord Esher was never afraid or ashamed to reverse his views if later he thought he had been mistaken in them. Stamfordham was surprised by this change of opinion. He pointed out that, after all, the Government had a majority of 100 in favour of the Bill. To dissolve it, the King would create a precedent which the present Government could invoke if, in Opposition on some future occasion, it wished to rush through an extreme measure. Besides, the Prime Minister would surely say to the King, 'You are anticipating events. The Bill has not yet passed. We may be turned out on some other issue before your turn comes.' In any case, Stamfordham felt certain that Rosebery would not consent to step into the breach.[91]

Oddly enough, 1913 was a deceptively peaceful year in western Europe. Rumblings from Germany were less ominous than in previous years. It was the lull before the storm. Regy was perturbed by Asquith's speech in the Commons in March denying that Great Britain was under any commitment to France. He wondered how the statement could be reconciled with honour to the commitments of the General Staff. Meanwhile the Germans were busy with their Navy Bill, building more and more ships. Spender, a commanding figure in Fleet Street and deep in the confidence of Asquith and Grey, warned Regy that France was ready to ignite. She had got it into her head that the Triple Alliance was rocky, although Grey refused to be drawn by French jingoism.[92] When it came to writing his memoirs Spender paid very handsome tribute to Regy's behind-the-scenes activities in these years. 'Lord Esher seemed to know everything and to know it correctly,' he wrote. His fund of knowledge and complete detachment from all political factions was extraordinary.

> He seemed to be handling all the axes and yet to have none to grind. He judged us all, Liberals and Tories, with a serene impartiality which enabled him to form the shrewdest opinions on points in the political game at home; and at the same time he seemed to be keeping watch over the whole European scene, and calculating the play of its forces and personalities with the same unruffled serenity.[93]

Spender believed that Lord Esher had rendered great services to his country. He praised his wisdom in declining office and remaining detached from party interests. 'He was one of the most remarkable men of his times, playing a unique part in affairs only to be compared to that of Colonel House under the Wilson regime in America.' It was when Regy stepped out of his unique role during the war and started criticizing Asquith and Kitchener that Spender attacked him rather savagely in *The Westminster Review*.

The year 1914 opened, not in fear of immediate war with Germany and continental carnage, but in near certainty among many statesmen that there would be civil strife in Ireland. The situation was as grave as it could be. Regy played an active role in the wings, informing the King directly of the trend of actions and deliberations within the Cabinet and the armed forces, and proffering advice, either in letters to the monarch or through Stamfordham, how the King should act in the parliamentary crisis ahead. On this particular issue Regy did not distinguish himself. He vacillated, at first condoning civil war, then withdrawing that opinion, thinking it would not be in the best interests of the monarch. For in every national crisis throughout his active life he put before all other interests that of the Crown.

On 3 January 1914 he wrote to Stamfordham admitting that his advice to him on 28 December last was likewise premature.[94] In suggesting that the King should ask for a dissolution and send for a neutral statesman he had not meant to suggest he should do so then, but in the event of an armed crisis suddenly arising. He thought now that the King could not take any action over Ireland until it was clear that the Government had forfeited the country's confidence. When that happened, 'the mass of the King's subjects will expect him to throw down his truncheon and cry, "Hold!" All reasonable people must now desire Ulster to be excluded from Home Rule.'[95] He forwarded to Stamfordham a letter he had received from Morley, Lord President of the Council, announcing that the conversations had ended in smoke and were not likely to be resumed; that Grey kept saying the door was still open, whereas the diabolical truth was that all the doors, windows and chimneys were shut.[96] To Regy's letter Stamfordham replied that Asquith must be bold and leave Ulster out of Home Rule at present in order to avoid civil war.[97]

On the 8th Regy wrote to the King personally. Haldane, he informed him, had said that Asquith and Bonar Law were in complete understanding that Ulster might be left out of Home Rule; and that Asquith had been keeping all his conversations secret after Churchill had twice informed Northcliffe of what the Prime Minister had discussed with his colleagues.[98] This letter was followed by another to the King on the following day, announcing that agreement had been reached between the Prime Minister and the Leader of the Opposition, and that the prospects for accommodation were not as black as they were painted. Asquith and Bonar Law would settle matters between themselves without consulting the leaders of the Irish faction.[99]

On the 20th Regy sent the King a memorandum of a conversation with Morley, to whom he had pointed out that the Cabinet were deceiving themselves if they supposed the King would sit back and allow force to be used against a million of his Ulster subjects, 'rightly struggling to be free', and that the man in the street was all for compromise. He doubted whether Morley would pass on this information to Asquith, of whom he and all the Cabinet seemed in awe.[100] After receiving the memorandum the King sent for Regy and questioned him severely: 'What made you change your mind? Almost the last words you said to me at Balmoral were, "Let these people fight it out." ' Regy explained that circumstances had changed. It was impossible to have any doubt now that the forces of resistance in Ulster were so large and well organized that resistance would mean, not a riot or a protest, but civil war; also that the Army could no longer be depended upon to fight Protestant Ulstermen. This was a somewhat lame explanation, as the King seemed to imply. The King then said that some of the best and wisest of the Opposition had told him his interference would ruin the Unionist party by making it into a King's party, and the day would come when they would be beaten, and the King with them. His Majesty could not emphasize too strongly that he was neither Liberal nor Conservative, Home Ruler nor anti-Home Ruler. He got on splendidly with Asquith now, and thought Grey the ablest Foreign Secretary in Europe. He would be sorry to lose them. Regy brought the topic to a close by saying it was impossible to come to a decision yet, and he begged the King not to worry himself to death; whereupon 'the King turned away with some emotion'.[101]

Regy was seriously worried over the King's distress and wrote to Asquith begging him, when he got the chance, to explain to the King with the utmost clarity his constitutional position, and to alleviate the anxieties he was suffering in the desire to do his duty.[102] Regy's attitude to George V was ostensibly that of a benevolent uncle towards a vulnerable and well-intentioned nephew. But Asquith's reassurances did little to mitigate the monarch's worries. The so-called Curragh Mutiny in March, when a number of officers surrendered their commissions in anticipation of being ordered to use force against Ulstermen, plunged him into deeper despair. He told Regy, who dined with him at Windsor on 4 April, that Ireland caused him to lie awake at nights. For a week he summoned Regy every day for an hour's discussion, unloading himself of his unhappiness and pessimism. On the 8th he rode in the Park without pleasure, and in the afternoon picked primroses for his mother. He met Nellie in the Long Walk and talked to her for a long time: 'The first time I ever knew of a Sovereign doing so simple and homely a thing,' wrote Regy.[103] On the 26th Regy even implored Margot Asquith to get the Prime Minister to settle with Ulster without delay. Otherwise the Army would get no recruits, and Ulster would resist. Each day of hesitancy brought an explosion nearer. He gave vent to his inmost feelings: 'I have always wished the Catholics in Ireland to govern themselves. We have shown ourselves unfit to govern a *community* of Catholics: this over centuries. But we are not half as unfit to govern Catholics as they are to govern the Protestant community.'[104] He often reiterated that the Irish were an impossible people, who could neither rule nor be ruled.

There was fear that, once the Home Rule Bill was through both Houses, the Government would introduce an Amending Bill in the Lords embodying their old plan for the four counties to be excluded for six years only, which in its turn would be rejected by the Conservatives of the Upper House. Fortunately this did not happen. Grey reluctantly agreed that Ulster should be permanently excluded. Two days before the Home Rule Bill was passed in the Commons for the third time – the Conservatives and Liberal Unionists having united – Regy was with the King. His Majesty was admirably clear about the situation. 'His intellectual grasp of the intricacies of the political position is as good as that of any minister,' Regy wrote.[105] On 26 June the King sent for Regy to tell him about the conversation he had just had with Morley. He had asked Morley whether, if the amended Amending Bill were rejected by the Commons, it would be fair for him, the King, to be presented with the Home Rule Bill for approval (the Lords, since the passing of the Parliament Act, no longer having the power to veto a third reading). Morley said it would be most unfair. 'That is enough for me, Lord Morley,' the King said. 'You are an old friend, and the oldest and most experienced of my ministers. I am content with what you say, and shall remember it.' He said he could not ask for more than to be treated fairly, and at once added a written record of the other interviews he had given that day to ministers. The King was in the middle of his seventh volume of written matter connected with the Home Rule controversy. Every conversation, Regy noted, was scrupulously chronicled.[106]

Regy was aware that he was not in good odour with either the Prime Minister or the Secretary of State for War. Both considered that he was interfering with critical matters outside his province, and stirring up trouble by alarming the sovereign. Indeed, Stamfordham had been sent an anonymous letter complaining that Lord Esher, the Lieutentant and Deputy-Governor of Windsor Castle, a courtier and a colonel, ought not to write so many letters to the press giving vent to his political views. Civil servants were quite rightly prohibited from doing so, and he was a sort of servant to the King. The public assumed that Lord Esher's views reflected those of the sovereign. It was the same old charge that had been levelled against him before. Regy exacerbated the situation by a letter to *The Times*[107] in which he declared that half the officers and men of the Territorials would resign sooner than be sent to Ireland to put down Ulster rebels, and he considered it monstrous that the men as well as the officers were not permitted to express their feelings. As a consequence, volunteers would be slower to enlist at a time when they were badly needed. Regy asked Stamfordham to tell him if he had overstepped the mark. He pointed out that, although he had been criticized for expressing personal views as a member of the Defence Committee, this was the first time to his knowledge he had been hauled over the coals as a servant of the King. Stamfordham's reply does not survive.

Regy's position of independence very seldom prevented him speaking his mind in private or public. On 27 March he delivered a lecture at the Sorbonne which gained him considerable publicity and approbation in Paris. Its title was *La Guerre et la Paix: Quelques Facteurs Nouveaux de la Politique Internationale*, and the theme that an aggressive war is doomed to failure. He told his audience that France and England were the two most highly civilized and progressive nations of the Western world. In Europe excessive armament-building and war would be a retrograde step leading to disaster. Aggression was doomed to failure. It was, indeed, the thesis of Norman Angell's *The Great Illusion*, and no less than an exposition of what the Garton Foundation stood for. The movement had no anti-patriotic or disarmament tendencies, he said. But war could not bring to nations, whether conquerors or conquered, any of the goals they pursued. The commerce and industry of a country were no longer confined within political frontiers, for fortune depended on a country's credit and commercial contracts. If such contracts were broken, that fortune or wealth disappeared. Every conquest was a vain enterprise, economically speaking, for the riches of a conquered country remained in the hands of the inhabitants. War no longer assured the survival of the strongest. On the contrary, it was the strong who perished and the feeble who survived.

Regy urged his listeners to establish clubs and societies to air the theories he had just expounded to their astonished ears. He ended by telling them, notwithstanding, not to let the Triple Alliance falter; at present the system of alliances, he said, was still the best preserver of peace. Splendid isolation was as futile as an ostrich burying its head in the sand. For a foreigner and citizen of an allied country to demonstrate to a French audience menaced, as they thought themselves to be, by the neighbouring might of Germany, Regy had chosen a spirited and courageous theme.

When it came to writing a letter to *The Times*[108] criticizing Lloyd George's budget speech, which announced increases in taxation, Regy was laying himself even more open to stricture. When it came to voicing his views about a highly controversial matter of national concern, a man of Esher's standing, closely associated with the court, was in a sense committing the court to taking politicial sides. In writing that he had no personal objection to being taxed for the benefit of the poor, he added that in his belief the poor would not benefit from the Chancellor's proposals – because, he argued, the rich would be obliged to throw servants out of employment. This notion was not absurd in 1914, for up to the First World War over 50 per cent of the working class was in domestic service. By way of dissociating himself from self-interest in his objection, he wrote, 'I am too old to have many vices. . . . Such as I had I have regretfully abandoned.' The words delighted many friends, and provoked others to speculate what those vices had been.

Regy spent much of the spring and midsummer at the Roman Camp, which became more and more dear to him and which he regarded as his only home and retreat. Never had the rhododendron blooms been more spectacular than during that May and early June. He never felt lonely or missed the excitements of London except, he wrote to his younger son, occasionally when Maurice was absent. The improvements which from year to year he carried out at the Camp were, he liked to think, for the benefit of Maurice, who would live there when he was dead. His one misgiving was that Zena might not want to bury herself in the north. In 1909 he had got Gerald Dunnage to add new wings and build a tower at one end of the new library. In 1910 he was putting up a reproduction Jacobean ceiling, inserting fifteenth-century panelling in the library and making a new staircase for Nellie. In 1911 Nellie's large north-facing bedroom, with a high chimneypiece carved with fruit and swags, was finished. The grand-children were never admitted to the library, which they called the 'mystery room', where the precious papers, letters and secret journals were kept in their immaculate leather bindings on the dark book-shelves. They had their own premises when they came to stay – an ugly villa on the High Street, approached through the garden; it was called the Bairns' House. The children regarded their grandfather with admiration and awe. He had his favourites and never attempted to disguise his preference. His was the dominating personality of the place; he chose, he gave the orders. Nellie in the background merely smiled and assented, although many of the improvements were the result of her sure taste and discernment. Even in his absence Regy's formidable spirit haunted the house, so his grandson Lionel has recorded.[109]

Regy's love of the Scottish scenery was almost mystical. He would often walk up the hills and on dry days lie in the heather for hours on end, just looking and absorbing. 'Such a day. An absolutely cloudless day,' he wrote to Maurice. 'Not a speck in the azure. [Loch] Lubnaig was like Como. No movement of the deep blue water, except an occasional ripple, when the lightest of breezes touched the loch.'[110] The tranquillity soothed him. 'Today is one of those quiet Sundays which I enjoy here. Not too many bells,' he wrote another time. The silence broken by the river rippling below the windows. Battalions of misty vapours sweeping over the crags. He pondered on the dour history which had fashioned Scotland, whose hills yet did not lack romantic passion. Often he would go forth with gun and dog, clad in his Forbes tartan kilt to which, strictly speaking, he had no right. But he made his own rules. He was a very good shot and liked to sit behind a stone and have a few birds driven over him – a slightly alarming business, for his companions never knew exactly where he might be.

In July 1914 the weather, as is frequently the case before a catastrophe, was perfect. Zena and Sylvia were staying, with their children. Angela, the Maurice Bretts' eldest child and one of her grandfather's avowed favourites, remembers with dread the meals when distinguished people such as Mr Balfour might be lunching. The grandchildren were huddled together in the window embrasure at a separate table, but they would not be kept out of the conversation. During a pause while the grown-ups were discussing world events, Regy would turn to the children and ask one by name his or her opinion. The child picked on would blush and stammer with shyness. When Lawrence Burgis first went to the Roman Camp just before the war, the house was lit by candles and oil lamps. A tipsy butler and a handsome footman, Alfie, waited at table. Alfie, the old coachman's son, also acted as chauffeur of a motor car called a Métallurgique, with a long brass serpent horn.

Meanwhile Regy was writing from Scotland that the Irish news was getting worse and worse; although it was impossible to make out from the newspapers what really was happening. Actually the King, in desperation, had called at Buckingham Palace a conference of two members each from the Cabinet, the Opposition, the Irish National-ists and the Ulster Loyalists, with the Speaker of the House of Commons as chairman. Its task was to debate what area of Ulster could be excluded from Home Rule; nothing came of it except criticism of the King for circumventing the Parliament Act. 'You see that the Conference having broken down', Regy wrote to Maurice on the 25th, 'the Radical papers go on kicking the King. What will Asquith do now? What he *ought* to do is to pass Home Rule by agreement, together with the clean cut [i.e. leaving Ulster out of the measure] – and meet his fate.'[111]

As it happened, other more dire events intervened in lightning succession: the assassination by a Bosnian fanatic of the Archduke Franz Ferdinand of Austria at Sarajevo on 28 June; Austria's ultimatum to Serbia; the declaration of war by Austria on Serbia; the declaration of war by Austria's ally Germany on Russia, which stood by Serbia; the German ultimatum to Belgium; her declaration of war on France; and finally, on 4 August, Great Britain's reluctant declaration of war on Germany. The royal assent did not have to be given to the Home Rule Bill. It was placed on the Statute Book and in October a Suspending Act deferred its operation until the end of the war. Regy left the Roman Camp hurriedly, reaching Tilney Street on 3 August. He was in the thick of things. During the eleventh-hour indecisions within the Cabinet over whether or not Great Britain should go to war with Germany, Regy had no doubts that his country was morally obliged to do so. He immediately got himself invited to luncheon with the Asquiths at Downing Street, where he found the Prime Minister in splendid spirits. On the very eve of the declaration of war he saw the King, who assured him that he had done everything possible by personal approaches to the Emperors of Russia and Germany to maintain peace; but it was all in vain. The progressive civilization of Europe had been suddenly shattered, and the continent was ablaze from end to end.

10

THE GREAT WAR: CIVILIAN SOLDIER

1914–1916

When on 4 August 1914 Great Britain declared war on Germany Regy was sixty-two, but although he was now in advanced middle age he still enjoyed robust health. This was largely due to the care he took of his body, which remained slim and upright; he never drank wine or spirits, and smoked expensive Turkish cigarettes only moderately. Old or not, at such a time he was not going to sit idly at the Roman Camp or even in Tilney Street. He had always been an extremely busy man, working to his own dictation and glorying in his independence; he would not change his methods now. For the past ten years his chief and most important preoccupation had been the Committee of Imperial Defence; but on the outbreak of war that body's functions were at once taken over by the Cabinet. It turned out to be an even more cumbersome substitute – Lord Chancellor Haldane's hopes that the Cabinet would turn into the great General Staff of the Empire, a real War Council, were not to be realized yet.[1] The CID had done a good job in making up-to-date war preparations, and for this it deserved great credit. Throughout the war it continued to digest the ideas and memoranda put to it, but did not originate strategy or offer high-powered advice to the War Office. As for Regy, he would again create for himself roles which he was successful enough to justify. The rest of the world might be mystified by what he was doing. That was their business. He did not care.

In his position as President of the County of London Territorial Army Association Regy had the urgent task of encouraging volunteers to join the services. He was fully aware that, of all the nations involved on both sides, Great Britain had an Army that was – though the most highly trained – by far the smallest numerically. Immediately he established an office in the Duke of York's Headquarters in Chelsea and organized his staff. His daughter Sylvia wrote:

> My father was in a turmoil of organization, flashing like a meteor from the King to the Army, from the Navy to the Flying Corps, dispensing wisdom. Many were jealous of him, for he had no scheduled work and was not bothered by red tape. Lord Esher may not always have been welcome, but they had to admit they could not do without him.[2]

Regy's recruiting was broken by a lightning trip up the east coast of Scotland to inspect defences and a one-night visit to Dover to his regiment, the Royal Fusiliers, of which he was honorary colonel. These exploratory jaunts were a kind of preliminary essay before hitting on what was to be his settled purpose.

He lost little time in communicating with Kitchener, who had been made Secretary of State for War. This appointment gave Regy satisfaction, provided K. was the same man as of yore, which he questioned. Whereas most generals were predicting that the war would not last longer than three months, because beyond that period it would be impossible to feed the troops, K. thought three years would be the minimum time needed to see the thing through. Although Regy feared that K. might destroy the morale of the Territorials by raising his New Army so soon, he fully realized that the great man must be given his head, and he begged those high-ranking officers of his acquaintance at the War Office not to oppose their chief. It would be utterly useless, he said; instead, they should endeavour to explain things to him, and if they failed they should accept his decisions without demur. On the 12th Kitchener sent for Regy to talk about 'his rotten Army. He is damaging the whole organization of the country, from not understanding, and from impatience,' he confided to Maurice.[3] His New Army could not be ready for eight months, by which time anything might happen. 'There never was such a wild elephant. *And yet*, his instincts are true enough.'[4] Kitchener would not listen to Regy, who admired and was often swayed by the man's undeniable charisma while at the same time being repelled by his manner. According to St John Brodrick, Regy was asked by Kitchener, at the Cabinet's behest, to sit on an *ad hoc* committee with himself and three prominent generals to organize the distribution of officers. They sat for fifteen hours a day. Regy dissented from his colleagues because they would not support his efforts on behalf of the Territorial Army, and he soon persuaded Kitchener to dismiss the committee.[5]

Then Kitchener asked Regy to cross over to France 'with a view to smoothing out those constantly recurring difficulties that were invariably the world of tittle-tattlers and mischief-makers', in other words to sort out the Secretary of State's differences with the Commander-in-Chief of the British Expeditionary Force to France, Sir John French. This was the ticklish kind of task at which Regy was adept, and it set him on the course which he pursued practically throughout the war – that of liaison, now between Kitchener and French, and afterwards between the British and French General Headquarters.

Sir John French may in peacetime have been a dedicated and competent general, but he was of such limited imagination and intelligence that when faced with war he made an indifferent commander. Vain, too fond of smart ladies and society, of which he himself was no adornment, he was self-opinionated and yet lacking in self-confidence. He was, however, fond of Regy, whose son had been his ADC and exercised considerable influence over him; of this Kitchener was well aware. Between Kitchener and French there was no sympathy. French was extremely irritated by Kitchener's visits to the front – dressed in field-marshal's uniform although he was a Cabinet minister – which he regarded as an intended slight to himself. Kitchener was utterly contemptuous of such touchiness. 'Lord K.'s big nature, his indifference to all men beyond a very contracted circle of intimates, renders him impervious to the sensitive reactions of Sir John,' Regy wrote. 'I delve down into the psychology of both men, being strongly attracted to them, and try to find solvents for the acids that lie about their hearts.'[6] He found it a hard and trying task. This state of affairs between the Secretary of State for War and the Commander-in-Chief was, at such a critical juncture, unfortunate to say the least.

Regy was from the first opposed to the Expeditionary Force being sent overseas on the outbreak of war. So too was Kitchener, but he was over-ruled by Sir John and the French General Staff. It had been the considered policy of the Defence Committee that only when a German advance was held up should the British land some 150,000 men on German soil to create a diversion, lower morale and cut off the enemy army from the Fatherland. Regy considered it a risky strategy to tack a small British army on to the French one in case it should be cut off if the Germans reached the Channel ports. By the end of August the situation looked exactly like that. Besides, he thought it exposed Britain to the menace of Germany taking advantage of the fact that the Expeditionary Force was heavily engaged across the Channel, and landing a small force on the Norfolk coast. As it was, the best-trained British officers were now in France, and Kitchener was left with raw, inexperienced ones. Even so, Sir John French was clamouring for more troops. The war had begun badly for the Allies. By the end of August the Germans had taken Liège and occupied Brussels. The Battles of Namur and Mons resulted in British retreat.

Now Sir John was showing temper. In wanting to attack the whole German Army he was put out when his impetuosity was checked by the War Office. He was also at loggerheads with the French Commander-in-Chief. Sir John could only see issues immediately in front of his nose, and ignored Kitchener's long-distance view. At the beginning of September Kitchener went to France to see matters for himself. He was very tactful with Sir John, in which he was greatly assisted by the French Minister for War, Alexandre Millerand.

September witnessed further German advances on the Western Front. They destroyed Louvain and took Amiens. By the end of the month Regy was again in France acting as intermediary between Kitchener and Sir John. Because of the rapid German advances the French Government withdrew from Paris to Bordeaux, and the staff of the British Embassy went with them; the American Ambassador remained behind and acted on behalf of British residents. Regy stayed in Paris, making his headquarters at the Hôtel Westminster in the Rue de la Paix, and sometimes at the Hôtel Meurice. The majority of hotels were closed, and practically all the shops had their iron shutters pulled down. There were no horse vehicles or motor taxis in the streets. When Regy descended the steps of his hotel a crowd collected in surprise at the sight of a British officer in uniform.

He wrote to Lawrence Burgis that he was having a tremendous time, both sad and thrilling. With Guy Brooke[7] he drove from Paris in an armoured car through silent villages and across the Marne battle-field. Bridges had been destroyed and the peasants were dispersed, yet the country was all smiling. Here and there dead men and horses lay with just a wisp of straw over them. Such sights were to be familiar as the war progressed, but in September 1914 they were still a novelty. It was impossible not to be fascinated by the terrible beauty of the battlefield scenes, and he wrote in his journal, 'No one could stand among the trees overlooking the Aisne valley, and not remember the description of Tolstoy, or forget the passions, the philosophic musings of Prince André on the field of Austerlitz. On a starry night it is all so infinitely great, and yet so infinitely little.'[8]

Regy stayed with Sir John in the château which he had made his headquarters at Fère-en-Tardenois. He had a long talk with the Commander-in-Chief, who voiced his resentment of Kitchener's coming among the troops masquerading as a soldier when he was now a civilian; Regy made light of the matter and mollifed the touchy little man. He mused upon the distressing story that an army chaplain had told him of a callow country lad who was court-martialled for leaving his trench by only a few yards. His CO did not have the courage to tell him that he was going to be shot. Early the next morning the chaplain woke him by putting his arms around him. All the boy begged was that his people at home 'would never know'.[9] In church Regy saw a dozen nuns and one British officer receiving the Sacrament. All down the nave and aisles lay about 150 British wounded, perfectly quiet, some smoking cigarettes. Regy was deeply disturbed by the state of the wounded, who were attended by a single overworked RAMC officer and fed on scraps of beef between hunks of bread. 'Disgraceful,' he wrote to Burgis. 'I have made a tremendous fuss, and have got Lord K. to back me.'[10] He asked himself whether the immense sorties to capture some little hillock were worth the appalling casualties. The savagery, the waste and the cruelty were anathema to his fastidious sense of what was the proper treatment of the simple soldier.

Regy was determined to follow the course of the journeys made by the wounded from the front. He discovered that, after lying on bare church floors and in barns, they had a twelve-hour trek in wagons, huddled on straw and cruelly jolted, to the nearest railway station. There they lay about on stretchers until piled into horse boxes or cattle trucks which reeked of disease, tetanus and gangrene. The train might take two or three days to reach a base hospital. The worst casualties destined for England took at least thirteen days to arrive, during which time their wounds were unattended and their dressings seldom changed. After the Battle of the Marne Regy helped the Editor of the *Westminster Gazette*, J.A. Spender, and his wife to see for themselves the conditions endured by the wounded at the front. Spender drew attention to this state of affairs in his paper.

Athough the United States was still neutral, it had established units for the care of wounded belligerents in northern France. The kindness and efficiency of these units, in contrast to the British ones, were overwhelming. The American hospital at Neuilly was a marvel of organization, and even luxury: the nurses and orderlies wore spruce white coats, and the wards were light and airy. Regy attributed the muddle and lack of vision of the British organizers to War Office incompetence. His influence with Kitchener resulted in mobile Red Cross hospitals, ambulances and medical personnel being sent immediately to Paris. Regy arranged for Arthur Stanley, Lord Derby's brother and chairman of the Red Cross Society, to pay a further visit with him to the front, and he also wrote a memorandum on the subject which Lord Kitchener circulated to the Cabinet.

On his frequent return visits to England Regy was struck by the way the British public seemed not to have grasped the gravity of the situation overseas. Society people were still regarding the war as a picnic, like the South African war. He was shocked by the contrast between the rich Londoners dining at the Ritz – men in tailcoats and white ties, and women in low-cut dresses, plastered with jewellery – and ordinary Parisians eating in bistros in their everyday clothes. In

France, unlike England, there was no petrol allowance for private motor cars. On the other hand Regy also noticed how the grass in the London parks was worn threadbare by drilling feet; the lamps were all painted over, and only half the usual number were lit. Experience was to reveal to him that in the long run the rich wasters were hardier and readier to suffer discomfort and extreme danger than were humbler and more meritorious persons. How was that seemingly incongruous paradox to be explained?

Regy was in Kitchener's confidence, constantly at his elbow and ever ready to proffer advice, which was usually accepted. He was in and out of the War Office at all hours. Kitchener appreciated his friend's contribution to the extent of recommending him to be appointed Chief of the Imperial General Staff. The Cabinet of course would not hear of it, which did not surprise Regy in the least; he was quite happy composing memoranda for Kitchener and sending copies to the King. At the end of the year he pointed out to Kitchener that Britain's greatest weakness was a lack of co-ordination between the naval, military and political forces of the Empire. The evil did not end there, however, because there was no proper co-ordination between the Allies either. It was difficult to keep in close touch with Russia owing to the great distance between the two countries and to the repugnance to normal diplomatic channels of the Grand Duke Nicholas, the Russian Commander-in-Chief. But with France there were no such excuses. The French were under far greater strain than the British, whose authorities just did not understand how to handle them. Regy, who was after all half French and spoke the language perfectly, knew that it was useless to haggle and bargain with French generals, as you would with Americans; but if you appealed to their friendship or sentiment they would do anything for you. He advised Kitchener to give of his best to the French people and ask for nothing in return; he would, he said, be amply repaid. Regy's usefulness as a go-between was to be proved again and again during the war. By January 1915 he was the recognized liaison between the British Secretary for War and Millerand, his counterpart in France. He had wormed his way, so to speak, into this unofficial position which he had foreseen to be absolutely necessary. As a result of his success his role was soon to be confirmed officially.

At the end of the month he was writing to Maurice that he had decided to 'take personal action'. He was, he explained, 'working for a sort of *Allied Council*. Very small. Russia, England, France, Japan.'[11] He had been talking with Millerand in Paris about the lack of co-ordination between the Army, the Navy and the diplomatic corps in Britain, her failure to make any use of her sea power, and the lack of co-operation between the Allies. To rectify these shortcomings was, he assured the French Minister for War, one of his major aims. Millerand complained to him of the lack of complete frankness between the two countries' leaders, and of the refusal of Sir John French – in spite of professing to work under the French Commander-in-Chief, General Joffre – to obey his instructions. Regy heeded Millerand's complaints. He urged Kitchener to come out frequently to France and discuss matters with Sir John, Millerand and Joffre, the last two of whom were working closely together. Kitchener replied that the War Office was so weak that he dared not leave it as often as he could wish, and he told Millerand that Regy would from time to time deputize for him. Millerand was satisfied and from that time onwards summoned Regy to come to him often and at short notice. The French Government was now in favour of a concerted attack on the German submarine bases at Zeebrugge. In February Regy crossed to Paris to inform the French War Minister that Kitchener did not favour such an attack, and would prefer to open a new assault on the enemy through Serbia. Millerand agreed with the first proposition but considered the second premature. In the same month he complained to Regy that Auguste Huguet, the popular French Military Attaché in London, was too 'English' and too submissive to Sir John. Regy defended Huguet, pointing out the great respect in which he was held by his countrymen and the fact that no man, French or English, had contributed more to the British Expeditionary Force being sent to France in August 1914.

Maurice, fully aware of the nature of his father's activities, wrote from Paris where he was established as Assistant Provost Marshal:

> I suppose K. is going to make you his representative here. Get authority from the P.M. too if you can. It will open doors much more easily in this country, where the first question is always: 'What position does he hold?' They do not yet understand, I mean the people who matter here, who you are and why they should see you! They are very hide-bound.[12]

This was sound advice. But Regy was touchy on the subject and replied to his son:

> I am not going to put myself out. I never do. Nor am I going to *regularize* my position which means that someone can give me orders. I never have. . . . It is such a new idea to the French, and it makes them sit up. There are now only two members of the Defence Committee who are not *officials*, Arthur Balfour and myself. It is a position of honour and complete freedom from everything and everybody excepting our responsibility to the King and the country. On these terms I will meet any of the French, soldiers or ministers. But on no other terms. . . . Very soon a moment will come when independent judgment from the standpoint of the *French*, will be very useful to Lord K.[13]

Again Maurice pointed out that the French would not understand this attitude. Then, deeming filial discretion the better part of valour, he submitted. 'Of course I agree with all you say about your position. The fact that you are free and responsible to no one is the source of half your power in England.'[14] To this his father responded that they must either treat with him as he was, or not at all. Regy relished the fact that he could and did snap his fingers at anyone, of low or high estate. To a telegram from the War Minister himself: 'When are you coming back? Kitchener', despatched on 19 March, he replied curtly: 'Never, unless you send for me.' But the result of adopting this high-handed and recalcitrant line was that many people, British as well as French, did not appreciate the important position he held and often subjected him to ridicule.

By March Regy was *de facto* head of the British Intelligence Service in France. In this capacity he wrote long, weekly letters to his friend Maurice Hankey, Secretary of the War Committee, in London on the question of alternative strategy to break the deadlock in the West. These letters were intended to be shown to the Prime Minister, Asquith. Indeed throughout the war Regy kept Hankey in close touch with affairs in France. Hankey was, moreover, a man of his creation. Originally discovered by him and Admiral Fisher, he was given the job of Assistant Secretary to Ottley at the CID in 1909. Known as 'the man of a million secrets', Hankey had one of the most brilliant brains of his day. J.A. Sylvester, who was his private secretary from 1914 to 1921, said that he was by far the finest man on the administrative side of Whitehall and that his mind was like that of a German razor.[15] It also resembled a cold, calculating computer; Asquith described him as 'the most useful man in Europe . . . he has never been wrong'.[16] He was an absolute fiend for work, acknowledging no limits to drudgery – a man, according to Stanley Baldwin, who 'had no bowels'. In 1912 he had been promoted to Secretary of the CID at the early age of thirty-five. The outbreak of war brought him further responsibilities of the most important kind – secretaryship of the Dardanelles Committee, the War Committee and in 1916 the War Cabinet Secretariat, to which was added the clerkship of the Privy Council. His greatest achievement was the formation of the Cabinet Secretariat, which brought him immense power, for no man was in closer touch with the Prime Minister in wartime. Since Hankey regarded Regy as guide, philosopher and friend, admitting that he owed practically everything in life to him, he could hardly have had a more valuable contact with the French Government.

By the beginning of 1915 Regy shared Kitchener's extreme pessimism about the outcome of the war. To his friend Chat he wrote privately, 'We are going to lose this war. A stalemate and a peace that is only a truce. No flattening out of Germany or reinstatement of Belgium is possible. . . . The French are splendid but they cannot bear more than a certain amount of strain. Our soldiers grand but our people flaccid.'[17] When Chat protested, Regy replied, 'The *facts* are obvious. Look at the map and see what Germany has done and is doing.' On 29 January he presented the CID with a memorandum, marked 'Secret', called *The War after Six Months*, which gave an up-to-date situation report on the belligerent and Allied countries. The advantage lay quite clearly with the Germans. Haldane's reaction was that, since Germany was making more effort than the Allies, she might wear herself out sooner; and Balfour politely reproved Regy for his depression on the grounds that the German casualties were as high as the British.

One of the criticisms levelled against him by the British Ambassador in Paris, Lord Bertie, was that he was morally, politically, militarily and financially pessimistic. Another objection was that he was the spreader of false rumours that the French were about to make a separate peace. But Regy's detractors were often ignorant of his ability to trail red herrings before the representatives of neutral countries and persons whose loyalty to the Allied cause he had reason to suspect. As for the British Ambassador, he loathed Regy from the very start. Frank Bertie had held his post in France since 1905. He saw Regy as a freelance rival with no responsibilities, but with a blank cheque from Asquith and Kitchener, undermining his authority. 'To make matters worse', he complained, 'Esher was equally at home with the French politicians as he was with the British Generals.' It was most exasperating, no doubt. Professional diplomatist and courtier were the antithesis of one another.

A further cause of intense annoyance was Regy's close co-operation with the only man at the Embassy who, he maintained, knew what was going on – Colonel Herman Le Roy-Lewis, who without consultation had been thrust upon Bertie as Military Attaché. A good-looking, mysterious figure, able and efficient, Le Roy-Lewis had the utmost contempt for his boss, who never deigned to address a word to him. At first Regy was disposed to admire Bertie for his understanding of the French; then the Ambassador's overt hostility changed his tune. Regy's perceptive antennae soon sensed that Bertie was a weak man who allowed himself to be swayed by personal likes and dislikes.

There are plenty of disparaging references to Regy in Bertie's published diaries. The first, dated 12 February 1915, begins, 'Esher came in fancy dress.' This was a common gibe. Arnold Bennett, dining in a restaurant at Meaux, likewise wrote that 'Lord Esher came in, wearing a fancy military costume – perhaps that of Constable of Windsor Castle. A star was depending from his neck. As soon as he saw my eye on it he tucked it inside his double-breasted khaki coat.'[18] Not for nothing did the mocking British Embassy clique dub him 'The Dog at the Fair'.[19] Lord Castlerosse related that the first time he came in contact with Regy was in the Ritz Hotel in Paris.

> His lordship was gorgeously caparisoned; round his neck hung a cross, and his breast was so covered with medals that I came to the conclusion that not only must he be at least a Commander-in-Chief, but also must have played a prominent part in the Hundred Years War. I asked who he was and was told that he was a modern 'Eminence Grise'. We were introduced and I said, 'There is a certain affinity between us. I understand that you have your finger in every pie, and I, on the other hand, go the whole hog and spend my life in hot water.' He enjoyed the joke and we became friends of a kind. I fear, though, that he never thought I was respectable.[20]

After all, Regy had some excuse not to wear civilian clothes. He was flitting from embassies and ministries to the French and British Army headquarters, and from there to the front and back; and he was honorary colonel of a reputable British regiment as well as – his card proclaimed – Chef des Territorieux Britanniques. He was also Sub-Commissioner of the British Red Cross Society in France. It does not strike the modern reader as wholly ridiculous for a distinguished official of sixty-three to be thus 'caparisoned'. Still, his precise position puzzled people. In the autumn a question was asked in the House of Commons as to what department Lord Esher represented. Lord Robert Cecil's nebulous reply was that he had no definite appointment, but was 'charged from time to time with particular tasks of a military character'. It was a cover-up of the important and secret role Regy was playing as head of the British Intelligence Service in France.

Lord Castlerosse also talked of Regy's devotion to his son Maurice, for whom he had managed to obtain the position of Assistant Provost Marshal of British troops in Paris, with the rank of colonel. 'He could not, in fact, have done a crueller thing, because every fighting soldier on going there sang a little hymn of hate against Maurice, who, I believe, was really a kindly, simple fellow, who would, if he had only been left alone, most certainly have been in the trenches.'[21] It was through his father's friendship with old Joe Duveen that Maurice was lent the art dealer's luxurious offices and gallery in Paris for his headquarters. In the same way Regy got Oliver into the Military Intelligence department of the War Office, where he spent the four years of the war in Whitehall. A determination to keep those he loved – and if he did not exactly love Oliver, he respected him as the heir to his honours – out of the fighting was also exemplified by his getting

Lawrence Burgis made ADC to Brigadier-General John Charteris.

Maurice's devotion to his father was no less sound now that he was safely married to Zena and, helped by the war, had cut himself adrift from Regy's over-demonstrative affection. He found time to write to Regy from the office a letter which warmed the ageing man's heart.

> The memories I have are very sweet. There is not one which I would obliterate if I could, and they are all connected with you and Zena. Do not ever dream that I could forget the past, for all my life has been a cloudless joy and all owing to your love for me. As far back as I can remember you have been the one dominant figure in my existence, my father, lover, friend, what you will, the only being to whom I have turned for what is good in this world. . . . I am undemonstrative I know, even with Zena, but you know in your heart that there is nothing in the world I would not do to try and make a small return for what you have done for me. . . . My heart never alters. And I feel today towards you just as I have felt any day for the last 20 years. My love is just as strong as in the days before Zena came into my life. My heart is big enough for two. . . .[22]

Regy continued to keep in touch with the King by letter when he was in France, and by audiences when he was in London. In January the King sent for him to tell him that Kitchener should be allowed to have Sir Henry Wilson, if he wanted him, as Chief of Staff. Nothing, he intimated, should be denied the one man who was capable in his view of saving Britain and the Empire, difficult though His Majesty sometimes found the Field-Marshal. He complained that Kitchener never allowed him to get a word in edgeways, and reduced him to silence. Regy was impressed by the King's remarkable knowledge of what was going on.[23] Furthermore, he too favoured Wilson being made Kitchener's Chief of Staff, for he was the only British general liked and trusted by the French.

In May the King was depressed and hoping for the Americans to join the war. Regy told him that the Archbishop of Canterbury had expressed the hope that the Allies would not follow the Germans in using poison gas. The King took a diametrically opposite view, holding that the question was a military, not an ethical, one.[24] In July Regy went to Windsor

> and met the King at the door. He made me walk with him and the Queen to Adelaide Cottage. Princess Mary joined us, and we four had a cosy tea. The Queen and Princess Mary laid the table. . . . When it came to the making of tea there was no urn. But the King would not allow the tea to be made in the kitchen, and to the obvious indignation of the servant, he was made to bring up a very heavy and dirty

tea-kettle. . . . Then we walked back to the Castle. The King read me a letter from the Czar. Full of firm determination and unbounded confidence.[25]

In September, in a letter to Stamfordham, Regy was urging the King to come to France, where his presence would be a tonic to the troops.[26] There was much gloom at the Palace over the devastating loss of men in the massacre at Loos. And when the King consented, Regy begged him on reaching Paris to give President Poincaré a word of praise about Millerand, who had been the best possible friend to Britain and was Kitchener's firm ally; it was more than probable that the Cabinet crisis in France might lead to his disappearance.[27] The King did as he was requested, but Poincaré retorted that Millerand was so unpopular in the Chamber that he had to go. In October Regy received a letter from Stamfordham on the King's behalf, thanking him for all his help during His Majesty's visit to France. Regy was touched by the letter. 'You are always extraordinarily kind to me,' he told Stamfordham. 'I have never in my life thought of the King as being "indebted" to me for the smallest thing.'[28]

Kitchener's differences with Sir John French, apparent since the very outbreak of war, were extremely detrimental. In January 1915 Kitchener complained to Regy that Sir John was writing behind his back to ministers at home.[29] By the end of the month Sir William Robertson was appointed Chief of the Imperial General Staff. This bluff, reliable, direct Lincolnshire village lad, who dropped his 'h's' and was referred to patronizingly but affectionately by his colleagues as 'Wully', was deeply loyal to Haig but had little use for French. Nevertheless Sir John was obliged to accept him. Regy, who was fond of Robertson, applauded his appointment, although towards the end of the war he became critical of his increasing ineffectiveness. Kitchener and Robertson made a formidable and united partnership. In his diary for February Bertie recorded that Esher told him friction between Kitchener and French was constant: whereas the former had no likes or dislikes, but was tactless and persistent and did not always do the right thing, the latter had both favourites and pet hates. Sir John thought himself justifiably angry with Kitchener for having an officer – meaning, presumably, Regy – at Joffre's headquarters in direct communication with London instead of with GHQ at St Omer. Moreover, Kitchener would not increase Sir John's forces.[30] A few weeks later Esher lunched at the Embassy on his return from a visit to Sir John. He said that Sir John, was full of confidence but complaining that Kitchener continually interfered with his plans and details. Relations between the two leaders were more strained than ever.[31]

On 14 May Kitchener sent a note to Regy: 'I am deadly sick of this system of intrigue with Headquarters, and if I get an excuse shall take it and get out of it all.'[32] Alarmed by this prima donna-ish outburst, Regy hastened to see him after dinner. They talked till eleven o'clock, and Kitchener was very forthcoming: he admitted to being overworked and yet incapable of delegating. Regy decided that Sir John was to blame for being explosive and surrounded by hangers-on who magnified his grievances; he himself knew Kitchener to be the least vindictive of men. On a recent visit to the front Winston Churchill had exacerbated Sir John's susceptibilities by discussing matters which should have been within Kitchener's sphere. Regy concluded that the problem had two causes: French's rank, which was inferior to Kitchener's; and the fact that Kitchener, as Minister of War, liked to hold all the strings in his own hands. Any attempts to patch up the quarrel, he thought, could be no more than temporary. He agreed to submit a memorandum for the CID, entitled *Unity of Command*, in which he proposed that Lord Kitchener, the people's idol, should be promoted to Commander-in-Chief of Imperial Forces in addition to being Secretary of State for War.[33] Anything was better than Kitchener's retirement at this stage, but the Cabinet rejected the proposal.

Regy was being pulled in all directions. The King, much disturbed by the War Minister's threats, kept sending for him. So did Kitchener. Guy Brooke, writing from France, begged him to come immediately to see Sir John, who was in deep need of his counsel. Haig, too, urged Regy to visit him at the front. Because of the crisis at home and the formation of the first Coalition Government under Asquith, Regy felt unable to leave London; however in mid-June, after Sir John had resolutely refused to accept proposals emanating from the French GHQ, he was obliged to cross over to St Omer to act as intermediary between the two field-marshals. Regy managed to do a little first-aid, but took a far from sanguine view of the situation.[34]

It was not only with his chief that Sir John was at loggerheads, but also with Joffre, as Millerand complained to Regy. In this particular Regy considered that the fault lay with the two Governments, who ought to settle the question of precedence among the British and French commanders. As usual, it was unity of command that was lacking.[35] Millerand sent for Regy to discuss this very question – which had already been discussed *ad nauseam*. He, being hand in glove with Joffre, not unnaturally wanted his compatriot to be Commander-in-Chief of Allied Troops; but Kitchener would not hear of it.[36] 'Your Government should have the moral courage to insist,' Millerand told Regy, who reflected on the absurdity and terrible waste of life involved in pouring vast numbers of men into the flat country round St Omer. Kitchener, thinking along the same lines, sent for Regy to ask why with so large a force of men the British were not doing better on the Western Front. It must be Sir John's fault. Kitchener wanted to send out yet more men, but Regy deprecated this idea, saying that there were too many men and not enough ammunition. Again, lack of central control was the underlying cause of all the muddle. It was not his business to issue commands; he could do no more than point out what he had observed from his repeated visits to the front. He had already written sharply to Kitchener: 'Either you desire the Field-Marshal to be under Joffre, or you do not. If you do not (which I venture to hope is the case), you should say so . . . and explain that our system of government makes it impossible, quite apart from the military sentiment. They would understand.'[37]

In her diary for 21 May, Nellie Esher wrote 'We were to have gone to Scotland but Lord Kitchener wanted R. to go to France, so our plans were changed.' Regy went straight to see Sir John French at Hazebrouck and talked to him man to man. He warned him against allowing his staff to leak news to the press and bring about attacks on Kitchener. Regy told him that his successes entirely depended on keeping on good terms with Kitchener and Joffre. All that his foolish friends' carping had done was to enhance Kitchener's reputation. Kitchener did not want to interfere with Sir John's functions, Regy said, and merely asked that he should not interfere with him as Secretary of State for War and head of the Army on all fronts. It was agreed that the best solution to the present difficulty was for Sir John not to communicate direct with Kitchener but to send all written communications via the General Staffs in the field and at home; also that Kitchener should not be expected to send further divisions, which might be needed elsewhere, until the German lines showed signs of being broken. There and then Regy drafted and despatched a letter of apology from Sir John to Kitchener.[38]

There is no doubt that Regy did an excellent job in bringing French and Kitchener temporarily to terms. He concluded that the war was being conducted by admirable old men in both France and England, most of whom he had known all his life, and all of whom had passed their heyday twenty years ago. Passion was what was needed in time of war, and it was lacking, as were inventiveness, boldness and action. If each of these old men could be replaced by another under the age of forty, he felt, the Allies would defeat the Germans in no time.

On his return to London, Regy told Kitchener that French had undoubtedly been hurt by the tone of some of his despatches, and by his coldness and lack of appreciation. 'I have given him most absolute assurances that you have always wished to be loyal to him, and that his own warm-hearted, impetuous, loyal nature will respond, I feel sure.'[39]

Sir John had certainly been guilty of whipping up the outrageous press attacks on Kitchener: had complained to the influential war correspondent of *The Times*, Colonel Repington, about the shortage of shells, which he attributed to the Minister of War. Repington's subsequent despatches in *The Times* created a major political row, and were followed by hysterical demands in the popular press for Kitchener's resignation. General Sir Henry Wilson, who was largely responsible for the work of General Headquarters, added fuel to the flames by spreading rumours that Kitchener was mad and unfit for service. Lord Northcliffe, owner of *The Times*, told his fellow press baron that he intended, 'to go on attacking Lord Kitchener, day in, day out, until he drove him from office'. It was this persecution that provoked Kitchener to write to Regy the despairing note of 14 May quoted above. Sir John excused his conduct by referring to Asquith's famous Newcastle speech in which he had said that the Army had all the ammunition it needed. 'When I read this speech, after all my public and private appeals, I lost any hope that I had entertained of receiving help from the Government as then constituted.'[40] He had then, he said, received at his headquarters a telegram from the Secretary of State directing that 20 per cent of his already inadequate reserve of ammunition should be shipped to the Dardanelles. It was at that juncture that he had aired his grievances to Repington, who happened to be at Headquarters. Paul Cambon, the French Ambassador, told Regy that he supposed the British nation had gone mad to allow the censor to pass articles and correspondence against Kitchener at such a time of crisis.

Regy was so disturbed by the ugly clamour being raised against Kitchener over what became popularly known as the 'Shells Scandal' that he begged Asquith to shut down Northcliffe's newspapers. The King sent for Regy, and while they walked round the gardens at Buckingham Palace told him he would support Kitchener to the bitter end. Regy dined the same evening with Kitchener, who declared how impossible it would be for him to remain at the War Office were Lloyd George ever to become Prime Minister. The personal attacks in the newspapers continued, and at a *tête-à-tête* dinner with Regy in July their victim actually showed signs, Regy wrote, of being 'rattled'.[41] The truth was that the legendary K. was beginning to lose his grip. As Violet Asquith wrote to a friend, Aubrey Herbert,[42] about this time,[43] her father loved him but the rest of the Cabinet foamed at the mouth at the mention of his name. 'At Cabinet meetings he smokes his cigar and talks the whole time. Starting off with, "I can't see why you want to do away with the Welsh Church" or "I don't see it's very important if we pass Home Rule now, or not." ' Kitchener was unreceptive to new ideas. He was obliged, she wrote, to have the differences between the territorial, reserve and special reserve forces explained to him over and over again. Yet Kitchener at sixty-five was not senile, and the public regarded him as a giant of strength, a bulwark against the enemy. To have ousted him during the summer of 1915 when Britain's stake in the war was at its lowest ebb – progress on the Western Front nil, casualties colossal, the Dardanelles fiasco a tragedy on an epic scale, the Russians in retreat from Hungary – would have been disastrous.

If Lord Kitchener was not senile, seventy-four-year old Lord Fisher very nearly was. His was the naval counterpart to the other's military legend, and in him all able-bodied seamen and most Tories had implicit trust. When, in October 1914, Prince Louis of Battenberg was cruelly obliged to resign as First Sea Lord on account of his German birth, Churchill, then First Lord of the Admiralty, invited Fisher to take his place. 'My beloved Friend Thanks for your dear letter,' Jackie wrote to Regy.

> Isn't it fun being back? Some d——d fools thought I was dead and buried! I am busy getting even with some of them! I did 22 hours work yesterday but 2 hours sleep not enough so I shall slow down! *Secret*. The King said to Winston (I suppose dissuading) that the job would kill me. Winston was perfectly lovely in his instant reply, 'Sir, I cannot imagine a more glorious death!' Wasn't that delicious? But burn please. Yours for ever more.[44]

At first all worked well. Then came the Dardanelles campaign, an operation about which Fisher from the start had grave doubts.

With a view to causing a distraction from the Western Front the British War Council had decided that communications should be opened from the Mediterranean to the Black Sea. The immediate aim was to assist Russia, already hard pressed by the Central Powers on her western flank. Naval operations began in February. But before land forces could arrive to secure the communications of the fleet, the naval attack of 18 March had failed. Instead of a shock victory over the Turks, a prolonged stalemate ensued with fearsome casualties for the Allied forces. To Fisher's embarrassment and distress Winston Churchill, his chief, nevertheless continued to pursue what Fisher himself felt sure was a lost cause. As the campaign drew out its weary length Fisher wrote to Asquith on 13 May 1915 that he could no longer subscribe to a ceaseless diversion of the British Fleet to a costly and worthless pursuit. At an acrimonious meeting of the War Council on the 14th he walked out. The next day he wrote again to the Prime Minister, 'I am off to Scotland at once so as to avoid all questionings.' Asquith replied by return of post, 'In the King's name I order you at once to return to your post.'

Bonar Law sent for Regy to say that Fisher must not be allowed to go, and that as one of the Admiral's oldest friends he must persuade him to remain. Fisher explained to Regy that since he considered Churchill an absolute menace he could not work with him a moment longer. Now Regy acted irresponsibly and wrote to him saying, 'My dear dear Jackie, you will never permanently patch up these quarrels. The only thing to be done is to revive the office of Lord High Admiral and take it yourself. Otherwise we are beaten at sea; and unless Lord K. takes the war into his own hands, ditto on land.'[45] It was a frivolous letter that disregarded the seriousness of the situation, and it encouraged Fisher to become still more unreasonable. He wrote to Asquith agreeing to remain at his post on stringent conditions which would ensure his absolute authority over the strategy of the Fleet. These terms, which would remove the War Council's control of the war at sea, were totally unacceptable and Asquith scornfully rejected them in a cold, curt letter which reached Fisher at Crewe station on his way to Scotland. The King, who had consistently cold-shouldered Fisher ever since his row with Lord Charles Beresford, one of George V's dearest friends, was so furious that he declared he would like to have him hanged at the yard-arm for desertion. Extraordinary as it may seem, Fisher then continued his journey and disappeared into Scotland where he could not be reached by telegram or letter.

Bonar Law now presented an ultimatum to Asquith, insisting on a change of government. The Prime Minister promptly sacked Churchill and also, to propitiate the Northcliffe press who were accusing him of pro-German sympathies, the Lord Chancellor, Haldane. As a result Haldane left the Liberal party and began attending Labour party meetings. Fisher's conduct, however reprehensible, brought about the fall of the Liberal Government and the introduction of the first Coalition Government. It also caused the end of the old War Council and the initiation of a new War Committee of the Cabinet.

From behind the scenes Regy had been fighting like a demon for unification of control. On 12 October he had a note circulated to the CID, imputing the lack of any striking success by the Allies so far to the fact that the war was not being centrally directed. The remedy it proposed was an inter-Allied Council.[46] Lord Selborne, a member of the Cabinet, was strongly in agreement with its principles, but amended Regy's note by suggesting that the conduct of the war should be entrusted to a Joint Committee of six, selected by the British and French Governments, to meet twice a week, once at Calais and once at Dover. On the 31st Regy wrote to the Prime Minister more or less endorsing what Selborne had propounded, and advocating a permanent secretariat on the lines of the CID. Only three French ministers, he advised, would be suitable: Briand, Galliéni – who had succeeded

Millerand and greatly favoured Selborne's recommendations – and Admiral Lacaze. Sir Maurice Hankey, the powerful Secretary to the Cabinet, was in agreement with the scheme. On 5 November the first meeting of the War Committee took place. At least eleven people attended, the British contingent including the Prime Minister, Balfour, Lloyd George, the Chief of the Imperial General Staff and the First Sea Lord. Regy kept Lord Stamfordham, the King's secretary, closely informed of these developments, telling him of his great hopes that the scheme on which he had worked for so many months would shortly bear fruit. Stamfordham replied that he deserved canonization for establishing a combined Franco-British General Staff.

In spite of all his various interests Regy did not neglect the Territorial Army Association of the County of London, of which he was President. In March he was able to tell General Huguet that he had already raised 80,000 territorials in London alone;[47] within less than a year the number increased to over 122,000. In August 1915 Geoffrey Robinson of *The Times* drew Regy's attention to the unpatriotic behaviour of the radical press over the conscription issue. Since Regy was one of the very few to have influence with Lord Kitchener, why did he not persuade him to bring the issue before the country with the agreement of Asquith and Balfour? Would he not ask him to change his method and appeal to the country on behalf of a national service at this desperate moment?[48] Robinson's letter had been provoked by one from Regy published in the *Glasgow Herald* on 10 August, entitled 'Equality of Sacrifice'. It was widely read in the south as well as the north. Regy stressed that all the politicians except Lord Kitchener had underestimated the length of the war. The British owed the Army to him. Germany was stronger than Britain. The aristocracy and the working classes had done magnificently. Still there were the war profiteers, whose gains could not be measured against the sacrifice of the fighting men. But this venture into jingoism did not meet with universal approval, and Lord Curzon, who was Lord Privy Seal and in favour of conscription, took Regy to task for his jeremiads about Britain's public figure.

> When you clamour for compulsory service as I understand you do, you write I think in ignorance of the fact that a group in the Government, of which I happen to be the spokesman, has been agitating for it ever since the new Government was formed, and that the reason for our failure up to date . . . is that we have hitherto been opposed, and from all indications are likely still to be opposed, by the Secretary of State for War. Convert him and the battle would be won.[49]

This was in fact what Robinson was suggesting. Lord Newton, for one, could not understand why Regy's important letter had to be sent to the *Glasgow Herald*. Why not raise the matter in the House of Lords? And why could not Lord Kitchener say in public exactly what he wanted?[50] J.A. Spender did not believe that conscription would result in the enlistment of more than 20,000 men, whom anyway we could get voluntarily, but agreed that it might have a moral effect upon the Allies.[51] It would convince them that we were taking the war seriously. And Balfour feared that a Compulsion Bill might defeat its own purpose because of opposition from Ireland, still seething with Anglophobia over the deferment of Home Rule on the outbreak of war, and the trades unions which would be bitterly resentful of a measure calculated to coerce its members.[52] His views bore out Lord Haldane's contention that the Northcliffe press had antagonized the working class on the issue. 'The workmen have no fixed bayonets,' he said.

The King was not pleased with Regy's letter. He thought the conscription question ought to be decided by Lord Kitchener, and he hoped Curzon was not going to cause a split in Asquith's Government over the issue. Howard Sturgis, representing the average intellectual with Liberal instincts, did not understand what Regy was getting at. He was dismayed by Regy's declaration that the German Army was superior to the British. Such information, if true, was bound to depress the French. Regy's denunciations were a little vague; did Kitchener agree with him? Was it true that he was not given a free hand? And what did Regy expect the ordinary civilian like himself to do?[53] Oswald FitzGerald, Kitchener's Personal Military Secretary, always in attendance on his master and deeper in his confidence than any man, affirmed that the Secretary of State for War did want conscription.

The disappointing truth was that voluntary enlistment was reduced to a trickle, a mere 12,000 a week which did not keep pace with casualties. Regy calculated that there were at least 1,200,000 young men between the ages of nineteen and twenty-four who would not enlist, and there were altogether 4 million men fit to serve who had not come forward. This seems an exaggerated number when one takes into account those engaged in important reserved occupations such as shipbuilding and munitions.[54] The Cabinet was still divided over this issue.

At the request of Lord Derby, who had been appointed Director-General of Recruiting, in October Regy went from Paris to London to take charge of recruiting in the capital and the Home District. It was the last attempt to fight the war on a voluntary basis. On 23 October the King issued a moving appeal to his people to join the forces voluntarily. The appeal had been drafted by Regy and, according to

Stamfordham, not a word was altered by the monarch. But the response was diminutive, and in May 1916 conscription was brought in by Lloyd George, who in the meantime had succeeded Asquith as Prime Minister.

It would have been unlike Regy not to keep an eye on the Prince of Wales in France. The young Prince had not ceased hankering to see active service. On the morning of 18 July 1915 the Prince drove forty miles to see Regy at General Headquarters in Blendecques village.

> He walked in the garden for a long time, and he told me what he had written to me, of his keen wish to be in the trenches with the Guards. Nothing could look better than the boy; his very clear skin is tanned, and this throws into relief the unusually bright and clear blue eyes. When presently the Field-Marshal's [French] motor drove up, he had a funny look of shyness, and hid behind an oleander bush until I dragged him out. The F-M treats him with a sort of paternal affection which makes their intercourse quite easy.[55]

At the beginning of October the prince narrowly missed being killed. He had just left his car to walk with General Lord Cavan when a shell exploded close to the vehicle, damaging it and killing his chauffeur.

> When Sir John heard of it he ordered the Prince of Wales away from the Guards division, to join the H.Q. of the 11th Corps. Two days afterwards, when he was driving along a muddy lane, he met the P. of W., walking dejectedly alone. He stopped and spoke to him; the boy, with deep emotion, begged to be allowed to stay with his Guards, adding that he would never be able to look them in the face again. Sir John, moved himself, yielded. When he told me of it he asked me what the King would say; and I really have no idea; but for the sake of the boy, for his own future happiness and the future of the Monarchy, I have no doubt whatever that he should take his share of the war as it comes . . . the boy's own popularity may preserve the throne for him, and if it does not, he will have splendid memories.[56]

When they were not meeting they were corresponding. The Prince, who, like Regy, became a close friend of Douglas Haig's secretary, Sir Philip Sassoon, told him he relished Lord Esher's letters, which were the best in the world. The Prince's letters abounded in laments that he was not allowed to go through the campaigns in the ordinary way, and what hell it was for him to know that his friends were being killed without his taking the same risks. He hated leading an isolated, comfortable, almost luxurious life close to the trenches. On the outbreak of war he had said to Kitchener, 'I have plenty of brothers, so what does it matter if I am killed?' Kitchener is alleged to have replied, 'I don't mind your being killed, but I object to your being taken prisoner, and you have no experience.'[57] The Prince never forgave him. The misery of the civil population over whose grounds they were fighting also worried the Prince considerably. Regy tried to console him, pointing out that he was the heir to duties which in the future would be hardly less onerous than those that his companions were now enduring. Regy flattered his intelligence by conveying information which he asked the Prince to treat as secret; he told him, for instance, about the differences betwen Sir John and Kitchener and the foul press attacks on the latter. 'One knows what a hot and impulsive little man he [Sir John] is!! Lord K. certainly behaved most awfully well & was so dignified about it all,' the Prince said.[58]

Regy wrote to Queen Mary about the praise the Prince was receiving from the French and the manner in which they quoted his sayings. When asked by a General what he thought of the prospects of the war, the Prince replied that he did not think there would be any *courbe* (bending) of the enemy's line, but that it would suddenly collapse. This was deemed a felicitous phrase. It certainly amused the Queen. 'I think she is very proud of him in a dry, unsentimental way,' Regy wrote.[59]

By the spring of 1915 Regy was seeing a good deal of Douglas Haig, and the two men were to be closely associated until the end of the war. When he first witnessed him, fresh from the Boer War, giving evidence before the Esher Committee, Regy had been struck by the brilliant, handsome young cavalry officer who spoke so haltingly but so sincerely. Even then Regy wanted him to be appointed Chief of General Staff, but Haldane and others thought him too young. In August 1914 Haig took the First Army Corps to France. Throughout the war Regy remained consistently loyal to and uncritical of this efficient soldier. On 4 April 1915 Brigadier-General John Charteris noted in his diary that Lord Esher had been visiting Haig at General Headquarters, 31 Boulevard des Invalides.

> He has some kind of unofficial mission in France. He is a most acute observer, and a very entrancing conversationalist. But his chief characteristic is that he is always close friends with those that matter. So his visit probably means that D.H.'s star is in the ascendant. It can only be a matter of time before he takes over the chief command out here.[60]

Charteris, who was Haig's Chief of Intelligence, was not wrong. He was a controversial figure, and Haig had a higher opinion of his efficiency than did many others. At first Regy thought him a capable soldier who had spies on the brain, and spying was ultimately a demoralizing business. Later he told Hankey that Haig had been greatly inconvenienced by Charteris's incompetence.[61] The man was pushing, self-confident and power-hungry; fat, outwardly good-natured and too consistently optimistic for an intelligence officer. Burgis, who became his secretary in October 1916, wrote that 'he was really a horror of a man'. As his unpopularity grew with all the Army commanders except Haig, Charteris became regarded as a national danger and known as the 'U-Boat'.

On 14 July 1915 Regy wrote for CID *A Note of a Conversation with General Girodon, Chief of Staff to General Gouroud.* Girodon, a man of alert mind and brilliant attainments, doubted the success of the Gallipoli enterprise unless it was accompanied by a landing on the Asiatic shore strong enough to occupy the coastline on the eastern side of the Narrows. He listed some disturbing examples of the lack of close contact and rapid exchange of information between the naval and military forces engaged in these operations. A decision, he emphasized, ought to be arrived at before the autumn weather set in. But this advice came too late. By September the public accepted the Dardanelles fiasco as having been brought about by the muddled actions of politicians and soldiers alike. In Regy's opinion the tragedy could have been avoided; rather, could have been brought to a glorious conclusion, but by one man only – Kitchener – if his colleagues had given him a free hand.

In June Kitchener's control of events was brought to a virtual end with the appointment of Lloyd George as Minister of Munitions. The Cabinet were unanimous in their decision to send Kitchener to see conditions in the Dardanelles for himself. On 5 November he passed through Paris and sent for Regy, to whom he complained that he had been driven out of the Cabinet. Affairs in the Eastern Mediterranean filled him with anxiety. 'I cannot see light,' he said. Yet he had his seals of office with him for he was still Secretary of State for War, and that office was loyal to him. At the Embassy FitzGerald read out to him a letter of farewell from his private secretaray, Creedy. Kitchener stood with his back to the fireplace, his eyes filled with tears. He talked to Regy about his colleagues' dislike of him. Regy attributed it to what he called his 'oriental ideas' – the autocratic methods he had acquired from long service in Africa and the East. Humbly he said, 'Yes, I suppose it is so, but I am an old man and I cannot change my habits now. It is too late.'[62] The display, however brief, of humility in a proud man is always poignant, and Regy wrote in his journal:

The vision of Lord K., massive, inarticulate, *émotionné*, haunts me. The man is a noble creature, and all of good, wholesome colour, in spite of the darker threads that traverse the tapestry of his character as they do in all of us. It is amazing to me that his colleagues fail to see his bigness, and misconstrue the forceful instinct of the traveller soldier, experienced in men and lands, human passions and volcanic forces, of which they know nothing beyond what educated men know who read books and newspapers.[63]

'Asquith', Kitchener said, 'is my only friend in the Cabinet.'

In at once passing on these words to Asquith, Regy put his own cards on the table. He told the Prime Minister that for twelve months he had identified his views with Kitchener's, and had worked for him as hard as he could; he had his complete confidence. In view of the odium in which Kitchener stood with his colleagues, he did not know what the Prime Minister wanted him to do. 'If you desire that I should continue in the groove in which I am, would you write me a formal letter – not too formal – to say that I possess in a minor degree your confidence.' The phrase was calculated to force the Prime Minister's hand. He went on:

Of course I want to make absolutely clear to you that I am very much attached to K., that I shall continue to do all I can to strengthen his hands and keep in close touch with the people who believe in him, but that I should be very glad to do all that I can during his absence, which may be indefinitely prolonged to work for you, should you wish it.[64]

Regy lunched with Haig on the 14th and had a long talk on the general situation at home. He asked what should be done with Kitchener, and Haig replied succinctly, 'Appoint him Viceroy of India.'[65] Anything to get him out of the way – but that proposal had already been made, and scotched in 1910.

One of the more disagreeable tasks into which Regy was drawn on Lord Kitchener's behalf was to persuade Sir John French that he should retire from his position as Commander-in-Chief of the British Expeditionary Force in France. Kitchener, Haig, the Prime Minister and the King were convinced that French's series of failures to break the German lines was the result of incompetence and the burden of command proving too great for his age. The heavy casualties preyed woefully upon his mind, and he held himself responsible. This was not the sort of talk expected of a general launching thousands of troops into battle. A note in Asquith's hand, written in November 1915, ran: 'I entrusted to Lord Esher as an old and most attached friend of Sir John French the duty of conveying to him my views and decision that owing to the strain of the previous months he was no longer able to conduct the campaign.'[66]

But first of all Sir Henry Wilson recorded in his diary that at 10.30 on 15 November he went to French's headquarters at Blandecques.

Like Regy, he had heard rumours of the Government's intentions to sack the Field-Marshal, and the two men endeavoured to get Sir John to anticipate his dismissal by resigning. The Field-Marshal, who had been unwell, was in bed, but better. Esher was already in the room.

> He led off by saying that he had been suggesting to Sir John that he should draw up a paper showing that it was the detachment to Gallipoli and Salonika which had ruined our offensive power in the West, and that if this continued he could not remain responsible for the operations in this theatre. Sir John and Esher asked my opinion. I said that in the present condition of the Cabinet they would jump at this and ask him to resign, but that, if we could get Joffre to endorse Sir John's views, we had got the Cabinet fixed. This was much approved.[67]

It was then decided that Sir John would immediately write 'the big despatch' which Wilson would take to Joffre the next day. 'Sir John took the whole thing most awfully well.' But to no avail. Joffre would not play. It is somehow unlikely that Regy inwardly subscribed to this whitewashing of Sir John and desire to retain him, fond though he had long been of him.

On the 22nd Asquith telegraphed to Regy in Paris asking him to come over to London immediately. He took with him a plan of campaign, concocted by himself and General Galliéni and approved by Briand, Joffre and the French General Staff. Asquith accepted the plan, saying that he felt sure the Cabinet would approve. He then told Regy that he had sent for him to explain that physically Sir John was not equal to the work, a change of command was imperative, and he must be dismissed. 'It is damnable having to deliver it, and friendship has its curse as well as its blessing,' Regy noted.[68]

Back Regy went to Blendecques, feeling like an assassin making a second attempt on a victim who would not die. He imparted the unpleasant news frankly. Sir John said he could think of nothing he had done to deserve this blow; that no successor to him would have better control of the Army. Regy passed on Asquith's offer to Sir John of a peerage, a grant from Parliament at the end of the war and the immediate command of the Home Forces. Sir John then went to London where he had an amicable discussion with Asquith who, taking the feeble line again, assured him that he was not being recalled and suggested that he resign.[69] Regy wrote to Asquith, 'I know you will make things as easy for him as possible. He is a poor man, and he has served his country well.'[70]

By the end of November Kitchener was back in Paris, having made up his mind on the necessity of withdrawing from Gallipoli. Regy had a long, straight talk with him, and told him candidly what everyone thought of him. Kitchener was petulant and pessimistic. He was doubtful whether the Government would heed his advice when he reached London; they really wanted to get rid of him. 'They want to use my name and deprive me of authority,'[71] he said, which was not far from the truth. Regy wrote to Asquith saying that he had discussed with some of the wisest Frenchmen the hypothetical question of Kitchener's retirement from the War Office: all deprecated it.

Regy knew how to deal with the stubborn, sensitive and proud Kitchener, and he took it upon himself to advise Asquith. 'My dear Prime Minister,' he wrote:

As for K., you will never get the best out of him as a sedentary S. of S., but as S. of S. and C-in-C of all the King's Armies *overseas* combined, and moving freely into any theatre of war, he would stand throughout the Empire, as a 'fixed point', after the manner of Joffre here, and give you his best instead of his worst. He would be his own liaison officer with France, Italy and Russia. He would, by his occasional presence, impose great confidence upon the East. I have for months urged this idea upon him, and upon the King. K. has been, from the first, submerged by the disturbed waters of political controversy, inseparable from Cabinet government. He exhibits under these conditions his *worst* side. . . . K. and Galliéni might together hold their own against the Germans. If K.'s position and powers could be more closely defined the definition of Galliéni's would follow.[72]

In other words Kitchener should be made Commander-in-Chief and given supreme responsibility for the conduct of the war. This was not a proposition likely to appeal to Asquith or any of the Cabinet – and it did not.

Regy had not yet finished with Sir John's predicament. On 8 December he drafted for his old friend a letter of resignation to Asquith. 'The thing I told you about', he confided in Lawrence Burgis,

is now a *fait accompli*. I am deeply grieved for my poor little friend. To leave so great a task unfulfilled is a tragic end to a fine soldier's career. . . . I feel rather depressed tonight, and am writing this at the little F-M's table. He has gone to bed. The room is full of maps – all the traces of a life that so far as this sphere is concerned is practically at an end.[73]

Asquith wrote to Regy that he had received French's letter. It was a moving document, and in every way worthy of him. 'I wish to thank you with all my heart for the good offices which you have rendered in a very trying and delicate situation. No one else could have done what you have done.'[74] This sentence alone was a positive answer to Regy's enquiry of the Prime Minister, a month previously, as to whether he was fulfilling any useful office by remaining in France. 'It was a painful affair,' he told Stamfordham, 'and I do not wish to go through anything like it again.'[75]

On 9 December Kitchener, with Robertson, was once again in Paris. Robertson consulted Regy about the proposition that he should become Chief of the Imperial General Staff at home. Kitchener consulted Regy about his unsatisfactory relationship with his Cabinet colleagues in spite of the fact that they adopted his advice to evacuate the Dardanelles; and he asked him to speak on his behalf to Robertson. He was, he protested, inclined to leave the War Office and remain generalissimo, but Regy persuaded him to remain Secretary of State. Robertson assured Regy that he would work happily with Kitchener. And so this 'fine unselfish soldier' became Chief of the Imperial General Staff in the place of Sir Archibald Murray.[76] As the years went by Regy became critical of Robertson's ineffectiveness, and in 1918 he sided with Lloyd George in the row between them.

With the resignation of Sir John French and his replacement as Supreme Commander of the Forces in the West by Sir Douglas Haig, Regy made great friends with a spirit who was more congenial to him than any other whom he had come upon during his war duties. Sir Philip Sassoon, 3rd Baronet, member of an extremely rich family and related to the Rothschilds through his mother, was then a young man of twenty-seven. With his bent nose and rather shapeless mouth, filled with prominent teeth, he was not handsome. Clever, talented, French-speaking, a connoisseur of the arts, darling of London society and very good company, he relished harmless gossip and had a sense of humour which appealed to Regy. On the last day of 1915 his first letter to Regy announced that he had just been appointed Haig's private secretary. Until the end of the war he was to remain with the Commander-in-Chief, to whom he was consistently loyal – which does not mean that he did not see the funny side of his master's earnestness and conventional habits and tastes. Whenever Regy went to Head-quarters Philip found time to take him aside and indulge in outrageous jokes. They corresponded regularly, usually every three days, their official business invariably giving way to scandal and teasing on both sides. By 1918 both men's letters had become very intimate. Regy, typically, started the correspondence with advice. Philip must shield his chief from visitors to the front, and not let others interfere with him once he had made up his mind. But this schoolmasterly manner was soon abandoned. Sassoon needed no guidance from anybody, was full of self-confidence and thoroughly experienced in worldly matters. Moreover, there was not a shadow of romance in their relationship.

Philip was, besides, self-sufficient and extremely rich. Throughout the war he hankered for his Park Lane house and Port Lympne
and Trent, his country houses, all of which he filled with treasures and
bric-à-brac, and delighted in sharing with his friends.

In his autobiography Kenneth Clark gives a vivid portrait of
Sassoon's 'idiosyncratic and infectious *style*. He moved quickly and
always seemed to be in profile, like an Egyptian relief.'

> His mind moved equally quickly, and as his most unexpected com-
> ments were made without any change of inflection, they often took
> people by surprise. He saw the ridiculous side of Port Lympne. Going
> round the house we came upon a particularly hideous bathroom,
> panelled in brown and black zig-zags of marble. Philip said, without
> altering his tone of voice, 'It takes you by the throat and shakes you.'[77]

He was by descent Indian, from Bombay, and his tastes were
decidedly exotic. To Regy he wrote in self-mockery:

> Of course the sort of house I like & pine for has no comforts, nothing
> but stone floors and stone walls, moth-eaten 14th-century fragments –
> draughts – and a few stiff chairs against the wall with a string attached
> across to prevent anyone from sitting down on them. You would think
> it easy to realise this ideal. But it isn't, and I find myself the reluctant
> possessor of Park Lane with its *leitmotiv* of sham Louis XVI, Lympne
> which is Martini *tout craché*, and Trent which isn't even Lincrusta
> when my period is Merovingian or Boiling Oil. *Le monde est toujours
> mal arrangé.*[78]

He made no excuses for his love of luxury and the soft way of life,
and he had few ambitions beyond the upkeep of his palatial houses
and the entertainment of his friends. 'To have slept with Cavalieri
[Michelangelo's friend], to have invented wireless, to have painted *Las
Meninas*, to have written *Wuthering Heights* – that is deathless life. But
to be like me, a thing of nought, a worthless loon, an elm-seed
whirling in a summer gale,' was another matter altogether. Regy was
enchanted by this odd, sophisticated, self-indulgent creature who was
the very antithesis of the type of serious, callow youth by whom his
paternalistic soul was moved. Philip stood no nonsense, spoke his
mind, was from the beginning on an equal footing, and played the fool
with him. Besides, Regy was impressed by Philip's surprising efficiency, usefulness to his boss, and his physical courage.

Meanwhile with the New Year of 1916 Regy was in England and,
like nearly everyone else there, profoundly depressed by the course of
the war. He told Chat that the outcome was most doubtful. A
stalemate was the best that could be hoped for. He was made even

more disconsolate by the imminent departure for France of Lawrence Burgis, to whom he paid a farewell visit at his parents' house at Bishop's Stortford. To him he sent a cry of anguish:

> How super damnable is this war, for people like you and me. . . . You have no idea how I hate and detest it. No 'glorious panoply of war' for me. It does not exist. I admit that the marvellous qualities it brings out in the men actually at the front are stimulating, but everything *behind* the front is odious to me.[79]

He seriously believed that the sorrow and destruction let loose upon innocent humanity were caused by a few ambitious and stupid – or were they malevolent? – men; and that to the inhabitants of Mars the objectives of the fighting must seem piffling.

To Sir John French he sent a word of rebuke. For some months now the little Field-Marshal had been Commander-in-Chief at home, and yet no one seemed to know, if London were to be raided from the air, what precautions had been taken, and whether he, Balfour, now First Lord, or Herbert Samuel, the Home Secretary, was responsible. It was an unsatisfactory state of affairs; after a crisis no explanations would be accepted by the public. From his old friend Howard Sturgis, to whom he had written in the same pessimistic vein complaining of the lax way in which provincial tribunals were allowing able-bodied men to retain civilian jobs, and explaining how he had written to every conceivable authority in protest, he received a characteristic straight letter: 'I didn't "pit into" you, darling, for wanting to "organize" but for not saying clearly what you *did* want, for being vaguely denunciatory & pessimistic, and for abusing people for being led away by "phrases", and then talking of "equality of sacrifice", which seemed to me to come under that head.'[80] Whatever his shortcomings, Howdie had a clear mind and hated vague insinuations and half thought out remedies. He continued:

> You may say you 'despise democracy' but when it comes to the point you trust the people rather than the politicians like Ll. G. who flatter and betray them. . . . You are with old Fug [Asquith] and me against the Cowdrays [Lord Cowdray was a press baron]. . . . I cling to liberty, even the liberty to make mistakes, as against the Wellses [H.G.] & Lloyd Georges who want to dragoon me *for my own good*.[81]

Were equality of sacrifice to mean making the rich do their bit, he would be a conscriptionist. But what the conscriptionist wanted, even more than to win the war, was in his opinion a weapon against the trades unions, so as to be able to say to the workman: 'Do as I say; accept my terms & go to the trenches.'

There was one poor little rich boy who, not for the first time, was badgering Regy to help him do his bit and exemplify the meaning of the term 'equality of sacrifice'. The Prince of Wales relished the 'long, kind and very interesting' letters which his old friend found time to write him. 'Yes, thank goodness they have left me in peace with the Guards Div. I simply couldn't leave it at such a time,' he had written the previous October.[82] He deplored being kept ten miles from the trenches, but was glad his father was coming out to cheer the troops. In March he was to be withdrawn from the Guards division and sent to Egypt, away from the fighting. Deeply grieved, he was so angry that for the first time in his life he wrote rather testily to the King and refused to speak to him for three days. Regy had a long discussion with him in London on the subject. He advised the Prince not to tie himself up with one regiment or set of men, to which the Prince replied that it was 'beastly bad luck' and he cursed the fate which had made him Prince of Wales. Of course he held Lord Kitchener responsible for this new transfer. That evening, when he got back to Tilney Street, Regy wrote him a letter. In spite of his hard manner, Kitchener, whom the Prince held responsible for this new transfer, was below the surface a tender man, Regy said,

so that when he takes a firm line upon a matter in which he knows you feel deeply, it is only because he is convinced that it is necessary and right. . . .

I wonder if you remember our talks at Balmoral when you were so miserable at leaving the Navy. If you do, you can realise that I understand and have understood all along exactly what you are going through and have gone through!

It is so difficult to judge exactly where one's duty lies, when one's inclinations are very strong. This country which may presently be going through very difficult times – I mean some years hence – will require leadership from you, and if the Empire is to hold together, you, thanks to what you are, and what you have done and are doing, will provide a rallying point that no one else – not one of your brothers, for instance – can provide.

I know this sort of blunt statement which looks like flattery, but is *not*, vexes you. But it is true, and therefore for England you must sacrifice much, all your inclinations, your companions, your secret wishes. It is a big sacrifice, but a noble one! . . .

It was a tall order. In truth there was to be no equality of sacrifice in the case of the young Prince of Wales. The sort of sacrifice which Lord Esher urged upon him was to be accepted by him for another twenty years, when it proved too burdensome to be borne longer.

But at this moment Regy had other more urgent matters to worry about. He did not hesitate to tell Haig that a passive attitude in the West would mean a disastrous peace before the following winter. He complained to Stamfordham that, in spite of the French plan for joint discussions which he himself had brought over the previous November and which Asquith had approved, nothing had been done about it. No meeting had taken place between Robertson, Haig, Joffre and Galliéni, who, when it came to strategy, excelled the lot of them. Furthermore, since Robertson had been appointed Chief of the Imperial General Staff in December not a single meeting between the Army chiefs had taken place.[83] Yet the War Office machinery, now manipulated by Kitchener, Robertson and Haig, had never run more smoothly. Regy sent Stamfordham a copy of a letter received from Robertson to show the King what a noble, disinterested old fellow Robertson was. Asquith must be made to realize that speed was the essential element of decision.[84] To several other correspondents Regy deplored the fact that the War Committee, set up in November 1915 to exercise the functions of the Supreme Command, was in effect conducted by twenty-two elderly Cabinet ministers; and that Lord Kitchener was by no means the autocratic leader which his critics liked to surmise. Even he, Regy, was showing signs of disillusion with his hero.

By February Kitchener's friends were again worried about him. Regy at last believed that the time had come when he should leave the War Office altogether. 'He possesses a bigness of heart and character that few give him credit for,' he told Robertson, 'and his military and political instincts are vastly superior to those of any of his colleagues.'[85] Nevertheless he felt that in his judgment of men Kitchener failed. As a critic of administration he was singularly blind. Within the first months of 1916 the Cabinet was riven by the French scheme to stake all available effort and manpower on one almighty offensive. If Lloyd George were to resign from the Ministry of Munitions on a question of vital military importance, it would be awkward for Kitchener to remain. Kitchener begged Regy to postpone going to France until the crisis was over, because he was sure to need his guiding hand. In the event Lloyd George did not resign, but remained in office until transferred to the War Office after Kitchener's death.

Before the Compulsory Service Bill was passed in May Regy experienced at first hand what one of the big cities thought of the inadequate war effort. In Glasgow the feeling of its leading citizens was profoundly anti-Government. The Lord Provost complained to Regy that ministers treated the city's leading businessmen like children. He considered that Asquith was deplorably weak and Kitchener going downhill. The Lord Provost and an intelligent

Socialist had recently had an interview with Kitchener in which the Secretary of State had been deeply unimpressive. 'If that is our only strong man', said the Socialist to the Provost afterwards, 'God help us.' On another occasion the Lord Provost and several prominent Glaswegians were kept waiting a quarter of an hour outside the Prime Minister's office at No. 10 Downing Street. When the door opened for someone to pass in or out they caught a glimpse of Asquith idly chatting to two ladies, who were smoking cigarettes, and buttoning the glove of one of them. 'Imagine', the Lord Provost commented, 'Mr Gladstone, Disraeli or Mr Pitt behaving so, at such a juncture.'[86]

Once conscription was a foregone conclusion and the break-up of the Government on that issue averted, Kitchener relaxed. On 21 April Regy told Lawrence Burgis that he had dined alone with him; he had been rather tired, but glad that the political row was over for the moment. 'He gets rattled by these lawyers, and has no idea how to deal with them.'[87] The respite enabled Regy to return to France. On 4 May he had an hour's talk with Briand, who was then enjoying one of his eleven premierships. Briand considered that the Compulsory Service Bill was a rude shock to the Germans, as it was an earnest to the French that the British meant to fight to the bitter end – for there were still some people in France who doubted Britain's good faith. Regy told Lawrence that he had taken rather a fancy to Briand, in whom he saw some traces of noble blood animating a low stock; he was very charming; in figure and shape like Lloyd George, but with a beautiful voice, fine eyes and a delightful smile.[88] Regy also told the King that the enthusiasm of the French on receiving the news about conscription was overwhelming. Briand said that he and his colleagues had been 'amazed at the skill with which Mr Asquith has managed Parliament so as to engineer such a measure into law without a disruption of national unity'. There was also universal praise of Douglas Haig.[89] There is little doubt that it was Regy who was largely instrumental in getting the conscription law passed. Apart from Robertson, the military were not in favour of an inrush of raw and possibly recalcitrant troops; and Parliament was deeply divided over the wisdom of the measure. Esher, however, from his contacts with the generals and politicians across the Channel, was in a position to stress the need to revive France's flagging morale.[90]

On the 25th Regy had a further interview with Briand, who considered the Germans more and more anxious to make peace. The interview was instigated by Haig, who was concerned lest French General Staff officers might be changed at the bidding of a political group. He begged Regy to put in a word with the French Premier to prevent anything of the sort happening; it would seriously affect the Allies' mutual plans were it to happen during operations.[91] Meanwhile

FitzGerald (Fitz) asked Regy to find out what the French were really thinking about Salonika, where Anglo-French forces had maintained a stronghold awaiting the opportunity of advancing against the enemy's combined strength in the Balkans. Kitchener was unhappy about affairs in France generally. The prolonged and costly Battle of Verdun was draining their reserves, and the politicians were bent on an offensive from Salonika. Kitchener deemed it premature.

Regy went by appointment to see President Poincaré at the Elysée Palace.

> The President's room is on the ground floor, looking over the garden. It is not the room occupied by President Faure, but is the last of the suite, with a private staircase communicating with the floor above and the private apartments. Monsieur Poincaré has not much personality; he is just a very intelligent lawyer, but he speaks with authority, and he takes great pains to make himself acquainted with the facts, so that he presides over the Council in rather a formidable manner. At the present time he strongly supports Briand and Joffre. He talked mainly to me about Salonika. . . .[92]

Indeed Salonika was the object of the audience. Regy informed the President that Haig was not always certain what Joffre's intentions were. The President replied that some activity must take place on the Serbian Front if what was left of the Serbian Army was not to lose morale. Regy told Kitchener that the French politicians and generals were in agreement that the offensive should be taken at Salonika. The difference between the French and British was deep-rooted in this matter. 'Remember', he wrote to Fitz, 'that I know [Briand and Poincaré] *very well*, and they talk as freely to me, almost, as Lord K. does.'[93] When Haig was informed of this he told Regy that Briand's only reason for continuing to keep troops at Salonika was fear that the Serbs would make a separate peace if they were withdrawn. He considered it a most short-sighted policy. But the real reason of the French was very different: they did not believe their country could survive the financial strain of another winter, and felt they must try to settle the war that year. The only way of bringing that about was by creating a diversion in the Balkans with the help of Russian forces. The Salonika issue was the cause of much contention in England. While Kitchener at Whitehall and Haig in the field were bitterly opposed to it, Lloyd George was in favour – if only because he was appalled by the unprofitable carnage on the Western Front.

At the end of the year Regy was staying with Haig at General Headquarters, for the first time since his host had taken over command, in order to find out how he was viewing the future. Regy told Stamfordham that he was immensely impressed by Haig's thoroughness and method. 'Douglas himself is unchanged. Perfectly calm and collected; orderly, reflective, obstinate. Haig's conference with Joffre indicates that an Anglo-French offensive in the west is imperative.'[94] Indeed, as the two friends walked round the ramparts of Montreuil Haig disclosed his plans for the offensive; but he wanted to postpone it until August since he had not sufficient men, reserves or guns. It was absolutely essential to prevent a French collapse, save Verdun and prevent a German victory in the West. Regy lamented that Haig had not been able to start his offensive on 10 February, the day Germany had launched her attack against Verdun. Then his achievement might have been definitive.[95]

Notwithstanding the decline of Kitchener's powers and his increasing unpopularity with his Cabinet collegues, he was still recognized by the Government and public alike as a charismatic figure. At the beginning of June he was sent, at the express desire of the tottering Russian regime, to give the Tsar's demoralized Army the benefit of his advice.

In the first week of that month Regy received a letter from one of the private secretaries at the War Office, informing him that Kitchener's séance with a group of MPs on Friday the 2nd had turned out very well. He had read them a long statement about his early war difficulties, which they had obviously not hitherto appreciated. He explained the object of his mission to Russia, and answered with great good temper a lot of rubbishy questions. 'I saw them off on Saturday afternoon for Thurso by special train. They are to call on Jellicoe and probably put out to sea last night on the *Hampshire*. . . . K. after saying goodbye, looked at the clock and said very gently, "I don't think we need wait any more", and stepped into the train.'

On Tuesday the 6th Regy was lunching with Briand at the Foreign Office on the Quai d'Orsay. Briand came in holding a telegram, and announced to his guest Kitchener's death. 'He was really moved, partly because of his regard for K., which seems to have been very genuine, and partly because of the effect of the catastrophe upon the results of the war. We hardly talked of anything else.'[96]

Regy was shattered by the news. The following day he could do nothing but walk alone in the Bois de Boulogne, thinking of his friendship with Kitchener. Sadly he murmured to himself Scott's lines on the death of Pitt:

> How is the stately column broke,
> The beacon-light is quench'd in smoke,
> The trumpet's silver sound is still,
> The warder silent on the hill.

Galliéni's death at the end of May – Kitchener had telegraphed Regy to represent him at the funeral – had been a severe blow for France and the Allied cause. He was a great force in reserve. But Kitchener's death was far worse. He had been a moral force in England, the stamina of his country. He had been the focal point of the whole national aspiration and war effort, so Regy told Lawrence Burgis. He could not imagine who would now rally the country. Anyway, no one could deprive Kitchener of his role as the legendary hero of the war. He could not keep himself from dwelling upon the tragedy, the drowning in those sullen waters made more poignant to him by the recollection that the hero was at the end of his life belittled by his compatriots. 'Then I am worried as today is Wednesday and there is no letter from you,' he wrote. 'Altogether I am unhappy.'

Regy was twice asked by Briand to accompany him to London to Kitchener's memorial service. But he refused in case it made Bertie jealous at the Embassy. Besides, he decided he would be more useful to Robertson by remaining in Paris where he could help smooth relations between England and France.

Regy wrote an article entitled 'Lord K.' for the July issue of *The National Review*, in which he explained that his hero's mind worked in an oriental way. After all, since the age of twenty-four he had served as a soldier and ruled as a governor in Palestine, Egypt and the Sudan. The years of his life spent in England had been few and far between. The Arabs had taught him to read the thoughts of others while concealing his own. He was no organizer. He was unduly reluctant to cause pain. For carelessness or neglect of duty he was ruthless, and had no compassion for incompetence. He inspired devotion in the few, including Fitz, that natural celibate who died with him and, apart from two months in India, had never left Kitchener's side since becoming his ADC in 1904. He was variable: in the morning he could be incisive and brilliant; in the evening of the same day contradictory, garrulous and muddled. He was naturally imperious. Had Britain's institutions allowed him to act autocractically the Allies might have won the war by the time of his death. At a gathering of the Allies he dominated generals and politicians by a cubit in stature; yet he was inarticulate, and not even clever.

In writing to congratulate the author of the article the popular novelist Marie Corelli was not alone among thousands of British people in saying that she did not believe Lord Kitchener was dead. It was utterly beyond the realms of reason to suppose that such a thing was possible.[97]

11

THE GREAT WAR: SOLDIER CIVILIAN

1916–1918

Within a matter of days after Kitchener's death Regy received a very civil letter, totally unsolicited, from Asquith asking him to continue 'the valuable work you have done for Lord K. and the country during the last two years'.[1] He replied that the Prime Minister could always rely on him to do everything in his power to help. Regy lost no time in passing on that the French desired it to be kept a profound secret that they had received feelers of peace from Germany. The stiff answer they gave was that they would not discuss peace terms before all French, British and Russian prisoners were repatriated and all German troops removed from French and Belgian soil. As it was, Briand and Joffre were preparing for an offensive. They protested that their confidence had never been higher.[2] Maurice Hankey wrote to Esher expressing delight that he was not going to give up his liaison work;[3] and Sir William Robertson hoped he might rely on Regy keeping him informed of useful news in the same way in which he had supplied Kitchener. When he wanted any particular views to be circulated, he would tell him. [4] Haig, too, wrote that he was pleased the Prime Minister had renewed Regy's credentials for the sake of the country's relations with France.[5] Regy promptly urged Hankey to improve British press communiqués; also to feed the French press with information about the activities of British troops and their losses.

For a man of sixty-three Regy undoubtedly performed a hard and useful job. In addition to his liaison work there were the Red Cross demands, no less stringent this year than the last. He was constantly inspecting hospitals in France, reporting to headquarters and making recommendations – about the position and condition of VADs in French hospitals, about getting adequate compensation for wounded men, and pensions for those invalided out of the Army. Many of his contemporaries were aware and appreciative of what he was doing. Colonel Repington was perplexed about the precise nature of his mission and expressed his curiosity. He was not enlightened. Whatever it was, Repington was sure no one was better informed of what was going on in Paris; Lord Esher knew all the French politicians and generals and was very shrewd, discreet and industrious.[6] Geoffrey Robinson of *The Times*, with whom Regy kept up a regular correspondence, thanked him for his invaluable help and said he would often see his own words embodied in that newspaper's leaders. But of course Regy had his detractors, too. Northcliffe wrote to Geoffrey Robinson from Paris:

> Nobody knows what he does here exactly. The Ambassador does not know, and asked me. He is dressed as a Colonel and wears the Grand Cross of the Legion of Honour all day long and probably all night too. He is always going backward and forward between Paris and the GHQ, writes for the papers, sees everybody who comes to Paris directly they arrive, is mixed up with some very queer Jews, but is really, I believe, only a busybody. Still, what he says, as the Americans say, 'goes' among the French. His visiting card is a most extraordinary production; it is in French – 'Le Vicomte Esher, member of the War Council (or some such words), Governor of Windsor Castle, Commissioner of the Red Cross.' There are about seven lines of it.[7]

As things were, with colossal French losses being reported from Verdun, and the British General Staff fearful lest the French might pull out of the fighting altogether, Paris in June 1916 was a very disagreeable place for a British civilian, albeit one wearing khaki. All Regy felt able to do was to urge Haig to stimulate press propaganda in the capital about the efforts of the British Army. In his last letter to Regy Haig had excused its brevity because he was about to go into battle. In fact the fearful Battle of the Somme was being launched, with ensuing casualties on an unprecedented scale. On 1 July Regy, in his capacity as a sub-Commissioner of the Red Cross visiting his units, was viewing the scene from GHQ, a pretty country house outside the village of Beauquesne. He stood with Haig listening to the preparatory rumble of guns and watching the puffs of smoke billow across the plain. Conscious of what he knew to be coming, Regy dashed off a communication to the Foreign Office urging them to release all over France films showing the gallant part British troops were playing and calling on General Charteris to indoctrinate the French press with the same propaganda. By the 14th he was back in Paris for Bastille Day. During the review of troops he received an urgent message from Douglas Haig that his concentrated attack had begun that morning at

3.20. He asked Regy to tell the French President, which he did on the tribune, during the review. Poincaré solemnly shook hands with him and was followed by the other ministers present.

On the 17th Maurice Hankey wrote to him, 'Well, you have got your big offensive, and on the whole it has not gone badly, though it remains to be seen whether the advantages gained compensate for the heavy casualties.' He feared that British losses would be much heavier than those of the Germans. Hankey, like Lloyd George, was an 'easterner' in that he favoured the Salonika policy of striking a blow at the Central Powers through the Balkans. In his opinion the static slaughter on the Western Front would not bring Germany to her knees. He believed the best way of defeating the enemy was by gobbling up German colonies and then the Balkan allies piecemeal, and so starving them.[8] This letter was followed by one from Haig thanking Regy for conveying so dramatically to Poincaré news of the British offensive and saying that military history would never forgive the French for bottling up so many troops in Salonika.[9]

On 3 August Regy wrote to Hankey that he had just returned from the front, and begged him to tell the Prime Minister that the battle was going extremely well. He was in fact certain that the Germans would soon crack.[10] Haig, however – already dubbed by the politicians 'The Butcher' – was beginning to be concerned by criticism at home of the huge losses of men, already 139,000 in the month's engagement. Regy, ever prone to leap to the defence of his heroes, advised him that if called to England he should explain that the casualties were worth the candle – in other words the increased morale among the surviving troops. Regy assiduously visited Haig every other week and kept writing home about the tremendous achievements not to be measured by inches on the map. The British Army had prevented the French from making peace, enabled the Russians to advance, and wrested the initiative from the enemy.

During these hectic weeks of going and coming between Paris and the front Regy did not fail to notice other candidates for high rank and distinction. General Tom Bridges possessed 'great charm of manner, and has a handsome and attractive face'. As well as being a first-class soldier, he was a very cultivated musician. These attributes, however, were eclipsed by his phenomenal courage, as Regy wrote to Burgis:

I remember one afternoon at Albert where he and I sat in his garden having tea. It was laid just as if we had been in the garden at Pinkie. About 60 shells fell into Albert that day. He did not seem to notice when a shell tumbled into the garden of the adjoining house. And I don't really think he did. He did not know what fear was. *I* could not keep my attention fixed upon what he was saying! A splendid *looking* creature as you know. The last time I saw him we went to a concert together in Paris.[11]

There was also Henry Rawlinson's Chief of Staff, Major-General Archie Montgomery. Regy considered him the handsomest soldier he had seen in France.

> Just a year ago I picked out Douglas as the future C-in-C because of his blue eyes and knowledge and Scottish coolness. So now I feel sure that Montgomery is *the* soldier who will command the British Armies of the future, after Douglas and Rawly [Rawlinson] have given up their charge. He is very tall, and has the frankest face you could wish to see; dark blue eyes, and a delightful smile. His capacity is obvious after two minutes' talk in spite of his disconcerting charm. They say he is tenacious, and even masterful.[12]

His perceptive forecast was to be realized. The object of his admiration was in due course to become Field-Marshal Sir Archibald Montgomery-Massingberd, Chief of the Imperial General Staff. Certainly his prognostications proved more often right than wrong. Early in 1916 he prophesied that if the war went on Clemenceau would end up as Prime Minister of France ('I am seventy-five years old,' he told Haig, 'and the whole future is before me.') and that Russia would sue for peace without consulting her Allies.

One of Regy's abilities was to look ahead. When, at the beginning of August, Lloyd George was on a secret mission to Paris, he sent for Regy who immediately interrogated him about Britain's peace objectives. Lloyd George admitted that no one at home had considered them. Regy observed that Briand was served by intelligent advisers who were working out the terms of an eventual armistice and France's claims and post-war policies. Regy feared that in the councils of the victorious nations Britain would be left behind France, who would be in a position to dictate terms to her advantage – which would not necessarily be to Britain's.[13] So he suggested to Robertson, the CIGS, that he should acquaint himself with Briand's peace views, then, when a conference was summoned, Britain would not take a back seat.[14] Robertson replied that he had no time to work out peace problems himself; he was far too busy trying to win the war.[15] Regy was not satisfied. He decided that the War Council would shilly-shally when it was too late and Germany would eventually revive under the influence of the best of tonics, discord among her foes.[16]

Regy saw similarities to Briand in Lloyd George. Both had Celtic origins and temperaments. Both had been educated in a village school. Both were radicals. Even their personal appearance and gifts of eloquence were not dissimilar. But he concluded that Lloyd George was the bigger man. His bigness could not be denied, in spite of glaring faults; one, undoubtedly, was that he did not know how to behave. Regy was present when Lloyd George and Asquith visited Haig at Beauquesne. The impression left by Asquith (his son Raymond had been killed the day before) was unexceptionable; that of Lloyd George deplorable. The Welshman seemed to seek the cameras and elicit the cheers of the soldiers. He was insolent and off-hand. The French were appalled by his vulgarity and bad language on his visit to Foch. Regy prayed that he would not succeed in dislodging Asquith. In his cool summary of Lloyd George's behaviour he decided that it was not altogether surprising; the man was a 'phenomenal little cad'. After all, one could not 'make a silk purse out of a Welsh solicitor's ear'.[17] Foch told Haig after the interview that he was amazed when Lloyd George examined him, a Frenchman, on the British generals and what he thought of them. Foch declined to express an opinion.[18] According to Stamfordham, however, Lloyd George stoutly denied having spoken to Foch at all.[19] In spite of his poor opinion of the Minister for War, only a week later Regy conceded that he did possess brilliant gifts, and political and military flair. He got things done. He stuck at nothing. He even summoned Sir John French to the front, as the best soldier available to report on artillery training and artillery tactics. It was an insensitive thing to do in the circumstances, and infuriated Haig, but Lloyd George did not care because it was the right thing to do. His opinion of Esher likewise was untainted by prejudice. He described him as 'general adviser to everybody and liaison officer between everybody and anybody – a most useful kind of person'. He praised him for his 'tact, discernment and experience' in a 'superlative degree'.[20]

Regy's confidence in Haig was unshakable, though he lamented the occasional differences between the Commander-in-Chief and the CIGS. While admitting that in Britain military supremacy was out of the question, nevertheless the military staff should stick together to combat unwise instructions from politicians. He was indignant when Joffre wrote an insufferably rude letter to Regy's 'dear Douglas' regarding Haig's modification of some tactical plans. Joffre pointed out that he was Generalisssimo, and expected obedience from his subordinates. Haig replied courteously but firmly, pointing out that he alone must decide whether his Army could carry out orders from above. Joffre's staff was so alarmed by Haig's letter that they delayed showing it to the Generalissimo until they knew the two men were about to meet at a conference. After luncheon Haig referred to the letter, and Joffre said, greatly to the other's surprise, 'When you get a letter of that kind from me, pay no attention to it. Do not answer it.'

Haig interpreted this extraordinary remark to mean that the Marshal wrote such letters purely for record purposes.[21] Less than two months later Joffre was succeeded as French Commander-in-Chief by Nivelle.

By November Regy was so concerned by Haig's need for more troops that he wrote from Paris to Lord Murray of Elibank,[22] the honorary Director of Recruiting for Munition Workers. He begged him to get Lloyd George, with whom he was very intimate, to establish one ruthless businessman – just as he had appointed Sir Eric Geddes (a master-stroke) to be Director-General of Military Railways – to circumvent all committees and superfluous paperwork and raise 1½ million men. Haig needed this number before the autumn if his and Joffre's scheme of concentrating on the Western Front was to be implemented; and he must be free from War Office control. The plea was presumably ignored, because a week later Asquith approved Lord Lansdowne's memorandum urging peace terms. Lloyd George resigned, and the First Coalition Government fell.

On 7 December the Second Coalition Government was formed, with Lloyd George as Prime Minister. Regy was the first to applaud the composition of the new War Cabinet. It consisted of only five members, all Secretaries of State. The conduct of the war was, as far as Great Britain was concerned, virtually confined to these five. Lloyd George's new broom swept away many anomalies. Most of the reforms he introduced answered the anxious questions which Regy had lately been raising. Regy wrote to Hankey, 'The War Council was a farce. I am heartily glad it is dead, and I hope it will not be revived in another form. The old CID was buried under that amorphous excrescence. It was a sad pity.'[23]

With Joffre's removal a similar ministerial crisis took place in France. Briand sacked his ungainly Cabinet and formed another, likewise consisting of a handful of leading national figures. General Lyautey was summoned from Morocco to become War Minister. Regy informed Haig that, although he was not personally acquainted with the French General, all he had heard about him was in his favour. He was, moreover, a close friend of his former ADC, Captain Doumayrou, now acting as French liaison officer to Hankey, and Regy assured Haig that through Doumayrou he and Lyautey could be brought together.

The year 1917 ushered in the general European disintegration. Both the Allies and the Central Powers were near the end of their tether. There were mutinies in the French Army and the German Fleet, and the catastrophic Revolution broke out in Russia. Amongst the Allied commanders there was friction and muddle. One bright ray of hope lay in the declaration of war against Germany by the United States. Even so, there was much doubt whether the military machinery of that great country could be organized in time to save the Allies.

Regy continued to cross and recross the Channel. He was mostly in France, sometimes with Nellie, who was Founder President of the Territorial Branch of the St John Ambulance. Having before the war set up classes in London in first aid and nursing, she was now running a unit of canteen workers and about eighteen ambulances on the French front beyond Noyon. She took her responsibilities extremely seriously and was frequently on tour with her husband, visiting the twenty-five Anglo-French hospitals under her jurisdiction.

On the first evening of the year Regy dined with Haig and Nivelle, the new Commander-in-Chief. Haig liked, and was able to talk on equal terms with, the half-English, bilingual Nivelle, which he had not done with Joffre. He was also duly impressed by Lyautey, the new Minister for War, who, though highly nervous in speech and movement, was shrewd. Most important of all, the two commanders were in agreement in favouring the Western offensive. Haig's prestige was much enhanced by the receipt of a New Year telegram from the King awarding him a field-marshal's baton. In spite of the improved relations brought about by these changes, Regy firmly believed that the French must be deprived of their political and military lead. 'Do not miss this psychological moment,' he counselled Robertson. He should establish Haig's powers and authority vis-à-vis Nivelle at once.[24] To this end he urged Lloyd George to send either Alfred Milner or George Curzon to be always at Briand's elbow, in the role of Ambassador Extraordinary.[25] Within a month Regy was having reservations about Nivelle's too vehemently expressed optimism. Any serious check by the enemy to his operations would be met with a violent French reaction.[26] To Haig Regy awarded rapturous praise for his acceptance, without a murmur of objection, of the thankless role of 'making a great holding attack while others try to win the palm'. It was worthy of the Great Duke.[27]

Regy was convinced that Frank Bertie was completely useless as Ambassador, and set about trying to get rid of him. He began by supporting the Military Attaché Le Roy-Lewis's idea that he might be promoted and freed from Embassy control so as to take up the work of a military commissioner; so able a man needed far more authority than he was enjoying. To both Robertson and Haig Regy wrote endorsing this idea. Haig sent for Regy, greeted him almost affectionately for so dour a man, and turned down the idea flatly. The CIGS was of the same opinion as the Commander-in-Chief. Le Roy-Lewis was not popular with the English community – he had been mixed up in a spy charge – and was considered mischievous. Regy was right, however, in judging him extremely clever and capable.

Notwithstanding this rebuff, Regy set about preparing a memorandum on Bertie's relations with the immensely rich Baron Jacques de Gunzburg, a man of Russo-German Jewish extraction who was associated with international pacifist organizations. What he had to say against this individual came from Le Roy-Lewis, who informed him that Gunzburg had promised the Ambassador chairmanship of the Central Mining Company at £5000 a year on his retirement. This charge may seem innocuous, and Regy may rather have lost his head over the whole Bertie affair; however, during a two-hour walk in the Bois Lewis disclosed further damaging details, including the Ambassador's friendship with Murray of Elibank who gave stock exchange business to Vere Bertie, his son. The Ambassador had quarrelled with Murray because he would give none of the proceeds to Gunzburg. Also confidential missives from Charles Hardinge, British Ambassador in St Petersburg, criticizing the Russians as Allies, had leaked to Germany through – Le Roy-Lewis affirmed – Gunzburg. Le Roy-Lewis assured Regy that, rather than be a party to these suspicious dealings, he preferred to leave the Embassy altogether.

Regy's increasing contempt for Bertie led him to quarrel with his old friend Viscount French, as Sir John had now become, for dining with the Ambassador, instead of with him, one February night while passing through Paris.

I imagine that because I am friends with Douglas and am very fond of him, as I always have been and always shall be, you think me faithless. But this absolute refusal on my part to accept your loves (and they have been many) or your hatreds (and they have not been few) is no new thing. I went through it all when Lord Roberts and Lord K. were anathema maranatha. We came through all right, and we shall come through this 'feeling' of yours about D.H. fanned as it is by your friends who are not real friends, and by your queer, suspicious, but really very nice nature.[28]

He meant what he said; he had always been irked by the man's touchiness and hot temper. But there were other reasons for his displeasure. He had not forgiven French for failing to respond to his request for promotion for his son Maurice, which it was within his power to grant. In consequence, when French took his seat in the House of Lords, Regy declined to be his sponsor.

In February Lyautey sent for Regy, who was impressed by his brilliant success as Resident Commissioner-General in Morocco. He was a gentleman, Regy decided, unlike most French politicians and generals of those days, and well bred; also avowedly royalist, his wife being the god-daughter of the Empress Eugénie – attributes not lost on Regy. He wore a signet ring inscribed with Shelley's words, 'The

Soul's joy lies in doing', which appealed to Regy who asked to have an impress of it. He appeared to be cunning and adroit, with an eye for humbug; he could not be taken in. He was also covertly homosexual, which Regy may have detected. Lyautey endeared himself to him by revealing that he had advocated setting up a committee of imperial defence for working out peace terms, such as Regy had submitted to Asquith the day that French was sacked. It had been ignored. Regy wrote to Robertson that Lyautey was worth his serious attention. 'His qualifications and authority are not absolute, but relative, and should be so estimated.' He was sure Lyautey would stand as the military representative of France just as Robertson was that of England.[29] He was greatly distressed, therefore, when his new hero resigned in March.

Meanwhile the Germans were rashly threatening the Americans that if Great Britain refused to entertain President Wilson's peace proposals they would intensify their U-boat campaign against British merchant shipping. The result was the opposite of what they expected. Wilson was horrified. On 3 February the United States broke off diplomatic relations with Germany, though without immediately declaring war. On the 17th Regy had an interview with the American Ambassador in Berlin, Gerard. He believed the German peace feelers were meant to split the Allies, regain the sympathy of America – which was bitterly opposed to their submarine warfare – and rally their own public. Gerard told Regy that any peace but a victorious peace would be fatal to the German monarchy, and that shortage of food would finish the country within a year.[30]

On the 27th a conference between the Allied commanders took place at Calais; its importance was brought about not by design, but by accident. Nivelle distrusted Haig ('*Evidemment on ne peut pas compter sur lui*', scribbled in pencil by the French Commander, was detected on a document inadvertently forwarded to Haig's headquarters). Ostensibly the conference had been called to discuss problems of transport. Suddenly Nivelle assumed without any previous warning that he was to be Generalissimo. Neither Haig nor Robertson had an inkling that the question of supreme command was to be raised, and whether purposely or by oversight the King had not been informed in advance. To Haig's and the British representatives' consternation Lloyd George, who had come determined to have Haig superseded, supported the French proposal. Lloyd George, in extraordinary ignorance, was under the illusion that Nivelle was a second Napoleon, whereas his own countrymen knew him to be a good average soldier. Haig, stupefied, asked Regy to come to him at once. Regy saw the situation as more than grave. Friction between the two chiefs of armies at such a time was intolerable. The British Army could not be put under the French Commander-in-Chief. Besides, he argued, Nivelle might be superseded by someone of even less calibre than himself. As it happened, he was succeeded by Pétain in May.

Regy dashed off a letter to Lord Murray of Elibank. Rumour in Paris was rife, he said, that Lloyd George was determined to get rid of Haig; this would be utterly disastrous. Lloyd George and Haig must be kept together in mutual confidence. If he, Regy, were to write to Lloyd George it would be supposed 'that my sole intention is to score off poor old Frank Bertie. This you know perfectly well is not the case, as although he hates me, I have no feelings about him personally, other than that of mild amusement. The PM ought to strangle this '*potin*' at once.'[31]

On 9 March Lyautey sent for Regy and disclosed what had really happened. It was Lloyd George, abetted by Hankey, who to the astonishment of Lyautey and Briand had prearranged Nivelle's announcement. The French could scarcely believe that the British Prime Minister had not previously informed either Robertson or Haig of his intention. Actually Lloyd George had tried to persuade Lyautey to tell them, but he refused and went off to spend two hours with the Duchess of Sutherland.[32] It was the French delegates who modified the scheme. Lyautey agreed with Regy that no one in their senses, French or British, would suggest that command of the British armies should be usurped by French officers. In the eyes of the French, Lloyd George's tactics were abysmal.

Regy passed on this information to Haig; and Briand felt moved to confirm that Lloyd George had been the author of the intrigue. The outcome was that Henry Wilson was posted to Beauvais as Chief Liaison Officer. Wilson urged both Lyautey and Robertson to meet and work out a means of amicable joint command. Haig, meanwhile, quietly handed in his resignation to the King, who persuaded him to withdraw it.

Regy was in close touch with Stamfordham over these embarrassing events. He pointed out that French politicians were worse than British ones in that they absolutely dominated the soldiers. So if the direction of the British armies had been yielded to the French, they would have been at the mercy of the Chamber of Deputies and their unstable vanities.[33] It was these people who then forced Lyautey's resignation as War Minister, for the simple reason that in debate in the Chamber he refused, for very necessary security reasons, to disclose the proceedings of the Calais conference. He was succeeded by a professor of mathematics, Paul Painlévé. In offering his condolences to Lyautey Regy wrote that his respect for him would not extend to his successor. He felt overcome by helplessness. Without Lyautey, he said, exaggerating a little, the London arrangements were '*ratés* [a failure]; *jamais l'entente ne tiendra, et l'unité de commandement (sterilisée de sa naissance) ne tiendra après votre départ du Ministère.*'[34]

The rock-like quality of Douglas Haig was emphasized during this critical time by its contrast with the irrational and often hysterical behaviour of most of the leading politicians and soldiers, whether British or French. Throughout their tantrums, irresponsible conduct, disloyalties and sheer pettiness Haig remained unmoved, calm, determined, resolute – on a plane above them all.

Henry Wilson was an old friend of Regy's. He was brilliant but mercurial, Irish and unpredictable. Repington called him an 'intriguing impostor' and hated him. Other officers despised him as a 'low-class schemer whose sole aptitude is for worshipping rising suns'.[35] Regy, who enjoyed his company and was amused by his facetious letters, considered him the cleverest general in the British Army. A very close friend of Foch, he was a leading exponent of firm co-operation with the French in matters military and political. It is not surprising that some people criticized Wilson's appointment as Chief Liaison Officer with the French headquarters. General Charteris thought it a great mistake, in spite of Regy's assurance that Wilson was always loyal to the man he was serving – that man now being Haig. Anywhere else he would be highly dangerous.[36] But Wilson did not accept the commission eagerly. When Regy lunched with him at his château at Beauvais he explained how he had refused both Robertson's and Haig's requests that he should become Chief Liaison Officer, telling them that they both distrusted and disliked him. He intimated that he would go only if Haig pressed him, if Robertson, the King and Nivelle begged him, and if he might retire whenever he pleased. When these conditions were granted the temperamental Irishman consented. Regy felt obliged to write a stern letter to Robertson in Wilson's favour, explaining that no man had more imagination or staff knowledge. 'I am not sure that he [Robertson] relished it. But after all I have achieved my one aim in life, independence, and I can fight for my friends regardless of the opinions or acts of any living man.'[37] Henry Wilson need not have bothered to impose his stringent conditions, for Painlevé and Pétain between them got rid of him in June. Regy much regretted the loss of this most intelligent general. By the end of the year, however, Wilson was in his bad books, as was Lord French. Regy was horrified by their joint report, made at the Cabinet's request, in which they spoke of Haig being 'quite unable to grasp the facts of the present situation', and as being 'obsessed by his own optimism'.

Perhaps the most serious disaster for the Allied cause in 1917 was the disintegration of the Russian army, followed by the whole imperial regime. Regy was appalled by the outbreak of the Russian Revolution, its excesses and implications. 'I am very sorry for the Czar,' he wrote to Stamfordham on learning of Nicholas II's abdication.

> He may have been 'weak' but he was conscientious and kind, and 'up against' a proposition in the Russian bureaucracy that no man alive could have coped with successfully. The whole tragedy is curiously like that in France a century ago. The German proclivities (so called) of the Empress and her unpopularity recall '*l'Autrichienne*'. The goodness of the Czar and his weakness are so like Louis XVI. Even between the poor child and the Dauphin there is the resemblance of delicate health.[38]

There was shortly to be a still more terrible resemblance between the two royal families – in the manner of their deaths. Although still a Liberal by inclination, Regy was dubious of true democracy, and democracy run mad terrified him. He felt in his bones that if the Allies failed to defeat the enemy in this war there would be revolution in England in which the monarchy, the Church and Victorian institutions would founder. He did not think the aristocracy in England had been loyal to the King. The pro-monarchical forces had not presented a united front over the 'detestable Russian outbreaks' and the abominable treatment of the Tsar and Tsarina. Asquith and Lloyd George, for example, had given the King bad advice from the outset of the war regarding his and his own sons' activities. He deplored all the kow-towing to democracy and telegrams to the Premier of the Provisional Government, Kerensky. They were doing incalculable harm in sapping the foundations on which the British Empire stood. They would incur the loss of India and the adoption of republican fashions which would make Great Britain a dependency at best of the United States and at worst of the Russian Soviet.[39] When Kerensky was deposed by the Bolsheviks in November he was delighted. 'The adulation [by our country], he wrote, of that neurotic self-seeker has been one of the worst features of the war.'[40]

From Beauvais Regy wrote at this time to the Prince of Wales, giving him as much inside information as he dared in a letter. In April they met in Paris. 'I had a delightful talk with [him], the sweetest thing in uniform in all the Armies. It was a real affectionate little talk, as if he were Lawrence ['Thrushy']. He goes back today to his XIVth Corps.'[41] The young man regarded this polished older man of the world as a surrogate father. In July he confided in him that he had had his first *amourette* six months ago – a little French girl who had brushed aside his extraordinary shyness.[42]

This month Regy condescended to meet Lyautey's successor; Le

Roy-Lewis took him to lunch with Painlévé at the War Ministry. Regy found the Sorbonne professor intelligent and, he guessed, more honest than his colleagues, contemporaries and entourage – but not above the average. He showed no profound knowledge of affairs, although his judgements seemed sound and considered.[43] Painlévé was up in arms to substitute Pétain for Nivelle, whose April offensive had proved a total failure. In this he was successful, in spite of Briand's support of Nivelle. Pétain's known policy was to spare French lives at the expense of American ones now that President Wilson had at last declared war on Germany. Haig maintained complete silence on the subject of Nivelle's dismissal, which he felt acutely.

The women of France were worn out, tired of war. The people were showing signs of being affected by the Communist plague from Petrograd. They were made unhappy by the constant changes of government and disillusioned with their own ministers. Regy prophesied, wrongly, that the nation would collapse in October or November. Only Lloyd George's popularity kept them together. When the volatile Welshman, known as the Chanticleer of France, arrived in Paris in August the citizens gave him a resounding welcome, withheld from their own premiers who lasted too short a time to inspire affection or confidence. The Chanticleer sent a note asking Regy to meet him at the Crillon Hotel, where they lunched on the balcony of his sitting room. He appeared amazingly alert and full of spirit, even laughing at jokes made at his expense. More surprising still, he praised Haig to the skies. This provoked Regy to comment: 'It is almost comic to see how much the balance has turned. . . . This instability of vision . . . is Ll.G.'s great weakness. With his tremendous vitality and indestructible spirit, it is a source of danger. But luckily he never displays infirmity of purpose. He suffers from over-elasticity of mind.'[44]

After the Prime Minister's return to London Regy composed a letter confirming what he had told him face to face, namely that he was badly served in Paris. The British Embassy was utterly useless, with the exception of Le Roy-Lewis. In such a crisis it was essential that Lloyd George had someone of authority to represent him in the French capital, for his popularity with the French was at its height. What was required was daily communication, interchange of information and the conveyance of moral support to French ministers.[45] It is unlikely that Regy had himself in mind, for reasons that will emerge presently. As he told Haig, Ll.G. had no ambassador other than a senile old gentleman whose ignorance was phenomenal.[46] The old gentleman was alive enough to fume with indignation when Le Roy-Lewis was promoted by the military authorities to brigadier-general, which he took as a slight to himself. 'The Bull [Bertie's nickname] has flown to Ll.G. protesting,' wrote Regy, 'and calling Le Roy-Lewis every name under the sun.'[47]

In May Regy again wrote to the Prime Minister, complaining that Bertie had refused to speak to Le Roy-Lewis. It was a scandal. He advised Lloyd George to place the Embassy under a chargé d'affaires and put Le Roy-Lewis in charge of a secretariat responsible to him personally for all business relating to the war. The Embassy was quite out of touch and busy belittling the Government at home.[48]

Lord Derby, the Minister for War, felt obliged to cross over to Paris to investigate matters for himself. He sounded Regy out on whether, if the Embassy were to be split in two for the duration of the war, he would consent to become one ambassador, or minister-extraordinary, with Henry Wilson his chief expert adviser on military matters and Le Roy-Lewis charged with looking after civil matters.[49] Wilson favoured the proposition, and so apparently did Haig. But Regy was doubtful of the wisdom of either appointment. He told Lawrence Burgis in confidence that the PM and Derby wanted to sack Bertie and put him, Esher, in his place. He was against the idea; he would make an unconventional ambassador. But if Lloyd George pressed the matter hard he would take over, though only on terms which he doubted would prove acceptable. In the first place Bertie must go. Then he would insist on certain rearrangements of the Embassy buildings and redistribution of work and personnel, which he was sure would not be agreed to. Nothing but patriotism would induce him to consider the proposition for a moment. Lawrence became so enthusiastic that he could think of little else; he did not yet know his patron very well. Bertie did not go – when the suggestion was broached he absolutely refused. And Regy knew Bertie would refuse, just as he knew that his own conditions would not be accepted at such a critical time. But to advance them looked better than downright refusal.

On the contrary, Bertie mocked Regy's pretensions. He informed Stamfordham that Esher was telling everybody his work was so important that he had been unable to leave Paris for a year, and quoted preposterous prophecies made by him to *The New York Herald* that the end of the war was in sight.

> Everybody asks what Esher is doing here. He gives people to under-stand that he is the official agent of many important persons. One of his functions is to convey messages from Sir Douglas Haig to the President of the Republic who, until I told him that Esher is merely a friend of the Field-Marshal, thought him to be a distinguished military officer attached to GHQ.

This was mischievous of Bertie, for Regy was in fact the very thing which the Ambassador pretended he was not – namely the agent, and not so unofficial, of many important persons, including the Prime Minister and the King.[50]

Regy in his turn wrote to Stamfordham, before learning of Bertie's refusal to leave the Embassy, that there should be no replacement until peacetime; and that, instead, Wilson ought to be sent to Paris as head of a military mission. He was a friend of Foch, and he was supremely intelligent. At a time of great crisis the traditions of the official hierarchy, including embassies, should be subordinated to the dire necessities of the country and monarchy. Both were under threat. France was being shaken by Communist agitators, and things were not going well. The British would do well to make efforts in Government commensurate with the military efforts which Douglas Haig's splendid troops were making.[51] In fact Regy's views, like those of everyone else on what should be done to transfer the conduct of the war from French into British hands, differed from day to day.

Regy found the intrigues in which he was involved this summer frustrating and unrewarding. He had never relished not getting his own way, and hitherto had fought hard to make sure he did. Now he had reached a stage when he no longer cared. On learning that there was resentment among high-ranking officers at headquarters of his frequent and direct correspondence with the Commander-in-Chief, he was also hurt. He told Haig, who in the Bertie battle had ostensibly been on his side, that there was no longer any need for his services in France. He had come only at the request of Lord K., who recognized the weakness of the British representatives in Paris, and he now wished to discuss his future with the Field-Marshal.[52] He would abide by his advice on what he should do. There is evidence that secretly Regy wanted his friend to persuade him to stay. Haig certainly did write, 'You are still doing such useful work in Paris in keeping an eye on our French Allies, and your new idea of working with the Americans seems excellent.'[53] It was nice to be told he could not be spared, even if it was in rather tepid terms.

Regy's capacity for work and his grasp of what needed doing were as extraordinary as they were commendable in a man of his years. Nevertheless it is hardly surprising that many people found him meddlesome. In July he made it his business to get to know General Pershing, recently appointed Commander-in-Chief of the American Expeditionary Force in Europe. They got on so well that Pershing asked Regy to act confidentially between him and the British Commander-in-Chief. Regy assured Haig that he would like Pershing very much. He was courteous, friendly and capable; moreover he was anxious to learn from his British counterpart. 'Discipline to [the

Americans]', Regy wrote, 'means the control of a man over himself, and very strict it is in all essentials. The Yankee rod will swallow up all the other rods before the War is over.'[54] The French, he reported, were already disenchanted with the Americans, finding them slow, their technicians inferior to their own, and their equipment not forthcoming. They were having to supply them with rifles. But this was a sort of jealousy, considering that a mere month ago the French Xth Army had been in a state of rebellion caused by inaction and the 'hopelessness of War'. No wonder that Pershing told Regy he would rather learn from Haig than from the French.[55] Besides, he found the French language and character obstacles. He modestly admitted to knowing little of the war up to date and nothing of the Allied plans. Regy was enthusiastic about the Americans. 'The most impressive thing in France just now is the American mouth and jaw. These thin-lipped, clean-shaven fellows have brought a new atmosphere with them,' he told the CIGS.[56] He fully realized that it was only this arrival of Allies from the New World that would redress the stalemate in the Old, and bring ultimate victory.

Next came Henry Morgenthau, President Wilson's close confidant and secret agent. After meeting him Regy at once wrote a memorandum to Haig and Lloyd George. The moral regeneration of America, which was floundering in material prosperity and worldly competition, was the over-riding objective of their leaders. The war to them was a crusade on the part of democracy against autocracy, through the torments of which their people must be cleansed of the filthy lucre of Mammon.

> There is an element of pathos in the simple and serious faith of these people. They are like early Christians in some well known picture attending white robed in the areas hemmed in by wild beasts and shouting crowds. The unpleasant reflection is that these same early Christians destroyed the Roman Empire and plunged Europe into the darkness of the Middle Ages. I am not sure whether Wilson or Kerensky is the more dangerous.[57]

The cynic in Regy was never far from the surface. He told Morgenthau that he did not believe in Wilson's practical efficacy. He did not believe this was a war to end wars. He, Regy, was a confessed materialist. He believed that the Allies must get hold of all the material guarantees they could, so that when the next war came they would find themselves stronger than they were in 1914. Morgenthau was shocked, and replied that no American would subscribe to this view.

Regy was not slow to realize that Wilson was equating British navalism with German militarism, both of which were abhorrent to him; and though the President could no longer justifiably keep America out of the war once Russia had gone Communist, he could make the price of his country's participation a settlement of the sort of peace he felt was righteous. This was the cause of the unpopularity with the Allies of his attempts at mediation before and after America joined the war. Yet he could not be alienated, because of the Allies' absolute dependence upon American intervention.[58]

Alarmed though Regy was at learning what was in Wilson's mind, he advised Lord Murray that the British must confide in the Americans instantly. At the same time he strongly urged him to caution Lloyd George not to be deceived by Wilsonism. Milner, he now cried out, was the only man qualified to become the British counterpart of Morgenthau in Paris. Let him come out. 'I feel like Nelson when he used to pray for frigates! Milner, Milner, Milner!'[59]

By September Regy was ill with worry and overwork. Nellie, who was living at Senlis working for French soldiers and evacuating villagers, took him to recuperate at Biarritz. Regy thought it the most beautiful seaside place he had ever visited. They had a hotel room that hung right over the great Atlantic waves, with only a few yards of sand between. But he found the sea noises disturbing. Having no war work to contend with, he returned to worrying about Chat's future. He was determined to devise some scheme whereby Chat, after his mother's death, might live comfortably at Tomperran, the Williamsons' dower house, at Comrie. Chat must rely on him to see it through. He also had time to write again to Milly; their correspondence had lapsed after her second and third marriages. It was not that Regy disapproved. He merely found it sad that this once exquisite woman had to find solace with such second-rate husbands. 'I wish she would grow old gracefully,' he wrote to Maurice.

Once back in Paris Regy was concerned with the peace proposals made by Germany, via Spain, to Briand. With Italy and Russia now almost out of the war, and Pétain with no will to attack in the West on a big scale, Regy had changed his tune. The sooner the various leaders set about discussing terms the better, he decided. Lloyd George should scrap the Paris Embassy temporarily and establish Milner there as British plenipotentiary so as to galvanize the Western Allies into some sense; in other words transfer the Foreign Office to Paris, which was now the nerve centre of Europe.[60]

Regy lunched with Briand and Bunau Varilla, editor of *Le Matin*. From Briand he learned how favourable were the peace terms offered by Germany, including the evacuation of Belgium and France. These negotiations were known to and approved by King Albert. Here were clearly grounds to work on. But the Foreign Minister, Ribot, instead of forwarding the proposals in a letter which Briand had drafted, sent such a garbled telegram version to Balfour, giving a lead for rejection, that he and Lloyd George refused to consider the terms. On 24 September the negotiations were abruptly broken off. The French were then told by the Spanish intermediary that as a result the Germans would fight to the finish. Briand added that, when he gave the Chamber, in secret session, a guarded account of what had happened, the feeling against Ribot was so strong that he had to go. Regy told Lawrence that he was amazed by the folly of the French and British Governments. The underlying motive was jealousy on the part of the French Foreign Minister that the offer had been addressed not to him but to Briand.[61] Regy also told Lord Lansdowne that he felt sure the Allies could have detached Austria from the Central Powers had we had the skill to make her definite peace offers six months earlier.[62] Philip Sassoon revealed a year later that this indeed was the case. The Austrian Emperor had actually made overtures in March of 1917, but the Italians would not hear of them. When Regy learned about them he wrote to Lloyd George in April 1918, informing him that the Italian Foreign Minister, Baron Sonnino, had put pressure on Ribot and Clemenceau to support him. He warned the Prime Minister that Clemenceau was untrustworthy; he invariably put French considerations first, even if they were not in the interest of ultimate victory.[63]

Regy had been corresponding with Lansdowne since the publication of his courageous letter of 29 November to the *Daily Telegraph*, advocating a peace and deprecating the Foreign Office's refusal to come to terms with the Kaiser. Regy read it while he was at Hesdin near the front lines. He knew that the Allies were weaker and the Germans stronger than they had been six months before. 'I cannot share the sentiments of those who would pour out oceans of living blood upon the altar of the future,' he wrote in his journal, 'a future remote, say 50 years. . . . How many men died of old in order that we should enjoy privileges that are quite valueless to us?' His was the sentiment of a man who had witnessed too much slaughter and destruction at first hand to see any longer the justification of national prestige.

> Why should a youth lose his life for another youth a generation hence? Even if you could be sure that the sacrifice would not be in vain, there might be something to be urged in its favour. . . . But when the impossibility of forecast is measured by past experience, surely there is no sane reason why a single life should be lost today for problematic security fifty years hence. In war 'enough for the day' is the safest maxim, while in peace it is the most dangerous of fallacies. To buy future peace by the extinction of the German nation is a futile dream.[64]

He was sick of the whole ghastly, fatuous, evil business. It had been brought home to him forcibly while driving back from Cambrai two nights earlier. He had met a battalion of fresh troops coming up into the line. They were singing, the poor innocents, the well-known music hall songs, and shouting as they marched. It was doubtless a fine illustration of the spirit and indomitable morale of the British Army. But why should these youths be asked to endure the conditions – the wet drizzle, the rough road, the heavy packs – as they pressed forward through the night to certain massacre? What did they suppose they were fighting for? How many of them knew or minded? Did they care a fig for *civilization* as expressed by their betters, freedom of the seas, the League of Nations, these English, French *and* German youths? It was a miracle, beside which that of the loaves and fishes sank into insignificance, the way they met death with calm courage and even good cheer. To Lawrence he wrote, 'I am sure that you thought none of these things when you jumped into that ditch under the shadow of the Vimy Ridge. Just the sporting instinct or that indescribable social pressure, so difficult to analyse, catches hold of young men's hearts, and makes them perform miraculous deeds.'[65]

The violence of the gutter press against Lansdowne sickened him. The *Daily Mail* accused him of being guided by personal motives, thinking of the preservation of his estates. 'Lansdowne! whose beloved son was killed in battle, and whose whole unblemished life has been passed in the service of his country.'[66] Lansdowne had been deeply wounded by his son Kerry's letter to his constituents denying his father; but consoled by the hundreds of letters from unknown people telling him he had written what all of them had been thinking for some time past, but not liking or daring to put into words. On the other hand Regy believed Lord Lansdowne's letter to be imprudent, if not inopportune, at a moment when the fortunes of the Allies were about to turn. He was not the only liberal-minded man to think so. Geoffrey Robinson (who had now changed his name to Dawson) refused to publish it in *The Times*, even going so far as to call it 'mischievous'.

The year 1917 ended on a note of discord. It is true that the Allied General Staff was an accomplished fact. Regy was amused that the scheme which he had devised exactly two years earlier, whereby the Staff was to be composed of three representatives of each country – the Prime Minister, a military member and one member of the Cabinet – had at last been adopted to the very letter. In Britain's case the three were Lloyd George, Jan Smuts and Henry Wilson. On the other hand quarrelling among the Allies and even among the British was rife. After the first inter-Allied conference at Versailles Lloyd George took Regy up to his room. He seemed satisfied with his recent bout with

Clemenceau, now French Premier, who was very hostile and wanted Pétain to command the Allied forces. Bertie, it appeared, was backing Clemenceau in whipping up the support of the French press. Then Lloyd George launched out about the intrigues against himself. He complained bitterly of Charteris and his fallacious advice to Haig. All Haig's plans, he maintained, had failed. He had promised the capture of the Channel ports of Zeebrugge and Ostend, and then victory in the November offensive against Cambrai. He had failed in all at a cost of 400,000 men. Now he wanted to embark on fresh offensives and was asking for more men. He would not get them. Robertson was also anxious to be rid of Charteris. And as for Lloyd George, Robertson said he was impossible to work with; he was capricious and frivolous. Robertson was also against Wilson, and criticized Haig. Lloyd George was vehemently against both Haig and Robertson. Regy told Lord Derby that this squabbling was deplorable; it was a sign of decadence, and reminiscent of France in 1870. It would lead to the triumph of Germany unless it ceased.[67]

At the beginning of January 1918 Regy informed Robertson that he definitely wanted to return home. Now that Henry Wilson was always in Paris and Milner often there he no longer saw the necessity for himself to remain. Besides, he was genuinely homesick for Scotland. Haig wrote that he was very sorry indeed to hear of Regy's departure. He would arrange for General Cox, Charteris's successor, to keep Regy's cypher; Regy could thus continue to communicate direct to the Commander-in-Chief from home. The privilege was immensely flattering, especially since it was Haig's own suggestion. Yet Regy was still worried about the confusion that reigned in the Supreme War Council. The taking over of more of the front line by the British Army was giving a good deal of trouble. The question had been referred to Allied headquarters, but should have been settled by the Council. Clemenceau was of one opinion, Lloyd George of another. The latter referred it to Robertson and Haig. This meant that it was impossible to pronounce where the real seat of authority lay.[68]

On 11 February Regy and Nellie, having met at Boulogne, crossed the Channel together. He had brought with him Haig's war notebooks which the Field Marshal had lent him on condition that no one else had access to them. After reading through them, Regy had them typed out.[69]

It was nearly two years since he had been in England. Lawrence, wearing his staff uniform, met the Eshers at Victoria station. Both Regy and Nellie were surprised by the changes in London, which they found hateful. The capital was down at heel like a pair of old boots, he declared. The people talked of nothing but the constant air raids. Not a single taxi cab was available. The few private limousines were propelled by gas from large bags floating above the roofs. Regy's old associates were much worn and aged. Nellie recorded that London was very depressed. The lake in St James's Park was a complete village of Government huts, and Kensington Palace Garden had been turned into allotments growing vegetables. Food was strictly rationed and nasty; there was less of it than in Paris; the minimum of sugar was allowed and there was the maximum of discomfort everywhere.

Conditions elsewhere in Great Britain were scarcely better. There were railway stoppages, strikes by munitions and dockyard workers, by coal miners and even the police. Regy, recalling the sufferings and evil conditions of the troops in France and Flanders, was deeply shocked by the attitude of the civilian workers at home. He attributed it to the British 'Bolsheviks' who were mobilizing against the war. Yet it was inconsistent of Regy to complain to Maurice that he was being deprived of his male servants in the great call-up, which he had been so instrumental in bringing about. Eventually the War Office sent back Taylor, his chauffeur, which was some consolation for the dyspepsia he was suffering from eating too much grouse.

One of the first people Regy saw was Lord Lansdowne, with whom he dined alone at Lansdowne House. His host saw no advantage in destroying the Government, for there was no alternative to it. On 16 February Randall Davidson, the Archbishop of Canterbury, who was ill in bed, sent for him.

> Lambeth was bathed in a cold sunight. The Primate's bedroom is not austere – it is full of flowers. His dark eyebrows and piercing eyes were the most conspicuous and effective furniture in the chamber. I remained with him for over an hour. He explained how often he had urged before the King and Queen the necessity of taking a firmer stand, and of coming into closer touch with realities. But he found the King obstinate and the Queen unimaginative. Virtue dominates that household, but not wisdom.
>
> The Primate yearns for peace, but sees no machinery available just now for procuring it. . . . If he or Ll. G. would negotiate with Prince Max of Baden, we might obtain a reasonable peace. But the forces of stupidity are overwhelming
>
> At five I went to Buckingham Palace. It was a Rip Van Winkle appearance upon the scene. Either the world has stopped still, or Buckingham Palace remains unchanged. The same routine. A life made up of nothings – yet a busy scene: constant telephone messages about trivialities.[70]

From now on Regy's private journals are often critical – almost carping – when referring to King George and Queen Mary. He may not have been fully conscious of it, and he certainly gives no explanation. Whether the King had reprimanded him for some mischief of which he did not think himself at fault, such as his letter to the *Glasgow Herald* in August 1915 about conscription or whether he was tarred with the brush of insubordination so conspicuous in Admiral Fisher and regarded askance because of his close friendship and alliance with him, is uncertain. Jackie Fisher did not hesitate to mock Their Majesties in letters to his friends and to repeat unkind things, such as the epigram quoted by the soldiers at the front that the King was futile and the Queen only fertile. Again, Regy's experiences of the front may have made him impatient of the pettiness of the life he now witnessed at court. The King's pledge to drink no alcohol he thought merely silly, and his refusal to offer it to his ministers positively unkind. Asquith found meals at the Palace without stimulant a purgatory, and on one occasion Rosebery contracted such an attack of hiccoughs from drinking ginger beer that he could not speak a word to the Queen on his left.

Regy always put the monarchy before the monarch. It was the welfare of the Crown that mattered to him more than the wearer of it. When the reigning sovereign made a mistake he said so to those members of his Household who were his special friends and who he hoped might agree with him and rectify the matter. He told Sir Bryan Godfrey-Faussett[71] that the Harmsworth press, which was acting like the Inquisition in Spain, ought to be controlled by law.[72] When a furious Colonel Repington told Regy that he had been so scurvily treated by *The Times* that he had resigned, Regy was indignant on his behalf.[73] Although he thought Repington mischievous and not wholly trustworthy, he recognized him as a sound patriot of great intellectual ability. And now he was a wronged victim of press monopoly. When therefore the King created Northcliffe, who was already a baron, a viscount he thought the Palace was being too stupid and feeble for words. Knowing that the Palace objected to a newspaper proprietor being a member of the Cabinet, he thought the royal action pusillanimous. He passed on these objections to Stamfordham, 'in the hope of doing some good. . . . It is impossible not to be anxious about the future of the monarchy and of the imperial traditions. I am fortunately at an age and in a position from which I can speak very freely to you and the King, without offence.'[74] Here Regy may have been overreaching himself. Monarchs do not relish unsolicited criticism even from respected advisers of twenty-three years' honourable standing.

At all events, when Regy came back to Tilney Street from Scotland in April he deliberately refrained from letting the court know, so as not to have to visit Windsor. On re-reading some pre-war royal letters he jotted in his journal, 'How well King Edward stands out compared with our poor little King, who is of so small account.'[75] And he showed irritation with the Household for saying how overworked and overtired the King was. 'They think of him as though he were Queen Victoria *after* her Diamond Jubilee. He is younger than D[ouglas] H[aig] and dozens of other people who never fuss.' His references to the King in letters to friends betray a new coldness this year. Concerning King George's proposed visit to France he wrote to Philip Sassoon in a condescending vein: 'Poor little King! I think he is right from the point of view of saving what skin he has left, to go out. . . . It is wonderful that the whole edifice has not crumbled under an avalanche of ridicule. . . .' He will in all probability 'be laid up in bed with a pain in his tummy, having his head held by Derek Keppel'.[76]

In February King George was very worried by the disagreements between Lloyd George and Robertson, which were making the Prime Minister ill. It amounted to no more than incompatibility of temperament, but was none the less vexatious for that. Both men wanted to be master, which was absurd. The King discussed the problem with Regy *ad infinitum* one February evening. Regy was struck by the lack of vision of both the Palace and Downing Street. What was the use of complaining of things and then doing nothing about them? Surely the King and his Prime Minister had only to pull themselves together and replace Robertson? Regy's sympathies were with Lloyd George, who after all was Prime Minister. Robertson, having dominated the War Office and been inflated by the press into a demi-god, saw his prerogatives like those of Napoleon rather than the Duke of Wellington. Haig was called over at this critical juncture, but refused to take part in discussions about Robertson; he merely assured 'Wully' that were he to be sent to Versailles he would take orders from him.

At last it was announced on the 18th that Sir Henry Wilson had succeeded Robertson as CIGS. Robertson, having accepted the Eastern Command, remained at York House, fulminating.

A few months later the King asked Wilson why he would not take counsel over some new issue from Sir William Robertson, whose experience and unrivalled judgement must be so useful. The difficulty lay, Wilson replied, in the fact that when Robertson was CIGS he could not get on with Lloyd George. 'No wonder,' said the King. 'Robertson was too honest and straight to get on with him' – a remark which Regy called a backhander with a vengeance.

On 12 February Regy watched his beloved Prince of Wales take his seat in the House of Lords. The House was fairly full, and the Ladies' Gallery thronged.

The procession was more pompous than is usual when a peer takes his seat. Balfour of Burleigh, George Curzon, the Dukes of Beaufort and Somerset were among the tallest peers. The boy looked more boyish

than ever in such surroundings. A youthful fair figure, smooth as
Henry V. His blush is ready as ever on a fair cheek, but his eyes have
lost their dreamy *Weltschmerz* look. He was composed and modest.[77]

Regy wondered whether this traditional ceremony was being performed for the last time.

The evening of the 26th was spent with Thrushy at the War Cabinet
Office where he was working just above Regy's old CID room. The
next day he and Nellie went to the Roman Camp. It was a joy to be
among his old treasures and books again, and the two of them stayed
for six weeks. In the mornings he wrote interminable letters, as was
his habit – to Henry Wilson, Haig, Thrushy, the children and Philip
Sassoon. In the evenings he read copiously – Shakespeare's *A Winter's
Tale*, Victor Hugo's *93*, Alice Meynell's *Hearts of Controversy* and
Lytton Strachey's *Eminent Victorians*, recommended by Sassoon. He
thought it incredible that Asquith had praised Strachey's book. It was
clever, of course, but iconoclastic, and showed a curious lack of vision
in the writer. Philip's letters were full of amusing gossip. 'I meant to
show you a beautiful chair I had got in Paris with a wonderful Louis
XIV inkstain on it – on a par for interest with the blood of the young
Princes on the staircase of the Tower.' 'Writing to you', Philip said, 'is
second best to *talking* to you – and I needn't finish my sentences as I
know you will always understand.'[78] Regy replied that he hoped
Philip did not show his letters to anyone else.

> My letters are intended for *you*: and it would give me small satisfaction
> to think of some Edmund Gosse of the future going into *extase* over
> them, or the reverse. But when you mention Byron I do so agree with
> you. He was the prince of letter writers, because he was so perfectly
> natural, and never laboured an idea or a word. Keats, of course, was
> wonderful, but incomparably good as his letters are, he was bothered
> by Fancy which though he thought it less than the present palpable
> reality, was to him greater than remembrance. Sound enough in poetry,
> but too high a strain upon the post bag after breakfast.[79]

He scolded Philip for being bored, a thing he never should allow
himself to become. Let him read a book right through, the Hebrew
scriptures if needs be.

On Haig's fifty-seventh birthday his chief made a charming speech
of gratitude to Philip which brought tears to the eye. On the other
hand he dropped two priceless bricks while dining at the British
Embassy in Paris. He observed of the superb Louis XVI *boiseries* of
the dining room that they reminded him of Bombay; and when asked
to admire a beautiful *garniture de cheminée*, remarked, 'What a lot of
idle people there were in those days.'[80]

Haig was devoted to his house at Kingston Hill, Eastcott, a modern villa with no pretensions to beauty or interest. Philip described his first visit to it in a letter to Regy. It was approached by a short gravel drive which somehow made the house more ignoble than if it were actually on the road.

> The hall painted in shiny lint-white enamel is stuffed with foxes roaming through artificial grasses. Bitterns under glass domes, and various trophies of the chase and sport, like crossed swords that hang like the sword of Damocles over the nape of the shrinking guest. The whole freely interlarded with Benares work. You know the rooms are papered with photos of Kings and Queens. His study has a claret coloured wall paper. I didn't know you *could* get any now: not even a rich Burgundy that would have made one think of booze, but a dull brick, like an old wine stain. One is not even spared the conservatory leading out of the drawing room (never used) in which a few plants languish of the variety that bear a scanty crop of leaves which they wish they had never produced and can never succeed in shedding.[81]

On 21 March the Germans launched a great onslaught against the British Fifth Army. Regy received a letter from someone or other at GHQ practically every day, so he did not feel entirely neglected. On the 24th Haig sent him a letter by King's Messenger, expressing great anxiety about the offensive. The Germans had pitted seventy divisions against them and won back half of the territory they had evacuated after the Battle of the Somme, 'through which', Regy wrote, 'I have so often wandered during the past year, where Nellie helped so many of the peasants to return to their poor homes.' It was sad that it was once more a battlefield.[82] Yet he never lost faith in Haig.

> His coolness and detachment of mind under all forms of provocation are admirable, but they are only what I always knew were the qualities he would display. He trained himself in early days to self control as part of a soldier's equipment. It is the discipline of the mind; and is acquired; and is not innate as many people think. . . . He always gives credit for the best that is in a man, and realising that all human character is shot-silk, he looks at the brighter rather than at the darker colours. It is the saner and safer outlook always. Others are influenced by passion and prejudice, so they are apt to take wrong turnings. D.H. rarely does, if ever.[83]

By the beginning of April the situation on the Western Front was at least static. But relief was to some extent countered by fresh troubles in Ireland caused by the extreme Nationalists who, in spite of John Redmond's moving declaration in the House of Commons in August

1914 that all quarrels between Great Britain and Ireland would be suspended until the end of the war, had persistently pressed for Home Rule and opposed enlistment in the forces. Their activities culminated in the Easter Rising of 1916 by the Sinn Fein party and the Republican Brotherhood, with the encouragement of and supply of arms by Irish-American sypathizers. The rebellion was suppressed, fifteen ringleaders were shot and over a thousand participants interned in England.

Under the threat of further insurrections throughout the hazardous months of 1917 Lloyd George felt bound to attempt an immediate settlement of the Irish demands for Home Rule on the basis of the exclusion of the six Ulster counties. No solution could be reached. Meanwhile, Sinn Fein disaffection intensified. In desperation King George summoned a convention of all parties to reach a temporary settlement. It achieved nothing and in April 1917 broke down. Regy took an extremely pessimistic view of the situation, feeling that Britain could expect no further recruitment of men from Ireland for the forces. Britain's own reservoir of manpower was practically exhausted. Yet the French Chamber and people continued to belittle British war efforts.

From Tilney Street Regy wrote to Chat on 16 April, 'The news is bad. Very dangerous position. There *are* no reserves. The outlook is gloomy. Very.'[84] And then how shockingly Clemenceau had behaved in turning down the Austrian Emperor Karl's plea for peace and handing him over to the mercies of the Germans – Karl, who was disposed to be our friend. What hypocrisy in the Allies to revile him for seeking terms! Hankey, of whom he saw much these days, dined alone with him in Tilney Street. He told him that the War Cabinet had not considered what steps to take if the worst should happen on the Western Front, which was not reassuring.

Regy was also extremely anxious about the future of the Empire. The entry of America into the war was a mixed blessing for the British in the long run, he told Haig.[85] The Canadian ministers were already looking towards America and away from Britain. He told Stamfordham that his quarrel with Asquith and Lloyd George was that they never appreciated the strength of England if properly focused. In matters of high policy the British people were being dragged at the heels of President Wilson, and the British armies were under the command of a Frenchman. If Foch failed to bring about a military miracle, where would we be? Regy had once had faith in Robertson, who had failed. His lasting faith – and that a desperate one – was in the British fighting men. The politicians were all too old, as were some of the generals and most of the diplomatists.[86] These early months of the summer of 1918 saw the nadir of British hopes in the First World

War. Regy may be excused for his pessimism, being out of things as he then was, with no official work and little to do but sit at home, miserably contemplating Britain and the Empire going to the dogs.

On 27 May the Germans' second offensive began, and within three days they had crossed the Aisne. They were advancing about three miles a week. On the 31st Philip wrote that they might reach Paris, and Haig actually asked Regy to come over to GHQ. This was a flattering request to which he knew better than to accede. 'When I left France', he wrote in his journals, 'I knew that the sun had set on those visits. If duty takes me again overseas I should welcome it, but I shall not indulge myself in following an inclination I have so often blamed in others.'[87] Old men must not deceive themselves into supposing that their physical strength and mental equipment were unimpaired.

At least Regy could relish one satisfaction. That was the abrupt dismissal in April by Lloyd George of Lord Bertie from the Paris Embassy, which he had occupied for thirteen years. The Bull had been seriously ill, and recovered, but his days were anyway numbered. The immediate reason for his dismissal was Lloyd George's anxiety to get rid of Lord Derby from the War Office. He was sent to Paris, and Milner took his place at the War Office. This shuffle presented Regy with the opportunity of supplying the new Ambassador with some schoolmasterly advice.

> Presently, when you are more settled, there are one or two people I should like you to see on the quiet. In France the most powerful forces are not on the surface of the waters. . . . I have a friend who is past master, and who will explain to you all the personalities that count. . . . Mind you put aside all prejudice, whether against politicians or personalities![88]

He strongly counselled Derby to achieve unity of command in fact, if not in name.

The friend who was a past master was of course Herman Le Roy-Lewis. This mysterious figure was to remain Military Attaché until he got into some sort of trouble with Clemenceau and tried to put the blame on others, including Regy. Derby found him useful because of his admirable relations with the French General Staff, although few members of the Embassy worked happily with him. After two months in his new office the Ambassador received another letter from the self-appointed mentor. 'I hear both in London and from Paris nothing but praise of you, and the change in the atmosphere since you took over from that poor old relic of a totally different age, is indescribable.'[89]

In July the tide of affairs on the Western Front changed. This time it was the Allies who advanced eastwards, and they were not to be deflected or driven back. The end was in sight for Germany. Little could anyone in Britain, high or humble, have believed a month ago that the wheel of fortune would be put so suddenly into reverse. Regy made few comments on the Allies' impending victory, either in letters to his friends or in his own journals. He may in the way of intelligent purveyors of Job's news, have been so taken aback by the unexpected rebuttal of his forecasts that, feeling slight shame, he took refuge in silence. To Jackie Fisher he merely wrote that the approach of victory was largely due to him. Everything seemed so far away and yet so near. 'Where should we all be today, were it not for your foresight, your bold determination. . .? My dear, you have had a glorious life, and if there is such a thing as fame you have earned it.'[90]

On the other hand there was still much to deplore. In mid-July news came through of the murder of the Tsar and his family. Regy was deeply affected. He was also shocked by the lack of effort made by the Government and the court to forestall the tragedy. To his way of thinking both institutions had shown blameworthy negligence. *The Morning Post* published a letter from him on the 25th defending the Tsar and Tsarina against the libels that had been circulating about them in the British press. He received numerous letters of congratulation from all sorts and conditions of sympathizers, including Lady Bathurst, sister-in-law of the last Ambassador to the imperial court, and Jack Durham.

Even Stamfordham, whose position as the King's Secretary usually sealed his lips when in disagreement with his royal master, wrote applauding Regy's attitude. 'Has this country ever displayed such callous indifference to a tragedy of this magnitude? And what does it all mean? I am so thankful that the King and Queen attended the memorial service.' He deplored the fact that the British authorities had done and said nothing, and that papers like *The Times* were silent. 'Why didn't the German Emperor make the release of the Czar and family a condition of the Brest Litovsk Peace?'[91] Why indeed? Regy replied that 'the answer lies in the ignorance of the masses and the moral cowardice of the few. Those who should have known better have, from fear of abuse or criticism, allowed a false picture of what happened in Russia to pass as a true one.'[92] He added caustically that their neglect to speak a word of disgust about the vile calumnies against Nicholas and Alix, followed by the atrocious murder of the one and perhaps of both, was sheer moral funk because public opinion was in favour of the Revolution. The reason why the German Emperor had not made their release a condition of the Treaty was presumably the same as that which had prevented the British Government from obtaining the Tsar's release from Milyukov, the Foreign Minister of the Russian Provisional Government, which would have been easy: again, moral cowardice. And he ended with the words, 'The King will have to listen more to the dictates of his own heart, and less to political advisers. He will have to look more to the simple rules by which his private life is governed than to the political barometer. . . . I could say a great deal more, but even now I have perhaps said too much. However, the fault is yours, as you asked for the answer.'[93]

It is clear from the correspondence of these two old friends, both servants in their different ways of the monarchy over very many years, that they did not absolve King George from all blame over this lamentable affair. To Maurice his father put the matter a little more bluntly. 'There is as much weakness there [Buckingham Palace] as at Tsarskoe Selo.' And Philip Sassoon, with his acute assessment of motives and effects, wrote to Regy, 'I thought you would notice with me the 4 weeks mourning for the Czar – a quaint sequel to the congratulatory wire to the Revolutionaries.'

Regy noted in his journal: 'The news came in great gusts of victory, and today we have broken through the Boche defences at Quéant.' On 11 November Regy was on the moor with his ghillie when he heard the bells of Callander ring out, and knew that the Armistice had been signed.

'The war is over,' he told his journal. 'But what happens next? Congresses and conferences only mean repairing damage and little men on ladders putting tiles on the roof and new drain pipes down the walls. War is a tragedy. Peace Congress the farce that follows.'[94] Regy hoped that the Allies would be lenient and compassionate with the Central Powers, reserving punishment for the Germans. To crush 80 million souls would be a disastrous invitation to a second war. Only two days after the Armistice Regy was in a pessimistic mood again '*Everybody* is anxious; no one sees daylight anywhere. After all the War provided bread and butter, or death. Peace provides only the latter by starvation.'[95] Henry Wilson wrote that the British were now, or would be before very long, 'face to face with our friend, the enemy – Bolshevism, in all its various forms'.[96]

Sassoon wrote from Paris to Regy at Callander, 'I feel that I am like the Kaiser who was heard to say to Count Bentinck as the car drove away from the station, '*Und was sagen Sie dazu?*' [What have you got to say to that?] I wonder what poor Count Bentinck can have found to reply to this.' Philip had been in attendance on Haig on the train in the forest at Compiègne where the Armistice was signed. The German delegates were treated aggressively by Foch and Weygand. They were appalled by the terms imposed, but quite helpless.

Whatever reservations Regy may have had about the King's

conduct over the Tsar, the monarchist in him always prevailed. The day after the Armistice he wrote congratulating His Majesty on the outcome of the war and the stability of his throne.[97] To Stamfordham he sent a letter of warning: 'above all to avoid is any relapse into the old "display" . . . until the people begin to settle down and until they see prosperity reviving. It is the modesty and simplicity of the King that win hearts.' He compared these attributes to the champagne and luxury at the Peace Conference.[98] Stamfordham shared his friend's concern about the prevalent anti-monarchist feeling in certain extreme circles. Every sacrifice should be made to avert it. He deprecated the recent Victory Ball, which was set up under the sham pretext of being in aid of charity, as a most unfortunate, ill-advised, inopportune business that had done a good deal of harm in socialist quarters.[99] Even Maurice wrote to his father that the Victory Ball had had the worst possible effect on Paris. The newspaper headlines called it 'Dancing on the Dead'. He added rather portentously, 'In the end Diana Manners and her like will ruin the Upper Classes in our country. I look on her as a public danger!' To divert attention from Lady Diana and other unforeseen menaces to the cause of monarchy, Regy lost no time in suggesting reforms of the Royal Household to suit the democratic spirit of the time. He advised Stamfordham to abolish certain antiquated offices, or else subordinate them to departments under the Private Secretary. The Lords and Gentlemen in Waiting should be reduced in number. Ceremonial and dress should be simplified. A commoner should be appointed as a member of the Household – a son of, say, Arthur Henderson or George Barnes.[100] Finally, the royal finances should be taken in hand. These measures ought to come from the King himself if they were to create a popular impression.[101]

Indeed there was much republican feeling in the air, and people were heard to say there was no place for a king at that time. Regy was extremely sensitive to the uncertain future. Apart from the vast numbers of soldiers facing unemployment when demobilized there were the mass of civilian war workers whose jobs were suddenly at an end and who were confronted with poverty, discontent and the false promises of Bolshevism. He saw a grand future for the King in connection with the consolidation of 'imperial' control of British public affairs. But imagination and boldness were required on the part of the monarch. The King and Queen must be prepared to face risks, he advised Stamfordham. Before the war had ended Regy was concerning himself with the repatriation of officers of the New Armies, young men who, having won commissions and responsibilities, would have to return to the humble livelihoods of their origins, or starve. He was constantly taking up the cudgels on behalf of ill-used officers and men, investigating with scrupulous concern their various grievances.

Meanwhile he was anxious to get Maurice out of the Army and home again. The day before the Armistice was signed he wrote to Haig asking for his son's release from the job of Assistant Provost Marshal in Paris, to which he had been appointed by Sir John French at the beginning of the war. He had already found an opening for him in a rubber company, and arranged that the Garton Foundation should take him back as part-time secretary. He had persuaded Hankey to link the Foundation with the War Cabinet to help with the big demobilization issue. Within a few days Haig had agreed to relinquish Maurice, and it now only remained to procure his official demobilization through Winston Churchill and Henry Wilson. By 18 November Maurice received his discharge through Churchill, although his formal demobilization did not come through until March 1919. It was extremely quick work considering how many officers and men, with their old professions and business firms crying out for their return, had to wait for months before obtaining release from the services. Maurice and Zena were able to spend Christmas happily at Pinkie.

Regy still manipulated Maurice like a marionette, but he was not always successful in getting for him what he considered his deserts. In 1915 he had tried and failed to persuade Stamfordham to take him on the Palace staff. Politely Stamfordham replied that for the present he and Wigram[102] could carry on without extra help. Regy intrigued with the War Office to get his son the Military Cross, but was told it was most unlikely for a non-combatant. Undeterred, he then fished for a CMG and was offered an OBE. On learning that his name had gone forward for a decoration Maurice, to his credit, implored his father to see that he was not awarded the DSO or MC, for 'I should feel ridiculous.'[103]

Although Maurice's war may have been extremely boring, it was at least comfortable, and he was constantly lunching and dining out with Zena in Paris. He was by no means an uncourageous man and would doubtless have been happier and more fulfilled had he gone with his friends to the front. His letters to his father during the war were full of complaints, rather off-hand and condescending. He was incessantly cadging or dropping broad hints for money. Regy was aware that his son laboured under the delusion that his birth entitled him to such support. He warned him that after the war it would be as much as anyone could do to keep his head above water. No one should be choosy about jobs. Zena must not think of what was dull or amusing. Even Winston Churchill had bought a farm in Kent to provide essentials for his family.

Anyone whom Regy accounted his friend had a claim on his advice and assistance. Maurice Hankey, though lacking charm, was a man of extraordinary ability. Regy recognized that his future must be carefully considered if the country was to get the best out of his services. In October he went to see Hankey, begging him not to become a proconsul, not to be banished to Mesopotamia or some such abominable place, but to stay put. If an extreme left-wing politician were to become Prime Minister, he, Hankey, as head of the Cabinet Secretariat, would act as a bulwark against Communism. Hankey agreed with him. So when Lloyd George asked him to go into politics he declined.

Regy was vehemently protective of Douglas Haig's reputation. No recognition of his hero's achievements was too great; no reward for them too lavish. He was overcome with admiration when Haig refused a viscountcy until the needs of the disabled soldiers had been met. In fact he thought a peerage might be construed as a diminution of his glory – certainly if accepted from Lloyd George and his minions. A grant was another matter, because it would have to come from Parliament as a gift.[104] Haig himself said to Sassoon, 'What's the use of being a peer and having to live in hotels?' On 30 November he told Regy that he had received a peremptory demand from Lloyd George to go to London the next day for some kind of triumphal progress behind the Prime Minister, Foch, Clemenceau and a crowd of foreigners, in which he was to ride in the fifth carriage with Henry Wilson to the French Embassy, where a reception, to which he had not been invited, was to take place. Regy was incensed, and urged the Field-Marshal to refuse point blank. 'Years ago', he wrote to Haig, 'you believed this war to be inevitable. Years ago you trained for it, and your faith in your destiny to lead our British Armies to victory was never shaken. That, and its achievement, are fine rewards and quite imperishable compared with more material ones that must – in the end – cumber the dust bin.'[105] As for Regy's own future, Stamfordham wrote to ask whether he was going to resume his duties as Royal Archivist in the Round Tower and custodian of Windsor Castle.

12

ACTIVITY IN RETIREMENT

1918–1930

There was clearly more meaning in Lord Stamfordham's question than Regy's old friend cared to put into words. Regy at once grasped it, for he replied,

> I am sometimes harassed by the thought that the King would be glad to be free of me, as I am not much use now, even in so 'honorary' an appointment as Lt Governor, and I cannot see myself ever again 'in uniform'. But advancing years do not make it easy to cut a connection which has obtained for so long. . . . I trust absolutely to your friendship to tell me *at the first* moment you think it would please the King if I were to resign my appointment as Lt Governor.[1]

Without much delay Stamfordham wrote again that the King had decided he should retain the lieutenant-governorship – which was more or less an honorary post, in which the holder could do little harm and from which he earned no emolument – but resign the keepership of the Archives to John Fortescue. Since Regy had created the latter post, and at the age of sixty-six was by no means senile, he was understandably a little hurt.

A matter of greater moment was once again Maurice Hankey's immediate future. On 10 February 1919 he wrote Regy a long letter from Paris announcing that, in spite of his friend's repeated admonition, he had allowed himself to be made Secretary to the Peace Conference. The appointment would of course only last for a matter of months. He had always intended to stick to the Prime Minister, whom he admired intensely, and in this temporary job they would be together.

The position I had prescribed myself was one which Berthelot[2] of the French Foreign Office told me he designed for himself. '*Je ne serai rien et tout*', he said, 'I shall appear at the conversations of Prime Ministers; I shall appear in the Conference, and I shall appear nowhere.' That is exactly the position I designed for myself. I shall be Secretary of the British Empire Delegation, which would give me the *entrée* anywhere, but I should have no official post in connection with the Conference.

He begged Regy to let him know what he thought.

You are such a faithful and valuable friend and, correspondingly, you will be able to read into it the whole position pretty accurately.[3]

Regy replied that Hankey's work during the war had been splendidly done and he had steered a difficult course with consummate skill. He was nevertheless anxious.

The handling of the internal situation (by the Government) seemed nerveless, and to require your presence. Not for long, but sufficiently long to enable you to formulate for the Prime Minister certain definite principles. Mere adroitness, of which he is a master, will not carry us through the troubles of the next few months.[4]

Under Hankey's control the British delegation at the Peace Conference became, in the words of Harold Nicolson, who was a close witness of its machinery, 'a triumph of administrative efficiency and prevision'.[5] But Hankey was getting restless. He told his friend that he had an urge to throw up the Secretaryship of the War Cabinet altogether and no longer return to the Prime Minister. It was a flagrant contradiction of what he had written on the 10th. In short, he had been offered the post of Secretary-General of the League of Nations. He believed with justifiable self-confidence that only an Englishman could make a success of that post, and that that man was himself – standing, as he put it, 'midway between the materialism of the European countries and the idealism of the United States'. He wanted Regy's approbation more than anyone else's in the world, 'for you know my abilities and defects and have an intuition that has again and again served me in good stead'.[6] 'I understand your frame of mind,' Regy replied. 'You are tired, my friend. – It was only natural. But you must get your perspective right. There is no chance of the future resembling the past. That is the first point. England, and the Empire, can never again be the England and the Empire that you knew.'[7] Were he to become Secretary-General of the League of Nations he would be a wasted force for Great Britain. The League must be an organization of very slow growth. It would be unproductive for Hankey, with his immense capabilities, to tend its growth, for there would be endless debates on procedure and discussions on policy rather than matters requiring decision. For his part, he believed that the happiness and welfare of the human race was more closely concerned with the evolution of British democracy and our imperial commonwealth than in the growth of any international league. The Empire had come of age. He was certain that, whenever executive action in the League was required, the leverage would be in the hands of the Prime Minister. Therefore his strong conviction was that Hankey's place was beside the British Prime Minister of our country for the next ten years. After all, he had fashioned the home and imperial cabinets. He should stay on in order to tie the knots tight.[8]

This somewhat lengthy correspondence shows how indefatigable Regy Esher was in giving his considered advice, usually extremely sound, to those friends whom he knew to be worthwhile. When it came to public figures like Maurice Hankey, who undoubtedly was one of the great influences behind Britain's conduct of the war, Regy's counsel was motivated by the interests of the nation before those of the individual. Today Hankey's conviction that the League of Nations should be conducted by an Englishman, and Esher's that the welfare of the world depended on the successful outcome of British democracy, may seem laughable. But that was what stalwart Victorians of the upper and professional echelons implicitly believed. And though Regy knew in his heart that, just as the aristocracy had been superseded in the nineteenth century by the middle class, so now the middle class was about to be superseded by the lower, it still did not occur to him that the new rulers would not adhere to the creed of their predecessors in upholding the pre-eminence of British values as the guiding light of the brave new world.

An example of Regy's beliefs about the changing social structure of the country was his dedication of a little book of essays called *After the War*, actually written during the war, to the President of the Scottish Miners' Federation. Robert Smillie, born of Belfast working-class parents, was a dedicated trade unionist and had been largely responsible for the coal strike of 1912 which had established the principle of a minimum wage; although two of his sons had enlisted, he had been a pacifist during the First World War. In writing to thank Regy for his dedication, he said he disagreed with all its conclusions. He was convinced that private ownership of land and capital must be abolished. Somewhat surprisingly, Regy sent Smillie's letter to the King. Lord Stamfordham replied that if the expression 'wage slaves' was the correct term for manual labourers who received payment, then it was equally applicable to all wage and salary earners, from the humblest up to His Majesty himself.[9] In reply to Smillie Regy wrote at length, dissecting his correspondent's arguments one by one in the friendliest spirit. Without dismissing them, and while even agreeing that some of his proposals should be tried, he questioned the wisdom of total social reconstruction, the infallibility of economists and the enduring benefits to the masses of nationalization and decentralization. He advised Smillie not be become a dedicated iconoclast.[10]

In *After the War* Regy's chief arguments were that the press had usurped the functions of Parliament. It alone controlled the executive of Government and made and unmade ministers. Individual statesmen were so ridiculed or lauded by the press barons that the Prime Minister looked to the press, instead of the House of Commons, for direction on whom to dismiss from and appoint to ministries. Regy also criticized the Cabinet of the day for being completely out of date, the weakest members proving the best in that a strong Prime Minister could manipulate them, which he could not otherwise do. Asquith took great exception to these arguments, and Margot was furious with the not so oblique criticisms of her Henry's lack of control over his Cabinets. 'It made my blood boil with its inaccuracies and cheap writing,' she told the editor of *The Morning Post*.[11]

The war had not left Regy's attitude to social conditions unaltered. Unlike the majority of his patrician contemporaries he had discarded many of his pre-1914 class-bound prejudices. He confided in Chat how much the plight of the workers worried him. Now that they were educated they wanted to know the economic facts – whether there was or was not a big profit margin in the firms they were working for, which could be distributed more equably between employers and employed. It was something which ought to be considered and acted on by the captains of industry.[12] He went so far as to say to Chat, 'I love the Labour Party – so babyish and sanguine. It is all very well for Winston to taunt them with inexperience. Just the same things were said when the middle-class was first admitted to high office.'[13]

King George was, if not alarmed, then a little disturbed by the progressive views of his father's staunch mentor and pillar of Edwardian correct thinking. After reading an interview in *The Weekly Despatch*, entitled 'The Old Order Changeth', in which Lord Esher had declared that, 'The days of evening clothes and solitaire diamond studs are over', the King instructed Lord Stamfordham to remonstrate with his friend. The King saw no reason why evening dress and cleanliness should be dispensed with. Surely it was a mistaken idea to curry favour with the working classes by adopting their costumes and manners.[14] It was the very thing which was to happen in the reign of his grand-daughter.

Regy's most notable public service in 1919 was acceptance of the presidency of the Army in India Committee. In June he sent Edwin Montagu, the Secretary of State for India, a memorandum on the co-ordination of the Indian Army under the Imperial General Staff. On the 18th he received a letter of thanks from the Minister, who considered the memorandum so interesting that he would publish it. Montagu, recalling Regy's great services to Army reform, then invited him to become chairman of the India Sub-Committee to investigate conditions in that country. Regy declined, because he was unwilling at his age to visit India, and for other unspecified reasons. But Montagu was so anxious to have him that he agreed to send a delegation of one civilian and three soldiers in Regy's place, to report their findings for the sub-committee to adjudicate upon.

The terms of reference of the Army in India Committee were to inquire into the administration and organization of the Indian Army, including its relations with the War Office and the India Office; to consider the position of the Commander-in-Chief in his dual capacity as head of the Army and member of the Viceroy's Executive Committee; and to report on any other matters which it might decide were relevant to the inquiry. Part 1 of the Report was published in November 1919 and the remainder in June 1920. The hearing of evidence led to a row between Esher and Curzon, an ex-Viceroy and now Foreign Secretary, who was piqued at not being among the first witnesses to be called. When Regy explained to him that the time to call witnesses had not yet arrived, Curzon protested that the time had actually passed when his evidence might have been useful. The correspondence ended in good-natured banter. Regy pointed out that he was trying to spare him unnecessary worry, 'but you are so infernally omnivorous for work that I should have known you would never show the smallest sense of gratitude'.[15]

Regy and Nellie spent the greater part of 1919 in Scotland. They now regarded the Roman Camp as their only home, and had ceased to live at Orchard Lea which for the past ten years had been an incubus. Oliver and Antoinette lived there for a brief period; then Sylvia and her Rajah rented it when they were together, which was not often. In November Regy allowed Maurice to sell those contents which had not been what he called 'looted' by Dorothy and his other children. In Scotland he once again filled the house with visitors, especially theatre people and artists. David Young-Cameron, the Glasgow painter and an admirer of Dorothy Brett's work, was a frequent guest; in August he was engaged on one of his best-known pictures, *The Menin Road*. In September an unexpected couple turned up for a night. Bunau Varilla and the famous novelist Colette had left Le Havre for a cruise on his yacht; after coasting round the south and west of England they had made straight for the Clyde. They hired a car to Callander and telephoned the Eshers from the local hotel, the Dreadnought. Regy considered it a great compliment. Colette was about to have a baby; she had a doctor on board, and had brought an adopted child of three. They thought the country perfect and the house a marvel. Then they left for Greenock and back to France. 'Curious people,' Regy observed.

Invited to go to Balmoral for an eight-day visit, Regy refused. He pleaded a 'regime' which incapacitated him and made visiting impossible. He told Oliver that 'the entourage these days is too boring. I think the Queen wanted to know all about Freda. The K knows *nothing*! But I am not inclined to be pumped, or to put my nose into what some day will prove a hornets' nest.'[16] Freda Dudley Ward was his sister Violet's daughter-in-law, with whom the Prince of Wales had begun what was to be a long affair.

Regy was resuming correspondence with Oliver and they were ostensibly on affectionate terms, although Regy was always ready to carp. 'There was a mysterious allusion in Antoinette's letter about your "seeking something to do",' he wrote on 9 September. 'My dear, do not be misled by aphorisms or conventional hypocrisies. . . . You possess many gifts that you can turn to the advantage of this driven world, always provided that you rise superior to convention.' He cautioned his elder son against acquiring an estate. A capital levy was almost certain. Besides, the profligate spending of the upper classes on frivolities and the Government on armaments in spite of the late war to end wars was paving the way for a Labour Government. His friend, Smillie, though no Bolshevik, was intent on changing society. 'Altogether we are politically slipping off the rails down a steep embankment.'

His daughter Dorothy, having struck out on a life of her own, devoted her considerable talent to painting, although she never earned the acclaim she deserved. Her love-hate attitude to her father was the cause of recurrent rows, and she made repeated demands for money. Though she prided herself on becoming extremely unconventional, she nevertheless kept well in mind her background, which compared to those of the majority of her associates had been luxurious. Regy found her attitude to him insufferable. He complained in letters to the paragon Maurice of her idiocies and sponging behaviour. Even so, he was sufficiently broad-minded to excuse them up to a point, because she was an artist. And, indifferent father though he had undoubtedly been, he encouraged her to paint. It was the squalor of her friends and her repudiation of the basic decencies of living which irritated him.

Throughout and even after the war, when she was not at Garsington or in the studios which her father bought or rented for her, Doll would lodge at No. 2 Tilney Street. Regy did not mind her doing this. In fact, because of air raids he liked to think she was at home, so to speak, where what servants were at hand could keep an eye on her. However, when she brought in young men like Gertler, who slept on the floor in their clothes and made a hideous mess of the house, so that the servants were shocked, he objected. When her parents remonstrated with her she treated them to insolent letters, accusing them of being old-fashioned, out of date and incapable of appreciating herself and her art. Yet Regy's tolerance was unexpected and often commendable. To her aggrieved and bitter reproaches he would reply:

Dearest Doll. . . . I understand your aspirations and disappointments well. . . . I love and admire you. So lead your life in your own way . . . but there are orbits in which different lives cannot move without friction, therefore let us all be free in action and thought. . . . Interchange of the latter is always pleasant to me.[17]

Her extravagance riled her parents: she threw money left and right to her impecunious artist friends, who supposed that the Hon. Dorothy Brett had an inexhaustible supply. Her demands for a larger allowance provoked her father into sending a caustic letter which she thought was unfeeling.

Dear Doll, we are not so dull as you think, and you are not the first artist we have known, although you appear to think so. There are however other things in the world besides self-absorption and self-glorification.

If society – i.e. human intercourse – is to issue from the barbaric stage, there must be give and take. Your idea of an artist is that he should take everything and give nothing.

We have always been ready to give you *sympathy* and appreciation but when have you shown that you asked for either?

By your own free choice you have looked further afield for companionship than your family. No one complains. You have perfect liberty of choice. But you cannot have it both ways. I suppose the artistic temperament does not realise so elementary a proposition.

I am glad you find a Russian Jew [Gertler] more helpful than your brothers and relatives. It used to be the fashion for young men to go to the Jews when they got into scrapes. I fully realise both the equality and similarity of the sexes these days.

When you wish to come here [Roman Camp] you are always welcome, as you know. Perhaps after the next European war, we shall see you.

Till then,
Yours ever,
E.[18]

It was very difficult to get the better of Regy. But it is easy to see from this letter that the gulf between the generations and their ways of thought were in this case quite unbridgeable. By the mid-1920s Brett was making a permanent home for herself in New Mexico to be with D.H. Lawrence and his wife Frieda. 'Of course she may marry an Indian. Her deafness would matter so much less if the language is Chock Tow,' Regy told Maurice.[19] After a final visit to the Roman Camp in November 1925 Doll did not see her father again. 'When people have drifted away for some time they become negligible factors in one's life, whoever they are. At least that is my experience. Distance lends no enchantment at all, so far as I am concerned.'[20] These were to be Regy's last words on the subject.

His relations with his younger daughter, Sylvia, were scarcely more cordial. He told Oliver that she was a hopelessly silly creature, with no sort of perspective in life. And as for the Rajah, he was a perfect loony of a husband, and a man with even less regard for the decencies of life than poor Doll. Regy extended his distaste for both the Vyner Brookes to their children. He hated their coming to Roman Camp because he did not want them to encroach on what he regarded as the exclusive preserve of Maurice's and Zena's children, with whom he was all sweetness and with whom he ganged up against their cousins. To his eighteen-year-old grand-daugher Angela Brett he wrote that Vyner and Sylvia's children were deceitful and two-faced. And he mocked Oliver and Antoinette's for being soft. 'Well, you see what comes of high-browism. Those wretched Watlington children are mummified. They have no initiative, no sense of being alive. Why on earth don't they raid the woodlands and cut down trees and snare rabbits? Any mischief would be better than kid glove boredom.'[21] Domestic disloyalty and acrimony could hardly go further. Only Maurice and Zena and their offspring retained his lasting affection. It surprised him that his other children showed him so little love. 'Thanks, my darling,' he once wrote to Maurice,

> for sticking up for me when all the rest of the family pull me to pieces. That is always the result of keeping an hotel. The landlord catches it. But you – at any rate – are a friend, a real one, and I care not a fig for what others may say. . . . No one else, as I have long ago realised, cares an ounce whether I am alive or dead, except you and Nellie.[22]

Against this passage, when years after his father's death Oliver came upon it, he scribbled in pencil, 'They had very little encouragement to feel otherwise.' It was strange that so wise a man in so many respects could not grasp the simple fact that if a father wants his offspring to love him he must love them first of all. Somehow it is difficult to believe that Regy minded more than a very little that Oliver, Doll and Syv disliked him. The truth is that from their birth he had never really cared for them.

The death this February of Howard Sturgis reminded Regy that there was at least one old friend who had always liked him a great deal. Years ago Howdie had written in his peculiarly candid manner, 'I don't pretend there is no one I am fonder of than you, but there is no one for whose company I wish more often, when absent.'[23] His affection never wavered, even when they had disagreements. And now he had gone in his sleep, holding the hand of the faithful Babe, his inseparable companion. Regy remembered with nostalgia the recurrent visits to Tan-yr-Allt at Portmadoc with him and Ainger. The late summer evenings with the long, low, orange-tinted horizon; the expeditions by bicycle, the fun and the laughter over Howdie's 'delicate improprieties', as A.C. Benson called them, his total lack of reserve and reticence, for 'he was ashamed of nothing except of being ashamed'.[24]

In February 1920 Haig entrusted to Regy his notes on the inner history of the workings of the CQG and GHQ in 1917–18. They had been compiled by General Davidson of the General Staff, and considerably altered by Haig himself with the help of his diaries. Regy alone was allowed to read them, after which he sealed them and passed them to Sir Frederick Kenyon, the Director of the British Museum. Kenyon asked him whether they were to be kept secret and for how long; Regy, directed by Haig to choose a date, said until 1940. He was also directed to edit them for publication if alive at the time – an unlikely eventuality, which was not fulfilled. When he heard of this transaction the King cavilled over the year 1940 for being too soon. At the same time Regy mentioned his own war diaries to Kenyon, who urged him to safeguard their future, perhaps by depositing them in the Museum. Indeed, this had been Regy's original intention.

By March the invaluable butler Alfred, who must have been called up at the very end of the war, was back at the Roman Camp; the Eshers were still well supplied with servants. Nevertheless Regy complained vociferously to Maurice of straitened living conditions. Food and coal were scarce. Prices were inflated. Petrol was expensive. Everyone was poorer than during the war. How men with families managed to live on their wages he couldn't imagine. He was taking a lively interest in his own farms, rearing lambs and calves in order to make ends meet. He was not, however, so poor that he could not spend money on improvements to the Camp, in both house and garden. He was delighted with the Roman wellhead brought from Orchard Lea. He loved the Camp more than ever, and repeatedly expressed the hope that Maurice cared for it as much as he did. He had granted Antoinette permission to sell the sapphires he had given her. 'Personally I think that these young women will look shabby at big parties without "flashing" jewels, but then "parties" are receding into the memories of Edwardian England. You can jazz I suppose, on tea and sandwiches between 4 and 7 o'clock.'[25]

When one considers Regy's relations with his family it may not seem strange that he marvelled over life's great mystery that 'man should love his neighbour better than himself, and thousands and thousands of little corpses strewn over Flanders and France prove it. Who can explain the apparent conflict between what is called the soul and the natural laws which enable the fittest to survive?' he questioned Lawrence Burgis.[26] Their correspondence never slackened. Nor was Lawrence's marriage, unlike Maurice's to Zena, any impediment to their intimacy. There is no reason to suppose that Lorna Burgis resented Regy's love for her husband. She was fond of him, and after the war often had the old man to stay at their house at Crathorne. Regy even volunteered to remark to Thrushy that 'only Lorna and a few other people matter to any of us'.[27]

Regy's enforced leisure enabled him to review books. The July 1920 issue of *The Quarterly Review* contained a critique by Lord Esher of G.E. Buckle's Volume II of *The Life of Disraeli*. Based largely on the reviewer's memories of the great statesman, it elicited congratulations from many friends. John Morley said that he had got within the spirit and heart of the subject, which is always the test of a good critic. Tom Jones agreed with Morley in thinking it one of the best things 'his dear friend' had written. It was an admirable piece of portraiture, showing a fine and tolerant comprehension. Buckle, too, praised his skill in distilling within a twenty-page article the essence of Dizzy, and his just appreciation of Monypenny's Volume I which had not received its due.

Regy's concentration on Disraeli impelled him to write Lawrence a long letter describing London in his day. 'You have no conception how England has changed,' he began.

The St James's Street of today bears no resemblance to St James's Street as I recollect it when I was young. Dizzy in his light grey coat and brilliant waistcoat sauntering down to the Carlton leaning on the arm of Lord Barrington, everyone in faultless clothes, Duchesses in open landaus drawn by beautiful horses with ribbons in their ears, a Jack-in-the-Green dancing in the courtyard of Nellie's old home in Arlington Street, servants in plush knee-breeches and silk stockings clinging on to magnificent coaches, milk-maids in short petticoats carrying milk-pails slung on the shoulders – all this in a London that has passed into oblivion. Of all the men who were the real thing in those days only Lord Chaplin remains.[28]

In September Regy was staying at Balmoral, his first visit since 1913. He told Oliver that it was very agreeable. They were only eight to dinner each evening; the children were all very delightful, natural and full of fun.

> Of course I had any amount of jobation about Princess Freda [Dudley Ward], but I made a really good case for *her* with both the Sovereigns, although the bitterness against all her *friends* is intense. I fear that there is little chance of putting the thing on a satisfactory basis, although I have suggested a possible remedy when the boy gets back.
>
> I like the D. of York. He has much improved. I never cared for him as a kid. The girl [Princess Mary] is really a most delightful creature. . . .
>
> We had a Ball, and the Queen, having walked miles, danced without intermission for three solid hours: 'Circassian Circles', 'Flirtation Polkas' and all sorts of weird things. Lots of people turned up from neighbouring 'chateaux'.[29]

By now Regy was widely recognized as the wise old counsellor to whom eminent people of all sorts submitted the drafts of important speeches and articles they were about to deliver and write. Field-Marshal Birdwood sent him the speech he was to make to the people of Australia and New Zealand; and Hankey his forthcoming paper on *Diplomacy by Conference*, to be read to the Institute of International Affairs. On 10 September Hankey assured him that he would not change his job as secretary to the Prime Minister for that of Hardinge at the Foreign Office, although rumours had it that he might. He had never seriously questioned Regy's advice that his place was in England. Unfortunately, the many Conference strings to which he was attached had meant his being much abroad lately. He hoped that England might pull out of continental entanglements. He had always agreed with Henry Wilson that the League of Nations' weakness was that it encouraged everyone to interfere in other people's business.[30]

It was extraordinary, too, how the King's servants habitually consulted a man who had no appointment at court. Sir Frederick Ponsonby, Treasurer and Keeper of the King's Privy Purse, had always been on the best of terms with Regy. Each had a high regard for the other. Ponsonby wrote in his memoirs that 'No mere recital of offices held does justice to this remarkable man.'[31] For his part Regy acknowledged Ponsonby's good sense, loyalty and devotion to the three sovereigns whom he had served, while not overlooking his venial weaknesses. 'Poor dear Fritz *is* inclined to a certain pomposity, as you say, of style, which is odd, considering that he draws caricatures, and can appreciate fun. His most serious fault is an uncertainty of judgement, arising from an underlying love of argument, and this is a fault very difficult to cure,' he once told Francis Knollys.[32]

As the servant responsible for the King's expenditure Fritz Ponsonby was worried about the consequences of inflation since the war, and in June 1921 he sought Regy's advice. He pointed out that, with wages more than double what they had been in 1914, and liveries, forage for horses, brooms and brushes now nearly twice the price, the Civil List ought to be increased by 100 per cent. Nevertheless the King had ordered him to cut down costs as far as possible and only ask for a 25 per cent rise from Parliament. To reduce expenditure to this level would mean doing away with all horses and carriages, and sending away some eighty men in the mews and a hundred in the Palace. The question was whether the King was justified in abolishing all pageantry. The King thought it wisest to put his position unequivocally before the House of Commons. He, Fritz, was loath to cut down on the pageantry. On the other hand, unlike Regy and Stamfordham he deprecated the King's industrial tours. He believed the people regarded His Majesty as a sort of divinity; for him to step out of a dust-laden motor-car was a mistake.[33]

Regy agreed that the King should follow the example of Queen Victoria and lay questions frankly before the Prime Minister at every stage, and act on his advice. But he strongly opposed Fritz's suggestion to reclaim the surrendered Crown Lands. If he, Regy, were Prime Minister, he would advise the King and the Commons to recommend reductions in pageantry in order to keep within the 1910 estimates, pending improvement in the national economy. He believed the 'dusty road' image of the sovereign making himself known to his subjects as the simple, well-intentioned, sympathetic father of his people – which in truth he was – to be admirable.

Regy submitted his correspondence with Ponsonby to Lawrence Burgis who showed it to Tom Jones, First Assistant Secretary to the Cabinet and a close friend of Lloyd George. Jones thoroughly approved of Regy's sentiments and praised the tenor of his letters to Ponsonby. So Regy wrote again to Fritz, pointing out to this old-fashioned courtier that times had changed. Guests, he said, going to stay at Hatfield were no longer met at the station by a carriage and pair with outriders. It was only right that the King should adapt his manner of living to that of his subjects while the country was overburdened with debt. If prosperity returned, it would be proper to ask for the people's taxes to be spent on pageantry as of old. As it was, the King was setting an example to his subjects and it would be wrong for him to ask for an increase in the Civil List.[34]

If the horses and carriages were dispensed with, Ponsonby maintained, it would be forever. Since dismissed servants had to be pensioned, double the number would have to be dismissed if a saving in wages were to be made – on the argument that pensioned servants were cheaper than employed ones. What did Regy think of the idea of the King selling some of his treasures?[35] As an outsider Regy said he thought it a rotten idea. He could understand the view of the insider who felt bound to make economies somewhere. For the monarch to start selling parts of the royal collections would be a bad precedent. He wondered whether instead the King might not surrender to Parliament some privileges which brought little financial reward – just as Queen Victoria, on his advice, had surrendered the Ranger's House at Blackheath and the Lodge at Kew, and thus became free of their upkeep.[36]

There was a lull in the correspondence until 13 July, when Fritz wrote that the Chancellor of the Exchequer had agreed to make to the House a brief statement of the King's financial situation and ask for permission to sell £100,000 worth of securities from the Duchy of Lancaster. Before going ahead he again requested his friend's opinion. On the 17th Regy wrote that he agreed with this suggestion, which was adopted.

Regy, who genuinely wished to shed his duties one by one and retire into private life, was glad to resign the presidency of the Territorial Army Association of the County of London. At a farewell meeting in Westminster Hall he received high praise from the Association for having recruited in 1914 four divisions of troops. Nevertheless in December he consented, at the request of the Prime Minister, to serve as British delegate on the Temporary Mixed Commission on Armaments which had been set up by the Council of the League of Nations, mainly for the purpose of presenting a plan for a proportionate reduction of land armaments throughout the world, and more particularly in Europe. It was to be his last public duty.

Apart from worry about the coal strike, the general discontent, the march of Bolshevism and the slow recovery from a bad attack of influenza, all indicative of incipient senility, Regy had no personal troubles. The only fly in his ointment was the carping reception of his book published in 1921, *The Tragedy of Lord Kitchener*. It nevertheless went into five impressions before the year was out. Some who had served with and known Kitchener thought it disloyal and unfair, and Lord Derby and Lloyd George condemned it as 'a thoroughly mean book written by a man whom Kitchener trusted, who owed everything to Kitchener, and who seemed to go out of his way to pick out all that was detrimental to Kitchener in the administration of the War Office and nothing that was good.'[37] Asquith called it a 'dragon in shallow water', and Philip Magnus in his biography damned it as 'malicious and disparaging'.[38] Although no hagiography, it was fair and objective. Lord Esher saw, as indeed he had been in a position to do since he was in such close touch with him, that towards the end of his life

Kitchener had lost his grip, yet still towered above all others as a leader. He did not renege on the view he had loudly expressed in 1915, when Kitchener was still alive, that unless a greater man could be found he should be made Supreme Commander of the British Armies. Kitchener's fault was an inability to convince his colleagues and the politicians of his sincerity, which contrasted pitiably with the high place he occupied in the esteem of the public. The author held a view, shared by others who had worked with Kitchener, that the press had manufactured an image of him that never really existed.[39] As it was, Kitchener had little knowledge of ministerial machinery, which he totally ignored, and was an autocrat to his fingertips. 'I hold no brief for Lord Kitchener. It matters nothing to me whether he commands the united forces of the Empire or is hanged to a lamp-post in Whitehall. I care only for the success of the British Armies.' These views were written by Lord Esher in a *National Review* article of 1915. If Regy could be so outspoken about the man who was his friend and boss in the man's lifetime, then surely he should not have been arraigned for repeating these sentiments in a monograph five years after the subject of it was dead. Professor H.J. Creedy, who read the proofs of *The Tragedy* 'with enthralled interest', was not far wrong in his conclusion that Lord Kitchener recognized only two chiefs, the King and the Prime Minister, taking absolutely no stock of his Cabinet or military colleagues.[40]

In the spring Regy paid a visit to the Oliver Bretts at Watlington Park, the country house they had bought in the Chilterns, and was much taken with it. His son had employed Philip Tilden, a fashionable country house architect, to enlarge the early Georgian red-brick house within a walled park. Even so, Regy had to level a small criticism. His son had sacrificed books to what Regy called 'aestheticism' in his library. He had read Oliver's recent book, *A Defence of Liberty*, and wrote, 'It is very good.' But when Oliver's third daughter was born in May he bluntly expressed his disappointment that the child was not a boy; 'but such things can't be controlled as yet'. Although he did not say so, the fault lay of course with Antoinette. It had come to his ears that this young woman from across the Atlantic had had the temerity to refer to him as 'a court flunkey'. However, since he had been persuaded reluctantly to be a godfather, he would have to sent *it* a cup.

With Maurice his relations now ran less smoothly. The two argued over unarguable matters. Maurice disagreed with his father's attaching too much importance to friendship. 'Why do you fuss about friends? They drift away just as quick as acquaintances if troubles come. Besides I do not try and make friends. Women friends annoy your wife and men friends try to seduce her. Acquaintances are safer.'[41] These sentiments, which irritated Regy, were bound up with Maurice's endless grumbles about lack of money. He received only a small salary from his job as assistant director at the London Museum, for which he was indebted to his father and Loulou Harcourt. Selfishly, he was unwilling to forgo a luxurious holiday in order to pay for his children's expenses. Then he hinted to his father that, failing financial assistance, he would have to let Chilston (named after the seat of their Best ancestors in Kent), the rather ugly house near Orchard Lea to which they had moved from the Roman Camp in April 1919, board his children out and go with his wife to some cheap establishment as paying guests. Regy for once did not pay heed to this threat. 'I consider your scheme wholly impracticable,' he answered sharply. 'And furthermore it infringes one of the simplest rules of life which the experience of mankind has justified. It would break up your home.'[42]

In fact Regy had transferred his worship of Maurice to his grandson, Tony, born to Maurice and Zena in 1913. He explained to Maurice that this infatuation was not a pale reflection of old loves, but a new shoot, green and flexible, the image of the ash tree in Siberian springs. According to Tony's cousin and contemporary, Lionel Brett, as a child Tony was so angelically beautiful that Lionel could not possibly be jealous of him. Regy, prey to every handsome youth who crossed his path, lavished his affection on this grandson and spoilt him accordingly. 'Your nobility of character seems to shine in the eyes of Tony when they look at his mother,' he told Maurice when the child was only two years old. And when the child was eight Regy wrote again to the proud father, 'Tony is certainly a darling boy. So caressing and his voice is perfectly sweet. He is *clever*. Make no mistake about that. He thinks, remembers, and draws deductions.'[43] Tony played up like mad to these compliments, which were not withheld from him. He 'sleeps with your letter under his pillow and carries it about all day', Maurice wrote to the flattered grandfather.[44] Regy arranged for the boy to be educated at Stowe after he had failed to pass into Eton, and himself became a benefactor of this newly founded school.

For a man reaching his seventieth birthday 1922 was a year of activity. The Temporary Mixed Commission of Armaments kept him occupied; out of disinterested motives Regy undertook to be British Delegate. He was increasingly concerned by the bad relations between England and France, as his voluminous correspondence this year with C.P. Scott, Herbert Fisher, Leo Maxse and others testifies. He hoped that through the Disarmament Commission, from which he never had great expectations, he might help to restore better feeling between the two countries of his birth, the strong alliance of which with fetters of steel he knew to be the essential foundation of future peace in western Europe. But inwardly he feared that disarmament talks would be futile, because France was determined to occupy the Ruhr at any moment. Once again the Eshers crossed the Channel.

He and Nellie had had a splendid journey, he wrote from the Hotel Westminster in Paris to Maurice on 17 February. 'Harbour Master, Station Master and heaven knows who were awaiting us at Calais. . . . No *douane*, no passports, reserved carriage, etc.' All the attentions and privileges were offered to which he was accustomed and which he accepted as his due. 'Here we are in the same old rooms. All the same servants, not one change. . . . It is queer settling down in the same chairs in which we sat for two years without stirring.' He found Paris noisy now that the traffic had come back to the streets. The shops were dear compared with London ones. The Conference met in the lovely tapestried rooms of the Luxembourg Palace. René Viviani, French representative at the League of Nations, made a most eloquent opening speech and a three-hour debate ensued. Regy felt that he kept Great Britain's end up all right.[45]

The next day he launched his scheme for the limitation of armaments and handed it to the Commission at the plenary session. As he explained to Ramsay MacDonald over two years later:

> My scheme was an attempt to take a step forward and attain assent to certain principles of disarmament, leaving the discussion of *co-efficients* to follow. I found the French very sympathetic and helpful. I saw Monsieur Poincaré [Prime Minister] and M. Millerand, both of whom had been very friendly to me personally throughout the war. They were ready to discuss details and to endeavour to find a solution. So was Marshal Foch, and Colonel Réquin was particularly helpful. The Italians were more difficult. But, as was anticipated, the 'principles' were not disputed; many of the details were not questioned; and the controversy settled down into differences over the *co-efficients*.
>
> In my opinion we could have made progress. But when Lord Cecil was co-opted on the Commission he was so keen about adopting a different procedure, i.e. a preliminary Treaty of Guarantees; he was so strictly combatant on this point, and his influence with the Commission was so great, that I readily but somewhat regretfully gave way, and withdrew my scheme until he had threshed out his. Under the circumstances and unbacked by the War Office and the Government as I was, I retired from the Commission.[46]

Sir Charles Hardinge, who was British Ambassador in Paris, called Regy's resolution a 'bombshell'. It was an unexploded one.

The discussions, the luncheons with Millerand, the interviews with Poincaré, Viviani and Foch, were to no avail. When Lord Esher's scheme was discussed the general opinion of the Commission was that it was not their duty to propose a scale of co-efficients for the limitation of land armaments. It was going beyond the scope of the Commission's activities. It was for the respective Governments to indicate to the Council of the League their military needs. The Temporary Commission would have to examine theoretical aspects which could not result in the fixing of a scale of limited co-efficients or armaments.

In a thoroughly philosophical, even bored, way Regy tamely urged that Lord Robert Cecil (as he still was until 1923) should be the leading figure on the Disarmament Commission. He did not care a jot, he told Oliver, about his own position. It was true.[47] Later on, Herbert Fisher wrote to him from the Board of Education, hoping that he would attend a special sub-committee at Geneva to consider his scheme, together with those of other Powers, 'If only you may prevent the whole project going to sleep';[48] and Viviani and the British Ambassador appealed to him personally to do the same – but he refused out of hand. He felt he could do no more. As he explained to Cecil, he had never contended that limiting armaments would end the possibility of war. But he did contend that it reduced the possibility of sudden attacks by one nation upon another. For this reason the experiment was worth trying, always assuming that the people of the world seriously wanted to minimize the chances of war.[49] 'If the Government goes out I shall chuck that commission,' he told Maurice. I only went on to it, in order to please the PM. He has always been nice to me.'[50] Four days later Lloyd George's Coalition Government fell, and Regy was as good as his word.

In Paris he learned of the death by suicide of Loulou Harcourt on 24 February. He at once wrote to Maurice that either he or Oliver must represent him at the funeral. 'Another link broken. It is no use to write about it. I am so grieved for May[51] and the children. It is terrible to be left with all those responsibilities. What an incubus are "possessions". I cannot imagine what they will do. Stranded. No one to help them. . . . It is tragic.' And he urged Maurice to think of a replacement for 'poor dear Loulou' as joint trustee with himself of the London Museum. London was soon 'convulsed over the sordid tragedy', as Philip Sassoon was quick to inform him, for Loulou had made advances to young Edward James, who had just gone to Eton. James told his mother, who told the whole of society. The result was an overdose of sleeping pills.

Harcourt, in his youth extremely ugly – Regy told Maurice in 1897 that he always gave him the creeps – was prone to this sort of behaviour, which his friend never approved of. Regy did not like what he called 'harpies' who pounced on the young simply for physical gratification; for in every love affair there must, he maintained, be sentiment and romance. As long ago as 1894 he had lectured Chat about promiscuous people. 'They are the enemies of the whole joy in those things in which you and I delight,' he wrote to him. 'They degrade sentiment and romance. I know them well and I dislike them intensely.'[52] Regy was naturally monogamous. 'We all of us do things with people whom we do not care a snap of the fingers about,' he told Maurice while he was still at Eton. 'But that is always a pity – although as a rule the temptation is impossible to resist. With people you *do* care about, you can do anything you like.'[53] He had a terror of scandal, not merely because of the disgrace but because the world came to know of things that should be kept secret to the perpetrators thereof. Regy would have been horrified had he known that mothers of Eton boys warned their sons against solitary walks with him as well as with Loulou, whose inclinations were discussed in high society. Being bracketed with Loulou was in a sense unfair to Regy, who never attempted seduction or pressed his attentions where they were clearly unwelcome. In fact to Regy sex was the corollary, and by no means the essential corollary, of love.

Loulou's attempted seduction of Doll had put that young girl off men for the better part of her life. His eager partiality to photographs of naked boys shocked the less prurient of his male friends. Still, Loulou had his qualities. His devotion to and support of his father had been outstanding. In Lord Rosebery's opinion his political ability was immense. He genuinely loved the arts and archaeology. As Minister of Works he had done much to improve the London parks and embellish the Houses of Parliament. His relations with both Eshers had always been close and cordial. When Nellie's beloved dog Grizzle died, only Loulou knew how to console her. He was an infallible friend in a crisis. Regy was not only one of his literary executors, but godfather to his son, Bill. When Maurice wrote to his father, 'What do you think May did with Loulou's collection of improper objects? Would she give it to me? There were some very nice antiques among them!' Regy considered the request ill-timed and not in the best of taste.

A second blow was the assassination of Henry Wilson in June. An implacable foe of the Sinn Feiners, this brave Irishman at last fell victim to them. On hearing the news at the Roman Camp, Regy indirectly attributed his friend's murder to the press. He told Maurice,

> It is these fellows in newspaper offices who work up boys of 24 and make them think that they are heroes if they murder a political opponent. Why not let all these brutes have it? But no one has the courage. . . . I believe Ll. G. is the only statesman on record who ever

went for the Press in his trouncing of Northcliffe. Henry was ill balanced when it came to Irish affairs as all Irishmen are, without exception. But he was a dear. And of all soldiers I ever knew the cleverest and the most human.[54]

Regy had the highest opinion of this mercurial soldier's brain. He realized that his brilliant personality, aggressive in its sharp delineations, had always been too much for his contemporaries. Besides, he had the reputation of being an intriguer, a supremely Irish characteristic.[55] Regy considered him to be a bird of totally different plumage from the normal run of generals. A white blackbird, or a black swan; cerebral, detached, and too like one of Bach's fugues to the neophyte.[56] He had the ability to view events from a detached height. Regy attributed this capacity to his peculiar upbringing.

> Henry's father, a very nice old Irishman, when he saw his little boy *desoeuvré*, used to ask him what he was doing. When the reply was 'Nothing', he used to say: 'Come up in a balloon with me.' And they would sit together and the father would take a survey of the world and what was going on everywhere, in minute detail, political, floral, animal, etc. It is this habit that has remained with Henry as his most cherished possession, and it is from a 'balloon' that he visualised the war.[57]

Although correspondence with the Prince of Wales necessarily slackened after the Prince came of age and no longer needed fatherly advice, Regy saw to it that all communication should not cease. In 1921 he presented the sculptor E.S. Jagger, whom he had helped promote to the Rome scholarship, to His Royal Highness for the purpose of making a statuette of the young Prince wearing field service dress, complete with gas-mask and steel helmet. Jagger, overcome by his subject's charm, agreed with Regy that the prince should be modelled hatless.

Regy consistently stood up for the Prince against his parents' mounting criticism. When the Prince appointed as his ADC Major Edward Dudley Metcalfe, known to his friends as 'Fruity', whom he met on his Indian tour, the court and the King were furious. Fruity was considered by the staid a feckless good-timer, and his influence damaging to the susceptible heir to the throne. His critics were, as Regy expressed it, 'jealous as cats'. When staying at Balmoral in September Regy endeavoured to defend the Prince's new choice of confidant, who had taken the place of the more ambitious and serious-minded Lord Louis Mountbatten.

A sentence in a letter to Maurice of 23 October brings the acquaintance of Gladstone and Disraeli, and the counsellor of Queen

Victoria and King Edward VII, incongruously close to modern times. 'What a curious phenomenon is this mountebank Mussolini. A rocket. But he may do no end of mischief during his short career.' The phase during which European countries had been ruled by patricians and the upper-middle classes was nearing its end. The blacksmith's son from Predappio had just marched his blackshirts on Rome. Regy was disquieted and disgusted. Even so, he managed to look ahead with his usual percipience.

Inspired by Henry Newbolt's poem 'Ionicus', a valedictory tribute to William Cory's love of heroic English history, Regy wrote and published in 1923 his long-deferred memoir of the man who had influenced his youth, his philosophy of life and love; his liberal outlook on the world's affairs and tolerant judgement of events and men's endeavours; and who more than any other had instilled into him the Greek ideal of wisdom and temperance. Regy deliberately gave his book the same title, *Ionicus*, as Newbolt's poem, which was a variant of Cory's first volume of verse, *Ionica*, published in 1858.

Nellie faithfully typed out the book sentence by sentence. While she was thus engaged the author wrote to Maurice, wondering whether anyone would notice the autobiographical touches and the curious intellectual relationship between a teacher and so young a pupil. 'Of course I was not the only one. But what an uplifting for a young mind. What will the Eton masters who read it think of it? Also I cannot imagine how it will strike an outsider.' It is a pity that Regy did not write *Ionicus* while he was a young man, still magnetized by Cory, and before he became cautious about what he committed to paper.

In September, paying yet another visit to Balmoral, he found the King in good spirits and even affectionate. He drove one day over a hundred miles with the Queen, who was an indefatigable sight-seer and collector. In reply to his letter of thanks the Queen wrote graciously that she derived as much interest from their conversations as she always had. If Regy's relations with King George had since the outbreak of the war become less personal and more formal, with Queen Mary he remained on quite intimate terms. The two corresponded regularly, exchanging presents as before: she gave him a lock of Princess Charlotte's hair in return for a little bag which had belonged to Queen Adelaide; and a little box of Queen Alexandra's for a blue glass cross made out of a fragment of window from Rheims Cathedral by a French *poilu*. Relentless in her commissions, she was constantly asking him to find things for her: 'What I really want is a decent looking coal scuttle to go in my room anywhere, & at the same time to have a shovel attached to it in order to make it easy for the servants *not* to make a mess in one's rooms. It is not an easy combination I admit.' King George thought matters of this sort tommy rot.

The Eshers preferred more and more being at the Roman Camp. Nellie opened a shop called the Pedlar's Pack in a hut outside Callander on the main road to the Trossachs; here she sold antiques and curios to tourists, and the profits helped finance an extension to the public garden in Callander. They had Glyn Philpot and his friend Vivian Forbes to stay. Glyn made alterations to the portrait of his host wearing a felt hat turned down at the brim and a wide ribbon round the crown. Everyone was pleased with it. Vivian was commissioned to paint three idyllic pictures of shepherds and nymphs.

In May 1923 Bonar Law, obliged to resign the premiership owing to ill health, was succeeded to everyone's surprise and Lord Curzon's chagrin by Stanley Baldwin. Only three months before Regy had asked his son whether he had read a speech from this back-bencher, which had impressed him. The back-bencher had given his recipe for Britain's salvation: faith, hope, love and work. 'Stanley Baldwin', he added, 'might make a Prime Minister one of these days.'[58] Little did he think how soon. In the General Election which Baldwin called in December the Conservatives were outnumbered by an Opposition consisting of 158 Liberals and 191 Labour Members. On 16 May Stamfordham wrote nervously to Regy asking for his views on the likelihood of Ramsay MacDonald calling on the King for another election. Could the monarch ask for an assurance against such a course? Regy was just as worried as the King's Secretary about the ministerial inexperience of MacDonald and his associates. He suggested that Stamfordham might tactfully hold 'educational conversations' with the Labour leader. Stamfordham thought that on the whole it would be better for him not to make any overtures of the sort until MacDonald's advent was assured. He did not wish to appear patronizing. What he agreed to be of greater importance was Regy's suggestion that first-class and capable civil servants should be drafted as private secretaries to the various government ministries, especially the Foreign Office.

On 23 January 1924 Ramsay MacDonald duly formed the first Labour Cabinet. The King was extremely friendly and helpful, patient and completely devoid of condescension. In fact, when after a difficult few months Labour was thrown out in October, the King was genuinely sorry to part with MacDonald, of whom he had become quite fond. 'Radicals and Socialists are much nicer to Sovereigns than Tories,' Regy observed.[59] The people who came badly out of this interlude were the Liberal leaders, who were torn by jealousies and dissensions.

Regy was this year involved in Sir Sidney Lee's renewed request for letters among Queen Victoria's papers relating to the education and early manhood of Edward VII, whose life in two volumes George V had given him permission to write. Lee's article in the *Dictionary of National Biography*, published soon after Edward's death, had caused disapproval in court circles and considerable indignation on the part of Queen Alexandra. The Queen Mother and the court felt that Lee had made the King out to be a benevolent nonentity. In truth Lee had not been unfair, as Regy, who at the time was critical, later conceded. His facts were on the whole correct; it was only his summary of the King's character that was not entirely flattering. So when Lee asked to be allowed to look through the old Queen's unpublished letters for the forthcoming biography, both Regy and Frederick Ponsonby demurred. What, Fritz Ponsonby asked Regy, were they to do in the curcumstances? Lee had a tortuous mind and might write a pejorative book. Regy was of the opinion that when an accredited writer asked for help it should not be refused, but that it was the right of the guardians of papers to withhold any that they thought might be damaging to the subject. When the first volume of Sir Sidney Lee's *Life of King Edward VII* was published in March 1925, Regy praised it in the *Observer*; in fact he wrote an essay rather than a review. He gave an excellent exposition of the King's character and achievements. He dwelt on his sense of duty and minimized his social activities. He stressed Queen Alexandra's elevating influence on him. He pointed out that Queen Victoria's restrictive methods of upbringing, if at times irksome, were in many instances unavoidable. A ripple of approval spread amongst Regy's friends. The King and Queen's only reservation was over the reviewer's theory that human beings in general were decadent after the age of forty. Garvin, the *Observer*'s editor, wrote that all opinions of the review were golden, and that Regy himself ought to have written the King's biography. Lord Burnham even invited him to write fifteen articles of two thousand words each for *The Daily Telegraph* on his reminiscences of the past forty years. No man, he said, was so well informed on royal and political affairs as Lord Esher. Regy declined.

Fritz Ponsonby was faced with another royal problem. He begged Regy to come to Buckingham Palace and advise whether the Empress Frederick of Germany's letters to Queen Victoria about her differences with her son, the Kaiser William, ought not to be published. They were amongst the boxes of papers which Fritz had, at the Empress's urgent deathbed request in 1901, smuggled out of Germany under the very suspicious eyes of her son. Ponsonby was in favour, since the rows had already been referred to in books, and usually from the Kaiser's standpoint. These letters showed the Empress's side, and he felt sure she would have wished her views to be made known. Fritz had already consulted her sister, Princess Louise, who had vigorously blue-pencilled the script. The Princess thought the time not yet ripe because King George and Queen Mary's relations might one day be resumed with the Kaiser, whose sensibilities would be hurt. Regy cautioned delay.

In April Maurice went to Rome and Naples on Garton Foundation business. Had he been about to trek through the Sahara on foot Regy could not have worked himself into a more tremendous fuss. He inundated his son with directions about what to look at, what notes to take, what hotels to stay in and what clothes to wear. He dreaded the parting. 'I shall not really be happy till you are back again,' he wrote. His one consolation – a major one – was that Tony would stay with him at the Roman Camp. 'Thank you for all your goodness to me,' he told Maurice later in the year. 'You at any rate always try to do what I wish, whether my wishes are wise or foolish.'[60] Against this passage Oliver was to write, when both his father and Maurice were dead, 'He was aged 41!'

As far as Regy's health was concerned 1925 was not a good year. He suffered from recurrent attacks of what he believed to be gout, but may have been incipient heart trouble. In March Lord Curzon died under an operation for prostate, and Regy wrote to Maurice,

Poor old George. He had fallen in battle all right, his battle, gallantly sustained against ill health from boyhood. His early letters to me showed that from the first he was determined not to give in, and to obtain most of his heart's desires. After all he started heavily handicapped, and he obtained many of the prizes *he* coveted.[61]

Regy considered him to have been one of the greatest of viceroys, if not the greatest. No one else had possessed his qualities as administrator. He had a brilliant imagination with the supreme gift of expression. Besides, he had far more humour than he was given credit for. In August Ramsay MacDonald and his daughter Ishbel invited themselves to stay for two nights at the Roman Camp. Regy was delighted. Ishbel was shy and consequently rather brusque, though Ramsay was at ease and very communicative. The two men found that at heart their sympathies coincided: they were both versed in the humanities.

The year ended with hard luck letters, which Regy had come to take for granted, from Maurice. He had never been more down. The oil company he had put money into had gone bankrupt, and he owed £500. The official receiver assured him he had done nothing dishonest. He was full of self-pity. His father, without a word of reproach this time, merely asked for a list of his total liabilities and promised to make any sacrifice to help him.

With 'poor dear old Stamfordham' he corresponded more than with any other friend during the last years of his life. They discussed politics and personalities from every angle. Stamfordham would stay at the Roman Camp, bringing his daughter Victoria, whose husband had been killed in the war, and her son, Michael Adeane, then a boy at Eton. In his old age Adeane remembered Regy as very genial and kind, teaching him how to cast a line and organizing expeditions for him on the river. He described him as not very tall, but spare and what he called 'sandy'. He was dapper, always wearing a buttonhole, usually a carnation, even on the hills.[62]

In January 1926 Lord Stamfordham consulted him about portraits to be taken of the King and Queen for the Royal College of Music. Lord D'Abernon, he said, had plumped for Augustus John for the King, and McEvoy for the Queen. Stamfordham felt sure the King would never sit to John. Lionel Earle had suggested Sir James Guthrie, who was not available. Whom did Esher advise? The King might listen to his advice, but would not heed his Secretary's. Lord Esher suggested Orpen. To which came the reply, 'The King, I fear, will say No. I shall be delighted to luncheon with you and meet Cameron.'[63] The King's portrait was ultimately done by Cope. The College of Music were pleased with the result. The Queen then inclined to Cope for her portrait, but Stamfordham warned Her Majesty that Cope's portraits of ladies in that year's Royal Academy were not pleasing. To which the Queen remarked that she would sooner die than sit to Laura Knight.

In May came the General Strike, Baldwin's handling of which greatly impressed Regy. He called it a triumph of character over intellect, and was full of praise for Baldwin. But, exhausted by the strain of the crisis he had surmounted, the Prime Minister relaxed into lethargy and failed to take steps to pacify the coal industry. Five months later Regy was telling Stamfordham that Baldwin was 'quite hopeless' and a woeful disappointment. He referred to him scathingly as Billie Baldwin, and a year later as a 'rustic clown'. All his speeches were written for him by Tom Jones: he might easily muddle them up and read out the wrong one. As for the Labour people, he considered that they had distinguished themselves. The strike was unpopular with the mass of the workers. 'Yet they held together, which did them credit,' he told Chat, 'and have taken their beating like true sportsmen.'[64] To Stamfordham he said that a general strike was a weapon which broke in the hands of its users. The best way of fighting another in the future was to prove its futility.[65]

During the last ten years of his life Regy's chief recreation beyond very leisurely walks over the hills in pursuit of an odd blackcock or two, was abundant reading. In Scotland there was little else that he could do, and reading new books had taken the place of attending first nights at the theatre, which in the Tilney Street days had been his favourite pastime. With Chat and Philip Sassoon he continued his Eton habit of bandying opinions on current literature. He was both attracted and repelled by Lytton Strachey, who wrote about some great people whom he had known. He disliked *Eminent Victorians* – it was journalese, not literature. Compared with young G.M. Trevelyan, for instance, it was cheap iconoclasm. When *Queen Victoria* came out he read it three times. He agreed with Chat that it was full of faults, but admitted that it gave a vivid picture. By 1929 he had come to recognize its subtle craftsmanship. He considered Thornton Wilder's *The Bridge of San Luis Rey* over-rated. Somewhat surprisingly, for his literary tastes were conventional, he recommended *No Love* by the author of *Lady into Fox*. Harold Nicolson's 'grave' style he admired. He thought Logan Pearsall Smith's *Trivia* clownish. 'I visualise the writer,' he wrote to Philip Sassoon, 'an ineffable type of "Smith" – as he pictures himself, a chimpanzee with a great splodge of scarlet on the seat of his trousers,' which is not entirely inept. 'Catullus did the same thing better.'[66] Regy was always an avid reader of poetry, and urged Chat to read Rupert Brooke and Siegfried Sassoon. When Chat became inordinately enthusiastic about the former Regy called him silly for ranking him so high. He rated Brooke a minor luminary compared to Ernest Dowson. An early advocate of Siegried's *War Poems*, he wrote to tell Edward Marsh so.

> There is a rough splendour about your friend Siegfried. It is good for the character of our people that a picture of war should be presented by a man so close up against it in the crude manner of El Greco. I am astonished that the mollycoddling Censor permitted the publication of these poems. Literary censorship seems to have been based on the assumption that the British high-strung imaginative nature required truth to be carefully whitewashed with sugar and that Britain had been subjected by the Greeks and not by Caesar. These poems are bitter aloes.[67]

Whereas Rupert Brooke's patriotism appealed to the ebullient Regy during the first half of the war, Siegfried Sassoon's terrible descriptions of the carnage struck a compassionate chord in the scarified heart of the disillusioned Regy when the war was over.

Of all contemporary writers he pronounced no man to be George Meredith's equal. He revered him for his wit and craftsmanship, rather than for what he had to tell. But it was Thomas Hardy, though belonging to the older generation, who appealed to him the most. 'What an artist and thinker!' he told Lawrence Burgis. '*The Dynasts* is one of the really great epics in our language. *Jude* and *Tess* are masterpieces.'

Of his own books the best known and probably the best written was published in 1927. *Cloud Capp'd Towers* was a straightforward memoir of some of the great country houses he had stayed in, and their owners whom he had known in his youth. Occasional ambiguities of style and too frequent introduction of French words and expressions made some of his earlier books seem laboured, as though he were trying to be too sophisticated. *Cloud Capp'd Towers* does not suffer from any straining for effect. His journals and letters on the other hand, written without premeditation, flow easily and are, apart from their interest as commentaries on his long life, succinct, often witty and always extremely perspicacious.

Douglas Haig wrote to him now and again. He accepted an earldom and £100,000 from Parliament in 1919, and two years later the gift from his grateful countrymen in the Empire of Bemersyde in the Border country, where his ancestors had come from. Becoming the 29th Laird of Bemersyde gave him more satisfaction than all his other honours. When once again War Office reforms were afoot he was amazed and indignant that he and others like him, with their vast experience of organization in the field, were not consulted.[68] Geoffrey Dawson of *The Times* was eager to learn Regy's views, bearing in mind that the problems which the reorganization purported to solve were new since his day. Maurice Hankey too wrote Regy a sixteen-page letter, marked 'private and personal', about the central organization of the Government, Cabinet machinery and so forth. He felt strongly that the service of the Cabinet and of the Committee of Imperial Defence should be under one hat. A separate secretary for each was permissible, provided he had full access to the minutes of the other and direct access to the Prime Minister.[69] Regy's views were that the Prime Minister should have an inner Cabinet consisting of ministers without a department – the Lord President, the Lord Privy Seal, the Chancellor of the Duchy of Lancaster, the Secretary of State for Foreign Affairs and the Chancellor of the Exchequer. The inner Cabinet should really govern, but should call upon the respective ministers whose departments might be concerned in the deliberations of the moment; indeed, might when necessary summon the whole Cabinet to hear and discuss, or even alter, the decisions reached by the Inner Cabinet. He also advised that the Secretary of the Cabinet should be housed right on the spot in No. 12 Downing Street.[70]

With Stamfordham his correspondence never faltered. When the King had to make a speech in July, which was to be broadcast, on the opening of the Kelvin Hall in Glasgow, Stamfordham begged Regy to add something appropriate to his draft. He sent some splendid contributions, with historical touches, though some of his jokes had to be watered down.

In December Fritz Ponsonby conveyed to Regy the King's offer of the post of Constable and Governor of Windsor Castle, which dated from Norman times. It had customarily been held by a lesser member of the royal family. Unfortunately, Regy observed, the salary of £1000 which had gone with it until the death of the Duke of Argyll in 1914 had been docked by the King. The promotion involved a different uniform with gold lace on the collar, cuffs and tail, as well as new shoulder cords and possibly a new sash. In King Edward's day this would have entailed an entirely new and expensive outfit, but Fritz advised Regy to consult the royal tailor, who merely added a few embellishments to his existing Deputy Governor's uniform.

A tiresome worry related to Daisy, Lady Warwick's forthcoming memoirs,[71] the manuscript of which she submitted to him. He found the references to her affair with King Edward fraught with embarrassments, and expressed doubts about the retention of certain passages. In her frank manner Daisy explained that all the late King's compromising letters had been returned by her to King George through Sir Sidney Greville. The egregious journalist and womanizer Frank Harris had stolen them from her, and on going to America in the first year of the war had shown them to various disreputable people. She had had to negotiate to get them back, which had cost her several hundreds of pounds. It was a disgraceful business, in which she was entirely innocent. They were, she confessed, unprintable and would of course not now be published by her. She went on:

> Of course during the ten years of my mid-life the friendship was so intimate that it is almost impossible to write of those years without mention of this particular friendship; but I am now doing about 20,000 more words to fill up the omission of the letters from the MS. As I told you your opinion is paramount with me.[72]

Regy groaned aloud, but felt it his bounden duty to the Crown to do his best by insisting on judicious excisions.

Of more importance to posterity was what Regy still did unofficially. Stamfordham wrote to him early in 1928 in some anxiety about the condition of the huge collection of Stuart letters and papers which had come to the royal collection in George IV's reign; he wanted to know how important they were and what should be done with them. Regy paid a visit to Windsor Castle.

> I looked at all the Archives. Here is the whole story. It would be sacrilege to leave the Stuart papers, etc. in an unoccupied, unfireproof,

damp house. These are and will be some of the most valuable MSS in England. . . . If the King wishes to keep a collection of MSS obsolete except for scholars, at Windsor, then space will in a few years be required. This can only be provided by taking back Fortescue's old rooms and adding them to the library. An assistant will be wanted to hand out and recover from readers these MSS, as it would be difficult to forbid their use to accredited persons.[73]

Fortescue's long term as King's Librarian had ended two years previously. The King decided to retain the Stuart papers; and it is largely owing to Regy's recommendation that they are today sorted, kept in box folders, minutely catalogued and faultlessly preserved in dry rooms in the Round Tower. Accredited persons are, by permission of the Queen, granted access to them.

Then there were Regy's own papers to be sorted at the Roman Camp. In July he told Maurice that he was absorbed in old letters, seeking some record of matters which might fit into a book. Whatever book he had in mind did not come to anything. Nevertheless he wrote, 'What I find is an absorption is your early life, to the exclusion of most worldly things. It is curious how after all these years I live again through those romantic days. I wonder whether it was *temps perdu*. It would be crushing to believe it was.'[74] It *was* curious that after all those years he returned to Maurice's love as having been the predominant one of his life. In spite of his passion for Tony, and his enduring ·but platonic affair with Thrushy, in spite of Zena having totally won Maurice's love away from him, in spite of this very ordinary boy having turned into a very ordinary man, and in spite of the scales having to some extent fallen from his eyes, still his younger son remained the best beloved in retrospect. 'I live again through those romantic days,' he had written when he used to visit Maurice at Eton in the late nineties and re-enact his own adolescence on the playing fields and river banks. It need not be supposed that he remained 'in love' with Maurice. It was through memories of Maurice as he used to be that he fell in love again vicariously with Chat, Beak, Elliot, Charlie Fraser-Tytler and the other golden boys in Tute's Trap and at Halsdon during the 1860s, days so distant that through his dimmed vision they recalled an unbroken Elysium of boyhood innocence.

Regy did not go to Balmoral this September. He told Queen Mary that he was sad to decline her gracious invitation, but the previous year he had had one of his tiresome attacks of gout there, to which he was now subject. They struck at intervals and he feared a recurrence out of sheer nerves.[75] Stamfordham wrote to him that month for advice on the award of the Order of Merit. He was suprised that Regy suggested Archbishop Randall Davidson of Canterbury, and pointed

out that in the arts he had overlooked Lutyens. Regy replied that he
had pressed for the Archbishop because he had contributed more to
Christian philosophy than had the late John Morley, OM, to pagan
philosophy. Besides, his sermons were great, looked at as literature.
'You can define Science, but not Literature or Art. Would Cicero have
qualified? Or Demosthenes? Or Tillotson? Or Cranmer? Bridges is
venerable. If you wait for genius you make few appointments.'[76] He
agreed with his friend about Lutyens, and felt sure that in due course
he and Winston Churchill would be recognized as possessing genius.[77]

Stamfordham was extremely worried and sad about King George's
illness in November. On the 21st the King was taken so ill with lung
trouble that he was unable to enter the day's events in his diary, and
had to ask Queen Mary to do it for him. On 12 December he became
unconscious, but rallied after an operation. On the 14th Stamfordham
wrote to Regy: 'Like you I have been regarding today as one of the big
fences to be safely negotiated, though from the start I have believed
that our dear King will be landed a winner. . . . It is a great struggle.
He has fought bravely.' In his stress the faithful Secretary was
confusing the language of the turf with that of the fishing reel.

In February 1929 the King was sent to Bognor ('Bugger Bognor!',
as His Majesty once exploded to the strait-laced Stamfordham), a
dismal seaside resort in Sussex which accordingly earned the suffix
'Regis'. There he lay in a semi-comatose condition, making slow
progress. Regy told Chat that it was odd that the country seemed to
get along quite well without a sovereign and a primate, for the
Archbishop of Canterbury too was failing. He wondered what Mussolini thought of it all. He had seen the Prince of Wales, who had
journeyed to the north visiting depressed areas, and had been much
moved by the workers' plight. 'Nellie and I lunched with him the
other day. Just a little round table wheeled up to the fire in his
sitting-room [at St James's Palace]. Who would credit such a proceed-
ing, by the light of the P. Consort? This boy is a Stuart, and not a
Brunswicker!'[78] Regy never failed to be surprised, even after his long
acquaintance with royalty, that they could sometimes behave like
ordinary mortals.

Both Eshers were concerned by Chat's proposal to have a female
friend to live and keep him company in his house at Comrie. Regy
considered it a mistake, and bound to lead to friction.

I, of course, could never do what you contemplate. A ménage
presupposes according to my notions habit built up from youth. I
should never tolerate inevitable *tricks* unless I had grown up with them!
You know how easily small things get on one's nerves. For me, solitude
every time, varied by the companionship and friendship and love of

young things. Middle age is vexatious. Rather horrible! 'Freedom and
youth', believe me. And then, young things. 'The very reason I love
them, is because they die.'[79]

Regy always assumed that others thought along the same lines that he
did. But Chat in his old age was much more easy-going than his
friend. Moreover he had no family, and no longer a lover. He was
lonely, and felt isolated. Besides, what young thing was going to bury
himself with an old man of seventy-six in the depths of Perthshire?
Chat no longer wanted to get emotionally involved with a young thing
whose affection would die immediately, if it were to be born at all.
That the lady companion was established seems unlikely. In any case
Regy continued to cheer Chat with news of the royal patient. The
King's body was mending slowly, but his mind lagged behind. '*She* is
happy in fulfilling *his* functions. He prefers her services to those of the
young Prince – Natural.'[80]

After her faithful ministrations Queen Mary found it a boon to be
back on her own home ground of pictures, furniture, treasures and
bibelots. Fritz Ponsonby wrote Regy an amusing letter about the
drastic changes being carried out in the apartments, 'in the Castle
which you govern. A sort of wave of Bolshevism has swept over the
Queen. Nothing is sacred; even Gordon's Bible has lost its stand and is
now in its casket where no one notices it.' Visitors would get lost since
it used to guide them to their bedrooms. 'The dominating principle
[is] that busts of the royal family however bad should take the place of
busts of the rest of the human race however good.'[81]

In March both Eshers suffered a long bout of influenza, and Regy
was wretchedly ill. When he was better he drove down to Stowe to see
Tony. England was at its marvellous best. The avenues in Stowe park
were budding in pale green. Boys in flannels were playing cricket on
the new-mown lawns. Boys in small yachts were racing each other on
the lake. Tony was radiant. Mr Roxburgh, the headmaster, was
effusive in his thanks for the gift of a royal stall to the chapel from
Queen Mary, through Regy's persuasions. He sought his advice on the
wording of the inscriptions to be carved on the panels of the various
donors. It was gratifying to have one's advice still wanted.

Whether it was wanted or not, Regy still gave it. Ramsay MacDonald's return as Prime Minister of the second Labour Government in
May presented Regy with a glorious occasion to be helpful to this
semi-experienced statesman whom he had got to know well. In July he
wrote him a friendly letter of remonstrance. Rumour had reached his
ears that the Prime Minister was excluding his secretary from Cabinet
meetings; this would never do. 'The evolution of our Cabinet system
from "Cabal" has been slow but sure. . . . In all Cabinet discussions

there have been moments when an absolute secret session, free from even an onlooker, might seem tempting, but secrecy and Lincoln's aphorism on government are uncongenial bedfellows.'[82] He warned him to expect another missive shortly about the House of Lords. MacDonald, a good-natured man, replied in a bantering vein: 'A rose has fallen from your chaplet. Not only do you confess to being a reader of *The Morning Post* but you take as gospel whatever you see in its romantic columns. The Secretary of the Cabinet has never been asked to leave it, either habitually or occasionally.'[83]

On 24 September Regy and Nellie celebrated their golden wedding quietly at the Roman Camp. Only a small party was assembled there, and even Maurice was not present, though he remembered the occasion. 'Your telegram reduced us to tears,' Regy wrote the next day. 'Phyll [Phyllis Dare] choked. You are rather wonderful. The only other touching thing was Nellie's gift to me of that pretty dessert service from the Park with a scrap written, "Roses, roses all the way." *We* are a nice family. . . .' By which, presumably, he meant himself, Nellie and the Maurice Bretts, for no mention was made of the Oliver Bretts, Doll or the Brookes. He went on, 'I wished for you and thought of vanished years. This place is dear to me for your sake, and I should love to feel that Tony would gather up the threads for you. Of this we cannot be sure.'[84]

It was still Tony on whom all his hopes were focused since they had been transferred from Maurice. Regy wanted him to resemble Maurice, or rather to inherit those virtues with which he had made himself believe Maurice was divinely endowed. Thus he allowed his intensely romantic disposition once more to cloud his vision. Regy's judgement was curiously faulty over matters in which his heart was concerned. Among his last papers he left a character sketch of Tony. The qualities which he found to praise were a gracious disposition, a diffidence, a fear of ridicule (perhaps exaggerated), attention to the slightest wants of others and a readiness to subordinate his wishes to those of others. Indeed, throughout his life Tony's good nature made him desperately anxious to please all with whom he came in contact. On the other hand there was the grandson and ultimate heir to his honours, Lionel, a successful scholar, then at Eton where he was showing that independence of mind which distinguished his father Oliver. Yet Regy, despite his adoration of his old school, never once visited Lionel when he was at Eton.[85] He fairly lavished his attentions on the golden boy, Tony. He gave him money, paid for anything he wanted, and appointed himself his chief mentor. He even began addressing to him rapturous poems about youth and beauty. Until he was sixteen Tony answered Regy's recurrent need for someone, preferably adolescent, to worship, indulge and direct. But fortunately for him the grandson was to be abruptly spared the tragedy that befell his father. Fate ordained that henceforth he had to stand on his own feet.

Regy's last public act was in November to get the Palladian bridge at Stowe scheduled as an ancient monument. On the 11th Fritz Ponsonby told him he had received the agreement of GOC London District that the Guard at Windsor Castle should turn out whenever the Constable and Governor were to pass by in uniform. Such an occasion would have delighted Regy, but he did not live to enjoy it.

On the morning of 23 January 1930, Regy returned from staying with Maurice and Zena at Chilston. He brought Tony Brett with him to No. 2 Tilney Street. While Tony was out for a walk Regy was talking and laughing happily with Nellie. He was to give luncheon to Thrushy at Brooks's Club, where he had got him elected a member, and went to his dressing room which was on the ground floor. Without any apparent warning he dropped like a stone on to the floor behind the door. When Nellie found him she could not believe that he was dead. She at once telephoned to Sylvia who happened to be in London. She asked her to go into the room and find out if he were merely unconscious. Sylvia records:

> I had never seen anyone dead before. I touched his hands, and they were still soft and warm. He looked young, the lines gone from his face, and peaceful. I remember thinking to myself, 'You will never be able to hurt me any more.' I had no feeling of loss or sorrow because I had never really loved him. I remembered him saying once, 'As one grows older nobody cares whether one is on the earth or under it.'[86]

Far different were the sentiments of the hermit of Tomperran in Perthshire. The very day that Regy died Chat wrote: 'My dearest Maurice, my love for your father was inexpressible. You know that, but though you know part, it is only a very small part of what he was to me, and what he did for me all through my life. I won't say more. It is not the moment, but you will understand. . . . God rest his dear Soul.' Nineteen years earlier he had told Regy he would not like Maurice to read all his letters to Regy, and would prefer them to be destroyed. Regy replied that he would prefer his to Chat to be put under lock and key in the British Museum, not to be opened for a century. But this did not happen.

King George and Queen Mary sent a telegram from Sandringham informing Nellie that they were shocked to hear of the death of their old friend, whom they would much miss; and the Prince of Wales sent a cable from Cape Town referring to 'our great loss'. He followed it up with a letter by the first mail. He explained to Nellie what he had meant by 'our great loss' when he learned the bad news. 'I mean that I have lost a very good and kind friend which Lord Esher has been to me for many years now & particularly since the War.'[87]

Regy's ashes were desposited, not in the chapel overlooking Loch Lubnaig which he had built for that purpose, or in the rose garden at the Roman Camp, but within the canopied monument constructed for the remains of the 1st Viscount in the graveyard of Esher parish church.

Though all his Scottish property was left to Maurice, his sole executor, Nellie had a life interest in the Roman Camp and grounds, as well as the contents of the house, apart from his private papers which went to Maurice absolutely. Oliver inherited all the old family papers and objects that he had not already been given, in addition to monies settled on him in his father's last will of 1923.

In her widowhood Nellie did not spend much time at the Roman Camp; and as for Maurice, he never once went near it after his father's death. Most of Nellie's remaining years were passed in Tilney Street, where Maurice and Zena's children stayed with her over long periods.

Her relations with her own children were little better than her husband's. With the exception of Maurice she did not care deeply for any of them; and even of him she occasionally showed jealousy, making a sarcastic remark which she instantly regretted – not so much on her son's account as on her husband's. 'I know you think Nellie "tart" sometimes,' Regy wrote to Maurice, 'but it is a safer nature than that of a woman who – like the Ranee – is always sugar to your face, and disloyal behind your back.'[88] Her niece Enid Adair remembered her snubbing her children, which she later attributed to acute shyness. When Enid grew older she realized that Nellie had intelligence and a pronounced sense of humour.

There were no limits to which Nellie would not go to please Regy, or to promote his interests and self-esteem. When Lawrence Burgis first knew her in 1911 she wore a grey wig, although she did not have a grey hair on her head; she thought it brought them closer together in appearance. That she accompanied her husband only on rare social occasions was her own choice. She became immensely fat, and in consequence would not dine out because evening dress did not suit her. Lawrence, whom she held in great affection – in her widowhood she largely depended on him and his wife – would often take her out to luncheon, but never to dinner. She loved the cinema and would go with Lorna Burgis from one movie to another. She frequently stayed with the Burgises in their house at Warlingham. Frances, wife of the Ambassador Sir Eric Phipps, saw her in those days as very sweet and gentle, with kind brown eyes like a faithful dog's.[89]

In January 1932 Maurice began editing his father's journals and letters. Most of the papers were in his hands, for Regy had not only preserved all the letters he had received but had taken copies of nearly all the important ones written by him. But there were letters to such people as George Binning, Teddy Seymour and Ernlé Johnson of which he had not kept copies. Maurice wrote to these and other particular friends (or their heirs) with whom his father was not linked by politics, but none of them was able, or willing, to lend his letters.[90]

Maurice lived to complete the first two volumes of his father's *Journals and Letters*, but not to see their publication in book form, for he died suddenly in August 1934. He did, however, see the extracts serialized in *The Times*, beginning on 12 June. That autumn Nellie wrote to the publishers, Ivor Nicholson & Watson: 'Colonel Brett left no directions in his will as to a literary executor. Would you like me to read the remaining proofs? I did all my husband's literary work for him, and was his typist all through his married life, including the War, when I also was in France.' The proofs were sent to her as they came from the printers, and the two volumes appeared in the bookshops in September and November. It fell to Oliver to edit and see through the press Volumes 3 and 4 in 1938.

In 1940 Nellie died of cancer, and her ashes went to join those of Regy and Maurice in the Gothic Renaissance memorial at Esher. As Sylvia was to write: 'In my mother's heart there was no one greater than Reginald Baliol Brett. What Reggie said, where Reggie went, how Reggie felt, were of the utmost importance to her; the very air she breathed was enchanted by Reggie's rose-tipped cigarettes.'[91] Nellie's own feelings, her ambitions for him, she had put into a sonnet to be found in *Dreamland*, a slim volume of her poems. In 'A Second Fiddle' she addressed Regy, not in a subservient capacity but rather in one of resignation coupled with humility about her own discarded aspirations; and, more touchingly, with pride in her ability to support his duties and services to Crown and state.

> A high ambition; dream of what should be,
> A crystal soul that shines as bright today,
> A mind still full of wit, now sad, now gay,
> A heart unhardened to the world and thee,
> I drew around me this the panoply,
> While the great public at your proud feet lay;
> Thinking the while of that enchanting day
> When I should blossom to the world and thee.
> A futile dream! So now, for art's dear sake,
> With patient smile I do not strive to lead;
> But, while relinquishing the greater mead,
> I lay this soothing fancy to my soul:
> I make the harmonies! 'tis I who make
> The musical perfection of the whole!

Nellie's lines do not contribute to an assessment of her husband as a public figure. The opinions of his near contemporaries and the younger generation were freely expressed in memoirs and reviews of his *Journals and Letters*. His friend J.A. Spender saw him as an exceptionally skilful man, 'in a manner which sometimes made one think of an Italian of the Italian Renaissance'. This skill was much in evidence in his relations with King Edward, in the full enjoyment of whose confidence 'I never once heard it alleged that he made mischief or poisoned the King's mind against any individual.'[92] Harold Nicolson saw him as 'half a soldier, half a politician, half a diplomatist, half a man of letters, half a man of taste', whose influence was greater than his achievements. 'For it was Esher more than any other man who created the influence of King Edward's court.'[93] Nicolson thought him more than a bland, affable ambassador behind the throne. Remarkable for his good sense and the excellent advice he tendered to both King Edward and King George during the several crises of their reigns, he enjoyed the confidence of the leaders of different parties – Balfour and Curzon, Asquith and Ramsay MacDonald. 'No man has ever had his finger in so many pies. Nor would it be fair to suggest that he was a busy-body, an intriguer, or an adventurist. He was the most perfect of all lubricants. . . .' Nicolson detected in him a touch of inhumanity and something pronouncedly un-English. Lord Esher's lucid and correct vision, he felt, was strangely Latin.[94]

A.C. Benson, who worked very closely with him in editing Queen Victoria's letters, had a shrewd insight into what he called 'the unexplained secret of Esher's enigmatic personality'. He wrote:

> Perhaps he was subconsciously or even consciously aware that his subtle and adroit brain, critical rather than creative, feminine rather than masculine in type, was unfitted for the decisiveness demanded of proconsuls, and that his continued refusals of the highest administrative posts showed a justifiable distrust of himself in such capacities. . . . Certainly it afforded him undoubted ability for wider opportunities of exercising itself in central and imperial businesses. . . . The psychology of the author of these *Journals and Letters* is at least as interesting as the events which they record.[95]

NOTES AND REFERENCES

ABBREVIATIONS

C.W.   Charles (Chat) Williamson
E.   2nd Viscount Esher, after he inherited the title, 1899–1930
E.J.   Ernlé Johnson
J.L.-M.   James Lees-Milne
L.B.   Lawrence Burgis
M.B.   Maurice Brett
M.S.   Millicent, Duchess of Sutherland
O.B.   Oliver Brett (later 3rd Viscount Esher)
R.A.   Windsor Castle Royal Archives
R.B.   Reginald Brett (later 2nd Viscount Esher) before he inherited the title, 1852–1899
W.B.B.   William Baliol Brett (later 1st Viscount Esher)
W.C.   William Cory (formerly Johnson) after 1872
W.J.   William Johnson (later Cory)

Volumes I and II of *Journals and Letters of Reginald Esher*, edited by the Hon. Maurice Brett, were published in 1934. Volumes III and IV, edited by Oliver Viscount Esher, followed in 1938. They comprise selections from Reginald Esher's extensive papers (over 400 bound volumes), now the property of Lionel Viscount Esher and on loan to Churchill College, Cambridge. The published *Journals and Letters* were not only reduced (they had to be), but often bowdlerized and sometimes altered by the editors. The present author's quotations are taken from the original manuscripts and typescripts.

In addition to these sources, and others referred to in the Notes, the author has had access to: the Windsor Castle Royal Archives (Esher Papers, vols. W33, W38, W39, W40, and W41); the National Library of Scotland (Rosebery Papers, 10006-7, Elibank Papers, 8804, and Haldane Papers, 5906, 5908-5914); the Liverpool University Library (Brett Papers, 162807);

the Bodleian Library (Geoffrey Dawson Diaries, Lewis Harcourt unpublished diaries, Lewis Harcourt Papers, dep. 424); the British Museum Library (divers Brett papers); Magdalene College, Cambridge (A.C. Benson unpublished journals); Trustees of the Chatsworth Settlement (letters and memoranda of Lord Esher to the Marquess of Hartington, later 8th Duke of Devonshire); Hon. Christopher Brett (Eugénie Viscountess Esher's letters to Reginald Brett, 1860–92, 1st Viscount Esher's letters to his wife 1850–80, and Orchard Lea Archives, 1913); the Countess of Sutherland (Millicent Sutherland's Treasure Book and letters from Millicent Duchess of Sutherland to Reginald Esher, 1891–1912); and Sybil Marchioness of Cholmondeley (letters from Reginald Esher to Sir Philip Sassoon, 3rd Bt, 1916–18). Lastly, Peter Fraser's *Lord Esher* (1973) has proved an invaluable record of Reginald Esher's army reform work and political involvements.

1 CHILDHOOD AND CHEAM 1852–1865 (pages 1–6)

1   E. to L.B. 25 May 1917.
2   Enid, Lady Adair, in conversation with J.L.-M., 1983.
3   His friends addressed him as Regie, Reggy, Reggie, Reg or Redge, but since his parents used the form Regy this spelling has been adopted throughout.
4   Eugénie Brett to W.B.B., 1850.
5   R.B. to O.B., 5 October 1898.

2 ETON AND CAMBRIDGE 1865–1874 (pages 7-27)

1   'O.E.' (anon.), *Eton under Hornby*, 1910.
2   Hubert Paul, *Stray Leaves*, 1906.
3   Was it ever circulated?
4   W.C. to R.B., 1 November 1888.
5   E. to M.B., 7 September 1903.
6   For much of the ensuing argument I am indebted to Hans Licht's *Sexual Life in Ancient Greece*, 1932.
7   W.J., journal, August 1868.
8   W.J. to R.B., 18 August 1868.
9   R.B., journal, 28 October 1868.
10   W.J. to R.B., 25 December 1869.
11   Fanny Rice, third wife of the 10th Earl of Winchilsea.
12   Murray, afterwards 12th Earl of Winchilsea, 1851–98; Henry, her second son, afterwards 13th Earl of Winchilsea, 1852–1927.
13   Julian Sturgis to R.B., 20 June 1869.
14   W.J. to R.B., 7 August 1869.
15   R.B., journal, April 1870.
16   G.N. Dawnay to R.B., 21 April 1870.
17   W.B.B. to R.B., 7 April 1870.
18   E. to L.B., 14 July 1920.

19 R.B., journal, 4 September 1870.
20 Of which Arthur Benson was to remark: 'It takes one in for five minutes, and then one sees what rank sciolism it is.' Journal, 28 August 1905.
21 R.B., journal, 14 June 1871.
22 R.B., journal, 3 April 1871.
23 R.B. journal, 18 April 1871.
24 R.B., journal, 1 July 1871.
25 W.B.B. to his wife, July 1871.
26 Afterwards 4th Earl Grey, 1851–1917.
27 Albert Grey to R.B., 24 April 1872.
28 R.B., journal, 4 August 1872.
29 Alfred Lyttelton to R.B., 2 August 1872.
30 W.J. to R.B., 22 August 1872.
31 R.B., journal, 9 August 1872.
32 R.B., journal, 2 June 1872.
33 R.B., journal, May 1873.

3 YOUTH IN DISARRAY 1874–1877 (pages 28-43)

1 3rd Earl of Malmesbury, 1807–89. His grandfather, the 1st Earl, had been sent as special envoy to negotiate the Prince Regent's marriage in 1794.
2 R.B., journal, 9 August 1874.
3 R.B., journal, August 1874.
4 R.B., journal, August 1874.
5 Elizabeth Farren, 1759–1829, actress, married the 12th Earl of Derby.
6 R.B., journal, 4 February 1875.
7 R.B., journal, 12 February 1875.
8 W.C. to R.B., 13 February 1875.
9 R.B., journal, 6 March 1875.
10 R.B., journal, 1 May 1875.
11 R.B., journal, 12 August 1875.
12 R.B., journal, 12 August 1875.
13 R.B., journal, 20 September 1875.
14 R.B., journal, 20 November 1875.
15 R.B., journal, 20 October 1875.
16 A familiar name sometimes used by Howard Sturgis.
17 Howard Sturgis to R.B., 8 November 1878.
18 R.B., journal, 6 July 1876.
19 E.J. to R.B., 1 October 1876.
20 R.B., journal, 24 September 1876.
21 R.B., journal, 6 October 1876.
22 Howard Sturgis to R.B., 10 January 1877.
23 R.B. to O.B., 18 June 1899.
24 George Binning to R.B., 17 December 1878.
25 E. to M.B., 7 September 1903.

26   Julian Sturgis's novel, *An Accomplished Gentleman*, published in 1879.
27   R.B., journal, 1 June 1877.
28   John Oswald of Dunnikier, Fifeshire, 1856–1917. He entered the diplomatic service and remained a close friend until his death. Howard Sturgis was greatly attached to him.
29   R.B. to George Curzon, 14 February 1878.
30   *Superior Person*, 1969.
31   Ian Anstruther, *Oscar Browning*, 1983.
32   W.C. to R.B., 3 September 1877.
33   R.B., journal, 14 December 1877.
34   So christened because no bad monarch or pope had born the name. He got into financial difficulties and married a mulatto, which pleased his protector, Howard Sturgis. After doing well as a gunner in the First World War he was last heard of in Canada in 1927.
35   R.B. to C.W., 23 July 1893.
36   W.B.B. to R.B., 10 September 1877.
37   W.B.B. to Sir William Harcourt, 29 December 1877.

4 POLITICS AND MARRIAGE 1878–1885 (pages 44-69)

1   Alfred Lyttelton to R.B., 17 January 1878.
2   Sir Henry Ponsonby to Bernard Holland, quoted in B.H's *Life of the 8th Duke of Devonshire*, 1911.
3   Sir Charles Dilke, diary, 3 March 1878.
4   A daughter of the 10th Earl of Wemyss. She married St John Brodrick, afterwards 1st Earl of Midleton.
5   W.C. to R.B., 25 September 1878.
6   R.B., journal, 13 August 1878.
7   R.B., journal, 13 August 1878.
8   George Binning to R.B., 13 May 1879.
9   E.J. to R.B., 27 August 1879.
10   R.B. to Eleanor Van de Weyer, dated 30 July 1879 (copied 16 November 1935).
11   All her subsequent life she had a *prix fixe* with Worth for frocks. She ordered one, and it came unseen.
12   R.B. to Lord Hartington, 26 September 1879.
13   R.B., journal, 18 October 1879.
14   R.B., journal, 27 October 1879.
15   E.J. to R.B., 2 November 1879.
16   Léon Michel Gambetta, 1838–82, one of the proclaimers of the French republic on the fall of the Emperor Napoleon III in September 1870.
17   Lord Hartington to R.B., 4 December 1879.
18   Thomas George Baring, 1st Earl of Northbrook, 1826–1904, Governor-General of India 1872–6. Friend and patron of Edward Lear.
19   R.B. to Herbert Gladstone, 23 July 1880.
20   Became 5th Marquess of Northampton, 1897.
21   Peter Fraser, *Lord Esher*, 1973.

22 R.B. to Lord Hartington, 12 August 1880.
23 *Times* report, 26 March 1881.
24 E. to Sir Philip Sassoon, 23 June 1918.
25 Written by R.B. in the bound volume of Gordon's letters.
26 R.B., journal, September 1885.
27 Gordon to R.B., 13 January 1881.
28 Gordon to R.B., 16 January 1881.
29 John Harraton so closely resembled Regy in looks that the late Lord Durham believed he might have been his son.
30 Lord Durham to R.B., 1887, undated.
31 Sir Charles Dilke, diary, BM, 7 August 1882.
32 R.B. to 1st Marquess of Ripon, 2 November 1882 (BM 43544).
33 R.B. to Lord Hartington, 2 December 1882.
34 R.B., journal, 25 June 1883.
35 The African International Association was the status imposed by King Leopold II of the Belgians on the Congo, the forerunner of the Congo Free State.
36 It is unlikely that the trip came off.
37 Peter Fraser, *Lord Esher*, 1973, pp.47–9.
38 R.B. to Herbert Gladstone, 28 June 1884 (BM 45511).
39 R.B. to W.T. Stead, 10 June 1884.
40 R.B. to Lord Hartington, 12 December 1884 (Chatsworth Papers).
41 Wolseley to R.B., 20 December 1884.
42 L. Harcourt, journal, 19 February 1885.
43 R.B. to Wolseley, 26 February 1885.
44 Wolseley to R.B., 1 March 1885.
45 John Morley to R.B., 8 January 1885.
46 R.B., journal, 16 April 1885.
47 R.B., journal, 3 June 1885.
48 Dated 20 August 1885.
49 R.B. to W.T. Stead, 15 July 1885.
50 *Pall Mall Gazette*, 15 May 1885.

5 ORCHARD LEA 1886–1894 (pages 70-95)

1   King George V, diary, 31 March 1907.
2   C.H. Dudley Ward, *Quarterly Review*, obituary, 1930.
3   R.B., journal, 16 January 1886.
4   R.B., memorandum, 24 February 1886.
5   J. Chamberlain to R.B., 26 December 1886.
6   Regy feared that Britain might be dragged into European complications with which she had no concern.
7   R.B. to W.E. Gladstone, 25 December 1886.
8   R.B. to W.E. Gladstone, 25 December 1886.
9   W.E. Gladstone to R.B., 28 December 1886.
10 Lord Randolph Churchill to R.B., 2 January 1887.
11 G.E. Buckle to R.B., 6 January 1887.

12   R.B. to G.E. Buckle, 7 January 1887.
13   L. Harcourt, journal, 13 August 1887.
14   Horace Seymour, 1843–1906, Commissioner of Customs 1885–90.
15   L. Harcourt, journal, 12 January 1887.
16   E. to M.B., 24 August 1902.
17   Today's equivalents of these sums are approximately £40,000 and £80,000.
18   One of several assassination societies subsidized by American Fenians. They advertised their intentions openly in the US press.
19   L. Chester, D. Leitch and Colin Simpson, *The Cleveland Street Affair*, 1976.
20   In later years Arthur Newton was Lord Alfred Douglas's solicitor.
21   Lord Arthur Somerset to R.B., 10 December 1888.
22   Fourth son of the 7th Earl of Sandwich.
23   Henry Labouchere, 1831–1912, MP and founder of the weekly journal *Truth*, which was notorious for exposing frauds and scandals. He felt passionately that people of high social status should not escape the consequences of the law to which those of humbler station were subject.
24   Lord Arthur Somerset to R.B., 28 December 1889.
25   Henry Labouchere to R.B., 27 February 1890.
26   Howard Sturgis to R.B., 20 August 1898.
27   Lord Durham to R.B., 11 November 1890.
28   R.B. to Lord Rosebery, 27 November 1890.
29   G.E. Buckle to R.B., 31 March 1889.
30   The Land League, of which Parnell was president, originated in 1879. Its purpose was to protect Irish tenants against landlords, particularly absentee English ones. The National League went further by advocating the total obliteration of the landlords. Boycotting, introduced by Parnell, advocated the punishment of anyone who took over a farm from which another had been evicted, 'by isolating him from his kind as if he was a leper of old'. The Plan of Campaign instructed a tenant to offer his landlord whatever rent the tenant considered reasonable. If the offer was refused, the rent was to meet the expenses of the Land War. These combined movements led to repeated outrages and assassinations.
31   R.B. to W.E. Gladstone, 31 December 1890.
32   R.B., journal, 3 February 1891.
33   R.B., journal, 15 February 1891.
34   Howard Sturgis to R.B., 13 October 1891.
35   R.B., journal, 29 August 1879.
36   M.S. to R.B., May 1891.
37   R.B. to M.S., 4 September 1893.
38   R.B. to M.S., 25 August 1895
39   R.B. to M.S., 10 April 1900.
40   R.B. to C.W., October 1892.
41   R.B. to C.W., 6 February 1892.
42   R.B. to C.W., 8 February 1892.
43   Loulou Harcourt and John Oswald.
44   Tan-yr-Allt, Tremadoc, Caernarvonshire, which A.C. Ainger rented

annually for his friends and old pupils to visit.

45 Howard Sturgis to R.B., 7 April 1892.
46 R.B., journal, 7 September 1892.
47 R.B., journal, 17 August 1892.
48 Howard Sturgis to R.B., 2 February 1893.
49 *Extracts from the Letters and Journals of William Cory, 1897.*
50 E. to L.B., 14 and 15 January 1917.
51 R.B., journal, 14 January 1893.
52 R.B., journal, 21 February 1893.
53 Politician and sporting squire. Created 1st Viscount Chaplin in 1916.
54 R.B. to C.W., undated.
55 R.B. to M.S., 12 December 1893.
56 R.B., journal, 14 January 1894.
57 L. Harcourt, journal, 14 January 1894.
58 R.B., journal, 9 March 1894.
59 R.B. to G.E. Buckle, 15 June 1894.
60 R.B., journal, 9 August 1894.
61 R.B. to C.W., 1894, undated.
62 Lord Rosebery to R.B., 29 November 1894.

6 THE OFFICE OF WORKS AND QUEEN VICTORIA 1895–1901 (pages 96-128)

1   R.B. to M.S. 26 February 1895.
2   R.B. to Lord Rosebery, 2 June 1895.
3   W.J., letter, 14 April 1864.
4   W.J. to Francis Warre Cornish, 17 November 1872.
5   R.B. to Lord Rosebery, 11 October 1891.
6   R.B. to M.S., 1 September 1894.
7   R.B. to C.W., 22 January 1892.
8   R.B., journal, 13 March 1895.
9   R.B., journal, 14 March 1895.
10 R.B. to Lord Rosebery, 15 March 1895.
11 R.B. to M.S., 18 March 1895.
12 R.B., journal, 4 April 1895.
13 R.B. to Lord Rosebery, 6 April 1895.
14 R.B. to M.S., 8 April 1895.
15 Lord Durham to R.B., 21 April 1895.
16 As Lord Kelhead.
17 Raymond Asquith to H.T. Baker, 1 October 1898.
18 R.B. to Lord Rosebery, 27 May 1895.
19 R.B. to M.S., 27 May 1895.
20 Lord Rosebery to R.B., 25 April 1895.
21 R.B. to M.S., 2 June 1895.
22 R.B. to C.W., 4 June 1895.
23 R. Rhodes James, *Life of Lord Rosebery*, 1963.
24 R.B. to Herbert Gladstone, 2 June 1895 (BM 46056).

25	R.B., journal, 8 October 1896.

26	Alfred Milner to R.B., 3 January 1896.

27	R.B. to C.W., 18 January 1896.

28	R.B., journal, 31 July 1897.

29	W.E. Gladstone to R.B., 2 January 1897.

30	Howard Sturgis to R.B., 11 January 1897.

31	R.B. to M.S., 5 January 1897.

32	R.B. to M.S., 18 June 1897.

33	When it came to toasting the sovereign, Jacobites would stretch their right arm over the bowl, thus drinking to the King over the water.

34	R.B. to M.B., 2 July 1897.

35	On the library hearthstone of slate is incised 'Reginald Viscount Esher. In the evening we shall remember and in the morning we shall not forget', and the date 1930. The house, which today is an hotel, still retains some of the furniture that belonged to the Esher family – painted chests of drawers, Empire tables, a Queen Anne stool with faded needlework stitched by Nellie, and French provincial wardrobes and chairs.

36	E. to M.B., 26 August 1906.

37	In the published *Journals and Letters* the adjective 'handsome' is substituted for 'beautiful'.

38	The moment the Queen finished her soup, the plate was snatched away by a footman and she was served fish. Slow eaters might find themselves still chewing game when the Queen had finished her dessert.

39	R.B., journal, 24 November 1897.

40	R.B. to M.S., 27 January 1899.

41	Sylvia Brooke, *Queen of the Head Hunters*, 1970. Much of the early suffering was caused by Maurice's sulks, which his family called his 'black daemons'.

42	R.B. to M.B., 10 March 1897.

43	R.B. to M.B., 26 August 1895.

44	R.B. to M.B., 2 September 1895.

45	Afterwards 12th Viscount Valentia, 1883–1949.

46	R.B. to M.B., 5 November 1899.

47	R.B. to M.B., 24 May 1897.

48	M.B. to R.B., 20 September 1898.

49	R.B. to M.B. 22 February 1898.

50	R.B. to M.B., 13 March 1898.

51	R.B., journal, 18 January 1898.

52	Nathaniel, 1st Lord Rothschild, 1840–1915.

53	Montagu Corry, Lord Rowton, 1838–1903.

54	Disraeli's biography was undertaken by W.F. Monypenny, who published Vol. I in 1910. G.E. Buckle completed Vol. II in 1920.

55	Arthur Bigge to R.B., 27 January 1898.

56	R.B. to C.W., 9 March 1898.

57	R.B., journal, 28 May 1898.

58	R.B., journal, 2 June 1898.

59	R.B. to Arthur Balfour, 1 April 1898.

60 Afterwards King George V.
61 Prince Henry of Battenberg married in 1885 Princess Beatrice, Queen Victoria's youngest child.
62 R.B. to O.B., 26 January 1899.
63 R.B., journal, 16 May 1898.
64 Lord Rosebery to E., 27 May 1899.
65 E. to M.S., 3 January 1907.
66 E. to M.S., 1 August 1899.
67 R.B. to O.B., 16 May 1899.
68 Queen Victoria's Journal, 15 May 1899.
69 R.B., journal, 15 May 1899.
70 She became Queen Mary.
71 R.B., journal, 15 May 1899.
72 Ernst Ludwig, 1868–1937, and Victoria Melita, 1876–1936, a sister of Queen Marie of Roumania.
73 R.B. to M.B., 22 May 1899.
74 R.B., journal, 22 May 1899.
75 R.B. to Lord Rosebery, 23 May 1895.
76 After 24 May 1899 references to events taking place after he succeeded to the title will be changed from R.B. to E.
77 E. to M.B., 26 July 1899.
78 E. to M.B., 1899, undated.
79 R.B., journal, 4 December 1898.
80 E., journal, 24 November 1899.
81 Sir Edward Wingfield, KCB, 1834–1910.
82 E., journal, December 1899.
83 Sir William Harcourt to E., 12 December 1899.
84 E. to M.B., 14 March 1900.
85 E. to Lord Knollys, 28 January 1903 (W 38/65).
86 Succeeded his father in 1907 as 9th Viscount Midleton. Created 1st Earl of Midleton in 1920.
87 E. to O.B., 19 October 1900.
88 Earl of Midleton, *Records and Reactions*, 1939.
89 E. to O.B., 11 November 1900.
90 E., journal, 25 October 1900.
91 E., journal, 11 December 1900.
92 In 1902 he was to be awarded the sword of honour at Sandhurst.
93 E., journal, 22 February 1900.
94 E., journal, 28 November 1900.
95 E., journal, 28 November 1900.
96 Sir William Osler, created baronet in 1911, Professor of Medicine at Oxford.
97 E., journal, 1 December 1900.
98 E., journal, 28 December 1900.
99 Peter Fraser, *Lord Esher*, 1973, p.78.
100 E. to M.B., 19 January 1901.
101 E. to M.B., 21 January 1901.
102 E., journal, 22 January 1901.

103 E., journal, 31 January 1901.
104 King Edward allowed him to keep it. In 1983 the wreath, in a glass case, was still preserved at the Roman Camp.
105 E., journal, 9 February, 1901.

7 EDWARDIAN APOGEE 1901–1907 (pages 129-173).

1 E. to O.B., 24 November 1900.
2 A.C. Benson, journal, 16 October 1903.
3 E. to C.W., 17 March 1901.
4 E. to M.B., 6 February 1901.
5 According to E., who so informed Joel Duveen. Information supplied to J.L.-M. by Colin Simpson.
6 E. to M.B., 17 February 1901.
7 E. to M.B., 17 February 1901.
8 E. to M.B., 11 November 1901.
9 E. to M.B., 1 October 1901.
10 E. to M.B., 11 June 1901.
11 The wife of E.'s friend Oliver, Earl de Grey, and later 2nd Marchioness of Ripon.
12 E., journal, 20 June 1901.
13 E., journal, 20 June 1901.
14 Sir Arthur Ellis to E., November 1901.
15 Lionel Cust, *King Edward VII and His Court*, 1930.
16 E. to M.B., 5 December 1901.
17 E. to M.B., 19 February 1900.
18 E. to M.B., 27 January 1902.
19 E. to M.B., 26 April 1901.
20 M.B. to E., 24 April 1899.
21 M.B. to E., 28 August 1904.
22 E. to O.B., 12 June 1898.
23 E. to O.B., 13 June 1898.
24 E. to O.B., 4 May 1899.
25 E. to O.B., 4 May 1899.
26 E. to M.B., 12 June 1899.
27 Sylvia Brooke, *Queen of the Head Hunters*, 1970.
28 E. to M.B., 20 June 1902.
29 E. to King Edward VII, 12 October 1902 (R.A. W38/44).
30 Earl of Midleton, *Records and Reactions*, 1939.
31 Earl of Midleton, *Records and Reactions*, 1939.
32 E. to King Edward VII, 17 October 1902 (R.A. W38/43).
33 E. to King Edward VII, 27 February 1903 (R.A. W38/80).
34 E. to King Edward VII, 4 December 1902 (R.A. W38/61).
35 19 March 1903.
36 E. to King Edward VII, 21 May 1903 (R.A. W24/94a).
37 E. to King Edward VII, 6 September 1903 (R.A. W17/110).
38 King Edward VII to E., September 1903 (R.A. W17/111).

39 E. to M.B., 21 September 1903.
40 E. to Arthur Balfour, 25 September 1903.
41 Lord Rosebery to E., 23 September 1903.
42 Howard Sturgis to E., 29 September 1903.
43 E. to M.B., 2 February 1903.
44 E. to M.B., 3 February 1904.
45 E to H.O. Arnold-Forster, 2 March 1904.
46 Max Egremont, *Balfour*, 1980.
47 E., journal, 3 October 1904.
48 H.O. Arnold-Forster, diary, 21 January 1905.
49 See p.186.
50 Information from Anita Leslie to J.L.-M.
51 E. to M.B., 22 August 1905.
52 E. to M.B., 24 October 1901.
53 E. to M.B., 3 October 1904.
54 E. to M.B., 5 October 1904.
55 E. to King Edward VII, 17 April 1905 (R.A. W39/74).
56 E. to H.O. Arnold-Forster, 26 April 1905.
57 Charles à Court Repington, 1858–1925, military expert and journalist;
    L.C.M.S. Amery, 1873–1955, statesman and journalist; L.J. Maxse,
    1864–1932, Editor of the *National Review*; Field-Marshal Earl Roberts,
    1832–1914; Sir Guy Fleetwood-Wilson, 1850–1940, Director-General of
    Army Finance, 1904–08; Sir Henry Rawlinson, Bt, 1864–1925 (Lord
    Rawlinson, 1919); and General Douglas Haig, 1861–1928 (Field-
    Marshal Earl Haig, 1919).
58 E. to M.B., 8 January 1905.
59 E. to M.B., 14 February 1905.
60 M.B. to E., 8 May 1908.
61 E. to John Morley, 15 December 1905.
62 Margaret, daughter of Clayton de Windt, and wife of Sir Charles
    Johnson-Brooke, Rajah of Sarawak. Sir Charles's uncle, Sir James
    Brooke, was the celebrated first White Rajah of Sarawak. For suppres-
    sing a rebellion and rescuing the inhabitants of Sarawak from barbarism
    he was created hereditary Rajah of Sarawak by the Malay Sultan of
    Brunei.
63 E. to M.B., 3 August 1904.
64 E._to M.B., 2 September 1906.
65 4th Marquess of Salisbury to Arthur Balfour, April 1905.
66 E. to M.B., 26 June 1905.
67 E. to M.B., July 1905.
68 E. to M.B., 4 October 1905.
69 E., journal, 28 November 1905.
70 E., journal, 5 December 1907.
71 Charles Repington to E., 5 October 1906.
72 Peter Fraser, *Lord Esher*, 1973.
73 E., journal, 13 December 1905.
74 E. to King Edward VII, 13 December 1905 (R.A. W39/1237).
75 E., memorandum to King Edward VII, 18 January 1906.

76 E. to Knollys (W 40/1).
77 Fisher to E., February 1906.
78 Later King Edward VIII, and known as David to his family and friends.
79 E., journal, 24 January 1906.
80 E. to King Edward VII, 26 April 1906 (R.A. W40/26).
81 E. to King Edward VII, 15 June 1906 (R.A. W40/32).
82 E. to M.B., 5 March 1906.
83 M.B. to E., 8 February 1906.
84 E. to M.B., 8 March 1906.
85 M.B. to E., 8 March 1906.
86 E. to M.B., 12 December 1906.
87 R.B. to C.W., 5 March 1895.
88 E., journal, 4 February 1906.
89 E., journal, 8 December 1907.
90 E. to Kitchener, 1906, undated.
91 E. to Campbell-Bannerman, 1 March 1906.
92 *Times*, 27 March 1906.
93 E. to King Edward VII, 22 March 1906 (R.A. W40/21).
94 E. to Lord Knollys, 24 March 1906 (R.A. W40/22).
95 King Edward VII to E., 14 April 1906.
96 E. to King Edward VII, May 1906 (R.A. W40/27).
97 E. to King Edward VII, 12 August 1906 (R.A. W40/45).
98 Lord Haldane, *An Autobiography*, 1929.
99 E. to Lord Knollys, 24 September 1906 (R.A. W40/57).
100 E. to King Edward VII, 18 March 1903 (R.A. W38/85).
101 E. to King Edward VII, 23 August 1906.
102 E. to M.B., 17 November 1906.
103 E. to King Edward VII, 30 December 1906 (R.A. W40/78).
104 E. to M.B., 31 December 1906.
105 E. to M.B., 14 January 1907.
106 2nd Viscount Mersey, *A Picture of Life, 1872–1940*, 1941.
107 E. to Lord Knollys, 19 March 1907 (R.A. W40/103).
108 E. to Charles Repington, 22 March 1907.
109 E. to Lord Knollys, 9 October 1907 (R.A. W41/1).
110 E. to Lord Knollys, 1 December 1907 (R.A. W41/11).
111 E., journal, 16 November 1907.
112 E., journal, 3 December 1907.
113 E., journal, 17 November 1907.
114 E., journal, 17 November 1907.
115 E. to M.B., 7 June 1905.
116 E., journal, 18 November 1907.
117 E., journal, 18 November 1907.
118 E., journal, 12 April 1907.
119 Kenneth Rose, *King George V*, 1984.
120 Lord Knollys to E., 14 December 1907.
121 E., journal, 26 December 1907.

8 EDWARDIAN DECLINE 1908–10 (pages 174-208)

1   E., journal, 4 January 1908.
2   Lily Elsie, 1886–1962.
3   Howard Sturgis to E., 20 January 1908.
4   E. to M.B., 30 August 1908.
5   Dr W.N. Barron to E., 19 December 1906.
6   Published 1984.
7   A.C. Benson, *Journals*, Vol.110, p.28.
8   A.C. Benson, *Journals*, July–September 1924.
9   E. to Lord Knollys, 20 August 1905 (R.A. W39/105).
10 King Edward VII to E., 23 March 1908 (R.A. W41/37).
11 E., journal, 1 February 1909.
12 E., journal, 3 March 1909.
13 A furore was caused at court in 1839 when Lady Flora Hastings, a lady-in-waiting to the Duchess of Kent, was scandalously accused to being pregnant. In fact she had cancer, of which she died four months later. The 2nd Earl Granville was Foreign Secretary 1870–4 and 1880–5. To him Queen Victoria wrote very freely.
14 E. to Lord Knollys, 19 January 1908 (R.A. W41/27).
15 Dated 4 April 1908.
16 E. to King Edward VII, 8 April 1908 (R.A. W21/40). Edward, Viscount Cardwell, 1813–16, abolished purchase of commissions, and substituted tests of fitness, and promotion by selection.
17 F. Ponsonby to E. 11 April 1908 (R.A. W21/41).
18 E. to Lord Knollys, 14 April 1908 (R.A. W41/39).
19 E. to King Edward VII, 16 April 1908 (R.A. W41/40).
20 F. Ponsonby, *Recollections of Three Reigns*, 1951.
21 E. to Lord Knollys, 19 January 1908 (R.A. W41/21).
22 E. to Lord Knollys, 12 July 1908.
23 E. to Fisher, 1907, undated.
24 Fisher to E., 19 April 1908.
25 E. to King Edward VII, 2 November 1908 (R.A. W41/79).
26 *The Assistance to be given by Great Britain to France if she is attacked by Germany*, 14 December 1908 (R.A. W41/84).
27 The Kaiser to Lord Tweedmouth, 14 February 1908.
28 E., journal, 2 February 1908.
29 Lord Tweedmouth to the Kaiser, 21 February 1908.
30 King Edward VII to the Kaiser, 22 February 1908.
31 Fisher to E., 20 February 1908.
32 E. to King Edward VII, 19 February 1908.
33 E., journal, 1 April 1908.
34 It gave the title to a collection of essays published by E. in 1910.
35 E., journal, 7 May 1908.
36 E., journal, 1 May 1908.
37 E., journal, 23 April 1908.
38 E., journal, 23 April 1908.
39 E., journal, 23 April 1908.

40 E., journal, 22 November 1908.
41 The Hon. Sir Schomberg McDonnell, Secretary to the Commissioners of Works and E.'s successor. The 1st and last Lord Burghclere was chairman of the Ancient Monuments Commission.
42 E., journal, 26 September 1908.
43 E., journal, 28 October 1908. Soveral was convinced that it was carefully prepared in advance.
44 E., journal, 22 November 1908.
45 E., journal, 5 November 1908.
46 E., journal, 21 November 1908.
47 E., journal, 28 October 1908.
48 E., journal, 21 November 1908.
49 Prince of Wales to E., 4 January 1909.
50 E., journal, 18 April 1909.
51 E., journal, March 1909.
52 Keith A. Hamilton, 'The Air in Detente Diplomacy', *International History Review*, Vol. III, No.2, April 1981.
53 W.S. Churchill to Lord Haldane, 9 January 1909.
54 E., journal, 26 July 1909.
55 Lord Northcliffe to E., 26 February 1909.
56 Hon. C. Rolls to E., 22 March 1909.
57 Hon. C. Rolls to E., 25 October 1909.
58 E. to Kitchener, 8 July 1909.
59 E. to Kitchener, 14 July 1909.
60 Lord Haldane to E., 13 July 1909.
61 E. to M.B., 29 December 1909.
62 Commander S. Roskill, *Hankey, Man of Secrets*, 2 vols, 1970–2.
63 Duchess of Connaught to the Duke, 17 October 1907 (R.A. Geo. V Q1560/12).
64 E., journal, 8 September 1909.
65 E., journal, 8 September 1909.
66 E. to Lord Knollys, 4 August 1909 (R.A. W41/95).
67 King Edward VII to E., 10 September 1909.
68 M.B. to E., 27 July 1909.
69 E., journal, 26 November 1909.
70 E. to M.B., 6 December 1909.
71 E. to M.B., 19 December 1909.
72 E. to M.B., 23 December 1909.
73 E. to M.B., 18 September 1909.
74 E. to Lord Knollys, 18 September 1909 (R.A. W41/97).
75 E., journal, 12 September 1909.
76 E. to Lord Knollys, 8 October 1909 (R.A. W41/98).
77 Lord Knollys to E., 8 November 1909.
78 E. to Lord Knollys, 12 November 1909 (R.A. W41/99).
79 E. to Lord Knollys, 28 November 1909 (R.A. W41/101).
80 E. to Lord Knollys, 1 December 1909 (R.A. W41/102).
81 Lord Knollys to E., 29 December 1909.
82 Geo. V K 2252/1 5 and 6 Cabinet Minute, 11 February 1910.

83   E. to Lord Knollys, 1 March 1910 (R.A. W41/110).
84   E. to King Edward VII, 10 April 1910.
85   Lord Knollys to E., 15 April 1910.
86   Lord Knollys to E., 17 April 1910.
87   *Memorandum of a Conference at Lambeth Palace* on 27 April 1910, kept by E.
88   E., journal, 7 May 1910.
89   E., journal, 7 May 1910.
90   E., journal, 10 May 1910.
91   E., journal, 10 May 1910.
92   E., journal, 12 June 1910.
93   E., journal, 12 June 1910.
94   M.S. to E., 9 September 1902.
95   E. to M.B., 9 July 1905.
96   Fisher, *Some Notes*, 1918.
97   Earl of Midleton, *Records and Reactions*, 1939.
98   Lionel Cust, *King Edward VII and His Court*, 1930.

9 GEORGIAN AFTERMATH 1910–1914 (pages 209-254)

1   1st Baron Hardinge of Penshurst, 1868–1944, Permanent Under-Secretary of State for Foreign Affairs 1906-10, and Viceroy of India, 1910-16.
2   *Quarterly Review*, July 1910, Vol.213.
3   Arthur Bigge to E., verbally, 9 May 1909.
4   E. to M.S., 4 August 1908.
5   E. to King George V, May 1910, undated.
6   King George V to E., 22 May 1910.
7   Kenneth Rose, *King George V*, 1984.
8   E. to Queen Mary, 10 May 1911 (R.A. Geo. V CC47/227a).
9   E. to Queen Mary, 28 August 1910 (R.A. Geo. V CC47/214).
10   E., journal, 3 July 1910.
11   E., journal, 4 June 1910.
12   E. to Queen Mary, 28 August 1910 (R.A. Geo. V CC47/214).
13   E., journal, 12 May 1910.
14   E., journal, 16 May 1910.
15   E., memorandum, 9 October 1910 (R.A. Geo. V K2552 (2) 88).
16   E. to Lord Lansdowne, 21 November 1910.
17   E., memorandum for King George V, 14 November 1910.
18   E., journal, 13 August 1913.
19   E., journal, 23 October 1908.
20   L.J. Maxse to E., 11 August 1911.
21   Lord Knollys to E., 8 December 1910.
22   A.C. Benson, *Journal*, 20 November, 1903.
23   Lord Stamfordham to Lady Esher, 23 January 1930.
24   E., journal, 26 November 1910.
25   M.S. to E., 5 August 1910.

26 *The World*, 21 June 1910.
27 *The World*, 16 August 1910.
28 E. to Lord Haldane, 6 September 1910 (National Library of Scotland, Edinburgh).
29 Lord Haldane to E., 7 September 1910.
30 Lord Knollys to E., 8 September 1910.
31 H.H. Asquith to Lord Haldane, 9 September 1910 (National Library of Scotland, Edinburgh).
32 Arthur Balfour to E., 8 September 1910.
33 E. to Lord Haldane, 9 September 1910 (National Library of Scotland, Edinburgh).
34 E. to Lord Knollys, 10 September 1910.
35 Norman Angell, *After All*, 1951.
36 M.B. to E., February 1912.
37 E. to M.B., 1 October 1911.
38 E., memorandum, 10 January 1911.
39 E., journal, 4 February 1911.
40 E. to M.S., 18 April 1911.
41 Aunt Adèle Gurwood (d. 1911) and Regy were devoted to one another. She also gave him diamonds and rubies to make up the star for his Order of the Bath; when he saw it, King Edward VII pronounced it the finest ever heard of since the one worn by Sir John Moore. Regy called Aunt Adèle the nicest and kindest woman who ever lived, adding characteristically that it explained why she had never found a husband.
42 M.B. to E., 11 September 1911.
43 M.B. to E., 12 September 1912.
44 E. to M.B., 12 September 1911.
45 Anita Leslie, *Edwardians in Love*, 1972.
46 Sylvia Brooke, *Queen of the Head Hunters*, 1970.
47 E., journal, 6 September 1911.
48 E. to L.B., 3 September 1911.
49 27th Earl of Crawford, *Journals*, pub. 1984.
50 E. to King George V, 11 August 1911 (R.A. Geo. V K2552(2)/73).
51 E. to M.B., 14 August 1911.
52 Margot Asquith to E., 15 August 1911.
53 E., journal, 4 October 1911.
54 E., journal, 14 October 1911.
55 E., journal, 4 October 1911.
56 Under the Algeciras Treaty of 1906 France's mandatory rights over Morocco were confirmed. The Agadir incident was regarded by France, Italy and Britain as a dangerous infringement of the treaty and a threat to the balance of European power in the Mediterranean.
57 Sir John French to E., 8 August 1911.
58 C.P. Scott, diary, 6 May 1914.
59 E. to Arthur Balfour, 9 November 1911.
60 Arthur Balfour to E., 15 November 1911.
61 E. to King George V, 29 March 1912 (R.A. Geo. V Q724/6).
62 Alfred Dreyfus, a Jewish officer in the French Army, was falsely

accused and convicted of treachery in 1893; not until 1906 was his innocence proved and the verdict reversed. He was a victim of virulent anti-Semitism, and the French people were divided into Dreyfusards and anti-Dreyfusards.

63 See p.61.
64 E. to Mrs Stead, 20 April 1912.
65 W.T. Stead, *The Daily Chronicle*, 25 April 1910.
66 E., journal, 5 July 1912. Major the Hon. William Cadogan was appointed the Prince's Equerry in 1912, and was killed in action in 1914, aged thirty-five.
67 He had been a naval cadet at Dartmouth and Osborne, and was appointed midshipman in 1911.
68 E., journal, 20 September 1912.
69 E., journal, 20 September 1912.
70 E., journal, 17 November 1913.
71 Howard Sturgis to E., January 1913.
72 E. to Lord Knollys, 23 October 1912.
73 E., journal, 2 December 1912.
74 E., journal, 24 December 1912.
75 E. to Lord Knollys, 19 January 1913.
76 E., journal, 13 September 1913.
77 *The Education of the Prince*, 1912.
78 E., journal, 26 January 1913.
79 E., journal, 26 January 1913.
80 *Notes of a Conversation*, 14 February 1913.
81 Geoffrey Robinson, who was to change his name to Dawson in 1917, was the new Editor of *The Times*.
82 H.H. Asquith to E., 20 February 1913.
83 E., journal, 13 March 1913.
84 Lord Stamfordham to E., 15 February 1913.
85 E., journal, 11 September 1913.
86 E., journal, 13 September 1913.
87 E to Arthur Balfour, 13 September 1913.
88 E., journal, 14 September 1913.
89 E. to King George V, 29 September 1913 (R.A. Geo. V K2553 2/40).
90 E. to Lord Stamfordham, 28 December 1913.
91 Lord Stamfordham to E., 29 December 1913.
92 J.A. Spender to E., 14 March 1913.
93 J.A. Spender, *Life, Journalism and Politics*, 2 vols, 1927.
94 See E. to Lord Stamfordham, 28 December 1913, above.
95 E. to Lord Stamfordham, 3 January 1914.
96 John Morley to E., 1 January 1914.
97 Lord Stamfordham to E., 6 January 1914.
98 E. to King George V, 8 January 1914.
99 E. to King George V, 9 January 1914 (R.A. Geo. V K2553 (3), 60).
100 E., memorandum to King George V, 20 January 1914 (R.A. Geo. V K2553 (3), 71).
101 E., memorandum of an interview with King George V, 21 January 1914.

102 E. to H.H. Asquith, 5 February 1914.
103 E., journal, 8 April 1914.
104 E. to Margot Asquith, 26 April 1914.
105 E., memorandum, 23 May 1914.
106 E., journal, 21 June 1914.
107 25 March 1914.
108 11 May 1914.
109 Lionel Brett, *Ourselves Unknown*, 1985
110 E. to M.B. 9 September 1902.
111 E. to M.B., 25 July 1914.

10 THE GREAT WAR: CIVILIAN SOLDIER 1914–1916 (pages 255-288)

1   The CID was officially suspended until 1920, and survived until 1939.
2   Sylvia Brooke, *Queen of the Head Hunters*, 1970.
3   E. to M.B., 12 August 1914.
4   E. to M.B., 13 August 1914.
5   Earl of Midleton, *Records and Reactions*, 1939.
6   E., journal, 11 November 1914.
7   Lord Brooke, then ADC to GOC, BEF.
8   E., journal, 26 September 1914.
9   E., journal, 9 March 1915.
10   E. to L.B., 25 September 1914.
11   E. to M.B., 30 January 1915.
12   M.B. to E., 27 January 1915.
13   E. to M.B., 1 February 1915.
14   M.B. to E., 3 February 1915.
15   J.A. Sylvester to J.L.-M.
16   H.H. Asquith to Lady Scott, 26 July 1916.
17   E. to C.W., 16 January 1915.
18   Arnold Bennett, journals, 25 June 1915.
19   Information from Lord Adeane.
20   Lord Castlerosse, article in *Sunday Express*, undated.
21   Lord Castlerosse, article in *Sunday Express*, undated.
22   M.B. to E., 21 September 1915.
23   E., journal, 19 January 1915.
24   E., journal, 9 May 1915.
25   E. to L.B., 26 July 1915.
26   E. to Lord Stamfordham, 13 September 1915.
27   E. to King George V, 23 October 1915 (R.A. Geo. V Q724/45).
28   E. to Lord Stamfordham, 28 October 1915 (R.A. Geo. V Q724/51).
29   E., journal, 24 January 1915.
30   Lord Bertie, diary, 26 February 1915.
31   Lord Bertie, diary, 12 March 1915.
32   Kitchener to E., 14 May 1915.
33   E. to M.B., 15 May 1915.
34   Lord Bertie, diary, 19 June 1915.

35   E., journal, 5 March 1915.
36   E., journal, 10 March 1915.
37   E. to Kitchener, 21 March 1915.
38   E., journal, 22 and 23 May 1915.
39   E. to Kitchener, 23 May 1915.
40   E.G. French, *Field Marshal Lord French*, 1931.
41   E. to L.B., 4 July 1915.
42   The Hon. Aubrey Herbert MP, 1880–1923, younger son of the Earl of Caernarvon, traveller and expert in Near East affairs.
43   1915 but undated.
44   Sir John Fisher to E., 1 November 1914.
45   E. to Sir John Fisher, 16 May 1915 (Kilverstone Papers).
46   Two years were still to run before the Supreme War Council was set up.
47   E. to Auguste Huguet, 13 March 1915.
48   G. Robinson to E., 27 August 1915.
49   Lord Curzon to E., 20 August 1915.
50   Lord Newton to E., 22 August 1915.
51   J.A. Spender to E., 27 August 1915 (R.A. Geo. V Q724/44).
52   J.A. Balfour, memorandum, *Efficiency in War and Compulsion*, 19 September 1915.
53   Howard Sturgis to E., 21 August 1915.
54   Lord Bertie, diary, 6 October 1915.
55   E., journal, 18 July 1915.
56   E., journal, 3 October 1915.
57   E., journal, 18 December 1914. Information supplied to E. by King George V.
58   Prince of Wales to E., 24 June 1915.
59   E., journal, 23 February 1915.
60   J. Charteris, *At GHQ*, 1931.
61   E. to Maurice Hankey, 24 December 1917.
62   E., journal, 5 November 1915.
63   E., journal, 5 November 1915.
64   E. to H.H. Asquith, 7 November 1915.
65   Haig, diary, 14 November 1915.
66   Asquith Papers (Bodleian Library, 28/251).
67   Sir Henry Wilson, 15 November 1915, quoted in Bernard Ash, *The Lost Dictator*, 1968.
68   E., journal, 23 November 1915.
69   E., journal, 25 November 1915.
70   E. to H.H. Asquith, 27 November 1915.
71   E. to L.B., 30 November 1915.
72   E. to H.H. Asquith, 29 November 1915 (Bodleian Library, 15/159).
73   E. to L.B., 4 December 1915.
74   H.H. Asquith to E., 6 December 1915.
75   E. to Lord Stamfordham, 30 November 1915.
76   E. to Lord Stamfordham, 30 November 1915.
77   Kenneth Clark, *Another Part of the Wood*, 1974.
78   Sir Philip Sassoon to E., 6 May 1917.

79   E. to L.B., 1 February 1916.
80   Howard Sturgis to E., 9 January 1916.
81   Howard Sturgis to E., 9 January 1916.
82   Prince of Wales to E., 14 October 1915.
83   E. to Lord Stamfordham, 25 January 1916.
84   E. to Lord Stamfordham, 25 January 1916 (R.A. Geo. V Q724/66).
85   E. to Robertson, 7 February 1916.
86   E. to Lord Stamfordham, 19 April 1918 (R.A. Geo. V Q 724/105).
87   E. to L.B., 21 April 1916.
88   E. to L.B., 6 May 1916.
89   E. to King George V, 6 May 1916 (R.A. Geo. V Q724/76).
90   Peter Fraser, *Lord Esher*, 1973.
91   Haig to E., 16 May 1916.
92   E., journal, 24 April 1916.
93   E. to Colonel O. Fitzgerald, 26 May 1916.
94   E. to Lord Stamfordham, 1 June 1916 (R.A. Geo. V Q724/77).
95   E. to Lord Stamfordham, 8 June 1916.
96   E., journal, 6 June 1916.
97   Marie Corelli to E., 5 July 1916.

11 THE GREAT WAR: SOLDIER CIVILIAN 1916–1918 (pages 289-320)

1   H.H. Asquith to E., 13 June 1916.
2   E. to H.H. Asquith, 23 June 1916.
3   Maurice Hankey to E., 13 June 1916.
4   Sir W. Robertson to E., 14 June 1916.
5   Haig to E., 1 July 1916.
6   Charles Repington, diary, 15 June 1916.
7   Martin Gilbert, *Winston Churchill*, Vol.3, footnote, letter of 8 August 1916.
8   Maurice Hankey to E., 17 July 1916.
9   Haig to E., 18 July 1916.
10   E. to Maurice Hankey, 3 August 1916.
11   E. to L.B., 26 September 1917.
12   E., journal, 29 July 1916.
13   E., journal, 11 August 1916.
14   E. to Sir W. Robertson, 11 August 1916.
15   Sir W. Robertson to E., 23 September 1916.
16   E. to Haig, 25 September 1916.
17   E., journal, 17 September 1916.
18   E., journal, 17 and 18 September 1916.
19   Lord Stamfordham to E., 12 October 1916.
20   Lloyd George, *War Memoirs*, Vol.1, p.472. Quoted by Peter Fraser in *Lord Esher*, 1973.
21   E., journal, 26 October 1916.
22   E. to Lord Murray of Elibank, 28 November 1916 (National Library of

Scotland, Edinburgh).

23   E. to Maurice Hankey, 10 December 1916.
24   E. to Sir W. Robertson, 11 January 1917.
25   E. to D. Lloyd George, 10 January 1917.
26   E. to Sir W. Robertson, 2 February 1917.
27   E. to Haig, 2 February 1917.
28   E. to Viscount French, 7 February 1917.
29   E. to Sir W. Robertson, 12 February 1917.
30   E., journal, 17 and 18 February 1917.
31   E. to Lord Murray of Elibank, 3 March 1917 (National Library of Scotland, Edinburgh).
32   Charles Repington, diary, 26 April 1917.
33   E. to Lord Stamfordham, 16 March 1917 (R.A. Geo. V Q724/22).
34   E. to Lyautey, 15 March 1917.
35   Charles Repington to E., 19 August 1906.
36   Brigadier-General John Charteris, diary, 25 March 1917.
37   E., journal, 27 May 1917.
38   E. to Lord Stamfordham, 26 March 1917.
39   E. to Lord Stamfordham, 24 August 1917 (R.A. Geo. V Q724/97).
40   E. to Lord Stamfordham, undated (R.A. Geo. V Q724/98).
41   E., journal, 27 April 1917.
42   E., journal, 30 July 1917.
43   E., journal, 13 April 1917.
44   E., journal, 21 April 1917.
45   E. to D. Lloyd George, 25 April 1917.
46   E. to Haig, 28 April 1917.
47   E. to Lord Murray of Elibank, 7 May 1917 (National Library of Scotland, Edinburgh).
48   E. to D. Lloyd George, 9 May 1917.
49   Sir Henry Wilson, *Life and Diaries* (Sir C.E. Callwell, ed.), 2 vols, 1927.
50   Lord Bertie to Lord Stamfordham, 25 May 1917 (R.A. Geo. V Q1124/1).
51   E. to Lord Stamfordham, 1 June 1917 (R.A. Geo. V Q724/95).
52   E. to Haig, 7 June 1917.
53   Haig to E., 3 July 1917.
54   E. to Haig, 10 July 1917.
55   Indeed Regy introduced Pershing to Haig: E. to D. Lloyd George, 4 July 1917 (Lloyd George Papers).
56   E. to Sir W. Robertson, 18 July 1917.
57   E. to Haig, 12 August 1917.
58   D.C. Watt, *Personalities and Policies*, 1965.
59   E. to Lord Murray of Elibank, 12 August 1917 (Elibank Papers 8804, National Library of Scotland, Edinburgh).
60   E. to D. Lloyd George, 3 December 1917.
61   E. to L.B., 31 October 1917.
62   E. to Lord Lansdowne, December 1917.
63   E. to D. Lloyd George, 13 April 1918.
64   E., journal, 29 November 1917.

65   E. to L.B., 26 December 1917.
66   E., journal, 3 December 1917.
67   E. to Lord Derby, 2 December 1917.
68   E., journal, 22 January 1918.
69   Lady Esher, journal, 10 March 1918.
70   E., journal, 16 February 1918.
71   Equerry-in-Ordinary to George V, 1910–36.
72   E. to Sir Bryan Godfrey-Faussett, 15 February 1918.
73   E., journal, 4 February 1918.
74   E. to Lord Stamfordham, 28 February 1918 (R.A. Geo. V K1263/8).
75   E., journal, 7 July 1918.
76   E. to Sir Philip Sassoon, 1918, undated (Sassoon Papers). The Hon. Sir Derek Keppel, Master of the Household.
77   E., journal, 19 February 1918.
78   Sir Philip Sassoon to E., 30 March 1918.
79   E. to Sir Philip Sassoon, 19 May 1918.
80   Sir Philip Sassoon to E., 9 June 1918.
81   Sir Philip Sassoon to E., 6 May 1917.
82   E., journal, 24 March 1918.
83   E., journal, 30 May 1918.
84   E. to C.W., 16 April 1918.
85   E. to Haig, 21 June 1918.
86   E. to Lord Stamfordham, 19 April 1918 (R.A. Geo. V Q724/105).
87   E., journal, 30 May 1918.
88   E. to Lord Derby, 22 April 1918.
89   E. to Lord Derby, 19 June 1918.
90   E. to Sir John Fisher, 21 July 1918.
91   Lord Stamfordham to E., 25 July 1918.
92   E. to Lord Stamfordham, 28 July 1918.
93   E. to Lord Stamfordham, 28 July 1918 (R.A. Geo. V Q724/108).
94   E., journal, 11 November 1918.
95   E. to M.B., 13 November 1918.
96   Sir Henry Wilson to E., 9 November 1918.
97   E. to King George V, 12 November 1918.
98   E. to Lord Stamfordham, 26 November 1918.
99   Lord Stamfordham to E., 19 November 1918.
100 The Rt Hon. Arthur Henderson, 1863–1935, Labour leader and statesman, Foreign Secretary 1929–31. The Rt Hon. G.E. Barnes, 1859–1940, trade unionist and MP; Minister of Pensions in Lloyd George's Government in 1916, and member of the War Cabinet, 1917.
101 E. to Lord Stamfordham, 15 December 1918.
102 Clive Wigram, 1st Lord Wigram (1935), 1873–1960, Assistant Private Secretary to King George V 1910–31.
103 M.B. to E., 25 April 1918.
104 E. to Sir Philip Sassoon, 30 September 1918.
105 E. to Haig, 10 November 1918 (Sassoon Papers).

12 ACTIVITY IN RETIREMENT 1918–1930 (pages 321-355)

1   E. to Lord Stamfordham, 2 January 1919 (R.A. Geo. V Q1437/1).
2   H.-M. Berthelot, 1861–1931, French general and Joffre's collaborator.
3   Maurice Hankey to E., 10 February 1919.
4   E. to Maurice Hankey, 15 February 1919.
5   Sir Harold Nicolson, *Peacemaking*, 1933.
6   Maurice Hankey to E., 16 February 1919.
7   E. to Maurice Hankey, 18 February 1919.
8   E. to Maurice Hankey, 18 February 1919.
9   Lord Stamfordham to E., 3 May 1919.
10 E. to R. Smillie, 5 May 1919.
11 Margot Asquith to H. Gwynne, 1919, undated. Quoted by Daphne Bennett in *Margot*, 1984.
12 E. to C.W., 2 May 1919.
13 E. to C.W., 7 January 1920.
14 Lord Stamfordham to E., 24 March 1919 (R.A. Geo. V O1431/9).
15 E. to Lord Curzon, 9 November 1919.
16 E. to O.B., 23 August 1919.
17 E. to Dorothy Brett, 12 April 1919. See Sean Hignett, *Brett*, 1984.
18 E. to Dorothy Brett, 23 December 1920. See Sean Hignett, *Brett*, 1984.
19 E. to M.B., 9 April 1925. Doll's deafness, first apparent after her operation for appendicitis in 1902, steadily grew worse.
20 E. to M.B., 3 November 1925.
21 E. to Angela Brett, 14 April 1929 and 1 May 1929.
22 E. to M.B., 18 October 1911.
23 Howard Sturgis to R.B., 12 May 1877.
24 A.C. Benson, *Memories and Friends*, 1924.
25 E. to M.B., March 1920.
26 E. to L.B., 1 January 1920.
27 E. to L.B., 22 April 1917.
28 E. to L.B., 13 February 1920. Henry, 1st Viscount Chaplin, 1840–1923, held several minor offices of state and was a prominent member of the Turf Club.
29 E. to O.B., 5 September 1920.
30 Maurice Hankey to E., 10 September 1920.
31 F. Ponsonby, *Recollections of Three Reigns*, 1951.
32 E. to Lord Knollys, 10 September 1905 (R.A. W39/117).
33 F. Ponsonby to E., 7 June 1921.
34 E. to F. Ponsonby, 15 June 1921.
35 F. Ponsonby to E., 17 June 1921.
36 E. to F. Ponsonby, 24 June 1921.
37 R.S. Churchill, *Lord Derby*, 1960.
38 *Kitchener*, 1958.
39 Lord Sydenham to E., 14 August 1921.
40 J.H. Creedy to E., 31 May 1921.
41 M.B. to E., 20 June 1921.
42 E. to M.B., 10 December 1921.

43 E. to M.B., 2 March 1918.

44 M.B. to E., 16 November 1919.

45 E. to M.B., 17 February 1922.

46 E. to J. Ramsay MacDonald, 25 August 1924.

47 E. to O.B., 23 March 1922.

48 The Rt Hon. Herbert Fisher to E., 25 March 1922. H.A.L. Fisher was British Delegate to the Assembly of the League of Nations 1920–2.

49 E. to Lord Robert Cecil, 1 August 1922.

50 E. to M.B., 15 October 1922.

51 Loulou Harcourt had married in 1899 Mary, daughter of Walter H. Burns, of New York.

52 R.B. to C.W., 14 November 1894.

53 R.B. to M.B., 18 March 1899.

54 E. to M.B., 23 June 1922.

55 E., journal, 2 December 1915.

56 E. to General Sidney Clive, 13 March 1918.

57 E., journal, 13 December 1917.

58 E. to M.B., 20 February 1923.

59 E. to M.B., 5 November 1924.

60 E. to M.B., 8 July 1924.

61 E. to M.B., 22 March 1925.

62 From information given to J.L.-M. in 1983.

63 Lord Stamfordham to E., 17 January 1926. David-Young Cameron was a close friend of the Eshers.

64 E. to C.W., 19 May 1926.

65 E. to Lord Stamfordham, 7 May 1926 (R.A. Geo. V 1431/67).

66 E. to Sir Philip Sassoon, 28 June 1918.

67 Christopher Hassall, *Edward Marsh*, 1959.

68 Haig to E., 27 September 1927.

69 Maurice Hankey to E., 29 September 1927.

70 E. to Maurice Hankey, October 1927.

71 Daisy (Frances), Countess of Warwick, *Afterthoughts*, 1931, in which she wrote that a year after King Edward's accession E. paid her a visit. He kindly and tactfully advised her that it would be a good thing for her 'close connection with great affairs' to cease because it was distressing Queen Alexandra.

72 Daisy, Countess of Warwick to E., 5 January 1928.

73 E. to Lord Stamfordham, 9 February 1928.

74 E. to M.B., 19 July 1928.

75 E. to Queen Mary, 4 September 1928 (R.A. Geo. V CC47/893).

76 E. to Lord Stamfordham, 21 September 1928 (R.A. Geo. V 1431/95).

77 Both Lutyens and Churchill eventually received the OM.

78 E. to C.W., 6 February 1929.

79 E. to C.W., 13 January 1929. E. misquoted W.C.'s final couplet in 'Mimnermus in Church', 'But oh, the very reason why / I clasp them, is because they die.'

80 E. to C.W., 7 March 1929.

81 Sir F. Ponsonby to E., 15 June 1929.

82 E. to J. Ramsay MacDonald, 21 July 1929.
83 J. Ramsay MacDonald to E., 25 July 1929.
84 E. to M.B., 25 September 1929.
85 Lionel was never envious, and still less resentful, of the favouritism bestowed on his cousin Tony. He describes his grandfather's dignity and charm and the peculiar aura with which he invested the Roman Camp in his autobiography, *Ourselves Unknown*, 1985.
86 Sylvia Brooke, *Queen of the Head Hunters*, 1970.
87 The Prince of Wales to Lady Esher, 26 January 1930.
88 E. to M.B., 8 October 1913.
89 Information given by Lady Phipps to J.L.-M.
90 C.W. told M.B. (10 January 1932) that on entering the Oratory he destroyed nearly all E.'s early letters. He then regretted it.
91 Sylvia Brooke, *Queen of the Head Hunters*, 1970.
92 J.A. Spender, *Life, Journalism and Politics*, 2 vols, 1927.
93 'Londoner's Diary', *Evening Standard*, 22 January 1930.
94 *Daily Telegraph*, review of *Journals and Letters*, 1938.
95 A.C. Benson, *Journal*, Vol.176, p.30.

INDEX

Note: Ranks and titles are generally the highest attained within the period of the book

THE
ENIGMATIC
EDWARDIAN

£2

[signature]

Science Studies Unit
University of Edinburgh

Dec 1995